CRIMINALITY AND CRIMINAL JUSTICE IN CONTEMPORARY POLAND

This volume gives an excellent overview about crime and criminal justice from different aspects in Poland, the largest country in the region of the former Soviet Union. The authors present data about crime development in the last century and cover issues including social change, poverty and social exclusion on the one side, and the role of justice, the media, social perception of crime, and factors of international interest on the other.

Helmut Kury, University of Freiburg, Germany

Relations between social change and crime has been an important theme for criminology since the times of Emile Durkheim. In that respect experience of Central European countries after the fall of communist regimes in 1989 is something unique. This book offers comprehensive and in-depth pictures of crime and criminal justice in the largest country of the region, namely Poland. Highly acclaimed when published in Polish it becomes now available for broader readership. It should be an indispensable source for all those interested in the subject.

Krzysztof Krajewski, Jagiellonian University, Poland

This book provides a fresh perspective on the many facets of crime in Poland. Among many other factors, it looks at: crime over the space of a century; crime in different social systems; crime in a time of profound social change. Distinguished Polish criminologists draw a powerful picture of different aspects of crime in their country. Their analyses and views enrich our knowledge of crime in a part of Europe that has long been obscured.

Alenka Šelih, University of Ljubljana, Slovenia

This book provides an in-depth analysis of the crime situation in Poland during its different political eras. It reveals the factors that influence criminality, points out the changing faces of criminal policy and reviews the outcomes on further fields of criminological research. This fascinating study by outstanding Polish scholars, will show readers an image of the world of Polish criminality, and provide them with a complex understanding of the country's history, legal evolution and socio-political developments since the 1989 regime change.

Miklós Lévay, Eötvös Loránd University, Budapest and
The Constitutional Court of Hungary

This book provides a masterful equilibrium of theoretical and practical analysis of both causes of crime and the justice system's response in Poland. It is an excellent example of a holistic view on the determinants of crime within the context of political and social change in Poland and Central and Eastern Europe since the 1990s. The book represents a valuable study of cultural and political aspects of crime and criminal and penal policy in modern Europe, useful for decision makers, researchers and students.

Beata Gruszczyńska, University of Warsaw, Poland

Criminality and Criminal Justice in Contemporary Poland

Sociopolitical Perspectives

KONRAD BUCZKOWSKI, BEATA CZARNECKA-DZIALUK, WITOLD KLAUS, ANNA KOSSOWSKA, IRENA RZEPLIŃSKA, PAULINA WIKTORSKA, DAGMARA WOŹNIAKOWSKA-FAJST AND DOBROCHNA WÓJCIK
Institute of Law Studies of the Polish Academy of Sciences, Poland

Routledge
Taylor & Francis Group
LONDON AND NEW YORK

First published 2015 by Ashgate Publishing

Published 2016 by Routledge
2 Park Square, Milton Park, Abingdon, Oxon OX14 4RN
605 Third Avenue, New York, NY 10017

First issued in paperback 2021

Routledge is an imprint of the Taylor & Francis Group, an informa business

British Library Cataloguing in Publication Data
A catalogue record for this book is available from the British Library

Library of Congress Cataloging-in-Publication Data

Buczkowski, Konrad.

Criminality and criminal justice in contemporary Poland : sociopolitical perspectives / by Konrad Buczkowski, Beata Czarnecka-Dzialuk, Witold Klaus, Anna Kossowska, Irena Rzeplińska, Paulina Wiktorska, Dagmara Woźniakowska-Fajst, Dobrochna Wójcik.
pages cm
Includes bibliographical references and index.
ISBN 978-1-4724-5184-2 (hardback)
1. Crime–Poland. 2. Criminal justice, Administration of–Poland. I. Title.
HV7015.7.B83 2015
364.9438–dc 3

2014037345

ISBN 13: 978-1-03-209875-3 (pbk)
ISBN 13: 978-1-4724-5184-2 (hbk)

Contents

Notes on Contributors

Konrad Buczkowski is Assistant Professor in the Department of Criminology of Institute of Law Studies in the Polish Academy of Sciences and in the Department of Criminal Law of Institute of Justice, Ministry of Justice of Republic of Poland. His main subjects of professional interest are: economic crime, insurance fraud, money laundering, white-collar crime and cybercrime. He is a member of the European Society of Criminology and the Polish Society of Criminology.

Beata Czarnecka-Dzialuk is Assistant Professor at the Department of Criminology, Institute of Law Studies, Polish Academy of Sciences, and at the Institute of Justice. Beata specialises in the problems of reacting to juvenile criminality and introducing restorative justice into the justice system, especially mediation in criminal and juvenile cases. Beata is a member of the Social Council for Alternative Methods of Solving Conflicts and Disputes at the Ministry of Justice, the European Society of Criminology, the Polish Society of Criminology, and the Board of the European Forum for Restorative Justice.

Witold Klaus is Assistant Professor at the Institute of Law Studies in the Polish Academy of Sciences. His main subjects of professional interest are: migration and crime, hate crimes, victimization, relations between poverty and crime and juvenile delinquency. He is also interested in migration law, discrimination based on ethnicity, and migrants' integration in Poland. Witold Klaus is an executive director in the oldest Polish criminological journal – *Archiwum Kryminologii* (Archives of Criminology), the Secretary of the Board in the Polish Society of Criminology, and the President of the Association for Legal Intervention. He is a member of the European Society of Criminology and the Polish Society of Criminology.

Anna Kossowska is Professor at the Institute of Law Studies, Polish Academy of Sciences. She is a Sociologist and Criminologist, and Head of the Department of Criminology at the Institute of Law Studies, Polish Academy of Sciences. Anna lectures in Criminology at the Institute of Social Prevention and Resocialisation, University of Warsaw, and is President of the Polish Society of Criminology. She is a member of the Editorial Committee of *Archiwum Kryminologii* (Archives of Criminology). Her main academic interests are: issues concerning the links between social change and criminality; the functioning of social control; crime prevention; and criminological theory. She is a member of the Polish Society of Criminology.

Irena Rzeplińska is Professor of law and criminology in the Department of Criminology of the Institute of Law Studies in the Polish Academy of Sciences and in the Warsaw University. She is an author of research on deviance, self-report studies, crime and crime policy – historical and contemporary, foreigners criminality in Poland and, in the last years: youth crime – past and present. She teaches criminology and human rights at the Warsaw University in the Institute of Social Prevention and Resocialization. Irena Rzeplińska is editor-in-chief of the oldest Polish criminological journal, *Archiwum Kryminologii*, and member of the European Society of Criminology and the Polish Society of Criminology. In the Helsinki Foundation of Human Rights – non-governmental organization – she is an expert in refugee and migrants law. From 2004, Irena Rzeplińska is a Vice-Director in the Institute of Law Studies in the Polish Academy of Sciences.

Paulina Wiktorska is a lawyer and sociologist. She completed her doctoral studies at the Institute of Law Studies, Polish Academy of Sciences, and currently works there as an Assistant Professor at the Department of Criminology. She is a member of the European Society of Criminology, the Polish Society of Criminology and the Editorial Committee of *Ekonomika i organizacja przedsiębiorstwa* (Economics and Organization of Enterprise). Paulina works with problems concerning criminal law and policy, especially criminal executory law, adolescent criminality, violence towards next-of-kin, and the sociology of law.

Dagmara Woźniakowska-Fajst is Assistant Professor in the Department of Criminology, Institute of Law Studies, Polish Academy of Sciences, and Chair of Criminology and Criminal Policy at the Institute of Social Prevention and Resocialisation, University of Warsaw. Her research interests include victimology, harassment issues in an emotional context, deviant behaviour of juveniles and women, crime as presented in the media, and justice system policy. She is a member of the European Society of Criminology, the Polish Society of Criminology, and the Association for Legal Intervention.

Dobrochna Wójcik is Professor of Law and Doctor of Psychology, and she worked for the Department of Criminology, Institute of Law Studies, Polish Academy of Sciences, from 1963 to 2007. Wójcik has worked at the Institute of Justice since 1992 and directed the Criminal Law and Criminology Section for several years. Research interests include juvenile criminality, aggression, examining victims of crime, and mediation issues. Wójcik co-founded the Group to Introduce Mediation in Poland, and is an academic consultant to the Polish Mediation Centre. She is a member of the Social Council for Alternative Methods of Solving Conflicts and Disputes at the Ministry of Justice and the Polish Society of Criminology.

List of Figures

List of Tables

Introduction

Criminality has accompanied social life from its inception. It has appeared in every stage of the development of every society, whatever that society's organisation or form of government and in whatever historical epoch it has found itself. Despite having always been present, the concept of criminality has varied considerably in its extent. This variability relates to both the definition of criminal behaviour (specific acts that have been deemed prohibited) and the application of formal response mechanisms to unlawful conduct. Apart from acts 'conventionally' considered criminal (e.g. homicide, theft and fraud), new crimes and new ways of committing acts already specified by the criminal law as prohibited have emerged. These are related to technological changes and changes in the way society functions. The attitude of societies to conduct that has always existed is likewise subject to change. Hence societies are constantly criminalising, or, in some cases, decriminalising them.

Simply defining crime is a difficult and multi-faceted problem for the criminologist. The criminal law dogmatist, who uses the definition of crime in the provisions of the General Criminal Code, is not plagued with uncertainty. Criminologists, by contrast, pay heed to additional elements that help determine whether an act or omission is deemed a crime. These include the investigative and penal policies of the particular country, the level of development of civil society, and bonds between people (see Chapter 1, 'Criminality Today and Tomorrow: Structural Stability and Variability', by Dagmara Woźniakowska-Fajst).

Other factors have an impact on changing the composition of criminality, e.g. the social and political system of the given country, economic development, urbanisation and industrialisation, and changes in the structure of the population due to migration or age. These sorts of changes can be effected in an evolutionary manner and over a long period or they can occur suddenly as a result of rapid changes taking place in the particular society.

Poland has experienced a lot of pivotal watershed moments in the course of a history spanning more than a thousand years. The result of each may have been an amplification or attenuation of the scale of criminality in the country. This refers to every war, the period during which the country was partitioned, the regaining of independence etc. These were all periods that created new conditions under which society had to function and that were able to influence the differently specified norms that had to be protected by the state (see Chapter 2, 'The Status of Criminality in Poland since 1918', by Konrad Buczkowski).

The transformations taking place in criminality are connected with the general processes of social change that affect all societies. The influence that the processes of social change exert on criminality has long been a topic of sociological and criminological analyses, and features in older and contemporary criminological theories and survey analyses. The system transformation of 1989 brought changes to the incidence and nature of criminality, and to the way it was viewed by the public. The determinants of criminality in contemporary Poland can be analysed using the same factors as those invoked by criminologists in their descriptions of criminality in postmodern societies, i.e. social inequalities and exclusion, and cultural changes resulting from globalisation and the technical and information revolutions (see Chapter 3, 'Social Change and Criminality: Mutual Relationships, Determinants and Implications', by Anna Kossowska).

The belief persists in Polish society that poverty is linked with criminality. For many people, the relations between poverty and criminality appear to be obvious and even though they really are present, it is worth emphasising that poverty is not the main factor that drives people to commit crime. At the same time, society is afraid of the 'down and out' as a class. This is because they are only perceived as threatening people who make trouble. Consequently programmes ostensibly meant to assist this group have a de facto aim to control it as a dangerous population rather than to ensure that these people are given essential help and support (see Chapter 4, 'The Relationship between Poverty, Social Exclusion and Criminality', by Witold Klaus).

Social policy, appropriately implemented, and preventive activities undertaken as part of that policy, should prevent exclusion, and people already on (or outside) the margins of society should be included within its framework. These activities should be very deliberately planned and draw from the example of other countries while making sure not to repeat their mistakes. Survey findings show that the only activities that have a positive effect in preventing criminality are those that are not restricted to simply supporting perpetrators or victims, but which are additionally accompanied by measures aimed at reducing income inequality and promoting social cohesion (see Chapter 5, 'Preventing Criminality: The Social Policy of Preventing Social Exclusion', by Witold Klaus).

A suitably applied social policy is not the only thing that can have an effect on changes in the dynamics of criminality. Criminal policy and the associated concept of punishment are just as important. The system of punishing perpetrators of crimes is one of the most important aspects of the social fabric and should therefore be treated in a multifaceted and holistic manner. The concept of criminal punishment can be understood as a consequence of social solidarity combined with various interdependencies between individuals striving to ensure mutual safety and order. Punishment is simultaneously a tool of power and dominion, a certain technique to exercise supervision and control over the observance of generally approved rules and principles. It is a peculiar expression of social sensitivity, punitiveness and tolerance. Finally, it is a certain form of compulsory social assistance offered to, or forced on, individuals who refuse to behave in a socially acceptable manner (see Chapter 6, 'Justice and Its Many Faces', by Beata Czarnecka-Dzialuk and Paulina Wiktorska).

Penal policy, understood as what the courts do in order to counteract and curb criminality through applying the provisions of the criminal law, is expressed as many and diverse theoretical concepts. An analysis of the statistical data on the penalties that have been imposed allows certain conclusions to be drawn on penal policy as applied in Poland during the period of social change at the turn of the twenty-first century. These conclusions, however, only make it possible to sketch an outline of the modern conceptions of resolving the social issues associated with criminality (see Chapter 7, 'Controlling Criminality', by Irena Rzeplińska and Paulina Wiktorska).

The suspended sentence was the most frequently imposed penalty in Poland during the first decade of the twenty-first century. We can therefore speak of a 'controlled freedom' that is inseparably linked with the institutions of probation and which is executed by court-appointed probation officers, who specialise in rehabilitating offenders. Whether and to what extent probation is effective, and whether it really constitutes an alternative to incarceration, however, are debatable (see Chapter 8, 'Supervised Freedom', by Dobrochna Wójcik).

The problem is that increasingly more people see the criminal law as the best remedy for social problems, which obviously include criminality. This is partly because the functioning of modern societies relies on access to various kinds of information in which the world is depicted in a simplistic, black-and-white manner that contributes to a feeling of being under threat. These fears related to criminality are very often unfounded and are merely a reflection of the anxieties associated with social changes and uncertainty about the future. For this reason, it is easy for various groupings, especially politicians, to substitute anxiety about criminality for real fears. The main slogans of political parties tap into this kind of anxiety. Once these parties come to power they make these slogans a reality by increasing the severity of the provisions of the criminal law, often out of all proportion with the actual level of criminality (see Chapter 9, 'The Social Perception of Criminality', by Witold Klaus, Irena Rzeplińska and Dagmara Woźniakowska-Fajst).

The mass media, by depicting criminality in a selective manner, plays a major role in shaping this simplified picture of social reality, which is connected with greater punitiveness and an acceptance of authoritarian means of control. The media often focus exclusively on brutal, sensational incidents and scandalous examples of gross negligence on the part of the justice system. As a result, the public has a mistaken view about the extent and composition of criminality, as well as the risk of victimisation (see Chapter 10, 'Criminality and the Media', by Dagmara Woźniakowska-Fajst).

This book attempts to fill a gap in the Polish criminological literature by analysing modern criminality, its causes and the various responses to it from different points of view. For this reason, the focus is on the problem of criminality in Poland with a consideration of the broad comparative background (theoretical concepts, research conducted abroad etc.).

The idea for this compilation was adopted by a team of writers who work at the Faculty of Criminology, Institute of Law Studies, Polish Academy of Sciences. This allowed for a broad look at criminality as a social phenomenon. We are aware that this is our subjective point of view and do not hold ourselves out as only delivering valid conclusions. We have attempted to take a comprehensive look at criminality as an ingredient of every modern society. And while it is an undesirable ingredient, it cannot be completely eradicated from social life. This does not mean, however, that it is completely impossible to supervise and monitor. We treat this publication as a contribution to the debate on the problem of criminality and how the social and penal policy of the state should control it.

The authors
Warsaw, July 2014

Chapter 1
Criminality Today and Tomorrow: Structural Stability and Variability

Dagmara Woźniakowska-Fajst

There is a generally held view that crime is a certain identifiable form of conduct that can be defined by law and which is recognised as not conforming to the conventional behavioural model of a given culture. Governments therefore take steps to discourage individuals from engaging in such conduct and punish actions defined as criminal through the application of sanctions of various kinds. But that is where the consensus ends. Governments may well deem specific actions criminal but they are driven by different imperatives. Criminal law systems are based on religious and cultural systems as well as on different interpretations of morality (Ram 2012, pp. 23–4). There is no single definition of crime in the criminal law, let alone in criminology. An exhaustive look at just what is meant by criminality would seem warranted in a book devoted to its various contemporary contexts. What factors decide whether a specific action is deemed criminal? What would the constituent components of a definition of crime look like? Who decides which actions are to be subject to penalty and on what basis? And finally, why is the concept of crime subject to continuous change?

At this point, a criminologist would ask what, in that case, constituted the substance of a crime. Who decides what actions are to be included in criminal legislation? Why are some actions crimes and others merely petty offences? And where is the line to be drawn? Why is everybody not criminally liable to the same extent?

The sources of this 'substance of crime' have always been specified differently depending on time and place. In the canonistic doctrine (i.e. based on canon law) that prevailed in Europe until the seventeenth century, crime was understood as being identical to sin and as disobedience to the will of God. During the period of absolutism that followed, crime was seen as inimical to the wellbeing of society. The theory of natural law held that crime was incompatible with the laws of nature and detrimental to society and its citizens. Kant said that crime was a violation of moral law, while according to Hegel it was 'an intentional deviation of the will of the individual from the universal law' (Andrejew 1988, p. 59).

If we look at the issue of crime from an historical perspective, we can see that the principles of criminal liability have varied considerably. The idea of society having a general welfare could not have been conceived until some sort of state structures had been set up. It was statehood that gave rise to the problem of crime. But only those few actions intended to harm the interests of the authorities qualified as public crimes and only these were prosecuted by the state. The vast majority of crimes were considered private and the burden of prosecuting them lay entirely with the aggrieved party or his/her family.

The Criminal Code currently in force[1] does not have a clear-cut definition of crime, although it frequently makes use of the concept. The definition cited at the beginning of this chapter is theoretical and clearly follows directly from the rules formulated in the Code. The Criminal Code, however, defines a prohibited act as follows: 'A prohibited act is any conduct with features defined by the criminal law' (Art. 115 § 1). This is a broader concept than crime. Prohibited acts can be subdivided into petty offences, summary offences and indictable offences. Only the last two qualify as crimes; petty offences are not formally crimes and, as such, are subject to a lower degree of criminal liability. This type of classification has a tradition going back many centuries.

During the Middle Ages, crimes were distinguished from transgressions, although the criteria for this division varied considerably (e.g. the extent of the damage or injury and/or the nature of the penalty) (Sójka-Zielińska 2009, p. 153). This division has been strongly criticised in modern times (Andrejew 1988, p. 67).

---

1 Criminal Code of 6 June 1997, Journal of Laws 1997 No. 88, Pos. 553.

Despite these reservations, many European countries maintain this classification of crimes as being either serious or minor, e.g. the Austrian model classifies one group of petty offences as the most minor crimes and another as administrative infringements that are not regarded as crimes and which are adjudicated by the Administrative Courts (Bojarski and Radecki 2006, p. 5). This, however, is not the only model, e.g. petty offences are considered crimes in France, where crimes are classified as petty offences, summary offences and indictable offences depending on their gravity (Bojarski and Radecki 2006, pp. 5–6). Petty offences are not seen as being essentially different from crimes in Poland (Bojarski 2009, p. 56). It has to be conceded, then, that the nineteenth-century prison reformers were correct when they spoke of assigning acts to specific categories on a purely formal basis. This is because there are no clear-cut rules, and any general prerequisites, e.g. the harm to society resulting from the act, have been interpreted differently at different times. For this reason, some summary offences were automatically made petty offences in Poland in 1966.[2] Larceny, conversion, receiving stolen goods and damaging property were among the offences that were decriminalised. These same kinds of acts can be found in the Criminal Code, the only difference being the value of the property constituting the object of the crime. In any case, this value is flexible and subject to fairly arbitrary changes. Stealing property to the value of 400 PLN, for example, is a petty offence at the time of writing (2014) and is punishable by fine, community sentence or arrest for up to 30 days. Anything above that amount is a crime and is punishable by three months' to five years' imprisonment. This makes a huge difference to the perpetrator.

Petty offences, however, can also be upgraded to crimes. Driving a vehicle while under the influence of alcohol was a petty offence until 2000. As this type of behaviour was fairly common, all the more so as it enjoyed a great deal of social approval, the legislature decided to make it more serious by criminalising it, i.e. by upgrading it from a petty offence to a crime and substantially increasing the penalty (CC Art. 178a).[3]

Whether something is a crime is also relative with regard to the perpetrator. For the same or a very similar act, one person will be penalised, another will bear a partial or reduced liability, and yet another will not be liable at all. It all depends on *who* the perpetrator is, i.e. his/her age, judgement, mental condition and sanity at the time of committing the act. These are objective conditions that the court takes into account, along with any issues shielding the actions of some perpetrators from the justice system. There is more on this below.

Criminal liability for an action in respect of the perpetrator appears to have varied considerably at different times in history. The family, and sometimes even the neighbours, of the perpetrator were held collectively liable in early mediaeval Europe and householders were long held liable for the crimes of household members under their authority. Moreover, every person who participated in a crime was given the same punishment, regardless of the nature and extent of his/her participation (Sójka-Zielińska 2009, pp. 146–7). That men and women were equally aware of their actions, and that culpability for committing prohibited acts could therefore be ascribed to women, was first recognised in the late Middle Ages. Men and women were made equally criminally liable on the basis of this major turnaround in thinking (Sójka-Zielińska 2009, p. 160). Juveniles were treated more leniently, as they could not be credited with the same degree of culpability as adults. There was no upper age limit but awareness and intellectual development were taken into account (Sójka-Zielińska 2009, p. 160). Mental illness was an extenuating circumstance that mitigated liability in some fourteenth-century cases (Sójka-Zielińska 2009, p. 168).

In addition to 'forbidden act' and 'crime', is the concept of 'punishable act'. This is defined in the Act on Proceedings Involving Juveniles (1982).[4] A 'punishable act' is any crime, fiscal offence or petty offence enumerated in the Act and committed by a person 13 years and above but under the age of 17.

Juveniles form a special category. An act that satisfies the definition of a crime will not, as a general rule, be recognised as such in their case. Whether a given act formally qualifies as a crime therefore depends on the characteristics of the perpetrator as well. As mentioned above, the perpetrator's maturity and awareness of what he/she has done were taken into consideration in the past. The legislature currently applies an arbitrarily fixed age limit to determine whether the perpetrator is a juvenile or has to answer the charge(s) as an adult. Some legislatures acknowledge that children below a certain age limit cannot be made to answer for committing

2 Act on Delegating Petty Offences to the Penal and Administrative Jurisdiction (1966), Journal of Laws 1966 No. 34, Pos. 152.

3 Schedule to the Act to Change the Criminal Code, Journal of Laws No. 48, Pos. 548.

4 Act on Proceedings Involving Juveniles (1982), Journal of Laws 2002 No. 11, Pos. 109.

a prohibited action, e.g. a person who has committed an action and who is 14 years and over but under the age of 18 is considered a juvenile in Hungary, Germany and Russia, whereas a juvenile is a person between the ages of 10 and 18 in England and Wales (Woźniakowska-Fajst 2010, p. 20). Moreover, many European countries have special rules for criminal proceedings involving juveniles (Gaberle 2006, p. 175). In Poland, the term 'juvenile' refers to three age groups, there is no fixed lower limit for liability, and a punishable act can be committed by a person between the ages of 13 and 17, although every so often the necessity of lowering the age limit for criminal liability is raised, especially in the case of the most serious crimes. On the other hand, the Criminal Code (Art. 10 § 3) provides for educational measures in lieu of a penalty for 17-year-olds. Accepting an artificially specified age limit is obviously more convenient from the standpoint of the judiciary as it frees the judge from having to go through all the minutiae of establishing the maturity of the perpetrator on a case by case basis. There are, however, various classifications to determine age distribution and establish criteria to distinguish particular phases in psychologically different ways. Arbitrarily defining a juvenile as someone under the age of 17 and an adult as someone 18 years and above is difficult to defend from a psychological standpoint (Domachowski 2005, p. 69).

If a prohibited act of a criminal nature is not in fact a crime when committed by a juvenile, then what is it? This mostly depends on the age of the perpetrator. If he/she has not yet turned 13, then Polish law confines the act to one involving depravity. The indications of depravity are enumerated, e.g. in the Act on Proceedings Involving Minors (1982), and one of them is the commission of a prohibited act. Educational measures can be applied to the perpetrator. In the case of a person who has turned 13, however, a criminal act is involved. For practical purposes, this is not a significant difference. Apart from educational measures, juveniles can be sent to youth detention centres as a corrective measure.

There is, however, one exception to the rule that a juvenile cannot commit a crime, viz. in the case of a very serious crime (e.g. homicide, causing serious health damage, armed robbery, aggravated sexual assault and rape), a perpetrator aged 15 years and over has the same liability as an adult (CC Art. 10 § 2). This provision raises all sorts of questions. In particular, Andrzej Gaberle has pointed out that according to Art. 10, the maturity of the perpetrator has to be recognised before any culpability can be imputed to him/her.

It has to be acknowledged, however, that given what is known about human development, a person who has not yet turned 17 achieves physical, emotional and social maturity in a sporadic manner (Gaberle 2006, pp. 178–9). Gaberle (2006, pp. 181–2) plainly states that 'the seriousness of the act committed by the juvenile is generally manifest proof of his immaturity as it clearly expresses his inability to comprehend the social consequences of his actions'. The legislature might have accepted the premise that a juvenile perpetrator should bear a lesser degree of culpability than an adult perpetrator and consequently imposed lesser penalties (Hałas 2006, p. 116), but research shows that juveniles charged under the Criminal Code (Art. 10 § 2) are punished severely. The courts have even sentenced 15- and 16-year-olds to 10–20 years' imprisonment (Rzeplińska 2007, p. 518).

The definition of crime also contains the concept of an illegal act. An act that ostensibly has all the elements of a crime will nevertheless not be a crime if it complies with the law on the basis of other regulations (Gardocki 2008, p. 111). These situations include lawful defence (i.e. the defence of legally protected interests from direct attack), necessity (forfeiting one good to protect another), acting under authorisation or obligation (e.g. a police officer using force to arrest a suspect), and innovation risk (e.g. conducting medical experiments to test a new drug).

Apart from the justifications laid out in the Criminal Code and several statutes, criminal law doctrine describes a few extra-statutory justifications. The very existence of these is further evidence that the word 'crime' is anything but unequivocal.

Extra-statutory justifications must, however, have some sort of authority in law, as their admissibility cannot be left to the sole discretion of the prosecutor or the judge when raised in a particular case. They are actually defined on the basis of an interpretation that draws on the principle of negligible social consequences. Customs and sporting risks are accepted as extra-statutory justifications.

One issue that always crops up is that boxing is a sport that people can engage in legally. In fact, it has its own official rules and is even an Olympic discipline. So long as the 'perpetrator' observes the rules of the sport, however, breaking noses and other bones, damaging internal organs, causing contusions and inflicting other serious injuries are not criminal acts. *Vale tudo* bouts, on the other hand, are considered illegal and anyone participating in one is subject to criminal liability.[5] The sporting risks justification has no application here. Pretty much the same goes for customs. The interpretation of what behaviour is acceptable is subject to constant change. The Polish custom of pouring buckets of water over people on Easter Monday (Śmigus-Dingus) can now be considered a justification so long as those who take part are known to each other and the doused person expresses consent. If, however, these conditions are not met, it can be considered harm to somebody's bodily inviolability (CC Art. 217).

As mentioned above, despite the conditions of social harm being clearly set out in the Criminal Code, prosecutors and judges are given a lot of leeway in how they interpret them. In any case, this doctrine has not withstood the test of time due to changing customs and a new understanding of what conduct is acceptable and what should be prohibited outright. A good example of this is castigating minors, which was a justification until recently (Gardocki 2008, pp. 129–31). To put it bluntly, this concerned the issue of whether a parent or guardian could hit a child. Proponents of this justification even worked out an elaborate set of rules. According to them, hitting a child does not constitute battery when it is done by a parent or legal guardian for an allegedly educational purpose and does not exceed a certain limit of intensity. Despite the obvious absurdity of this sort of reasoning and despite the fact that the doctrine never recognised it, some criminal law experts argued for its existence. All these questions were rendered moot when Art. 96^1 was inserted into the Family and Guardianship Code in 2010. This plainly states that 'No person exercising parental authority over, or otherwise having care or custody of, a minor shall administer corporal punishment'.[6]

The Polish criminal law system is structured in such a way as to make the individual guilt of the perpetrator the basis of criminal liability (Marek 2010b, p. 5). Whether culpability for committing a crime (intentionally or unintentionally) can be ascribed to the perpetrator in a given case therefore mostly depends on whether crime and perpetrator liability are applicable. The perpetrator's degree of liability is also connected with the applicable penalty. This is because the appropriate and just response to the act should directly correspond with the degree of culpability.

Proving that a particular individual committed an act is not sufficient to have that act considered a crime. The key question is whether the act was the result of a decision on the part of the perpetrator and whether that decision was made through an exercise of free choice. The constitutional principle of justice requires the state to 'configure the foundations of criminal liability so as to exclude the application of repressive punishment to a person who was unable to avoid committing the act in which that liability lies' (Wróbel and Zoll 2010, p. 322). Before a perpetrator can formally be culpable of anything, he/she must have reached the age specified in the penal act (i.e. 17 or 15 in special cases). The material circumstances are those that prove that the perpetrator was capable of recognising the significance of his/her act and of making a free decision as to which act or omission he/she would undertake. A perpetrator who is not sufficiently mature mentally to recognise the significance of what he/she has done or who was non compos mentis at the time he/she acted, might therefore not be culpable, especially if the act was committed in circumstances that prevented him/her from making a free decision (e.g. threats, blackmail, fear or orders) (Wróbel and Zoll 2010, pp. 328–30). The criminal law also makes use of the concepts of wilful misconduct (a prohibited act qualifies as wilful misconduct when 'the perpetrator intends to commit it, i.e. when he/she either wants to commit it or can foresee the possibility of its being committed and is agreeable thereto' [CC Art. 9 § 1]) and unintentional misconduct ('when the perpetrator does not intend to commit it [i.e. the act] but nevertheless does so through failure to exercise due care in the circumstances, even though he/she foresaw or could have foreseen the possibility of committing the act' [CC Art. 9 § 2]). In other words, some conduct can also be punishable when the perpetrator demonstrates a certain lack of care in his/her actions, even though his/her level of maturity and intellectual development indicate that he/she should have assessed the consequences of his/her actions otherwise. There is a presumption in Polish law that the perpetrator is capable of understanding the significance of his/her actions. This presumption can only be rebutted by demonstrating that there were subjective circumstances that ruled out any possibility of a genuine understanding of the significance of the act (Wróbel 2006, p. 664).

5 *Vale tudo*, which originated in Brazil in the 1920s, is a combat sport with very few rules that is not officially acknowledged as a sport.

6 Family and Guardianship Code (1964), Journal of Laws 2012, Pos. 788.

The next assessment criterion of judging whether a specified act or series of acts can be considered a crime is its social harm.[7] Since the Enlightenment, there has been a general realisation that some conduct is harmful to society and its members. This is one of the justifications mentioned above for criminalising acts. For a long time, the criteria for assessing social harm were not laid out in the codes but were based on case law and doctrine (Bojarski 2009, p. 60). These criteria were not set out in the Criminal Code until 1997. They were inserted into the Petty Offence Code later. The Criminal Code (Art. 115 § 2) states:

> when assessing the social harm of an act, the court shall take into account the type and nature of the infringed right, the extent of the inflicted or threatened damage, the manner and circumstances in which the act was committed, the seriousness of the duties that were breached, the perpetrator's motivation and intent, and the type of rules of caution that were infringed and the extent to which they were infringed.

All these considerations, as well as those accounted for in the description of the prohibited act, make up its social harm.

It is also significant that the legislature clearly states that a given act can only be considered a crime when its degree of social harm is not negligible (CC Art. 1 § 2). The Petty Offence Code does not impose this limitation. The degree of social harm, then, is the major difference between the Criminal Code and the Petty Offence Code. In principle, petty offences are socially harmful, but to a negligible degree. The social harm of an act, figuratively speaking, is a safety valve installed to make the criminal law rational and just. The legislature decides which actions should be considered crimes and consequently punished. At the same time, it gives the bodies that conduct criminal proceedings the necessary tools to determine whether a specific human action was nevertheless not a crime in a particular case as it was not harmful to the members of society or to society in general. An example of such a situation is a family member forging the signature of a paralysed person on a cheque with that person's consent so that funds can be withdrawn from his/her bank account to pay for rehabilitation.

The criminal law approach to the concept of crime as described above shows that 'what is crime?' is not an easy question to answer. The issue of determining the elements that make up particular crimes is only one aspect of the problem. Moreover, the difficulty increases once we step outside the confines of the criminal law and examine what criminologists have to say about the concept of crime and how the state formulates criminal policy.

First, there is not, nor can there be, a single definition of crime from a criminological perspective. The criminological dictionary specifies three elements that determine whether an act is a crime, viz. '(1) harm; (2) social agreement or consensus; and (3) official societal response' (Henry 2006, p. 78). Harm is defined in terms of the nature and seriousness of the inflicted wrong and the aggrieved party. Consensus refers to the social agreement as to whether a victim has suffered material harm as a result of a given incident. The 'official societal response' means the specific criminal law provisions that set out the circumstances in which a given act is considered a crime. The legal definition of crime was created on the basis of two main models, viz. the consensus society and the conflict society. The consensus society is inclusive, has a fairly stable structure and is built on generally accepted norms and values. The members of such a society agree on principle with the fundamental definitions of right and wrong and the criminal law reflects the will of the citizenry. Acts that provoke a negative societal response qualify as crimes (Michałowski 1977, pp. 23–4). A conflict society per contra consists of disparate social groups having diverse norms, values and interests. Such societies are typically unstable and the criminal law is exploited by the more powerful governing groups to force the other groups to behave in a specified manner. The criminal law does not defend common values but merely protects the interests of those groups that wield power (Błachut 2007, p. 56). Many societies, however, have a mixed system. Certain conduct is criminalised on the basis of a common social accord but the parallel criminalisation of other actions may well arouse controversy as it only protects the values and interests of one of the co-existing social groups (Błachut 2007, p. 60). The criminal law often hits the weakest groups in

7 This was known as the 'social danger of an act' during the time of the Polish People's Republic.

society the hardest, i.e. the unemployed, the uneducated, the poor and the socially excluded.[8] It sometimes protects privileged groups as well.[9]

The fact that crime existed, however, went unchallenged most of the time. Nils Christie's (2004b, p. 3) radical statement has, however, given contemporary criminologists a great deal to think about: 'Crime does not exist. Only Acts exist, acts often given different meanings within various social frameworks. Acts, and the meaning given them, are our data.' Christie strongly emphases that the authorities (i.e. the legislature) arbitrarily define which actions will be considered crimes and which social problems will be solved using other methods.

Christie (2004b, pp. 16–20) indicates a few typical situations where society (formally or informally) flexibly comes to qualify specific conduct as criminal. The more we know about people who commit acts that go against generally accepted norms, the less inclined we are to define them as crimes. Christie comments that the 'limited amount of knowledge inside a social system opens for the possibility of giving an act the meaning of crime' (Christi 2004b, p. 5).

The last example of flexibility in qualifying conduct as criminal is our attitude to certain acts between next-of-kin.[10] Law, as well as custom, comes into play here. Polish law recognises 'relative application offences'. On principle, these acts should be prosecuted ex officio. However, given the special relationship between the perpetrator and the victim, the appropriate motion must be submitted by the aggrieved party before a prosecution can be launched. The Criminal Code states that these acts include unintentionally impairing the functioning of a bodily organ or causing a health disorder, larceny, burglary, conversion and fraud. So far as these acts committed to the detriment of a next of kin are concerned, the legislature has simply delegated the decision as to whether they should be treated as crimes to the aggrieved party. Should the aggrieved party decide that the matter can be resolved without the intervention of the state, he/she can waive the motion for prosecution.

When writing about the phenomenon that is crime, we should not lose sight of the fact that through the centuries and in various places around the world there is, and always has been, a catalogue of deeds that, without the slightest shadow of a doubt, bear the appellation of 'crime'. These include homicide, robbery and theft. The social assessment of other acts, on the other hand, has changed over time. As a result of changing ideologies, political systems and customs, some have become criminalised and others decriminalised. This is a vigorous and ongoing process. Lech Gardocki describes motives for criminalisation as being either rational or irrational. Gardocki (1990, pp. 53–4) sees a rational motive for criminalisation as one that has a specific purpose in mind and where criminalisation is expected to bring about definite results. The addition of stalking to the Criminal Code is an excellent example of rational criminalisation over the last few years. The phenomenon itself is nothing new – in fact it has been recognised for many years – but one result of the rapid development and increasing use of electronic messaging, especially by young people, is that increasingly more people are being emotionally harassed. Criminalising acts that new technology has made possible is likewise rational.[11]

Some acts have been criminalised because there has been a change in social attitudes towards the conduct in question, which, even though it had always occurred in society, was either tolerated or treated leniently. The Polish legislature has clearly and decisively declared that children cannot be subjected to corporal punishment and that there is absolutely no 'extra-statutory justification for castigating a minor' (as discussed above).

Gardocki (1990, p. 54) claims that irrational reasons for criminalisation are those where emotional considerations hold sway. The legislature frequently fails to cite any specific, rational purpose for criminalising something. Rather it invokes its 'intuitively felt reprehensibility of the conduct in question'. Conduct recently criminalised for primarily emotional reasons is mostly sex-related, e.g. publicly promoting, or expressing approval of, paedophile behaviour (CC Art. 200b), producing, distributing, presenting, storing and possessing

---

8 This is discussed further in Chapter 4: 'The Relationship between Poverty, Social Exclusion and Criminality'.

9 Death caused through duelling (a dangerous upper-class pastime), for example, was a mitigating circumstance in Poland prior to the Second World War. Cf. Świda (1989, p. 60).

10 According to the Criminal Code (Art. 115 § 11), 'next of kin means a spouse, ancestor, descendant, sibling, relative in the same line or degree, person related by adoption or the spouse thereof, or common-law spouse'.

11 This is discussed further in Chapter 2: 'The Status of Criminality in Poland since 1918'.

pornographic materials in the form of originals or copies of images, whether modified or not, depicting minors (this includes e.g. any representation of an adult made up as a child) engaging in sexual activity (CC Art. 202 § 4b).

Given the multiplicity of approaches to the problem of criminality and the diverse formulations of it that have been adopted in different parts of the world at different times, there is nothing for it but to admit that there is simply no good, comprehensive, universal definition of this phenomenon. The state responds to deviant behaviour in different ways: sometimes it criminalises it, sometimes it decriminalises it. Customs, morality and sensitivity to specific conduct are subject to constant change in any society. Social policy, the educational system, compensation, mediation and at times the criminal law, have all been used at one time or another to resolve societal issues. Experts in criminal law, criminology and sociology, and finally lawmakers responsible for implementing criminal policy have an enormous task ahead of them. How to measure, counteract, monitor and respond to criminality when the very phenomenon of criminality defies all definition?

Chapter 2
The Status of Criminality in Poland since 1918

Konrad Buczkowski

The phenomenon of criminality in society is inextricably linked with the existence of regulations that are accepted by the community as a whole and considered violated by the actions committed by criminal perpetrators. Criminality, under the impact of ongoing transformations in a given society that lead to, inter alia, political changes and changes in the state's criminal policy, will undergo substantial changes as a result of the transformations that go with socio-economic development or the evolution of the social perception of specific conduct that demands a response from the criminal law.[1] It should be borne in mind that:

> criminality is an aggregation of concomitant behaviours that have been ever present in human society 'since forever' and have always been held in check by a specific criminal law response. A crime is one, albeit a distinctive one, of many social behaviours, as it is prohibited by criminal legislation at the time it is committed. (Rzeplińska 2010, p. 195, author's translation)

There is no crime, then, unless there is a regulation to sanction the given conduct as such at the time.

The changes observed in the picture of criminality may hinge on any number of factors, including the specific socio-economic system of the given state, its economic development (including the effects of industrialisation and urbanisation) and changes in the makeup of the population brought about by internal (rural to urban) and external (labour immigration) migration and the population pyramid. These transformations can come about slowly through evolution or occur suddenly as a result of the given society being jolted by violent changes.

Poland has experienced many pivotal moments in the course of a history dating back more than a thousand years. The result of each may have been an escalation or a weakening of the scale of criminality in the country. Every war (of which there have been no shortage), the time during which the country was partitioned (1772–1918), the regaining of independence etc. all created new conditions for society to function and were able to influence the differently specified norms that had to be protected by the organs of the state.

The first period that needs to be mentioned and which may be referenced using statistical data is the two decades between the two world wars, i.e. 1918–1939. From the standpoint of the development of the criminal law, this can be divided into two periods:

- the first saw an endeavour to unify the substantive and procedural criminal law – completed in 1932 and 1928 respectively – inherited from the partitioning powers;[2]
- the second covers the period from codification until the outbreak of the Second World War in 1939 and is characterised by changes in the criminal law resulting from a transformation of the legal system of Poland, which was heading towards authoritarianism.

---

1 There is an important distinction between criminal policy and penal policy. The former encompasses a wide range of activities and methodologies primarily aimed at preventing or curbing criminality and minimising the effects of crime. The latter is restricted to counteracting criminality by having the courts and the various bodies that work with them (the public prosecutor, police etc.) apply the provisions of the criminal law. The extent to which state bodies, local government organisations, social institutions, NGOs and even citizens' groups can work together under the rubric of criminal policy when penal policy is implemented solely by investigative bodies depends on the perpetrator having committed a crime (or a punishable act) or being suspected of having done so. See Szymanowski (2005b, pp. 211–15).

2 *Rozporządzenie Prezydenta RP z 19.03.1928 r. – Kodeks postępowania karnego* (Decree of the President of the Republic of Poland 19 March 1928, Criminal Procedure Code [Journal of Laws R.P. No. 33, Pos. 213]). *Rozporządzenie Prezydenta RP z 11.07.1932 r. – Kodeks karny* (Decree of the President of the Republic of Poland of 11 July 1932, Criminal Code [Journal of Laws R.P. No. 60, Pos. 571]).

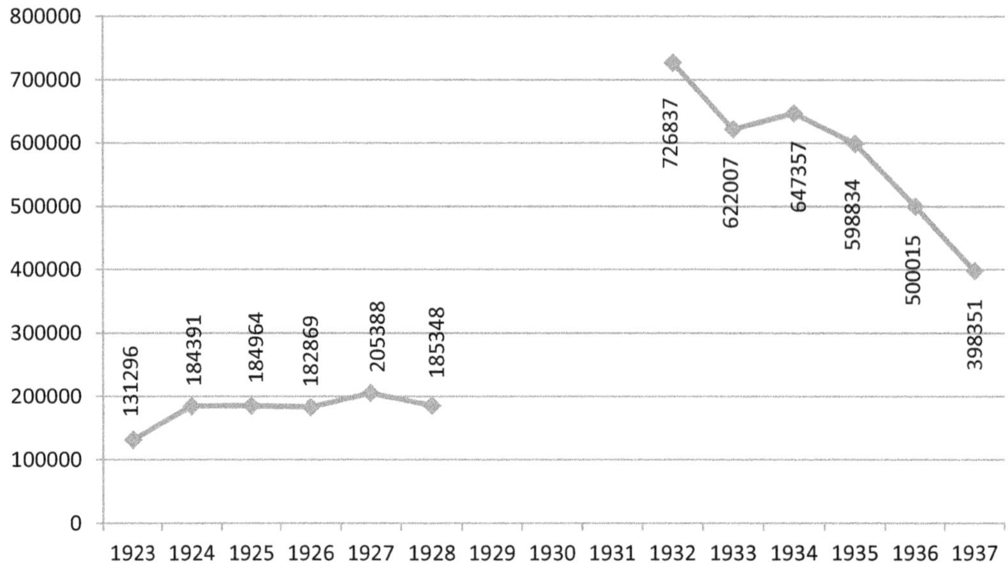

Figure 2.1 Finalised convictions in absolute numbers 1923–1937

Note: no statistical data were collected in 1929–1931.

Source: Author's figure based on data from Melezini (2003, p. 294) and Główny Urząd Statystyczny Rzeczypospolitej Polskiej (1936, p. 258).

In terms of the development of the criminal law, during the 20-year interbellum the clash between the opposing tendencies of aspiring for liberalisation and new proposals on the one hand, and increased harshness on the other was particularly evident.

The first found expression in the introduction of conditionally suspended sentences and conditional early releases as well as a remarkable lightening of penalties in less serious cases. The second led not only to a toughening of sanctions for particular crimes but also to the criminalisation of a greater number of activities. If the Criminal Code of 1932 alleviated the harshness of the criminal law by allowing the courts to exercise discretion in determining the size of penalties, then the extra legislation introduced since the May Coup in 1926 evinced the opposite tendency.

The regulations, made pursuant to delegated legislation, on summary proceedings issued by the President of the Republic of Poland in 1928 appeared especially harsh.[3] These extended the options for ordering the death penalty and made temporary arrest mandatory. Similarly with two pieces of delegated legislation from the President in 1934: Certain Crimes against the Security of the State;[4] and the Matter of People Threatening Security, Peace and Public Order.[5] The latter provided for repressive extrajudicial measures in the form of 'places of isolation'. It was this that allowed Bereza Kartuska prison to be set up (Melezini 2003, pp. 36 ff.).

Documented criminality increased during the Second Republic (for details, see Radzinowicz 1935–1937a, pp. 1–132; Radzinowicz 1935–1937b, pp. 361–439; Czernicki 1939, pp. 181–222). This was a variable trend until after 1935. By 1938, it had returned to what it was before 1929. The level of criminality, however,

3 *Rozporządzenie Prezydenta RP z 19.03.1928 r. o postępowaniu doraźnem* (Delegated Legislation on Summary Proceedings from the President of the Republic of Poland, 19 March 1928 [Journal of Laws R.P. No. 33, Pos. 315]).

4 *Rozporządzenie Prezydenta Rzeczypospolitej z 24.10.1934 r. o niektórych przestępstwach przeciwko bezpieczeństwu Państwa* (Delegated Legislation on Certain Crimes against the Security of the State from the President of the Republic of Poland, 24 October 1934 [Journal of Laws R.P. No. 94, Pos. 841]).

5 *Rozporządzenie Prezydenta Rzeczypospolitej z 17.06.1934 r. w sprawie osób zagrażających bezpieczeństwu, spokojowi i porządkowi publicznemu* (Delegated Legislation on the Matter of People Threatening Security, Peace and Public Order from the President of the Republic of Poland, 17 June 1934 [Journal of Laws R.P. No. 50 Pos. 473]).

remained about 25 per cent higher than what it had been in 1924 (the first year for which statistical data are available after Poland regained independence) (Krajewski 2007–2008, p. 120).

The above tendency is additionally confirmed by the statistical records of finalised convictions (i.e. no appeals pending) during the interbellum. Mirosława Melezini shows that in 1932, the number of sentences had increased by 292.1 per cent since 1928, before falling in 1933 and experiencing a slight upward swing in 1934. The number of sentences in 1937 amounted to 54.8 per cent of the number in 1932 (Melezini 2003, pp. 294–5). Detailed data are shown in Figure 2.1.

The makeup of criminality during the interwar period is also worth noting. Property crime, and especially theft, dominated. According to Krajewski:

> it generally made up a significant portion of all crime, but this increased to 70% in 1930–1934, compared with 'barely' 64% in 1924–1929. Consequently, this meant that the documented changes in the dynamics of criminality were mostly the result of changes in the incidence of theft. This situation changed somewhat after 1935. Criminality began to fall as of that year, but this did not affect theft, the incidence of which did not fall significantly until 1938. The incidence of theft was 26% lower that year than in the peak year of 1934 and only 6.8% higher than in 1929. The result was that theft became more prominent in the composition of documented criminality, constituting just under 80% of all reported crimes in 1935–1937. This share only fell to 68.1% in 1938, but this was still slightly higher than at the end of the 1920s. (Krajewski 2007–2008, p. 120, author's translation)

The cause of these fluctuations in criminality, and especially its precipitous rise from the late 1920s to the early 1930s, can be found in the economic situation in Poland during the Great Depression (1929–1933). This crisis affected the entire industrialised world as did the concomitant societal consequences (unemployment and falling living standards) whose outward sign was an increase in property crimes, especially theft.[6] Leon Radzinowicz was among those who described these conditions in detail. Radzinowicz added that the crisis led to 'a loosening of the ties of group solidarity, a strengthening of conflict and social friction, and a weakening of ethical restraints' (Radzinowicz 1937, p. 114, author's translation. See also Radzinowicz 1969, pp. 135–63). Śliwowski remarked that one factor that led to an increase in the number of 'crimes for profit' owing to poverty was 'anarchy and a lack of social discipline, an element of the lack of administrative harmony' (Śliwowski 1936, pp. 39–40, author's translation). Madey, Sztumpf and Mieszkowski likewise pointed to the decline in the moral standard of society. Mieszkowski even described the steps that were supposed to lead from unemployment to criminality (Madey 1936, p. 205; Sztumpf 1933, p. 2; Mieszkowski 1936, p. 95).

These theories on the rise in criminality spawned many ideas on how to bring it down, some of which found their way into criminal legislation in the 1930s. Most, however, concerned specific individual prevention issues and post-penitential care. A lack of resources, followed by the outbreak of the Second World War, destined them to remain nothing more than theoretical formulations (see further Rodak 2009, pp. 101 ff.).

Following the Second World War (1939–1945), Poland had its political system changed drastically (from a democratic state to a 'socialist democracy') and its borders redrawn (the country was shifted westwards and reduced in area). It also suffered an enormous population loss (through physical destruction and emigration) and a demographic transformation (from a multiethnic society to one that was ethnically homogeneous).[7] The communist authorities made very liberal use of the provisions of the criminal law to usher in and consolidate the new system. Indeed, the criminal law became one of the tools used to restrain, if not completely annihilate, any opposition to the new government. The liberal application of the penalty of confiscating property is one example of this sort of instrumental use of the criminal law. Irena Rzeplińska observes:

---

6 The economic crisis did not generally affect property crimes involving violence. Robbery barely made up 0.6 per cent of all reported crimes in 1924 and constituted just 0.2–0.6 per cent in the 1930s. See Krajewski (2007–2008, p. 120).

7 In the general census of 2002, 96.74 per cent of respondents declared themselves to be of Polish ethnicity, 1.23 per cent declared themselves to be of an ethnicity other than Polish, and the remaining 2.03 per cent declined to answer (Główny Urząd Statystyczny, *Rocznik Demograficzny 2010* [Demographic Yearbook 2010] 2010, p. 163).

> post-war legislation in the People's Republic of Poland extensively adopted the penalty of property confiscation. The legislature regarded this as an essential plank in a strict penal policy. ... During the forties and fifties, it was mainly directed towards two categories of accused: those who were politically opposed to the new authorities or who simply could not reconcile themselves to the new order ... and those who had been convicted of fascist and/or Nazi crimes or of deserting the (Polish) nation during the war. In the late fifties, the penalty of confiscation began to be used to victimise perpetrators of acts directed against public property. ... This extension in applying the penalty of confiscation – for crimes against the fundamental political and/or economic interests of the State and for appropriating public property – was transmitted to the Criminal Code (of 1969). (Rzeplińska 1997, pp. 79–80, author's translation)

The period 1944–1989 was a time when all sorts of information about the dynamics and structure of criminality served as tools for implementing the policies of the communist authorities. Any data from this period should therefore be treated with caution. There is no option, however, but to base analyses on official statistics, as no information is available from independent sources.

Several phases of criminal policy can be identified:

- 1944–1955: criminal policy and law were meant to consolidate the new political system and serve as weapons in the 'class struggle';
- 1956–1969: the Polish October and the 'Polish thaw', associated with the end of the Stalinist period, saw some degree of political and criminal liberalisation;
- 1970–1980: the years of 'prosperity' under Edward Gierek and the first years during which the new criminal codification was in force;
- 1981–1988: the socialist system was collapsing under a political and economic crisis.

During the period of the People's Republic of Poland (PRP), which lasted until 1989, the country was officially governed by many parties with the Polish United Workers Party as the senior partner. This period was characterised by a low level of criminality. Andrzej Siemaszko, however, points out:

> This state of affairs was, however, a direct result of the identifying features of a totalitarian system, viz. endeavouring to keep a tight control over every aspect of the lives of the citizenry, a disregard for human rights and democratic freedoms, and an extremely stringent criminal code and a monumental repressive apparatus typical of a police state. (Siemaszko in Siemaszko et al. 1999, p. 167, author's translation)

The immediate aftermath of the Second World War brought radical changes to the criminal law. The Criminal Code of 1932 and the Criminal Procedure Code of 1928 remained in force but were supplemented by a number of additional statutes that had the effect of changing the entire complexion of criminal legislation. Suffice it to say that more than 100 decrees, criminal statutes and other statutes containing criminal provisions were adopted in 1944–1953. These were meant to realise both political and economic aims of the new administration and were geared towards consolidating the new regime (Melezini 2003, p. 63 quoting Andrejew, Lernell and Sawicki 1954, pp. 231–43). The main effect of these changes was that the criminal law became considerably more punitive. This is evident in the increase in the options for applying the death penalty, introducing new types of crimes, including 'counterrevolutionary' crimes, e.g. sabotaging agricultural reforms or economic sabotage, increasing criminal sanctions, and summary proceedings intended to speedily inflict severe penal victimisation.[8]

---

8 It is necessary here to point out the extremely important role played by the *dekret z dnia 13.06.1946 r. o przestępstwach szczególnie niebezpiecznych w okresie odbudowy państwa* (Decree of 13 June 1946 on Crimes Especially Dangerous while Building the State) (known as the 'little criminal code'), which remained in effect until 1 January 1970, when it was replaced with the Criminal Code of 1969. This decree suspended the statutory effect of the provisions of the Criminal Code of 1932 that were covered by the decree. It introduced the new types of crimes mentioned above aimed at combating counterrevolution and was used with the general provisions to lend itself to a wide range of interpretations (e.g. public incitement to act to the detriment of the friendly union of the Polish State and an allied state). Moreover, it provided for the death penalty for 14 criminal offences, liberally applied life imprisonment, and additionally allowed for the

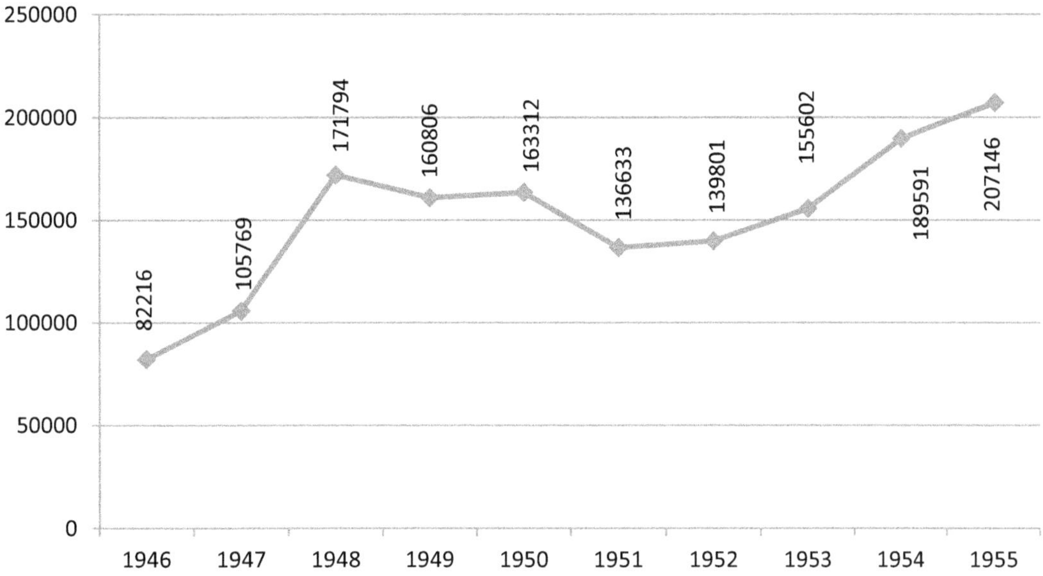

Figure 2.2 Finalised convictions in absolute numbers 1946–1955

Source: Author's figure based on data from Melezini (2003, p. 323).

It is impossible to discern any criminal trends during this period. Any attempt is impeded by the incompleteness, or complete lack of, available data. The only available information concerns finalised convictions and it is replete with errors (Figure 2.2).

These data show a clear upward trend in finalised convictions in 1946–1948 (there is no information for 1944–1945, which might be explained by the war and/or the chaos that followed in its wake). This may be a direct result of the increased stringency of the criminal law provisions connected with the campaign against opponents of the new system being waged by the communist authorities. The next two years saw a relatively stable 170,000 convicts or thereabouts per annum. This figure fell in 1951, which might partially be explained by the Act on Conditional Early Release of People Serving Prison Terms being adopted on 31 October that year.[9] This liberalised the provisions on early release. The following years, however, saw the number of convicts rise. The 1955 figure was two-and-a-half times the 1946 one.

One thing that has to be said when looking at the makeup of criminality in 1946–1955 is that perpetrators of property crimes made up the largest group of convicts, just as they did prior to the Second World War. Property crimes constituted 60.4 per cent of the total in 1946, 42.9 per cent in 1954 and 41.9 per cent in 1955. This downward trend can also be observed in subsequent years. Among this group, convictions for crimes against public property, mostly petty theft, were most prevalent. Theft was the dominant offence for those convicted for crimes against personal property (47.9 per cent in 1954 and 50.4 per cent in 1955) (Melezini 2003, p. 326). The rationale for this view of property crime convictions can be found in the new criminal policy foundations established by the communist authorities. These were especially intended to protect public property and make investigative bodies more active in that area.

The Polish October of 1956 and the 'Władysław Gomułka thaw' that followed brought certain changes to this view of criminality. Criminal policy was also slightly liberalised during this time.

---

confiscation of property owned by convicted persons and anyone with whom they were in marital or familial relationships (Melezini 2003, pp. 68–72, quoting Siewierski 1947).

9 *Ustawa o warunkowym przedterminowym zwolnieniu osób odbywających karę pozbawienia wolności* (Journal of Laws No. 58, Pos. 399).

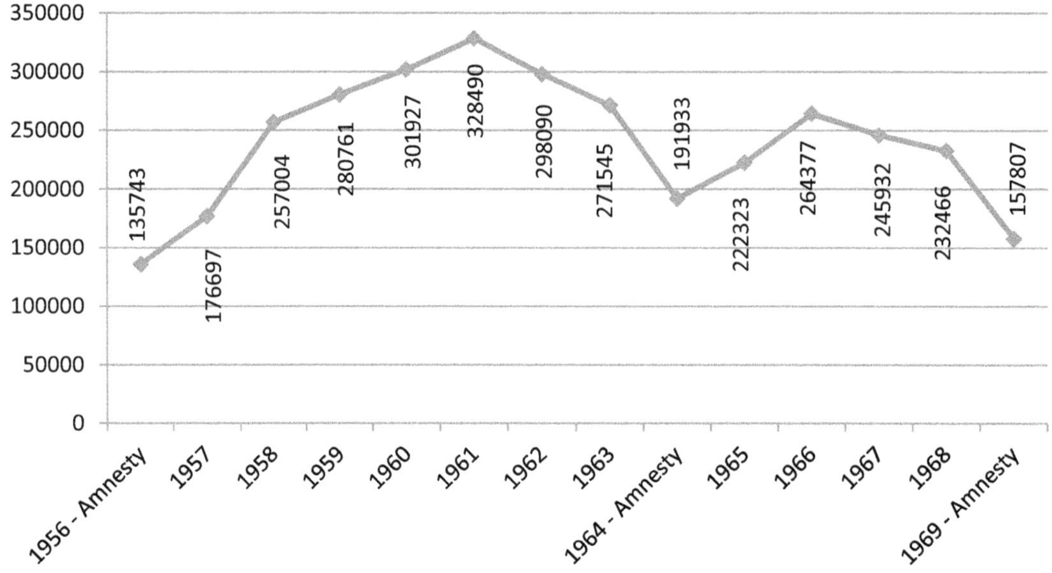

Figure 2.3 Finalised convictions in absolute numbers 1956–1969

Source: Author's figure based on data from Melezini (2003, p. 355).

The data on the number of finalised convictions in 1956–1969 reveal an upward trend until 1961, which then declines until 1969 except for a slight increase in 1966 (Figure 2.3). Similar trends can be observed in the statistics on confirmed crimes.

There were certain disruptions to the overall pattern of convictions, as presented in the data here, in 1956, 1964 and 1969. These were years in which a general amnesty was announced. A comparison of the data from 1956–1969 with those from 1944–1955 shows a considerable increase in the number of convictions. Leaving aside 1957 and the amnesty years, it can be seen that the absolute number of convictions exceeded the greatest number of the preceding period, viz. 207,146 in 1955.

The legislative changes during the period in question are worth noting as they had an impact on alleviating the harshness of the criminal law. The first was the Act on the Transfer to the Common Courts of Competencies Heretofore the Domain of Courts Martial in Criminal Cases Involving Civilians and People Employed by Public Security Bodies, Citizens' Militia and the Prison Service, which was adopted 5 April 1955.[10] This restored competencies in cases of crimes committed by civilians, with the exception of espionage, to the common courts. Rzepliński points out that this was the first sign that the Polish justice system was being de-Stalinised (Melezini 2003, p. 83 quoting Rzepliński 1989, p. 32; Rzepliński 1990, p. 42).

The next modifications were made by the Act to Change the Criminal Proceedings Regulations of 21 December 1955, which substantially reformed the model of preliminary proceedings with mandatory temporary arrest;[11] and the Act on Conditional Release of People Serving Prison Terms of 29 May 1957, which modified the material circumstances of conditional release by stressing the correction of the convict and amended its formal conditions by specifying the absolute minimum sentence that had to be served before it could be applied.[12]

10 *Ustawa z dnia 5 kwietnia 1955 r. o przekazaniu sądom powszechnym dotychczasowej właściwości sądów wojskowych w sprawach karnych osób cywilnych, funkcjonariuszy organów bezpieczeństwa publicznego, Milicji Obywatelskiej i Służby Więziennej* (Journal of Laws No. 15, Pos. 83).

11 *Ustawa z 21 grudnia 1955 roku o zmianie przepisów postępowania karnego* (Journal of Laws No. 46, Pos. 309).

12 *Ustawa z 29 maja 1957 roku o warunkowym zwolnieniu osób odbywających karę pozbawienia wolności* (Journal of Laws No. 31, Pos. 134).

The Act on Transferring Some Minor Crimes to the Criminal and Administrative Jurisdiction as Petty Offences was adopted on 17 June 1966.[13] This was the last Act to be adopted during this period. At the same time, it was the first Act to follow through on the idea of stratifying criminality and polarising criminal liability as espoused by exponents of the doctrine of the 1960s. The aim was to regroup acts from categories of crime into categories of summary misdemeanour and to alleviate the severity of the measures applied to them while maintaining the severe harshness meted out to perpetrators of serious crimes (Namiotkiewicz 1960; Ulman 1960; see also Melezini 2003, p. 97 quoting Rzepliński 1990, pp. 44–5, Skupiński 1967, pp. 105–6).

While some of the modifications made in 1956–1969 alleviated the harshness of the criminal law, others had the opposite effect. These mostly concerned strengthening the legal protection of public property and provided for harsher criminal sanctions (mainly imprisonment) for causing damage to such property as well as the optional additional penalty of either wholly or partially confiscating the property of the offender (further see Rzeplińska 1997). The option of a conditionally suspended sentence was additionally revoked in the case of any act against public property and both a fine and a prison sentence were made mandatory penalties in the case of a conviction for committing any crime intended to violate public property.[14]

As was the case earlier, property crimes were the most numerous in the overall composition of criminality. It should be noted, however, that, for example, the rate of incidence of theft in 1969 was 30 per cent lower than in 1956 (Krajewski 2007–2008, p. 121). The most numerous among the group of those convicted for this type of crime were convicted for acts against public property (16–28 per cent in 1955–1969). The proportion of convictions for crimes against individual property was 13–17 per cent. A significant fall can be observed in both groups at the end of the 1960s. This can be partly attributed to the partial depenalization carried out in 1966 (Melezini 2003, p. 360). Moreover, Krajewski points out that the fall in property crime, and especially theft, may have been a result of the impoverishment of society, as there were fewer things to steal (Krajewski 2007–2008, p. 121). This proposition may additionally be confirmed by the downward trend in the number of economic crimes in the overall composition of convictions (from 12 per cent in 1956 to 4 per cent in 1969) (Melezini 2003, p. 360).

It is further worth noting a certain new factor that appeared in the composition of criminality in 1956–1969. The Act of 10 December 1959 on Fighting Alcoholism criminalised any act connected with being in control of a vehicle while under the influence of alcohol.[15] A curious result of this was a marked increase in crimes against public safety and road safety (from 2 per cent in 1956 to 16.5 per cent in 1965) and a 14-fold increase in the number of convictions (Melezini 2003, p. 360).

The new criminal law codifications adopted in 1969, viz. the Criminal Code, the Criminal Procedure Code and the Sentencing Code, all came into force in 1970.[16] These made significant changes to the system of criminal law that prevailed in the PRP. Virtually all the criminal provisions issued prior to 5 September 1939, and most of those published thereafter (including the Decree on Summary Proceedings), were repealed.

One of the basic assumptions underlying the new codification was that the criminal law had to provide a remedy that was differentiated according to the gravity of the crime. This was already apparent in the Act on Transferring Some Minor Crimes to the Criminal and Administrative Jurisdiction as Petty Offences of 1966. As Mirosława Melezini observes:

> a code based on the principle of polarising criminal liability made it possible to conspicuously differentiate the severity of penal measures. On the one hand, there were severe penalties … that were reserved for perpetrators of serious crimes, repeat recidivists, and, to a certain extent, crimes of a hooligan nature. On the other hand, the

13 *Ustawa o przekazaniu niektórych drobnych przestępstw jako wykroczeń do orzecznictwa karno-administracyjnego* (Journal of Laws No. 23, Pos. 149).

14 These changes were put into effect by the *ustawa z dnia 21.01.1958 r. o wzmożeniu ochrony mienia społecznego przed szkodami wynikającymi z przestępstwa* (Act of 21 January 1958 on Escalating the Protection of Public Property from Criminal Damage [Journal of Laws No. 4, Pos. 11]) and the *ustawa z dnia 18.06.1959 r. o odpowiedzialności karnej za przestępstwa przeciwko własności społecznej* (Act of 18 June 1959 on Criminal Liability for Crimes Against Public Property [Journal of Laws No. 36, Pos. 228]).

15 *Ustawa z dnia 10 grudnia 1959 r. o zwalczaniu alkoholizmu* (Journal of Laws No. 69, Pos. 44).

16 All three codes were adopted on 19 April 1969 and issued, together with the introductory provisions, in the Journal of Laws No. 13, Pos. 94–9.

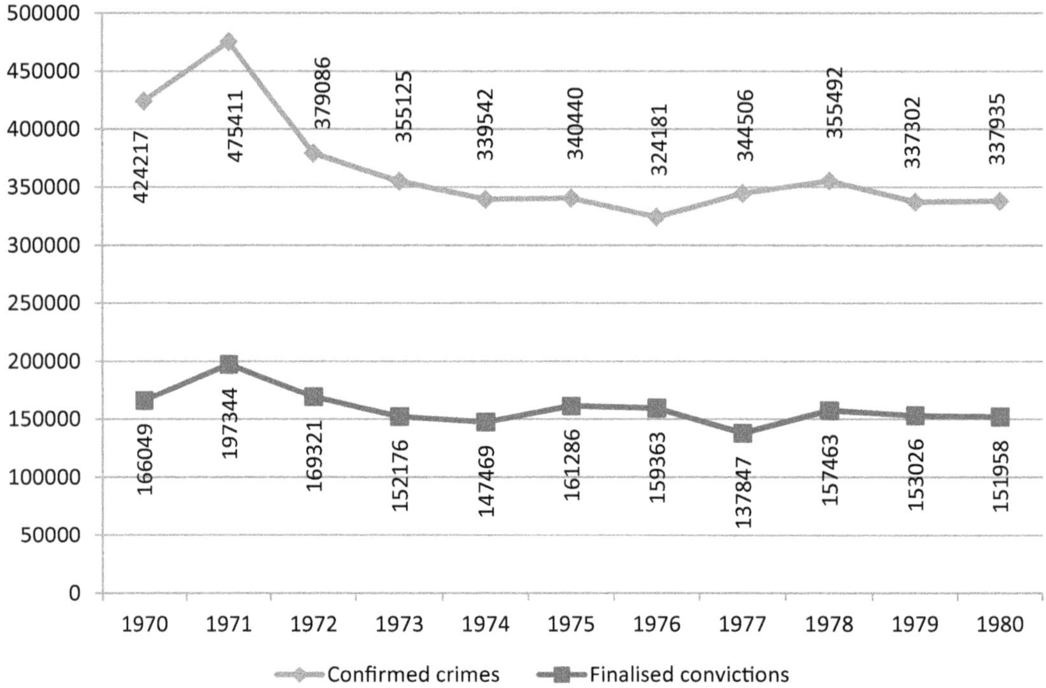

Figure 2.4 Confirmed crimes and finalised convictions in absolute numbers 1970–1980

Source: Author's figure based on data from Statistics Department, Ministry of Justice and Police Headquarters.

> code expanded the system of penalties and probationary measures that were not connected with imprisonment … and which were to be applied to perpetrators of minor crimes, leading to a radical limitation of short prison terms. … The Code laid the groundwork for applying a relatively flexible penal policy that left a lot of room for judicial discretion, especially in dealing with the most minor crimes. (Melezini 2003, pp. 125–6, author's translation)

The legal regime fashioned by the new codifications remained virtually unchanged until 1980. The only change was the Petty Offences Code, which was adopted on 20 May 1971 and came into effect on 1 January 1972.[17] This managed to redefine some minor summary offences (e.g. stealing, logging or receiving stolen trees to the value of 150 zloty or refusing to leave a public gathering despite being ordered to do so by a legitimate authority) as petty offences and hand their jurisdiction over to the Petty Offences Board (Melezini 2003, p. 122 quoting Marek 1975, pp. 14–15 and Marek 1996, p. 33). This measure, although theoretically alleviating criminal sanctions, actually gave greater scope for prosecuting perpetrators of such acts while the penal policy towards them became more stringent (see, further, Szumski 1980, pp. 102 ff.; Melezini 2003, p. 123 quoting Marek 1994, pp. 196–7). At the same time, it is impossible not to mention the judicial and jurisprudential guidelines issued by the Supreme Court. Although, these did not have the status of rules, they were unconditionally binding on the lower courts. Their purpose was to implement the criminal policy of the state by making penal repression more severe (see, further, Melezini 2003 quoting Jasiński 1982, pp. 37 ff.; Dukiet-Nagórska and Lubelski 1982, pp. 71 ff.).

---

17 *Ustawa z dnia 20 maja 1971 r. – Kodeks wykroczeń* (Journal of Laws No. 12, Pos. 114). The codification of petty offences additionally comprised the *kodeks postępowania w sprawach o wykroczenia* (Petty Offences Procedure Code) and the *ustawa o ustroju kolegiów do spraw wykroczeń* (Act on the Constitution of the Petty Offences Board) (Journal of Laws No. 12, Pos. 116–18). These were all adopted on the same day.

The 1970s was a time of stabilisation in terms of both confirmed crimes and convictions (Figure 2.4). There was a decline in both categories after the rise of 1970–1971, which was, it has to be acknowledged, a transitional period between the old and new criminal law regulations. The number of confirmed crimes decreased by 10.85 per cent and convictions by 10.25 per cent. A similar dynamic can therefore be said to be connected to the fall in both groups.

An analysis of crime by category reveals that property crimes made up the dominant share of overall criminality, accounting for as much as 40–54 per cent of the total in 1972–1980. Their dynamic during the period in question continued their downward trend, e.g. the incidence of theft in 1980 was 17.8 per cent lower than in 1972. This was not the case, however, with all types of property crimes. The rate of burglaries was 57 per cent higher at the end of the period than in 1969 and almost 30 per cent higher than the average rate during the 1930s. Burglaries accounted for as many as 20 per cent of all confirmed crimes at the end of the 1970s.

Krajewski points out that the decline in the number of thefts and the rise in the number of burglaries was a result of society slowly becoming enriched and that there was:

> the increasingly more common sight of more valuable potential targets whose theft required breaking down crush barriers (cars) or getting into premises where there might be property. (Krajewski 2007–2008, p. 123, author's translation)

The composition of burglaries likewise underwent certain changes. However much breaking into buildings that constituted public property might have predominated at the beginning of the decade, private property was mostly targeted by the end of it (the ratio was 46:54).

Convictions for the following crimes decreased as a portion of overall criminality during the 1970s: crimes against life and health (from around 15 per cent in 1972 to less than 10 per cent in 1980), against liberty and decency (from 2.2 to 1.6 per cent), against the activities of state institutions (8.3 to 3.7 per cent) and against public order (1.6 to 0.7 per cent). On the other hand, economic crimes, including speculative crimes, increased from 2.3 to 4.1 per cent. This may have been a result of changes in what the public owned and the approaching economic crisis of the 1980s.

The PRP was in terminal decline in 1980–1988. The communist authorities made one last ditch effort to save it as its political structures and centrally controlled economic system slowly crumbled. This was also a time of grave economic and political crisis that triggered an unprecedented outbreak of social conflict. By comparison, the 1970s was a time of prosperity and socio-economic stability.

This increased penal harshness was paying dividends by the beginning of the decade. The Act of 25 September 1980 on Combating Speculation introduced sweeping changes in punishing crimes and petty offences committed in trade and commerce.[18] The Act increased criminal liability for speculative crimes by means of additional penalties and accelerated procedures.

The criminal legislation introduced during the period of martial law made penal measures even more severe. Special mention should be made of the following decrees of 12 December 1981: the Decree on Martial Law; the Decree on Special Procedures in Matters Concerning Crimes and Petty Offences During the Period of Martial Law; the Decree on Transferring Certain Crimes to the Courts Martial and on Amending the Constitution of the Courts Martial and Military Units Organised by the Public Prosecutor of the Republic of Poland During the Period of Martial Law.[19] The Decree on Special Procedures was extraordinarily harsh. It provided for temporary procedures for as many as 143 offences typified as crimes in the criminal law, including 124 in the Criminal Code (Melezini 2003, p. 131 quoting Jankowski et al. 1982, pp. 10–19).

---

18 *Ustawa z dnia 25 września 1980 roku o zwalczaniu spekulacji* (Journal of Laws No. 24, Pos. 124 as subsequently amended).

19 *Dekrety z dnia 12 grudnia 1981 roku: o stanie wojennym, o postępowaniach szczególnych w sprawach o przestępstwa i wykroczenia w czasie obowiązywania stanu wojennego, a także o przekazaniu do właściwości sądów wojskowych spraw o niektóre przestępstwa oraz o zmianie ustroju sądów wojskowych i wojskowych jednostek organizacyjnych Prokuratury Polskiej Rzeczypospolitej Ludowej w czasie obowiązywania stanu wojennego* (Journal of Laws No. 29, Pos. 154, 156 and 157).

After the suspension of martial law at the end of 1982, the decrees listed above were replaced by the Act of 18 December 1982 on Special Legal Provisions During the Suspension of Martial Law.[20] While this Act mitigated some of the harshest measures introduced when martial law was declared, it simultaneously broadened the scope of criminal activity through its amendments to the Criminal Code. This especially applied to crimes against public order and to the addition of a new Article 282a of the Criminal Code that penalised 'engaging in activities aimed at inciting public unrest or disturbances'. This was supplemented by § 2, which criminalised organising or running a protest campaign directed against legal provisions.[21]

There is yet another Act adopted during the period of martial law that should be mentioned, viz. the Act of 26 May 1982 on Amending Certain Provisions in the Criminal Law and the Law on Petty Offences.[22] This significantly strengthened economic penalties by increasing e.g. fines (even by 10 times as much) and compensation payments.

The results of these changes can be seen in the dynamic of criminality in 1981–1984, e.g. in the significant increase in apparent crime. The statistics on convictions reveal very different tendencies. This picture is disturbed by the announcement of an abolition in 1981 and amnesties in 1983, 1984 and 1986 (Figure 2.5).

During the final years of the PRP, there was a significant increase in the severity and restrictiveness of the criminal law through what was known as the May Acts of 1985, i.e. the Act of 10 May 1985 on Amendments to Certain Criminal Law and Petty Offences Provisions[23] and the Act of 10 May 1985 on Special Criminal Liability,[24] which had something of a sporadic nature during the three years in which it was operative (i.e. until 30 June 1988). These were justified on the basis on an increase in the crime rate noted during the first half of the 1980s.

The harshness of these statutes is evident in the severe tightening of statutory fines (the lower limit was increased four times and the upper limit five times), which were not tied to any rise in inflation, and an increase in the bounds of payable compensation (by two-and-a-half times and 10 times respectively) while at the same time extending the conditions under which it applied.

The provisions of the sporadic statute that excluded the option of ordering conditionally suspended sentences for perpetrators of multiple crimes, that severely limited the option of applying the remedy of extraordinary mitigation of punishment and that disallowed the ordering of conditional early release of recidivists convicted under CC Art. 60 §§ 2 and 3 had a strong impact on the increase in punitiveness of the criminal law. This statute additionally broadened the application of the penalty of mandatory confiscation of property and introduced very strict rules for imposing fines. This was a departure from what was formulated in the Code, and assumed that the lower penalty threshold was determined by the value of the object of the crime multiplied several times over.[25]

The decline in criminality observed as a result of the amendments to the Criminal Code, the Petty Offences Code and the criminal provisions of other statutes in 1985 was used to confirm the validity of the theory that

---

20 *Ustawa z 18 grudnia 1982 roku o szczególnej regulacji prawnej w okresie zawieszenia stanu wojennego* (Journal of Laws No. 41, Pos. 273).

21 This amendment was effected by the *ustawa z dnia 28 lipca 1983 r. o zmianie niektórych przepisów z zakresu prawa karnego i prawa o wykroczeniach* (Act of 28 July 1983 on Amending Certain Provisions in the Criminal Law and the Law on Petty Offences [Journal of Laws No. 44, Pos. 203]). This Act extended the jurisdiction of the Courts Martial in cases concerning crimes defined in CC: Arts 122–33 (Crimes Against the Basic Political and Economic Interests of the PRP) committed by civilians. The Act also extended the range of prohibited acts by inserting Art. 278 § 1, which concerned belonging to a clandestine association, into the CC.

22 *Ustawa z dnia 26 maja 1982 roku o zmianie niektórych przepisów prawa karnego i prawa o wykroczeniach* (Journal of Laws No. 16, Pos. 125).

23 *Ustawa z dnia 10 maja 1985 roku o zmianie niektórych przepisów prawa karnego i prawa o wykroczeniach* (Journal of Laws No. 23, Pos. 100).

24 *Ustawa z dnia 10 maja 1985 o szczególnej odpowiedzialności karnej* (Journal of Laws No. 23, Pos. 101).

25 For a detailed description of these changes see Melezini (2003, pp. 134 ff.). The *ustawa z dnia 17 czerwca 1988 r. o zmianie przepisów prawa karnego i prawa o wykroczeniach* (Act of 17 June 1988 on Amending the Criminal Law and Petty Offences Provisions [Journal of Laws No. 20, Pos. 135]) came into effect when this ceased to be binding as a result of the sporadic statute of 1985. This new Act introduced a raft of amendments mitigating the rigour of the then prevailing criminal law provisions.

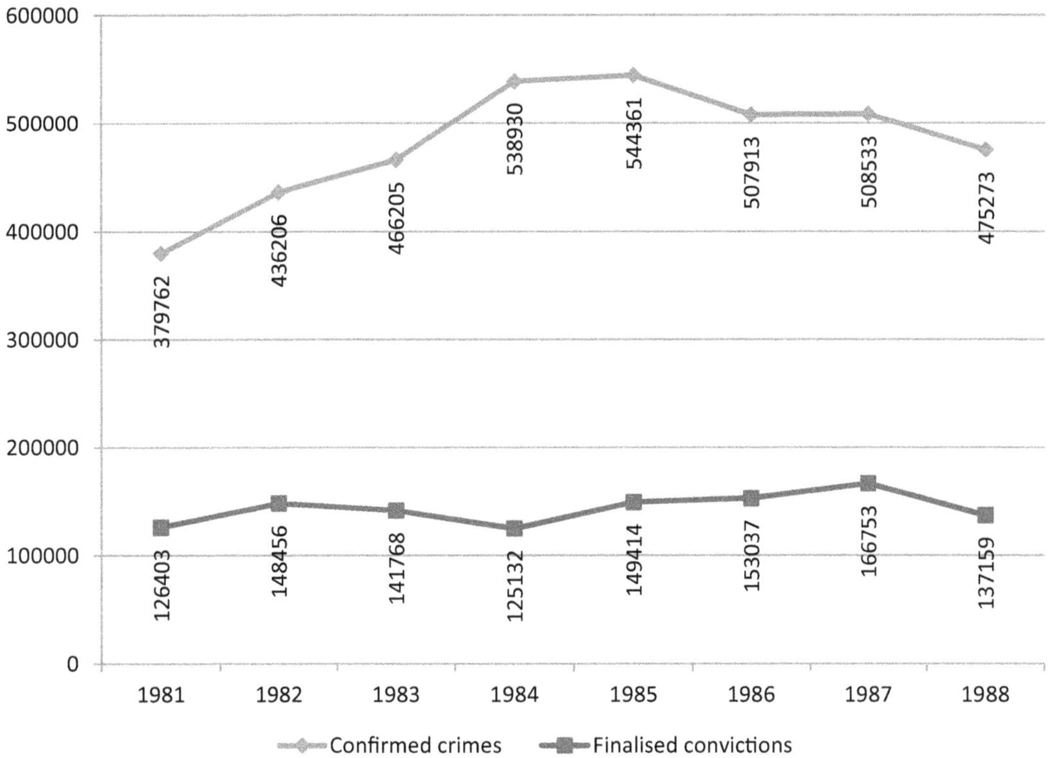

Figure 2.5 Confirmed crimes and finalised convictions in absolute numbers 1981–1988

Source: Author's figure based on data from Statistics Department, Ministry of Justice and Police Headquarters.

severe penal suppression can effectively restrain criminality and contribute to an increased feeling of security on the part of the public.

Property crime evolved in a similar way to the dynamics of apparent criminality in the 1980s (i.e. it rose until 1984 and then fell). A more substantial fall, however, is noticeable in the group of crimes aimed at public property than in the group aimed at private property (the number of crimes in the latter group began to grow again in 1987).

The greatest changes, however, occurred in the group of economic crimes and crimes against public order. The number of convictions for speculative crimes increased two-and-a-half times in 1981–1985 before falling below their 1981 level in 1988. The number of convictions in the second group, on the other hand, increased until 1987 (the 1987 figure was more than 14 times the 1981 figure). This has to be connected to the increase in convictions for crimes that contravened the Act on Combating Alcoholism and Temperance Education of 1982 (these accounted for almost 84 per cent of convictions for crimes against public order in 1987).

Jasiński analysed the breakdown of crimes resulting in convictions in 1980–1988 (indictable offences, serious summary offences, less serious summary offences, summary offences of little seriousness and trivial summary offences) and concluded:

> people convicted in the 1980s were generally perpetrators of increasingly less serious crimes. This occurred after the May Acts of 1985 were introduced and came into effect. (Jasiński 1993, pp. 53 ff., author's translation)

The most recent period of social upheaval in Polish history was that of the socio-political changes of 1989 and the constitutional and political transformations that followed. These could not have taken place without impacting the level and composition of criminality in Poland. The criminal policy of the state can be divided into two periods: before the new Criminal Code came into effect on 1 September 1998; and from the time the new provisions were introduced until now.

It bears repeating that crime statistics during the PRP were a propaganda tool. For this reason, actual criminality should be taken to have been significantly higher than what the official data reveal. The relevance of this proviso is confirmed by the marked increase in confirmed crimes after the constitutional and political changes of the late 1980s and early 1990s. The incremental increase was still not inordinately large in 1989, being no more than 15.2 per cent higher than in 1988. In 1990, however, it was over 61 per cent higher than in 1989. It was relatively stable, but remained at a high level, in 1991–1993 (Figure 2.6).

Attempts have been made to find the causes for this state of affairs in several factors. One is the already mentioned unreliability of statistics during the period of 'real socialism' (1945–1989). These were tweaked to suit current propaganda requirements. In particular, they were manipulated to show a high level of effectiveness in combating the kinds of criminality the authorities wanted to restrain. The changes of 1989 also made investigative bodies, which were trying to show their commitment to the democratic changes taking place in the country and which were keen to dissociate themselves from their negative associations with the Citizen's Militia in the mind of the public, agree to report every crime, no matter how trivial or how obviously incredible. A desire to obtain a greater budget allocation for the police might have been an additional motivation. A statistical increase in criminality was achieved in this simple manner. A greater desire on the part of the public to report crimes obviously might have had something to do with it as well.

Irrespective of the causes that might somehow have had an effect on the increase in the number of registered crimes, however, the spectacular growth of criminality in particular groups of acts, witnessed during the course of a single year (between 1989 and 1990), cannot be overlooked. A 100 per cent increase was recorded for burglaries, almost 80 per cent for robberies, over 50 per cent for theft, 30 per cent for crimes of violence or assault, over 30 per cent for homicides, and 20 per cent for crimes involving bodily harm (data from Siemaszko et al. 1999, p. 168). A general increase of approximately 80 per cent was recorded for property crimes (data from Krajewski 2007–2008, p. 127).

Organised crime was an additional factor that influenced the growth of confirmed criminality in the first few years after the constitutional and political transformations. This typically involved a lot of crimes being committed by the same people, so their confirmation would have resulted in a relatively small increase in the number of suspects. Moreover, new kinds of crimes associated with forging documents and racketing made their appearance.

Nor can it be overlooked that the knock-on effect of the economic transformations in progress, viz. social stratification and a precipitate rise in unemployment, might have had a certain influence on the rise in criminality, especially against property crimes, although this has not been confirmed academically.[26]

Siemaszko designates the following additional causes of the rise in criminality in Poland in the 1990s (Siemaszko et al. 1999, p. 170):

- increased emigration as a result of opening the borders and the appearance of more foreigners, who were both perpetrators and victims of crime;
- an increase in the value of goods possessed by the population, which had an effect on the number of property crimes;
- a weakening of social control connected with the considerable liberalism of investigative bodies and the justice system;

26 Szymanowski points out: 'Unemployment in Poland fluctuated from 1.126 million in 1990 to 3.217 million in 2002, and was 1.954 million at the end of 2010. It is interesting to note that the highest level of unemployment was recorded in 2001–2003, when there were 3.115–3.217 million unemployed and when the highest level of criminality, as measured by police statistics of confirmed crimes, was also recorded. The fact that up to 43.5 per cent of people suspected of having committed crimes were either unemployed or out of work and not looking for work is also established by police statistics. It might therefore be thought that being out of work is conducive to committing crimes. However, studies conducted in Poland do not corroborate the existence of any scientifically confirmed relationship between unemployment and/or destitution and criminality' (Szymanowski 2012, p. 26, author's translation).

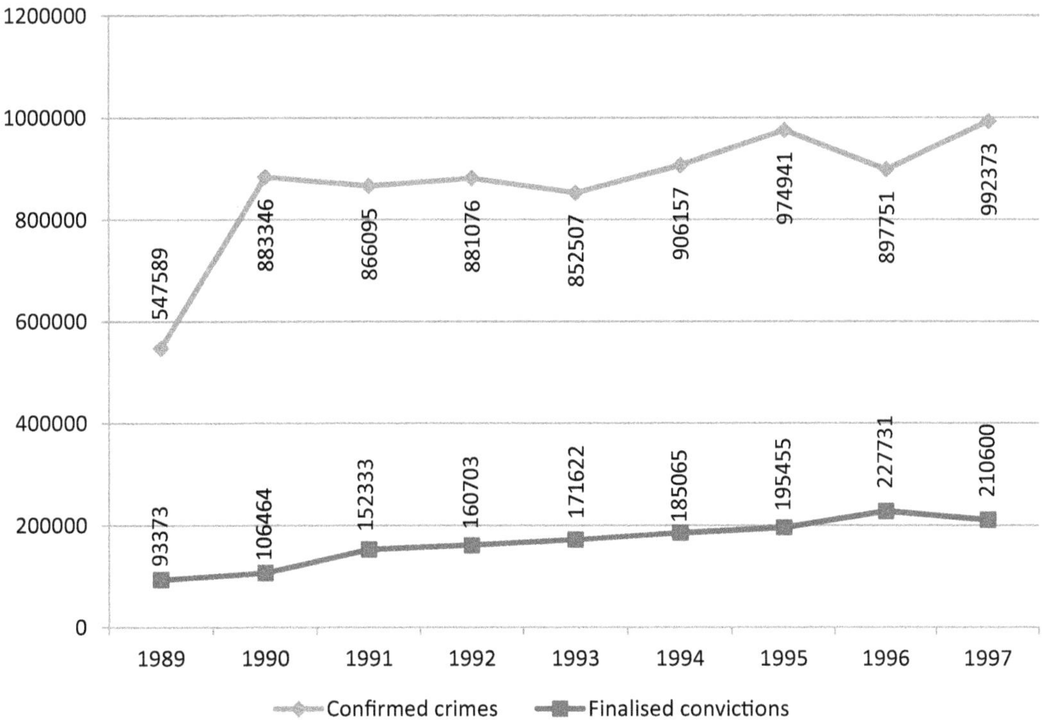

Figure 2.6 Confirmed crimes and finalised convictions in absolute numbers 1989–1997
Source: Author's figure based on data from Statistics Department, Ministry of Justice and Police Headquarters.

- a feeling of marginalisation on the part of large groups that had been socially favoured under the previous regime, which could have led to greater susceptibility to deviant behaviour;
- normative chaos, which might also have resulted in making people susceptible to criminal patterns of behaviour;
- the progressive stratification of society, typical of market economies, which led to a rise in beneficiaries of the system as well as groups of people who had no chance to benefit from the changes.

Criminality was relatively stable in 1991–1993, although it was not far below its 1990 level (the official crime rate per 100,000 people fluctuated between 2,216.7 and 2,296.6 compared with 2,317.3 in 1990).

Two substantial amendments were made to the Criminal Code at the beginning of the post-transformation period. The first was the Act of 23 February 1990 on Changing the Criminal Code and Certain Other Statutes, which made changes towards liberalising the legal provisions.[27] This mostly introduced regulations limiting or abolishing the differentiation in protecting public and private property (e.g. introducing aggravated theft of such property and lessening the penalties for the crime of appropriating public property of significant value) and abolished the additional penalty of confiscating property as well as the special penal measures associated with special recidivism (protective supervision and social adaptation centres). The provisions associated with what was known as the great economic affair were likewise abolished (CC Arts 134 and 135).

The second amendment was introduced by the Act of 29 September 1990 on Amendments to Certain Criminal Law and Petty Offences Provisions.[28] This had the opposite effect in that it increased fines and

27 Journal of Laws No. 14, Pos. 84.
28 Journal of Laws No. 72, Pos. 422.

compensation tenfold. This should not, however, be seen as deliberately increasing the severity of these penalties but merely as a desire to keep up with the rampant inflation, which in 1990, was at a record level (just under 586 per cent per annum) and twice as high as it had been in 1989. The increase in fines and compensation introduced in 1992, however, really did represent greater severity.[29] Fines had their lower limits increased 150 per cent and their upper limits 400 per cent relative to their 1990 levels.

The next rise in severity came in 1994. The dynamic index that year was 165.5 compared with 155.7 the previous year (1989=100) and was not much higher than in 1990 (161.3). Confirmed crimes also increased in 1995 (78 per cent relative to 1989 but only a little over 10 per cent relative to 1990).

The Act of 12 October 1994 on the Protection of Business Trading and Amendments to Certain Criminal Law Provisions came into force in early 1995.[30] This extended the range of criminality with new types of crimes previously unknown to Polish criminal legislation, e.g. money laundering, credit fraud, insurance fraud and crimes against creditors. It additionally made a series of amendments to existing valid types of crimes (e.g. mismanagement, and counterfeiting money and securities), and for some crimes (Arts 1, 5 and 6) it stipulated severe penalties while providing for cumulative fines, setting their upper bounds at 25 times the amount stipulated in the Criminal Code. Despite adapting the provisions of the criminal law to the conditions of a market economy, the Act on the Protection of Business Trading did not affect the rise in the number of confirmed economic crimes in any substantial way during the period in which it was operative (these provisions came into effect in the Criminal Code from 1997) (Buczkowski and Wojtaszek 1998).

The most sweeping changes to the criminal law during the period preceding the change to the Code were made by the Act of 12 July 1995 on Amendments to the Criminal Code, the Sentencing Code and on Increasing the Upper and Lower Bounds of Fines and Compensation in the Criminal Law.[31] This had a considerable impact on the decline in registered criminality in the following years. The Act managed to liberalise the criminal law while simultaneously making it more severe.

Liberalising changes can be found in, for example, the range of penalties for crimes of a hooligan nature committed by recidivists, a considerable extension of the legislative range of the application of the institution of exchanging the type of penalty for something more lenient, an almost doubling of the potential areas in which fines and community services can be applied (in the same extension), and a suspension of the obligation to order a fine with a custodial sentence and the option of replacing a fine that cannot be enforced with useful social work.

The changes intended to make criminal liability more severe consisted of increasing the sanctions for a range of crimes (including racketeering and extortion, assaulting a government official and illegal possession of weapons), introducing new types of aggravated crimes (e.g. traffic accidents, expropriating a motor vehicle for short-term use, and abuse) and introducing an extraordinary tightening of the penalties connected with committing a crime as part of an organised group or association.

There was an 8 per cent fall in registered crimes over the previous year in 1996 due to the impact of the provisions of the amendment of 12 July 1995. This was the result of yet another change introduced by the Act, viz. an increase in the threshold value of stolen goods and/or inflicted damage above which a prohibited act became a crime. Quite a few prohibited acts that had previously qualified as crimes were now summary offences. The greatest fall was in the category of theft, where the rate per 100,000 residents fell from 548 in 1995 to just over 408 in 1996. The decrease in the level of criminality in 1996, however, has to be understood as a result of legislative changes, as it generally reverted to its 1995 level a year later. It should be noted that the greatest number of confirmed crimes on record in 1989–1997 (992,373) occurred in 1997.

Of all the detrimental changes in the composition of criminality in 1989–1997, the rapid growth in crimes involving aggression should be noted (robberies increased three-and-a-half times, crimes of violence

29 *Ustawa z dnia 28 lutego 1992 r. o zmianie niektórych przepisów prawa karnego, prawa o wykroczeniach i o postępowaniu w sprawach nieletnich* (Act of 28 February 1992 on Amendments to Certain Criminal Law, Petty Offences and Juvenile Proceedings Provisions [Journal of Laws No. 24, Pos. 101]).

30 *Ustawa z dnia 12 października 1994 roku o ochronie obrotu gospodarczego i zmianie niektórych przepisów prawa karnego* (Journal of Laws No. 126, Pos. 615). This statute inspired a number of studies of which the following are worth mentioning: Górniok (1995); Buchała et al. (1995); Wojciechowski (1995).

31 *Ustawa z dnia 12 lipca 1995 roku o zmianie Kodeksu karnego, Kodeksu karnego wykonawczego oraz o podwyższeniu dolnych i górnych granic grzywien i nawiązek w prawie karnym* (Journal of Laws No. 95, Pos. 475).

or assault four-and-a-half times and crimes occasioning bodily harm two-and-a-half times). The exception was homicide, which after a huge increase at the beginning of the 1990s, had stabilised at a rate of three per 100,000 people. Juvenile criminality grew dramatically (approximately 15 per cent of suspects were juveniles) as did the brutality of the acts they were committing.

Poland is a country of relatively low criminality by European standards. As Siemaszko puts it:

> the list of 'crimes known to the police' shows that in terms of the homicide rate, Poland [in 1997] was ranked 10th out of 28 countries, in terms of the rate of crimes involving aggression – 22nd place, in terms of breaking into dwellings – 24th. Moreover, the results of the International Crime Victims Survey confirm this trend. And the 'general indicator of the risk of victimisation' places our country (for 1995) 23rd. This assigns us one of the lowest places in an international ranking involving 13 countries. … It can generally be said, however, that international comparisons show that the threat of criminality is still lower in Poland than in most Western countries. (Siemaszko in Siemaszko et al. 1999, p. 170, author's translation)[32]

Beata Gruszczyńska compared the crime rates among Central and Eastern European countries and noted:

> in first half of the 1990s, the rate of almost every type of crime (with the exception of homicides) was significantly lower in the CEE countries than in Western Europe but their growth rates exceeded the increase in crime in Western European countries. The rates of increase of robberies and drug offences were also decidedly higher in the post-socialist countries than in Western Europe in 1995–2000, although a certain stabilisation was observable in the case of theft and crimes occasioning bodily harm. Of the seven new EU member states, the growth rates of theft and robbery in Poland were similar to those in Latvia, Estonia and Lithuania, while the trends in the Czech Republic, Slovakia and Hungary were similar to those in the countries of Western Europe. (Gruszczyńska 2005, pp. 37–8; see also Gruszczyńska 2004, pp. 123–36)

The new criminal codification adopted 6 June 1997 came into effect 1 September 1998. This package of legislation comprised the Criminal Code, the Criminal Procedure Code and the Sentencing Code.[33] These made fundamental changes to the criminal law, generally by lowering the level of punitiveness.

Melezini assessed the new criminal codes and claimed:

> the liberalisation of the criminal law found expression in the number of legislative measures intended to limit the role of custodial sentences in criminal policy. This aim was mostly served by broadening the base of penalties and measures not connected with imprisonment in the Criminal Code while simultaneously modifying their legal complexion and adopting the principle that imprisonment was ultima ratio with reference to minor and medium criminality. In addition, the liberalisation of criminal sanctions manifested in the overall lowering of the upper and lower limits legislated for particular crimes and in the expanded range of alternatively structured sanctions created wide-ranging options for mitigating penal harshness. In principle, however, the courts were given a great deal of discretion in deciding the size of the penalty. It should also be noted that the Code adopted a relatively liberal conception of the criminal liability of recidivists. (Melezini 2003, pp. 200–201)

The Criminal Code, however, retained some of the measures that maintained severe sanctions: imprisonment for life and imprisonment for 25 years with the option of restricted responsibility (as part of conditional early release), criminal liability of juveniles aged 15 years and over for certain crimes, and for offenders involved in organised crime (Melezini 2003, pp. 200–201).

---

32 Differences concerning the statistical level of criminality between European countries may partly be the result of differences in the methodologies employed in different countries. As B. Gruszczyńska and M. Gruszczyński point out, the level of criminality recorded in Central and Eastern Europe was considerably lower than in Western Europe in 1995 and 1999. This might be explained by the more precise and restrictive system of police statistics in the 'old' EU countries than in the new member states (Gruszczyńska and Gruszczyński 2005, pp. 337–45).

33 Journal of Laws No. 88, Pos. 553, 555 and 557 as subsequently amended.

The Criminal Code began to be subjected to legislative changes the moment it was adopted. The first amended the provisions on infanticide (CC Art. 149) and terminating pregnancy (CC Art. 152 § 2) and criminalised wilfully causing harm to the body of an unborn child and wilfully causing a life threatening health disorder (CC Art. 157a § 1).[34] This was greeted positively by pro-life organisations.

Subsequent amendments in 2000 effected the following changes:

- Penal measures against perpetrators of traffic offences were made more severe, especially by introducing new kinds of prohibited acts that involved driving a motor vehicle under the influence of alcohol and/or drugs (CC Art. 178a).[35]
- Liability for corruption was extended with the introduction of criminal liability for passive bribery on the part of any person fulfilling a public function in a foreign country or an international organisation (CC Art. 228 § 6) and actively bribing such a person (CC Art. 229 § 5) as well as equating passive and active bribery.[36]
- The money laundering provisions were reworded (CC Art. 299 §§ 1, 2 and 7), the statutory penalty for the basic form of this crime was made more severe (the lower limit was raised from three to six months' imprisonment and the upper limit was raised from five to eight years).[37]

Moreover, in a concession towards the need to streamline preliminary proceedings, the Criminal Procedure Code was amended so as to transfer authorisation of temporary detention from the Supreme Court to the Appellate Courts.[38]

It is difficult to unambiguously pinpoint the causes of the harsher criminal policy of 2000. They may be the result of the precipitous growth in the number of confirmed crimes (the 2000 figure was almost 30 per cent above the 1996 figure), which had been observed since 1996, and the noticeable fear of crime on the part of the public (this had been observed in previous years), which in turn gave rise to calls for legislative changes. There was, however, one noticeable effect of these changes, viz. the amended Art. 178a of the Criminal Code brought about a sharp increase in the number of traffic offences. These constituted 13.5 per cent of all crimes in 2011 compared with only 4 per cent in 1997 (Szymanowski 2012, p. 62).

The amendments to the Criminal Code began to be perceived as a panacea to all sorts of social ills. The policy of changing criminal statutes in line with current events (not just political ones) and as a response to societal moods became the defining feature of the amendments of the first decade of the twenty-first century.

Obviously, not all amendments to the criminal codes need to be analysed in this context. It has to be remembered that Poland was undergoing rapid and profound changes in the early years of the new century in preparation to join the European Union, which it eventually did on 1 May 2004, and the country had to adapt its laws to EU regulations. The following may serve as examples of the kinds of changes made to the Criminal Code:

---

34 *Ustawa z dnia 8 lipca 1999 r. o zmianie ustawy – Kodeks karny oraz ustawy o zawodzie lekarza* (Act of 8 July 1999 on Amendments to the Criminal Code and the Medical Profession Act [Journal of Laws No. 64, Pos. 729]).

35 *Ustawa z dnia 14 kwietnia 2000 roku o zmianie ustawy Kodeks karny* (Act of 14 April 2000 on Amendments to the Criminal Code [Journal of Laws No. 48, Pos. 548]).

36 *Ustawa z dnia 9.09.2000 r. o zmianie ustawy – Kodeks karny, ustawy – Kodeks postępowania karnego, ustawy o zwalczaniu nieuczciwej konkurencji, ustawy o zamówieniach publicznych oraz ustawy – Prawo bankowe* (Act of 9 September 2000 on Amendments to the Criminal Code, the Criminal Procedure Code, the Unfair Competition Act, the Public Procurement Act and the Banking Law Act [Journal of Laws No. 93, Pos. 1027]).

37 *Ustawa z dnia 16.11.2000 r. o przeciwdziałaniu wprowadzaniu do obrotu finansowego wartości majątkowych pochodzących z nielegalnych lub nieujawnionych źródeł* (Act of 16 November 2000 on Counteracting Introducing Assets Values from Illegal or Undisclosed Sources into Financial Turnover [Journal of Laws No. 116, Pos. 1216]).

38 *Ustawa z dnia 20.07.2000 r. o zmianie ustawy – Kodeks postępowania karnego, ustawy – Przepisy wprowadzające Kodeks postępowania karnego oraz ustawy – Kodeks karny* (Act of 20 July 2000 on Amendments to the Criminal Procedure Code, the Preliminary Provisions of the Criminal Procedure Code and the Penal and Fiscal Code [Journal of Laws No. 62, Pos. 717]).

- Legal protection from any act defined in Art. 248 of the Criminal Code (electoral crime) regarding elections to the European Parliament and MEPs was extended by broadening the definition of a public official in the Code (CC Art. 115 § 13 Pt. 2a).[39]
- As a result of implementing the Convention on Protecting the Financial Interests of the European Community, the application of the unrestricted nationality rules (CC Art. 112) was changed by having the Polish justice system assume jurisdiction of crimes committed outside the borders of Poland, whatever the citizenship of the perpetrator, and make crimes punishable where they were committed, provided they result in a financial benefit being obtained in Poland, and in including all forms of obtaining European Community funds (subsidies, grants etc.) by deception or extortion under the statutory heading of credit fraud (CC Art. 297).[40 41]
- As a result of the Council of Europe Convention on Cybercrime, to which Poland became a signatory on 23 November 2001 (although it has not ratified it as at the time of writing), the provisions on computer crime were amended (CC Art. 268 § 2 and the new crimes enumerated in CC Arts 269a and 269b); the revised description of a prohibited act in Art. 202 § 2 of the Criminal Code, which extended the punishability of keeping pornographic content in an unsecured manner, thereby enabling minors to familiarise themselves with it, should be considered as it was partly due to these changes.[42]
- The following were implemented: the Act of 16 April 2004 on Amendments to the Criminal Code and Certain Other Acts;[43] regulations adjusting Polish law to the Council Framework Decision of 13 June 2002 on Combating Terrorism by defining a terrorist crime and tightening criminal liability for such an act (the changes were made to CC Art. 65, 110 § 1, CC Art. 115 § 20 and CC Art. 258);[44] and new regulations on enabling or facilitating another person to remain in Poland illegally with the aim of obtaining a financial or personal benefit (CC Art. 264a) and harsher penalties for arranging an illegal border crossing.[45]

Some of the amendments made it necessary to adapt the criminal regulations to changes being made in other areas of the law. The changes wrought by the Act of 29 June 2007 on the International Transport of Waste serve as a case in point.[46] This statute penalised crossing the border with dangerous waste without the requisite notification or contrary to the conditions set out therein (CC Art. 183). Other regulations had to be changed as a result of Constitution Tribunal decisions which held them to be invalid. One example here is the Act of 9 May 2008 on Amendments to the Criminal Code, which altered the wording of CC Art. 226 § 1 concerning the punishment for insulting a public official or a private individual.[47] Another example is the Act of 25 November

39 *Ustawa z dnia 23 stycznia 2004 r. – Ordynacja wyborcza do Parlamentu Europejskiego* (Act of 23 January 2004 on Regulations on Elections to the European Parliament [Journal of Laws No. 25, Pos. 219 as subsequently amended]), which was passed on 1 August 2011.

40 *Konwencja o ochronie interesów finansowych Wspólnot Europejskich z dnia 26 lipca 1995 r.* (Convention on Protecting the Financial Interests of the European Community of 26 July 1995 [Journal of Laws No. 208, Pos. 1603]).

41 *Ustawa z dnia 18 marca 2004 r. o zmianie ustawy – Kodeks karny, ustawy – Kodeks postępowania karnego oraz ustawy – Kodeks wykroczeń* (Act of 18 March 2004 on Amendments to the Criminal Code, the Criminal Procedure Code and the Petty Offences Code [Journal of Laws No. 69, Pos. 626]). This Act introduced other changes to sexual crimes by declaring sexual intercourse with a minor under the age of 15 to be a punishable act in itself and by extending the definition of the document.

42 Ibid.

43 *Ustawa z dnia 16 kwietnia 2004 r. o zmianie ustawy – Kodeks karny oraz niektórych innych ustaw* (Journal No. 93, Pos. 889).

44 Council Framework Decision of 13 June 2002 on Combating Terrorism (2002/475/JHA) (Journal of Laws L 164 of 22 June 2002, p. 3).

45 These changes came out of the Framework Decision of 28 November 2002 on the Strengthening of the Penal Framework to Prevent the Facilitation of Unauthorised Entry, Transit and Residence and Directive 2002/90/EC of 28 November 2002 on Defining the Facilitation of Unauthorised Entry, Transit and Residence.

46 *Ustawa z dnia 29 czerwca 2007 r. o międzynarodowym przemieszczaniu odpadów* (Journal of Laws No. 124, Pos. 859 as subsequently amended).

47 *Ustawa z dnia 9 maja 2008 r. o zmianie ustawy – Kodeks karny* (Journal of Laws No. 122, Pos. 782).

2010 on Amendments to the Criminal Code, which amended the regulation that made it mandatory for the courts to prohibit anyone convicted of a road safety offence from driving a motor vehicle (CC Art. 42 § 2).[48] [49]

The amendment to the Criminal Code of 13 June 2003, known as the anti-corruption amendment, realised both aims stated above.[50] On the one hand, this was part of a legislative package that adjusted Polish law to EU legislation prior to Poland joining that organisation. On the other hand, this achieved a correction of errors that both scholarly writers and practitioners had noticed in the original wording of a series of provisions in the 1997 Criminal Code. As Mik points out:

> thanks to the anti-corruption amendment, four forms of fundamental errors were removed from the criminal law, i.e. to name them as per convention:
>
> - desistance (e.g. ... refraining from embracing the definition of a personal benefit ... in CC Art. 115 § 4);
> - legal-symbolic, i.e. not actually contributing any normative content but creating the appearance of such and thereby raising interpretative uncertainties (e.g. the specification in that same definition of entities that might be beneficiaries of a financial benefit received by, or promised to, a perpetrator of passive bribery, although not intended for him, with a consideration between them of a completely legally amorphous and undefinable 'group of people conducting organised criminal activity');
> - destroying the internal coherence of the system (e.g. omitting certain kinds of confiscation in the catalogue from CC Art. 39 Pt. 4, in combination with, inter alia, the time bar rules on implementing penal measures as per CC Art. 103 § 2);
> - axiological (e.g. an unjustified and drastic lowering of the limits of the statutory penalty for influence peddling – from a range of 1–10 years' imprisonment as per CC Art. 244 to a range of 1–36 months' imprisonment as per CC Art. 230). (Mik 2003, p. 13, author's translation)

Among the adaptive provisions to EU law, the amendment made changes to the criminal law that enabled corruption to be combated more effectively, by, for example, including categories of corruption that had so far gone unpenalised (e.g. economic corruption), broke the solidarity between the giver and receiver of a financial or personal benefit, and additionally made important corrections to the mechanisms that allowed perpetrators of crime to be dispossessed of any financial benefits they had received. This last change especially needs to be stressed as its underlying assumption and intended aim was supposedly that the judiciary could obtain a real possibility of ordering the confiscation of the benefits derived, even indirectly, from crime – not just from the perpetrators of the act(s) themselves, but also from anyone to whom those benefits had been transferred (CC Art. 45 §§ 1–3).[51]

---

48 *Ustawa z dnia 25 listopada 2010 r. o zmianie ustawy – Kodeks karny* (Journal of Laws (2011) No. 17, Pos. 78).

49 The existing wording of this regulation had been impugned by the Constitutional Tribunal, on the grounds that it raised uncertainties as to how it was to be interpreted, in a decision handed down on 5 May 2009 (File No. S 2/09). Editing the regulation led to situations where road safety offenders driving vehicles other than motor vehicles were incurring stricter liability than offenders driving motor vehicles. This was a result of the former being given sentences banning them from driving mechanical vehicles as well as the vehicles they were driving when apprehended.

50 *Ustawa z dnia 13 czerwca 2003 r. o zmianie ustawy – Kodeks karny oraz niektórych innych ustaw* (Act of 13 June 2003 on Amendments to the Criminal Code and Certain Other Acts [Journal of Laws No. 111, Pos. 1061]).

51 Research conducted in 2009 on the effectiveness of the changes made to CC Art. 45 pursuant to the amendment of 2003 included cases from 2007 and 2008 in which orders to confiscate financial benefits on the basis of CC Art. 45 were finalised (i.e. all appeals had been exhausted) and in relation to which action was taken to execute the judgement. Statistically, there was a total of 1,921 executed prison sentences as against 2,455 people who had a financial benefit confiscated or were ordered to pay an equal amount as per CC Art. 45 § 1 during the period in which the research was conducted. Information obtained directly from the courts reveals that only approximately 25 per cent of the judgements ordering the confiscation of a financial benefit were either wholly or partly enforced, and in around half these cases, this was only because the offender paid voluntarily. The taxation office collected the remainder. Moreover, enforcement procedures were applied to collect financial benefits of little value (a significant majority of which came to 101–1,000 zł), with more than 80 per cent of judgments being for 5,000 zł or less. The data reveal that, in practice, security on property was seldom utilised in preliminary proceedings (CC Art. 291 ff.), despite this coercive measure being the simplest means of ensuring

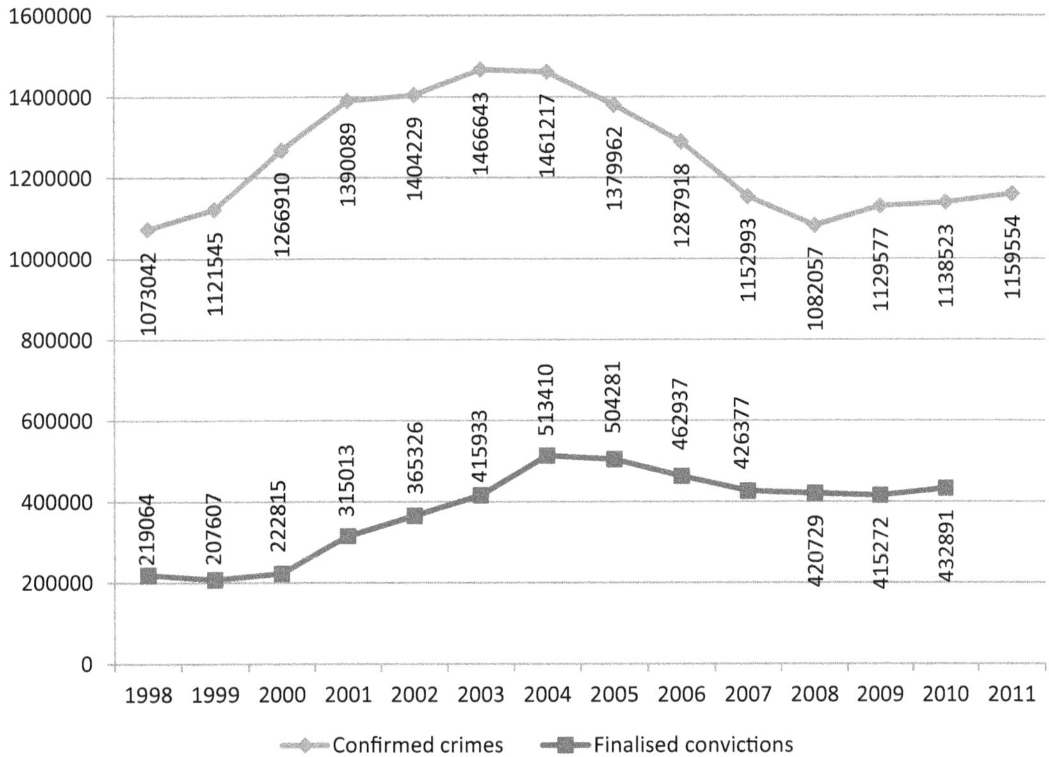

Figure 2.7 Confirmed crimes and finalised convictions in absolute numbers 1998–2011

Source: Author's figure based on data from Statistics Department, Ministry of Justice and Police Headquarters (available online at www.policja.pl).

The turn of the 21st century was a time when criminality grew systematically in Poland. Siemaszko observes:

> The magic number of one million confirmed crimes was passed in 1998. The general increase in crime was even more dynamic over the next four years, with a new record of 1.4 million being set in 2002. Criminality remained at an inordinately high level of 1,400,000–1,460,000 in 2002–2004. The growth trend started to be reversed in 2005 and there were 20 per cent fewer crimes in 2007 than in the record year of 2003. (Siemaszko in Siemaszko et al. 2009, p. 313, author's translation)

The number of confirmed crimes in 2008 was 1,082,057 – the lowest value for the first decade of the new century. This was more than 26 per cent lower than the figure for 2003 and not far off the figure for 1998 (1,073,042) when the 1969 and 1997 Criminal Codes were in force (Figure 2.7).

A slight growth in the number of confirmed crimes has been observed since 2009. The figure for 2011 was around 7 per cent higher than that for 2008, but still more than 20 per cent lower than that for 2003. The number of finalised convictions increased 130 per cent in 2000–2004, from 222,815 to 513,410. The amendments to the Criminal Code of 14 April 2000, mentioned above, were largely responsible for this prodigious growth. These came into force on 15 December 2000 and inserted Art. 178a into the Code. Being

---

that a judgement to confiscate a financial benefit will be satisfied without having to launch executory proceedings, which are frequently time-consuming (see further Buczkowski 2010; see also the research results for 2003–2005: Buczkowski 2007).

in control of a motorised vehicle on land, water or air, or some other vehicle (e.g. a bicycle) on a public road or in a residential area, while under the influence of alcohol or drugs, was upgraded from a summary offence to a crime by this provision.

It is worth pointing out that of the overall tally of people convicted in 2001, 24 per cent were convicted under CC 178a. This figure was over 28 per cent in 2004 and over 30 per cent a year later.[52] These convictions are mainly responsible for the highly significant change in the composition of the most frequently committed criminal acts, as traffic offences (including those under CC Art. 178a) ousted property crimes from first position. Traffic offences comprised 31.2 per cent of all crimes in 2010 compared with 29.3 per cent for property crimes. Offences against the administration of justice (8.2 per cent),[53] drug offences (4.8 per cent), crimes against life and health (4.7 per cent) and ill-treatment of family members (3.1 per cent) were next on the list (Szymanowski 2012, p. 75).

Nor can the amendments to the Act of 29 April 1997 on Countering Drug Addiction in 2000 be overlooked. This was replaced by the Act of 29 July 2005 on Countering Drug Addiction.[54] The number of confirmed crimes connected with breaching these provisions consequently increased considerably – from 7,915 in 1997 to 35,169 in 2003. The number of crimes committed under this Act more than doubled from 2003 to reach 74,535 in 2010.The number of finalised convictions started to fall in 2005 and reached its lowest value in 2009 (415,272 in absolute numbers), when it was 20 per cent lower than in 2004. This figure increased slightly in 2010.

This increase in the number of confirmed crimes noted in the first few years of the twenty-first century was conducive to bolstering the punitive tendency of the criminal law and strengthened the hand of those calling for the government to implement a tougher criminal policy. Paradoxically, however, amendments intended to tighten regulations – especially the Criminal Code – made their appearance just as the level of criminality in the country started to exhibit a downward trend.

The Act of 16 November 2006 on Amendments to the Criminal Code and Certain Other Acts[55] was a conspicuous example of this tendency, combined as it was with populist slogans about the need to combat rising crime rates.[56] This Act reinstated the idea of a summary offence of a hooligan nature in the criminal law (CC Art. 115 § 21) and obliged the courts to impose a penalty that was at least as great as the lower limit of the statutory penalty increased by a half on anyone convicted of an offence of this type (CC Art. 57a § 1) and to order that compensation be paid (CC Art. 57a § 2). The options of suspending either a community sentence or a fine (CC Art. 69 § 4) or waiving any penalty (CC Art. 59 § 1) were simultaneously revoked.

Another example was the revocation of the option of imposing either 25 years' imprisonment or life imprisonment for homicide as specified in CC Art. 148 § 2.[57] This was ruled invalid by the Constitutional Tribunal and subsequently amended in 2010 by introducing the option of imposing a prison sentence of not less than 12 years.[58]

Amendments that merit nothing but disparagement should not be associated solely with the populism that found its way into criminal legislation. The relatively high level of punitiveness exhibited by the Polish people needs to be borne in mind as well. The range of activities undertaken in response to the current socio-political

---

52 Incidentally, it is worth adding that inserting Art. 178a into the Criminal Code resulted in a sharp increase in the number of people for whom penal measures were ordered. This was a result of the prohibition on driving a motor vehicle while under the influence of alcohol in accordance with the crime notified above.

53 This mainly concerns CC Art. 244 and violating the CC Art. 178 prohibition on a convicted person driving a motor vehicle.

54 *Ustawa z dnia 29 kwietnia 1997 r. o przeciwdziałaniu narkomanii* (Act of 29 April 1997 on Countering Drug Addiction [Journal of Laws No. 75, Pos. 468]), *ustawa z dnia 29 lipca 2005 r. o przeciwdziałaniu narkomanii* (Act of 29 July 2005 on Countering Drug Addiction [Consolidated text Journal of Laws [2012], Pos. 124]).

55 *Ustawa z dnia 16 listopada 2006 r. o zmianie ustawy kodeks karny oraz niektórych innych ustaw* (Act of 16 November 2006 to Amend the Criminal Code and Certain Other Acts [Journal of Laws No. 226, Pos. 1648]).

56 For a further discussion of this issue, see Chapter 9: 'The Social Perception of Criminality'.

57 *Ustawa z dnia 27 lipca 2005 r. o zmianie ustawy – Kodeks karny, ustawy – Kodeks postępowania karnego i ustawy – Kodeks karny wykonawczy* (Act of 27 July 2005 to Amend the Criminal Code, the Criminal Procedure Code and the Sentencing Code [Journal of Laws No. 163, Pos. 1363]).

58 *Ustawa z dnia 26 listopada 2010 r. o zmianie ustawy – Kodeks karny oraz ustawy o Policji* (Act of 26 November 2010 to Amend the Criminal Code and the Police Act [Journal of Laws No. 240, Pos. 1602]).

situation can be considered justified and as having played a significant role in the country's penal policy. This was to affect the following changes:

- Extensions to the limitations periods for certain crimes (CC Art. 101 § 1) came into force on 3 August 2005.[59] This was admittedly a response to a range of charges in the Foreign Debt Servicing Fund (FOZZ) scandal becoming time-barred, but the change itself should be viewed positively.
- The introduction of a prohibition on entering a mass event (in the Polish context, this essentially means a football match) connected with a personal appearance in a police organisational unit (CC Art. 41b) and a possible sanction for non-compliance – as an answer to the increasing scale and seriousness of stadium brawls and the frequent scuffles between football supporters and police units trying to maintain order.[60]
- An amendment of the provisions on penal measures and protective measures in the case of a conviction for a crime against sexual freedom and/or morality to the detriment of a minor, and a simultaneous increase in the penalty for the crimes set out in CC Arts 197, 200 and 202 – so as to meet demands to combat paedophilia.[61]
- The criminalisation of behaviour that constitutes stalking, i.e. harassing someone persistently, and expanding the catalogue of cases in which the courts can issue restraining orders prohibiting people from being in specified surroundings or places for crimes against freedom not previously mentioned.[62]

Whatever the causes of the fall in criminality, they should not be seen in connection with onetime political campaigns, but rather with changes of a more general nature.

Siemaszko indicates three main – according to himself – reasons for the decline in criminality in 2005, viz. changes in the population pyramid, emigration and improvements in police work (Siemaszko in Siemaszko et al. 2009, p. 319). The recorded decline in criminality in Poland since the first decade of the twenty-first century is especially noticeable when the national and Eurostat data are compared. Poland is one of 30 countries whose crime statistics are published by Eurostat. In 2009, Poland had the lowest crime rate in Europe when it came to drug offences, car theft, breaking into property and crimes involving aggression, but was ranked 16th in terms of the number of homicides and robberies (Eurostat 2012; see also Gruszczyńska and Heiskanen 2012, pp. 83–102).

The frequently unnoticed change made to the increase in criminality on the basis of where crimes were committed cannot be ignored when describing the impact of the constitutional and political transformation after 1989. The societal changes taking place in Poland did not just affect the cities; rural areas were equally transformed. Detailed analyses of these processes are best left to sociologists. What are of interest to us are the diminishing differences between urban and rural growth in criminality.

Teodor Szymanowski points out:

> If this difference came to 27.4 points, determining the ratio [of people convicted of crimes in the city and in the country] 'in favour' of the cities, in 1987, it shrank to 11.8 points in 1997 and to just 8.6 points in 2010. This would therefore seem to be a consistent trend. It is not easy to interpret these undeniable changes without examining them. The following explanations, however, may serve as a hypothesis here:

---

59 *Ustawa z dnia 3 sierpnia 2005 r. o zmianie ustawy – Kodeks karny* (Act of 3 August 2005 to Amend the Criminal Code [Journal of Laws No. 132, Pos. 1109]).

60 *Ustawa z dnia 20 marca 2009 r. o bezpieczeństwie imprez masowych* (Act of 20 March on Safety at Mass Events [Journal of Laws No. 62, Pos. 504]). This was amended by *ustawa z dnia 22 lipca 2010 r. o zmianie ustawy o bezpieczeństwie imprez masowych oraz ustawy – Kodeks karny* (Act of 22 July 2010 to Amend the Act on Safety at Mass Events – Criminal Code [Journal of Laws No. 152, Pos. 1021]).

61 Act of 27 July 2005 to Amend the Criminal Code, the Criminal Procedure Code and the Sentencing Code (Journal of Laws No. 163, Pos. 1363).

62 *Ustawa z dnia 25 lutego 2011 r. o zmianie ustawy – Kodeks karny* (Act of 25 February 2011 to Amend the Criminal Code [Journal of Laws No. 72, Pos. 381]). See also Siemaszko 2010, pp. 45 ff.

- the ensuing evolution in social awareness and the assimilation of urban modes of behaviour in the country;
- the visible development of networks of all sorts of sales and services outlets has had an effect on evening out the differences between city and country, including the scale of criminality. (Szymanowski 2012, p. 87, author's translation)

The huge impact that Poland's joining the EU has had on the countryside should also be noted, especially through the receipt of subsidies meant to be directed towards rural development and ensuring the profitability of agricultural production, and yet often devoted to current consumption.[63] The rural population are endeavouring to ensure that they enjoy similar living conditions to those that obtain in the cities, and internalising and consolidating the standards presented by the mass media, which are still the main source of not only information, but also cultural standards. Unfortunately, these are becoming increasingly globalised and part of a homogenised mass culture. This equalisation with the city, which the data presented above seem to confirm, might also include criminality (while the number of crimes involving country people driving a vehicle under the influence of alcohol remain dominant) (Fandrejewska 2013).

The number of crimes dropped considerably in 2012. Police statistics on ongoing preliminary proceedings show a fall of 3.1 per cent over the previous year (950,860 cases, including 662,815 for criminal offences, had been commenced, compared with 981,480 the previous year) (http://www.statystyka.policja.pl/portal/st/840/83416/Raport_statystyczny_za_2012_rok.html, accessed March 2013; see also Zawadka and Blikowska 2013). The number of serious criminal offences fell, as did the number of petty theft and property damage cases.

Looking at particular groups, the greatest fall in criminality in 2012 was recorded for armed robbery – down 18.7 per cent on 2011, homicide – down 17.4 per cent, and predatory crimes (robbery, robbery with violence and extortion with violence) – down 14.4 per cent. The number of break-ins and property damage cases likewise fell – by 7.4 and 7.3 per cent respectively. The number of car thefts exhibited a downward trend as well – 5.3 per cent less than in 2011. It is also worth stressing the 7.4 per cent fall in the number of proceedings commenced for traffic offences (163,212 cases, of which 137,805 were for driving a vehicle under the influence of alcohol).

These downward trends in criminal offences in 2012 were accompanied, however, by an increase in economic crime, which was up 9.6 per cent over the previous year (a combined total of 83,124 proceedings in progress). The number of drug offences also grew by 0.3 per cent (23,001 proceedings). The increase in the number of cases belonging to the rather broad category of economic crimes may be an indication of the dominant trends in criminality over the coming years.

The constitutional and political transformation of 1989 may not have been the last of the abrupt societal changes to impact the scale and the scope of criminality in Poland. The next change has to be sought in the context of global transformations. It may be that we are not yet in a position to notice it, as the measuring tools we have been using so far cannot pick it up. This global change has been in progress for over 30 years, but has accelerated suddenly and rapidly since the beginning of the twenty-first century with the popularisation of the Internet. This is turn owes its existence to technological advances in facilitating long-distance communication. Simply put, the development of computers and methods of rapid data transfer (e.g. fibre-optic cable) has brought about radical social change not previously seen.

The widespread access to online content (the Internet is a global network of networks), the simplified acquisition and exchange of information, and the technological advances that have followed (suffice it here

63 Data from the Central Statistical Office on improvements in the standard of living in Poland in 2000–2011 reveal a significant diminution in the differences between rural and urban standards of living. Differences in furnishing apartments have especially decreased. And virtually every household, regardless of where it is situated, now has a TV, an automatic washing machine and a mobile phone. Cars and bicycles have also come to the countryside. Rural families are more frequently purchasing computers with Internet access, dishwashers, printers, DVD players and microwave ovens. If the differences between rural and urban standards of living have been narrowing over the past decade, then the effect of EU payments has led to considerable differentiation in the affluence of rural household. Large holdings have gained while small farms that only produce for their own needs have become impoverished. See also Fandrejewska (2013).

to mention tablets and smartphones), have all made us look at criminality anew and have indicated new areas that may constitute criminogenic factors.[64]

The Internet, which is increasingly more widely available, combines elements typical of both the press and television, while at the same time leaving an enormous field of action to the users. All sorts of information can be exchanged over the Internet, including information about criminality and particular kinds of prohibited acts. This can focus on thematically grouped interests (e.g. organised crime or cybercrime) and provide up-to-date commentary on media reports on criminality (Witkowska 2007, p. 159).

As with every technological innovation, the Internet, which has only been on our computers since the mid-1990s, initially aroused safety fears as well as fascination and admiration. Jewkes writes:

> postmodern media merge 'fun' and 'hate', 'cruelty' and 'playfulness', 'inclusive' and 'exploitative', 'accessible' and 'extremist'. The Internet celebrates a world of entertainment, spectacle, narcissism and performance, and – when it comes to privatized pleasure – it is surely the cardinal site of the carnival of crime. (Jewkes 2010a, p. 31)

The first link between crime and the Internet are culpable acts that have been made possible (even on a very large scale) by the mere existence of this medium. These include breaking into computers and computer networks and spreading viruses. This last can be a form of fun or malice, or it can be a means of committing crime, as some viruses infect computers in order to extract information stored on them (Bielska 2010, p. 158). The consequences of breaking into computers and networks can vary in seriousness, from hacking e-mail and social media accounts to playing jokes, through to stealing naked photographs of celebrities from their personal computers and posting them online, on to what happened in early 2010 when a hacker broke into the official website of the Spanish Presidency of the EU and put a photo of a smiling Mr Bean there (Bielska 2010, p. 158). If breaking into individual accounts can be distressing for their owners, then breaking into government websites or military computer systems can be a threat to everyone in society. Attacks on systems managing highly sensitive networks can have serious effects, e.g. interference with air or rail transport systems, or the theft of information on national security systems (Newburn 2007, p. 104).

Theft and intellectual property violations of various kinds constitute another kind of Internet crime. Computer piracy is a worldwide problem that has not spared Poland. This crime is defined as accessing files, not downloading them, on networks under Polish law. Despite that, there is no shortage of people willing to share their collections and portals offering free files with films, music and e-books are inordinately popular. Shutting one down changes little; another will appear in its place.

There is also a specific kind of fraud known as the Nigerian scam. An email, purportedly from a political exile in desperate straits, arrives in the inbox of the intended victim. The author claims to be heir to a large fortune in some African country (this was originally most often Nigeria; hence the scam's name) and to be seeking assistance in accessing his/her account to deposit money that he/she cannot withdraw for one reason or another. The letter mentions a princely sum, and the addressee is offered a generous share in exchange for his/her assistance. Should the addressee respond, he/she is requested to deposit a sum of money to deal with unforeseen contingencies (e.g. the need to pay bribes or bank charges). There are several variations on the Nigerian scam. Apart from the millionaire exile story, victims are lured into investing money or told that they have inherited a large sum from a long-lost relative or won a lottery.

Another means of online theft is phishing, i.e. defrauding customers of various institutions of confidential information (passwords, credit card numbers etc.) by impersonating those institutions. A bank customer receives an email, purportedly from his/her bank, regarding the need to update certain details. Clicking the link in the email brings up a page that looks like the bank's website. The customer is prompted to enter e.g. his/her credit card number and security code. The thieves can now use the credit card to make online payments.

There are also crimes that have long been known but widespread Internet access has changed their nature and scope and/or modified their modus operandi. This refers to the dissemination of pornographic materials, including those whose production involves the participation of children, the publication of abuse, defamation and/or threats, and various forms of online harassment known as cyberviolence. This is defined as 'the use of IT and communications technology by a person or group or people for the purpose of engaging in wilful,

64 The rest of this text was written in collaboration with D. Woźniakowska-Fajst.

repeated and hostile conduct intended to cause harm to others' (Wojtasik 2009, p. 8, author's translation). Cyberstalking (emotional harassment using the Internet) and cyberbullying (intimidation, ridicule, harassing peers in the case of children and youth) are two offences that come under the heading of cyberviolence. The Internet is also used to disseminate hate crimes – from users making comments, often anonymously, to visiting dedicated websites that promote racism, intolerance and hostility towards certain groups (the LGBT community, feminists, people with leftwing views etc.). Shutting down these sorts of sites is extraordinarily difficult as they are usually run on servers outside Poland.

The growth of the Internet is also connected with terrorism. Terrorist organisations clearly use the Internet as a communications tool in their operations, both between members of the same groups and as means of propagating their demands to a wide circle of people. The Internet is an excellent, widely available medium that is not subject to censorship. Terrorists can use it, not only to propagate their ideas, but to publish films showing hostages pleading to be freed and often being executed (Radosz 2007).

The Internet is also a source of information and this can be used to commit crimes. It is not difficult to find information on how to make bombs, prepare poisons and commit suicide effectively.

Many crimes committed using the Internet are never detected and prosecuted. This is due to a range of factors, such as the sheer volume of materials on the web and the technical issues involved in monitoring them, the difficulties involved in bringing formal proceedings (because e.g. the perpetrators might be anonymous or the offences might span several jurisdictions), and the fact that victims seldom report this type of crime (due to embarrassment, lack of confidence in the effectiveness of the police, and the fact that the results of such crimes are sometimes not discovered until many months after they have been committed).

There can be no doubt, however, that the preponderance of criminality will shift significantly to virtual reality – if not in the very near future, then definitely during the course of the next 20 to 50 years (more likely the former). This is not to say that people will stop committing ordinary crimes. It is just that as more areas in which particular individuals, or society as a whole, are involved are moved to the Internet, the number of crimes committed on it will naturally increase.

Chapter 3
Social Change and Criminality: Mutual Relationships, Determinants and Implications

Anna Kossowska

Introduction

The links between social changes and criminality and, although not always obvious, the processes and phenomena concealed behind these two ideas, have long been of interest to sociologists and criminologists. Against this backdrop, 'criminality' is most often taken to mean conduct defined as such in official registers (i.e. discourse on criminality is generally published). This may exclude a whole raft of relevant issues connected with the social perception of the dangers of actual crime, i.e. crime that now shows up in statistics and does not provoke a response from the state or its institutions. The concept of 'social change' finds application in the description of some very diverse social processes, both progressing on the macro level and observable at the level of local communities. We can discuss social change in its associations with criminality once we have analysed the effects of such events as wars, revolutions, peaceful regime changes, industrialisation, urbanisation and the economic situation. Mass migration, revolutions brought about by technological changes (and all their ramifications), demographic changes, lifestyle changes, the structure of the labour market, the way social functions are performed and the internationalisation of social problems often need to be considered in this context. To all this can be added changes taking place in social consciousness, such as attitudes towards social inequality (and to social organisation generally), the presence of risk in everyday life, 'truths' about criminality and how to control it, and cultural diversity. It seems impossible to cite a single commonly acknowledged and universal definition of social change. Piotr Sztompka lists a range of definitions that simultaneously apply in contemporary sociology and then proposes his own (Sztompka 2005). This is fairly general, but for that reason useful, in preliminary deliberations.

Sztompka takes 'social change' to mean 'the difference between the state of the social system (i.e. groups and organisations) at one point in time and the state of the same system at another point in time' (Sztompka 2002). The two states may differ in terms of the composition and layout of the system, and the functions performed by the various elements of society. Sztompka adds that social change can mean both an isolated incident and a process with a specific temporal dynamic and sequence of qualitative changes.

Anthony Giddens (Giddens 2009) puts the emphasis on the fact that social change is not a new phenomenon but something that can be found in every stage of development of every society. However, it is now occurring at a different pace and it is precisely this rate of change that is the source of our specific contemporary problems. Many societies can be observed to be in a state of confusion in a rapidly changing world (even those that are not going through drastic, revolutionary transformations, e.g. regime change), especially now that this change is taking place on many levels at once.

Social Change in the Light of Criminological Theories

Criminological deliberations on the link (generally cause and effect) between certain social and economic processes and criminality originally took on the complexion of fairly simple analyses (of both a theoretical and empirical nature) of the impact of changes in the economic situation on the size and nature of criminality. In a certain sense, this corresponded to the popular stereotype that 'poverty makes thieves'. A peculiar duplication of criminological considerations on the link between social change and criminality was then delineated. On the one hand, the range of criminological theories includes references to the effects of change and certain relative changes. On the other, several works have emerged on the basis of empirical studies. These are based on selected components of these theories and are not an attempt to verify them. Andrzej Mościskier's studies on the impact of urbanisation and industrialisation on criminality are a Polish example (Mościskier 1978b).

One concept frequently invoked in descriptions of the links between social change and criminality is that of 'anomie', especially in the sense Émile Durkheim ascribed to it. According to Durkheim, abrupt social changes result in confusion as to the binding normative system. This uncertainty towards normative substance in the new social situation is called anomie. Symptoms of anomie in this sense were distinctly noticeable during the initial period of the constitutional and political transformation of Poland. The special significance of the state of normative chaos was stressed in analyses of the reasons for the changing portrayal of criminality in Poland published in the 1990s (Siemaszko et al. 1999).

The concept of anomie, in the sense ascribed to it by Robert Merton, has to do with the ramifications of the discrepancy between aspirations and the expectations of their being satisfied. Despite its highly distinctive American pedigree, Merton's theory of anomie currently happens to be useful in analysing the state of social consciousness in countries going through transformations. Along with political and constitutional change, and all that follows from it in terms of consciousness, opening up to external, Western (essentially US) cultural models and progressive social stratification, there has been an awakening of new needs, especially in the area of consumption. Political and constitutional change did not, however, bring about the changes in the social structure that some idealists had expected. In his description of the transformations, Henryk Domański stresses that regime change reinforced existing divisions and raised social barriers (Domański 2004, pp. 69–96). The new political system was not more just. On the contrary, social inequalities became even more pronounced with the result that the general feeling of anomie became more pronounced. The essential problem is not, however, the level of inequality in itself, but above all the dissemination among specific social groups of the feeling of deprivation that goes with it and an awareness of the structural hurdles along the road to economic success and its attendant cultural trappings.

Manuel Eisner focuses on the usefulness of the theories of modernisation, opportunity and civilising process to analyses in this area in his discussion of the impact of long-term and far-reaching socio-economic changes on the level of criminality (Eisner 1995).

The theory of modernisation comes out of the work of Durkheim, who considered that industrialisation and urbanisation generates an increase in criminality, as these processes are distinguished by a high level of anomie, a severing of social ties, greater anonymity, a decline in social integration, and confusion at the individual level. The basic assumptions of the criminological theory of modernisation are: (1) in its initial phase, modernisation increases the incidence of both property crime and crimes against the person – this is a consequence of the traditional systems of integration and control being ruptured by migratory processes; (2) during the next phase, the socio-economic processes of modernisation decrease the incidence of violent crime (typical of rural culture) and increase the incidence of property crime, which is a form of crime typical of societies undergoing modernisation and is caused by consumption assuming increasing importance and goods in demand becoming more accessible;[1] (3) modernisation, by its very nature, brings about an increase in the incidence of crime, i.e. crime is an unavoidable cost of modernisation; and (4) the moderately proceeding modernisation of advanced societies should result in a standardisation of the socio-economic situation and an assimilation of the composition and incidence of crime.[2]

Eisner has combined opportunity theory with the elements of routine activity theory. As can be seen, the latter explains the incidence and specifics of crime in contemporary advanced societies where everyday activities are changing. These lifestyle changes are linked with a weakening of social control mechanisms. This is all the more important as, in line with the assumptions underlying routine activity theory, a crime will be committed whenever a sufficiently motivated perpetrator comes across an appealing and unprotected item in the right place at the right time. The theory assumes the number of potential perpetrators in society is constant. What is relevant is the number of opportunities, i.e. appealing items not under protection or

1 It should be borne in mind that a culture of violence is not restricted to traditional rural culture. The urban variety is very clearly in evidence in descriptions of the modern ghettos of large cities.

2 I have yet to see an attempt to verifying these claims empirically.

surveillance. The number of opportunities for crime has risen dramatically in postmodern societies. This is not merely due to pressure to consume more, which is what drives the production and availability of goods, but also to wide-scale activities designed to create needs and stimulate demand for luxury goods that are considered prestigious or superfluous for whatever reason, especially among the young. The incidence of crime, especially property crime, depends on the number of opportunities. This line of reasoning is not so obvious in the case of crimes against the person, although it has been accurate in certain instances.

The third theory Eisner analyses is the civilising process. This stems from the work of Norbert Elias (Elias 1976). Its basic claim is that, on principle, the incidence of violent crime in contemporary societies should decrease with modernisation and the development of an advanced capitalist economy. Elias derived his theory using an historical analysis of the formation of criminality in Europe from the Middle Ages to the present. Data on the inordinate incidence of violence in the Middle Ages and the progressive fall in the incidence of crimes employing it over time (Elias substantiates this on the basis of historical materials, mostly concerning homicides) supposedly confirm this hypothesis.[3]

Criminologists who invoke Elias's idea maintain that the consecutive components that characterise contemporary capitalist societies are relevant here, viz.: (1) increased external (formal) control due to the state assuming broader powers; (2) increased significance of self-control – at first, only relevant to the socialisation of social and cultural elites; and (3) a gradual diffusion of external control and self-control into society generally.[4]

The development of modern capitalism entails greater mutual interdependence, while full-blown self-control becomes the fundamental social and cultural resource essential to achieving success. Self-control then is a product of successful socialisation and a factor that should have an impact on restricting the incidence of crime, especially that involving violence. Violence between people is highly dysfunctional. It disturbs the social order and makes success in social and cultural life difficult to achieve. The reason for the incidence of crime being higher than expected for a particular level of civilisational development is that not every member of society has the same opportunities of acquiring the capability of self-control.[5]

Eisner considered, for example, the progressive weakening of social ties, the social disintegration that comes with modernisation, the greater number of opportunities to commit crime that flows from economic growth and the increased importance of self-control and formal control resulting from the development of modern capitalism to be the most relevant factors in explaining the changes in criminality that stem from long-term and wide ranging socio-economic processes.[6]

It should be borne in mind, however, that Eisner set out to verify the theory in question by analysing historical materials on criminality. Unfortunately, the general data on the dimensions of criminality do not correlate with the picture in the stages of modernisation he describes. Moreover, certain elements of his theory are not supported by the statistics.[7] In Eisner's view, this does not undermine the soundness of most of the theoretical concepts under discussion but attests to the complexity of the problem and the necessity of employing more refined methodologies.

Eisner's treatise also contains an attempt to describe the directions in which criminality is developing in Central and Eastern Europe. This is based on the fundamental assumptions of the theories he describes. These considerations deal with the actuality of the early 1990s and are based on data included in papers available internationally. They are more hypothetical in nature than analyses of actual phenomena but are nevertheless

3 The essential methodological limitations of this sort of analysis, however, cannot be ignored. The statistical data on which the fundamental assumptions of Elias's theory rest are not complete, the manner in which they were collected is not known, and their credibility is dubious.

4 For a review of the writers who refer to Elias's theory, see Eisner (1995, p. 21).

5 The convergence of Elias's views on self-control and those of Gottfredson and Hirschi in their general theory of criminality, published in 1990, are interesting. The two works are more than 10 years apart.

6 Eisner evidently does not refer to the considerable expansion of the disorganised areas of large-city environments, which assume the character of large-city ghettoes, together with their specific subculture of violence, at all. To some extent, this is a by-product of modernisation.

7 Using historical analyses of statistical data on crime taken from various periods and created using different, and not always known, means as a basis is obviously risky. For more on the problems associated with the statistical picture of criminality, see, e.g., Błachut (2007).

worth citing. And so Eisner states that economic and social transformation in Central and Eastern Europe has brought about a complete change in the level of self-control required to achieve success. As existing cultural resources have been partially destroyed, a large portion of society (especially young people) has experienced considerable difficulty in adapting to these changes. Moreover, the permanent marginalisation of certain social groups might have been expected as inevitable in the new state of affairs. Eisner next refers to the obvious consequences of stimulating needs (as a result of holding up Western models of consumption) that a significant proportion of the society cannot possibly have satisfied. He also stresses the importance of the inevitable weakening of existing control structures and social integration. Eisner believes that the foregoing observations warrant the hypothesis that the rapid growth in the incidence of crime in countries going through rapid transformations should be maintained at the rate applicable to the period immediately following the system change. As can be seen, this hypothesis has not been confirmed in the case of Poland (or other countries going through system change).[8]

The theoretical assumptions underlying the social control movement would seem to be especially relevant in analysing the links between social change and criminality. Many criminologists agree with Travis Hirschi that the most essential component of social control is the bond that ties the individual to his/her surroundings. Should this bond be weakened or broken, there is very little that can be done, apart from stepping up repressive formal control measures, to restrain people from engaging in criminal conduct. This allows the determinants of criminality in a situation of social change to be determined. Transformations in the economic, political and social conditions under which individuals function are accompanied by a rupture or a drastic weakening of social ties. This makes it easier to make criminal decisions, at not just the level of the individual, but also that of the social group. These mechanisms have to do with the changes associated with modernisation and other mass processes.

The significance of social disorganisation, which is an inevitable result of the social changes mentioned above, should be stressed when analysing the macro-social determinants of criminality. Sociologists are not in full agreement as to how to define social disorganisation, but it can be assumed that it has to do with situations where social change has led to the functioning of individuals and institutions being disrupted.[9] In certain special cases, social disorganisation at the macro level might cause, for instance, family socialisation (although seemingly appropriate) to become inadequate in the new social circumstances associated with, for example, political, social or economic transformations. Admittedly, disorganisation is generally considered the normal state of affairs in modern societies, but once a certain level is exceeded on the macro scale, the operation of the social control mechanisms is disrupted.

To recapitulate: the various analyses of the determinants of criminality in the constantly changing world of today all refer to the effects of disrupting the operation of social control mechanisms, the greater number of opportunities for crime and the impact of inequality, exclusion and deprivation. It seems legitimate to apply a specific combination of the main assumptions of social control theory and opportunity theory (i.e. taking the perspective of routine behaviour into consideration) with elements of different versions of structural theories when analysing the determinants of criminality resulting from social change.

Social Change and the Perception of Criminality

It is worth considering those components of social reality that distinctively affect both the social perception of the dangers of crime and the way it is currently depicted when analysing the links between social change and criminality.

Certain commonly occurring regularities generally crop up in descriptions of postmodern societies, where it is claimed that criminality is different now than it was in the 1960s and 1970s. The changes have been both qualitative and quantitative. Revolutionary changes have simultaneously occurred in the labour market,

8 For more on changes in criminality, see Chapter 2, by Konrad Buczkowski, in this volume. As for criminality in Central and Eastern European countries undergoing transformations, see Šelih (2012).

9 For a review of the definitions of disorganisation, see, e.g., Kossowska (1992, pp. 71–7). For a criminological interpretation of this concept, see ibid. (pp. 77–96).

the ways leisure time is spent, the use to which public and private places are put and the overall feeling of security. The conviction that victimisation is becoming increasingly widespread is gaining strength (Garland and Sparks 2000; Young 1999). Jock Young analysed certain aspects of the way advanced societies functioned in the 1990s and stated: 'Crime has moved from the rare, the abnormal, the offence of the marginal and the stranger, to a commonplace part of the texture of everyday life' (Young 1999, p. 30). This obviously raises the question as to whether Young and others would formulate their hypotheses the same way today, given the decline in the incidence of criminality over the last 10 or 20 years. It seems likely that social consciousness and stereotypes about dangers are changing more slowly than are the realities of life, including the measurable level of criminality, in contemporary societies. This may indicate the topicality of the foregoing assessment.

The threat of criminality, correlated with a subjective and objective assessment of that risk, is therefore a significant component in any description of the relationship between postmodern societies and criminality. By way of digression, there is a common conviction among the members of postmodern societies that everyday life involves a general risk of many and varied dangers. Crime is but one of many. David Nelken, in his mid-1990s discussions on the directions the desired changes in the development of theoretical criminality should take, states that risk is one of the issues whose analysis could contribute to an improvement in the level of criminological discourse (i.e. perception and control of 'risk') (Nelken 1994). Another direction of criminological reflexion postulated by Nelken is the social issue of the construction of 'the outsider'. These two issues are related. The view that a high (or considered high) incidence of crime, together with anxiety about it and a feeling of being threatened by it, is a fact that influences both individual conduct and attitudes to authority as well as, importantly, determining the enemy, can be found in the literature. This enemy is, obviously, an actual perpetrator of crime but is much more often, however, a potential, imagined perpetrator, i.e. someone considered a threat by virtue of being labelled an 'outsider'. This outsider might, for example, belong to a culturally different group. This would explain the incidence of hate crimes in some societies. It is worth noting that perpetrators of hate crimes are very often members of subcultures considered a serious threat by most of society. An interesting phenomenon can be observed in Poland recently where groups hitherto considered 'foreign' and dangerous are being reappraised for short-term political ends, e.g. 'football hooligans' are being redefined as 'true patriots' staunchly defending traditional values.[10]

The issue of anxiety about criminality (regardless of whether this has any rational basis) is not only important because it could make individuals change their behaviour and do things that are sometimes irrational to minimise the threat of crime. This also has an effect on social attitudes, intensifies the general feeling of distrust in the government, especially in particularly disorganised societies, and eventually makes people susceptible to falling prey to populist and radical sloganeering. The result is a stronger consensus for an expansion of formal social control and a tendency for social exclusion, in its various aspects, to increase.[11] In many countries, it is possible to speak of a distinct politicisation of the threat of criminality and the emergence of a 'populist punitiveness' manifested in changes made to penal policy on the basis of public opinion driven by popular impressions of criminality and its determinants. These changes are often made with a view to achieving short-term political ends.

Obviously, the problem of risk in postmodern societies does not solely depend on the general feeling of being threatened by criminality. As Ulrich Beck demonstrates, a hitherto unknown degree of risk is common in postmodern societies (Beck 2005). Despite its commonality, however, risk does not affect everyone to the same degree which applies also to the risk of victimisation.

Attitudes to social inequalities have changed compared to what they previously were in postmodern societies. Inequalities have obviously always existed. The distance that separates particular groups and social strata has at times been incomparably greater than it is at present.[12] However, social inequalities arouse far more opposition today. A sense of deprivation can affect the conduct of individuals and social groups in modern

10 In any case, this is the conclusion to be drawn from reports of organised demonstrations by extreme right groups at various national events and commemorations in which organised groups of 'football supporters' play a significant role.

11 The attitude of Americans to having their rights and freedoms drastically restricted in the wake of 9/11 is an example of this.

12 It is difficult to compare the social distance between, for example, a serf and a land owner vs. the upper and lower strata of contemporary Western societies.

societies. It delimits criminal motivations, is a source of social unrest and affects attitudes to the authorities and the state. Social inequalities are most often examined in the context of economic inequalities with all the attendant consequences in education, health, access to worthwhile occupations and opportunities for cultural participation. An increased likelihood of engaging in criminal conduct and a greater susceptibility to being victimised is another result of economic inequalities.[13] Chris Glover has analysed various manifestations of social inequalities in their association with criminality and stresses that although the issue of causative links between economic inequalities and criminality is a component of structural criminological theories, the mechanisms of these connections do not always appear to be obvious (Glover 2008). He nevertheless cites Steve Box's statement, 'Income inequality is strongly related to criminal activity – with the exception of homicide. It should be emphasised that no existing research has produced results which contradict this', with approval (although, in principle, he is referring exclusively to petty crime) (Box 1987, p. 96 cited in Glover 2008, p. 35).

Social inequalities are often linked with social exclusion in its various manifestations. According to the *Sage Dictionary of Criminology*, the term 'social exclusion' refers to the multifaceted process that involves barring individuals or groups from participating in social, economic, political or cultural systems designed to ensure social integration (McLaughlin and Muncie 2006). This process is dynamic and fluid – it is not a static state that lends itself to a precise definition. Trevor Bradley takes the view that the idea of 'social exclusion' can be used to refer to marginalisation, social isolation and lack of social affiliation in moving from modernity to post-modernity with all the changes that occur in social life and which are connected with an increase in social inequalities, a general feeling of uncertainty and the danger these changes unleash (Bradley 2005, p. 401). According to Bradley, social exclusion is now mainly manifested in three areas: (1) as economic exclusion of individuals denied access to standard employment; (2) as isolation from participating in social life through the mechanisms of social and spatial segregation; and (3) as a result of the increasing exclusionary policies and practices of the criminal justice systems. Exclusion in any of these areas is significantly linked with criminality in modern societies.[14]

The debate on the impact of the many and varied phenomena collectively known as 'globalisation' is an important part of any description of postmodern societies. There seems to be no consensus on how to define this concept. There is, however, some agreement on the importance of the influence of the outcomes of the information and technological revolutions – e.g. standardising cultural models in consumption and lifestyle requirements, facilitating capital flows and making it possible for supranational crime syndicates to collaborate – on the form it adopts in the context of criminality. The clear tendency to standardise the forms of official response to criminality at the supranational level is another important aspect of globalisation. As is the case with combating terrorism and illicit drugs, these are often imposed by the most powerful countries.[15]

Polish Criminology vs. Social Change

Criminality in former descriptions of change

While the links between social change and criminality have not been researched in great detail by Polish criminologists, there are nevertheless some fascinating studies that analyse some of the changes that have taken place in Poland over the past few decades. These discussions would be worthwhile from a historical perspective, starting from the beginning in 1918 of the Second Polish Republic, i.e. covering the integration of territories previously under the three partitioning powers, with their different legislatures and diverse ethnic and cultural compositions, into a single unit. Unfortunately, there are no criminological analyses of this process. There is, however, an excellent analysis on the criminality that occurred as a result of the Great Depression,

13 For more on this topic, see Klaus and Woźniakowska-Fajst (2012).

14 A broader introduction to the consequences of exclusion can be found in Chapter 4: 'The Relationship between Poverty, Social Exclusion and Criminality'.

15 For more on the links between globalisation and criminality, see, e.g., Franko Aas (2007).

or which was connected with it, by Leon Radzinowicz (Radzinowicz 1969). There is a dearth of analytical studies on the impact of the Second World War on the incidence and nature of criminality (or at least expressly devoted to this issue). Only a few studies examine the long-term effects of large-scale post-war migration associated with border changes. Witold Świda (Świda 1960) published a work, much discussed at the time, on the impact of post-Second World War regime change on criminality. Over the following years, Andrzej Mościskier (1978b) performed a more thorough analysis of the links between criminality and industrialisation and urbanisation in their various aspects. Finally, the social change associated with the transformation of the political system was discussed in a series of sociological, and very soon afterwards, criminological, works. An analysis of the period of aggravated social conflict that preceded and followed the introduction of martial law would also seem to be essential to understanding criminality after 1989.

In the introduction to his analysis of criminality in Poland in 1928–1934, Leon Radzinowicz states,

> It is not enough to state that crime has increased as a result of the Depression. It is necessary to explain why it has increased as a result of the Depression, and then explain what changes in the minds and social behaviour of individuals were brought about by specific changes in economic circumstances and how these changes in the minds of individuals could have led them to crime. (Radzinowicz 1969, p. 141)

The period analysed by Radzinowicz covers the years 1927–1929, which he describes as the greatest economic boom of interbellum Poland, and the first half of the 1930s, when the depression was deepest. He describes the economic indicators of both periods, as well as data on criminality, in the introduction. These sometimes show a dramatic fall in economic development indicators as well as a definite increase in the incidence of criminality in the 1930s. Detailed data on criminality, combined with a description of the economic conditions for the period in question (e.g. the unemployment rate and the fall in real wages), are then thoroughly analysed. Radzinowicz's observation that the number of crimes clearly increased in 1931–1934 while the tendency to report having been a victim of crime decreased seems curious. Radzinowicz describes this state of social disorganisation as an effect of the depression in that the high level of criminality made crime an everyday occurrence and people grew indifferent to it. Moreover, there was a widely held belief that it was futile to report crime to the authorities as the police were becoming increasingly ineffectual. The possibility of retaliation on the part of the perpetrator made it dangerous as well. Some of these allegations might explain the reluctance of contemporary Poles to report having been a victim of crime to the police.

Radzinowicz was not completely satisfied with the results of his analysis 'on account of certain inadequacies in the data on criminality and economic conditions' (Radzinowicz 1969, p. 158). Despite these caveats, Radzinowicz's findings cannot be understated. He claimed that the incidence of criminality in marginalised groups increased whenever there was an abrupt, precipitous worsening of their material situation, while the accumulation of the negative consequences of the Depression (unemployment, poverty, disruption of family life etc.) engendered hostility towards the existing social order. Radzinowicz invokes the results of many sociological studies, which show clear changes in the social attitudes in the study groups towards the system of norms, values and law as well as the state and its institutions. 'Our analysis entitles us to say that, all things considered, times of prosperity have a significantly weaker effect on diminishing criminality than periods of depression do in increasing it' (Radzinowicz 1969, p. 161).

Finally, it is worth quoting Radzinowicz's conclusion on the impact of the Great Depression on penal policy:

> States that fail to eliminate or neutralise the real cause of the rise in criminality, and that try to turn their penal policy and criminal code into palliatives meant to remedy difficulties, very often grasp an 'authoritarian' criminal justice system [and as a result] a depression – by way of a criminal crisis – will give rise to a reactionary justice system. (Radzinowicz 1969, p. 162)

It must be noted that most of Radzinowicz's determinations about the causal links between the Depression and criminality in the Second Polish Republic could – after a little retouching – be cited in an analysis of criminality during the political and economic transformation of Poland.

Witold Świda, when analysing the effect the post-Second World War 'political system change' on criminality takes the phrase to mean 'a range of political, economic, social and cultural phenomena' that can be divided into two groups (Świda 1960, p. 9). To the first, which Świda considers the essence of this change, is consigned

> the removal of the propertied classes from power, the nationalisation of banking and industry, the socialisation of trade and commerce, the socialist remodelling of the agricultural economy, the implementation of a planned economy, the promulgation of socialist education and culture and all the consequences that flow from that, viz. the eradication of depressions and unemployment, the creation of a new intelligentsia etc. (Świda 1960, p. 9)

To the second group of phenomena (which are, in a certain sense, an outcome of the first), Świda consigns mass phenomena, e.g. rapid urbanisation and industrialisation, and migration. He considers that although these processes are crucial to describing the transformations of a socialist society, they affect capitalist societies just as much, if not more. As a result, they are of no use in his analysis of the consequences of political system change.

The crux of Świda's studies was his comparison of criminality in the city and district of Kalisz in 1939 and 1952. This was based on an analysis of all the criminal cases in the court files for those years. A preliminary quantity analysis shows a considerable drop in the number of criminal cases in 1952 compared with 1937. In Świda's view, this was partly due to the population changes brought about by the war. These mainly involved the extermination of the Jewish population and the expulsion of ethnic Germans. The population had fallen more than 30 per cent in the areas in question, according to Świda's estimates. Świda, however, sought the main reasons for the decrease in the incidence of crime in political system change.

In the core of the work, Świda isolates everything concerning crimes 'directly connected with the regime as such' from the criminal case files in order to examine the influence of political system change on criminality (Świda 1960, p. 27). By these, he meant crimes committed in the fields of trade, industry and handicrafts, crimes connected with the agricultural system, crimes connected with urban housing, crimes committed against a background of unemployment, prostitution, anti-Semitism, and other 'crimes anticipated in the legislature set up with the change in regime' (Świda 1960, p. 28).

In conclusion, Świda states that 'analysing the selected materials demonstrated that the change in regime altered the makeup of criminality in a radical way. It had a fundamental impact on the factors that induce crime by entirely eliminating some, changing the nature of others, and bringing yet others to life' (Świda 1960, p. 149). It would be difficult to disagree with this statement. There can be no doubt that a fundamental social system change, e.g. a change in political system, has to bring about a change in the individual components of the system, including the sphere of unlawful behaviour.

Most of Świda's conclusions are convincing. By analysing detailed data on crimes deemed to be singularly associated with a change in political system, Świda explains the incidence of industrial crimes being greater in 1952 than in 1937 by falling unemployment (the lack of fear of being dismissed from work for committing crimes against employers) and by there being no education on the appropriate attitude to nationalised property (a completely new element of social consciousness). State policy to replace private with public trade and commerce (which likewise affected handicrafts and services) was what affected crimes in this area. According to Świda, this led to shortages, which were conducive to unlawful economic activities. He also refers once more to the inappropriate attitude to nationalised property as a cause of criminality.

The analysis of changes in criminality associated with the rural situation is interestingly presented. Świda shows that, in rural areas, the number of crimes associated with poverty fell considerably (through the transformation of proprietary relationships and the appearance of conditions conducive to lowering rural unemployment), although the number of crimes associated with the legal regulations binding in those areas increased dramatically (this obviously refers to regulations on rationing the sale of rural produce, land etc.). The number of crimes against a background of proprietary relationships in rural areas fell in 1952 compared to 1937. Statutory limitations on people disposing of their property and the fruits of their labour helped reduced conflicts associated with land possession (by restricting the feeling of ownership).

Świda attributes the greater number of crimes associated with housing issues in 1952 to the introduction of a specific socialist housing economy (e.g. the practice of populating flats with several families unknown to each other made conflicts inevitable). Obviously, there were virtually no crimes associated with unemployment recorded just after the war. Świda claims that 'unemployment was a powerful stimulus pushing the ranks of the unemployed on the road to crime in 1937, whereas in 1952, the change in regime had cut off that source so effectively that it was no longer capable of moulding the criminality of that period' (Świda 1960, p. 108). It would no doubt be interesting to compare Świda's views on the role of unemployment in the aetiology of criminology with the current labour market situation. The living conditions of the unemployed and their families obviously cannot be compared with what they were before the war due to, for example, the different levels of social welfare. Świda next puts the lack of prostitution crimes in 1952 down to the altered legal status of prostitution and the general improvement in living conditions (in his opinion, poverty and unemployment had not yet forced women into prostitution).

The above arguments in support of the hypothesis that changes to specific kinds of criminality are associated with the change in political system can so far generally be considered convincing. Those in the last category, however, i.e. anti-Semitic crimes, cannot be so treated. Świda does not raise the fundamental issue, i.e. the complete extermination of the Jewish population in the territories in question, at all. Instead, he writes that 'those crimes in 1937 appeared against a backdrop of certain contemporary political parties propagating fascist and anti-Semitic slogans. The change in political system has meant that this type of organisation no longer has any right to exist in People's Poland' (Świda 1960, p. 113).

Świda's analysis, for all its methodological anachronisms and ideologically coloured phraseology, contains many observations that may be useful in analysing certain aspects of the modern workings of social change, especially in the sphere of social consciousness, even now. The conclusion of the work (and a couple of the detailed discussions) raises the question of the peculiar disparity between the specific components of social change and the state of social consciousness, the extent to which changing regulatory standards are adopted, social functioning in the new circumstances, and culture (as broadly understood) generally.

In a 1970s work on the influence of economic development, industrialisation and urbanisation on criminality, Andrzej Mościskier tried to prove that these processes were of no fundamental significance to the level of criminality in Poland using factor analysis (Mościskier 1978b). 'By using an organising concept, the pattern of the reported studies was the proposition that while even a simple analysis of the coefficients might have suggested a correlation between socio-economic factors and criminality, this correlation would turn out to be merely apparent on a more precise analysis' (Mościskier 1978b, p. 135). As a result of a correlation analysis of the 62 variables that had been factored into the study and which characterised every voivodeship in terms of criminality, demographic factors, migration, the socio-cultural attributes of its residents, the development of basic economic branches, and other relevant characteristics, Mościskier claimed that the large-scale migrations that followed the redrawing of Poland's borders in the immediate post-war period had the greatest influence on criminality in the country. According to Mościskier, this exerted a long-term influence on the level and spatial diversity of criminality.[16] In other words, the fundamental influence on the level of criminality in a given region is not the level of industrialisation or urbanisation but rather the effect of the consolidated social disorganisation associated with rupturing or drastically weakening social ties and social control as a result of the administrative displacement of millions of people from what used to be the territory of the Polish Republic to the Recovered Territories.

> The social consequences of these migrations, manifested over several years, such as a relatively unstable incoming population, copious consumption of alcohol and greater susceptibility to the negative aspects of mass culture as a result of the weakening of social bonds and social control, were the main reasons why the incidence of criminality increased in certain parts of the country. (Mościskier 1978b, p. 142)

Mościskier could only discern a link between urbanisation and criminality in the case of juvenile crime. In conclusion, he categorically states that the level of economic development in a given region has no effect on the level of criminality.

16 This is one of the abovementioned attempts to analyse the effects of social change associated with mass migration. For more modern links between the effects of post-war mass migration and criminality, see Siemaszko (2001).

In another work on criminality in heavily industrialised regions, Mościskier analysed this phenomenon in rapid social changes, assuming that studies conducted in these regions would constitute a special experiment (Mościskier 1978a). The specifics of this analysis involved examining the results of the abrupt transformations that followed the building of huge industrial facilities in places that until then had not been industrialised. Mościskier's conclusions were basically that the increase in the incidence of criminality in rapidly industrialised areas is transitory (although this sometimes only happens after 10–20 years).[17] The processes to which Mościskier attributes this at least temporary influence on the incidence of criminality, however, are worth bearing in mind. These are a weakening of social control associated with an influx of building and construction workers into the area, conflicts between the local population and the newcomers, a state of moral loss, a conflict of cultural models due to a rapidly changing social reality, and a general state of disorganisation in its many and varied manifestations.

The analyses mentioned above on change processes in their connection with criminality were based on official data on criminology. Only Radzinowicz raises the question of the limitations that follow from that; the other researchers do not even mention the issue.

The authors of the analyses so far described mention the factors they consider relevant to criminality during a period of change and stress, e.g. the importance of social inequalities, disorganisation and the social and individual levels, the different rates of change in political and economic life relative to social consciousness, the weakening of social ties, and the profound rupturing of the functioning of social control mechanisms. Despite the passage of time, some of the conclusions in these works would seem to be common to any description of criminality during a period of transformation.

Criminality and the post-1989 change in political system in criminological analyses

The transformation of 1989 ushered in a whole raft of political and economic changes. Some of the consequences of these changes were unexpected and painful. Piotr Sztompka gives these negative results the appellation 'change trauma' (Sztompka 2002). The more sudden and abrupt the change and the more areas of life it encompasses, the more traumatogenic it will be. During the first stage of the transformation, the changes brought disorganisation and chaos at the institutional level (i.e. anomie in Durkheim's sense of the term) and cultural disorientation and a feeling of 'civilisational incompetence' at the individual level. The symptoms are a lack of trust (in institutions and fellow citizens), apathy, a feeling of impotence manifested in a lack of interest in public affairs, a tendency to live for the moment, idealising the works of the community, a general feeling of fear and unease and, finally, the emergence of phenomena associated with 'moral panic'. All these elements of social consciousness can be taken into account when analysing the determinants of the change in the picture of criminality in Poland.

Alenka Šelih has analysed the phenomenon of criminality and its control in Central and Eastern European countries undergoing transformation (Šelih 2012, pp. 3–36). She points out that all these countries were suffering to a greater or lesser extent from economic crises at the time they were being transformed, which raised its social cost considerably. Additionally, this was followed by a remarkable increase in social stratification and disintegration in all the countries studied. Šelih further stressed that the changes in institutions and social structures turned out to be more complicated than could possibly have been assumed beforehand.

Without conducting a detailed analysis of the picture of criminality during the transformational period of recent years, I would simply like to call to mind the general tendency. The fundamental qualitative change was between 1989 and 1990, when the incidence of criminality increased approximately 61 per cent. A period of relative stability then prevailed until 1994, after which criminality began gradually and steadily to increase. A clear downward trend was not noticeable until 2004.[18] The composition of criminality likewise clearly changed. Most noticeable was a fall in the share of property crimes in the overall composition of criminality, from close to 85 per cent in 1990 to approximately 54 per cent and still falling in 2007 (Siemaszko et al. 2009, p. 17).

17 It is difficult to say what the results of a repeat analysis of these phenomena over a longer period would have been. Mościskier's examinations took place 10–20 years after these projects had commenced.

18 Chapter 2, by Konrad Buczkowski, has a detailed analysis of the statistical picture of criminality in Poland during this period.

The level of fear of crime also changed during the period under consideration.[19] This level rose sharply when the political system transformations began. This might be attributed to both the actual increase in the incidence of crime and Polish society suddenly encountering the media image of criminality. It obviously has to be borne in mind that one of the trauma symptoms associated with sudden and profound social change is an increased feeling of being lost, uncertain and threatened in many areas of life, including the threat of criminality. We have now been observing a clear fall in the level of fear for some time, although the beginnings of this downward trend appeared before any noticeable changes in the incidence of criminality.

How then did criminologists most frequently diagnose the causes of the changes in criminality associated with the change in political system in Poland? When these analyses were carried out is crucial. Another perspective that has been adopted is to analyse the entire 20-year period after 1989, when the characteristics of the change parameters were set in the period immediately following the collapse of the system, in the face of a sudden, huge increase in the incidence of criminality.

Andrzej Siemaszko believes that the causes of the changing image of criminality in the 1990s 'had to be sought in the material and non-material domains' (Siemaszko et al. 1999, pp. 170–71). Among the former, he points to a fall in the effectiveness of policing, an increase in external migration, unemployment, easy access to firearms and 'an increase in the number of valuable goods in the possession of the public'.[20] Among the latter, he mentions social control (both formal and informal) being weakened, large social groups feeling marginalised, normative chaos and society becoming progressively stratified. These two groups are related in many respects. The fall in the effectiveness of policing has a variety of causes and is an essential component of the weakening of formal social control. Regardless of whether the cause is insufficient manpower and possibly ill-considered organisational changes, underfunding and/or inadequate training, the result of this state of affairs is an increased feeling that offenders are going unpunished and that society is under threat from criminality. Unemployment, especially when it is long-term or structural, can make people more inclined to improve their material situation by resorting to illegal activities, especially when conscious stimuli, e.g. feeling excluded and frustrated with increasing stratification, are taken into account. It is difficult, however, to completely agree that such factors as increased external migration or easy access to firearms are deemed essential in explaining the significant increase in criminality. These two factors were obviously frequently cited in the mid-1990s, but neither the greater relative ease of obtaining firearms illegally nor the 1,000 per cent increase in border traffic during the period can explain an increase in criminality on this scale.

Anna Kossowska distinguishes subjective causes, directly connected with the state of social consciousness, from objective causes, connected with the realities of social, political and economic life (although influencing the views and attitudes of society), when analysing the causes of the increase in the incidence of criminality after 1989 (Kossowska 1996). Kossowska includes the dissemination of special neutralising techniques and a tendency to rationalise criminality (mainly property crimes), as manifested in a series of stereotypes, among the subjective factors.[21] The first of these stereotypes was mainly present in the media and in statements made by politicians. This was basically the oft-repeated claim that unemployment (viewed as a social phenomenon, not as the providence of an individual) and an abrupt worsening of the overall financial situation cause an increase in criminality. Kossowska believes that the pervasiveness of claims of this kind in descriptions of the realities of Polish life during this period could have made it easier for individuals to make criminal decisions. The next stereotype, mainly trumpeted during election campaigns, was the assertion that the elite were generally corrupt. This found voice in the common view that since 'they' all stole and were not penalised for it, illegal activities on the part of private individuals could more easily be justified. And finally, the stereotype typical for the initial, pioneering period of the transformation, i.e. the permissibility of any activity not expressly forbidden, in a period where the law had not kept up with economic changes, justified making decisions that were on the borderline of the law or just outside it.

Kossowska counts the situation in the police force, the state of the law and the condition of the Polish family among the objective factors that influenced criminality in the first half of the 1990s. The sweeping staff changes planned for the police force in the initial period of the transformation brought about an unexpected

19 For more on the fear of criminality, see Chapter 9: 'The Social Perception of Criminality'.

20 The author had the increase in the number of foreigners in mind.

21 In a certain sense, these neutralising techniques are used more at the social than at the individual level.

result in that it increased the number of inadequately trained officers through the resignation (for a variety of reasons) of many existing staff members. Moreover, the police were not prepared for many of the new tasks that resulted from the change in the makeup and extent of criminality. The new economic situation, in particular, demanded skills from investigative bodies that took time to acquire as well as a change in the way they thought. Finally, one highly relevant factor determining the effectiveness of the police force was that of uncertainty as to the role of the force in the new system on the part of officers (and their superiors). One inhibiting factor of police work during the initial period following the transformation was their willingness to shed their former citizens' militia image and uncertainty as to what field of action the public would accept. This feeling of uncertainty was admittedly short-lived.

The state of legal regulations was an important factor influencing the nature of criminality and attitudes to the law in Poland. First, in one sense, the law failed to 'keep up' with political and economic changes and the changes to the law and the way it was applied were complicated and often made amid heated debates and controversies. This lessened the respect, which has never been particularly great in Poland, in which the law was held, as well as the motivation to act in accordance with it.

The last of the objective factors was (and still is) the situation of Polish families. This has a very important connection to the state of social consciousness. First, the initial transformation period was conducive to feeling confused about the standards and values that applied in the new system. The socialising functions of the family were disrupted in these circumstances. Second, on the one hand, the new economic situation meant that maintaining the material status of a family now required a greater effort (at the expense of education), while on the other, it made it more important to possess things deemed essential by society. Both these factors contributed to limiting the role of the family as an educational environment and strengthened the influence of peer groups, subcultures and the media. Finally, the impact of unemployment on the children of the long-term unemployed is material to any discussion of the links between the changes in criminality and the situation of the family. Feeling marginalised and being aware of being denied access to the opportunities made available by the new socio-economic situation was an important factor in becoming criminally motivated.

Irena Rzeplińska mostly emphasises social change as generally understood in her description of the changes in criminality and their causes during the transformation in Poland, although she does not expand on this idea (Rzeplińska 2010). Rzeplińska also stressed the importance of such factors as crimes being more comprehensively recorded by the police, a greater willingness on the part of victims to report their injuries and losses to the police, a more affluent society (which increased the number of criminal opportunities) and certain new criminal phenomena, e.g. cross-border crime, the criminality of foreigners, crimes associated with avoiding excise taxes in the goods trade, but most of all, the arrival of organised crime syndicates with their own special kind of criminality.

Teodor Szymanowski claims that the explanation for the inordinate increase in property crimes throughout the transformation has to be sought in the enormous increase in the number of criminal opportunities and the galvanising of consumerist attitudes in his analysis of the profile of this type of crime in Poland (Szymanowski 2012). The first of these factors is connected with the sudden appearance of huge quantities of goods that had previously been unavailable or heavily restricted on the market, along with the development of a commercial system, and especially those types of commerce that encourage customers to come into direct contact with goods. 'Fluctuating unemployment, especially structural unemployment, and destitution might have played a certain part as well' (Szymanowski 2012, p. 71).

Each of these diagnoses of the causes of criminality during the transformational period is to some extent correct. None of them, however, can explain what caused the rapid escalation of criminality between 1989 and 1990. No amount of change in social consciousness, normative chaos, social stratification or the law could have triggered the sort of rapid social behavioural response reflected in the number of reported crimes. So how is this phenomenon to be explained?

All the determining factors to change criminality mentioned above seem to be relevant (although obviously in varying degrees) but they only concern the change mechanisms after the period of stability in the first half of the 1990s. If this 60 per cent increase in criminality is to be properly understood, it has to be accepted as the outcome of the social progress of the 1980s, and especially the latter half of the decade. It can therefore be said that, in this respect, social change should be backdated to before 1989. This is not about the change involved in moving away from the Polish version of socialism to the Polish version of capitalism, but about the transformation itself being de facto a profound disorganisation of the country in terms of institutions, social attitudes and social consciousness. A certain amount of social disorganisation is normal in modern societies, but what we are dealing with in the cases described here is a state of disorganisation that is multi-faceted, long-term and deep-seated. That those in power agreed to dialogue with the opposition is, in any case, evidence that even they could see the country was falling apart. A lot of the writers who have analysed the state of criminality in Poland stress that the real level of criminality before 1989 was decidedly higher than that revealed by government statistics.[22] This was not just because statistics were intentionally fabricated but also because the citizens' militia were reluctant to register a lot of criminal incidents and victims were reluctant to file complaints. This last reason stemmed from a complete lack of confidence in the citizens' militia. Once the political system had changed, the police were more inclined to register even the most trifling incidents. The number of crimes definitely increased (although obviously not so significantly), while the police began to see the benefits of inflating statistics just as they had previously seen the benefits in understating them.[23] However it may seem, the 60 per cent change in the registered incidence of criminality between 1989 and 1990 does not imply any change in actual criminality. There was obviously an increase but definitely nothing like what the police statistics indicated. The fact that criminality was maintained at the same level for the first few years after the changes of 1989 supports this line of reasoning. Further, criminality only began to gradually, but distinctly, increase as a result of the mechanisms described above.

The discussions on the factors influencing the level of criminality during the transformational period have so far largely been of an historical nature. It is now 25 years since the transformations began and the determinants of criminality in contemporary Poland can be analysed using the same factors as those invoked by criminologists in their descriptions of criminality in postmodern societies, i.e. social inequalities and exclusion however measured, and cultural changes resulting from globalisation and the technical and information revolutions.

Conclusion

In summarising this chapter, it is necessary to consider a highly relevant aspect, and so far the only one that has been indicated, of the issues. The views on the links between social change and criminality detailed above refer to situations where the change has brought about an increase in the incidence of criminality. However, in many countries, including Poland, there is now a noticeable decline in the incidence of criminality.[24] Moreover, this state has prevailed since the mid-1990s in most of the countries where it has been observed. This decline, however, has occurred after a lag of about 10 years in Poland and some of the other countries whose political systems are being transformed.

The changes in the organisation and functioning of postmodern societies and the impact of these changes on the nature of criminality are a matter for speculation when considering the causes of this reversal of trends in criminality.

Jan van Dijk and Ben Vollaard, who wrote on the decline in the incidence of criminality internationally, believe that the reason for the decline in petty crime may lie in the change in the composition of criminal opportunities. They mostly attribute this to the dissemination of different methods of situational crime prevention. Van Dijk and Vollaard claim that we can speak of the result of a specific interaction between potential perpetrators and potential victims, especially regarding property crimes (van Dijk and Vollaard 2012, p. 261). The number of criminal opportunities has increased, as has criminal motivation, as a result of economic and technological development. The number of crimes has therefore increased as well. For understandable reasons, the response of potential victims has been belated, although it has nevertheless taken the form of situational crime prevention measures. There has consequently been a decline in the incidence of specific crimes.

---

22 For more on this topic, see, e.g., Siemaszko et al. 1999, pp. 167–8.

23 The high incidence of criminality might have been an argument in favour of increasing the police budget and/or expanding their authority.

24 The greatest decline has been observed in the case of property crimes.

Demographic changes associated with the changing age structure of postmodern societies and the development of new modes of performing external social control are among the other reasons that crime trends have been reversed. Obviously, this is merely speculative. This is an issue that definitely requires multi-faceted research. It is worth quoting Franklin Zimring on the cyclical nature of the fluctuations in the incidence of crimes which, in his opinion, cannot be explained on the basis of the existing criminological oeuvre (Zimring 2007). He terms these cyclical changes 'mysterious', although the editors of *The International Crime Drop* fairly categorically claim that there is nothing mysterious about this peculiar 'undulation' of crime trends and that it seems wholly explicable on the basis of the regularities mentioned above (van Dijk et al. 2012a, pp. 300–320).

In conclusion, the emergence of a fascinating new research topic connected with the rise of cybercrime should be mentioned. There is no way of examining the determinants of this new criminality on the basis of existing criminological theories. The profile of perpetrators is disparate. They are not infrequently completely socially well-adjusted young people for whom the time-honoured 'truths' about the aetiology of criminality and maladjusted youth simply do not apply.

Chapter 4
The Relationship between Poverty, Social Exclusion and Criminality[1]

Witold Klaus

Introduction

This chapter discusses the relationship between poverty and criminality and the various actions taken pursuant to public policies intended to counteract these two phenomena. The theoretical concepts underlying the historical approach the public authorities have taken both in helping the poor and socially excluded and in controlling them will be discussed. Social exclusion can become a catalyst for engaging in deviant behaviour, including criminality, or it can result in victimisation and thus contribute to making life less safe for people at the margins of society.

Historical Perspective: Controlling Vagabonds

Applying the various mechanisms of the criminal law to control the poor is by no means a recent idea. It is worth delving back into history to see how, since the middle ages, society has related to the poor, as well as people who have led lifestyles that differ from the norm. Even back then 'the Other' was feared and ascribed criminal characteristics. As Juliusz Makarewicz (2009, pp. 229–30) points out in his description of the history of criminality, poor people were basically synonymous with criminals in the distant past. The notions of 'poor person' and 'criminal' were used interchangeably in legal documents as well. Furthermore, the epithet 'vagabond', commensurate with 'rogue' and 'wanton person', was used in Poland to denote anyone who led

> an unsettled life in a manner that differed fundamentally from the norms and value hierarchies that are approved by eminent people and generally accepted. These were people who did not own real estate, had no fixed abode and were not employed in any designated occupation. (Kamler 2010, p. 30)

A broad group of people, therefore, lived apart from the majority of society. Some of them, being e.g. outlaws, fugitives from justice, army deserters, or, as happened in Poland and elsewhere, escapees from feudal estates (as bonded serfs), led their lives under duress. Often some became beggars, through the necessity of earning a livelihood, though some did so through choice, e.g. peddlers and wanderers seeking adventure.

Mid-thirteenth-century ordinances of the French King Saint Louis IX, based on Angevin customary law, considered as suspicious

> … people who could not show either property or an honest means of subsistence, and who frequent taverns. The magistrates should seek them out, and … open an official enquiry into whatever they were accused of, with the view to punishing them. Even if proof was lacking and even without investigation …, because it was the duty of the authorities to cleanse the country of 'evil people'. (Geremek 2006, pp. 13–14)

Vagrancy was generally perceived as more of a threat than a crime at this time.

---

1 Two sections of this chapter were written in collaboration with Dagmara Woźniakowska-Fajst: 'The Contemporary Definitions of Poverty and Social Exclusion' and 'The Other Side of the Coin, i.e. the Effect of Poverty on Victimisation'.

A change in attitude to vagabonds can be observed from the fourteenth century. Due to the epidemics afflicting Europe at the time, as well as significant depopulation wrought by wars and an emerging labour shortage, economic growth began to accelerate. Hired workers started to demand higher wages for their labour or simply refused work. Vagrants thus came to be looked upon as an untapped labour force, as did all poor people who had no fixed place of work and who spent their time sitting in taverns, playing games of chance, singing in the streets or begging. The lower classes were deemed to have had no right to have fun, and what little time they had away from work was expected to have been spent entirely on religious devotion. Thus a whole series of proclamations were issued in France, England and Castile ordering vagabonds to take up employment (including municipal jobs) immediately or leave town. The penalty for not complying with these ordinances ranged from a few days in prison (on bread and water) through to being pilloried and even being branded on the forehead, depending on the degree of 'recidivism'. Municipal officials and judges were ordered to combat vagrancy, beggary and other undesirable conduct and to force such people into gainful employment (Geremek 2006, pp. 29–39).

The attitude to vagrants changed again in the fifteenth century. They now came to be perceived as a source of criminality, i.e. as people who disturbed the social order. The legislature established at the time showed

> that the reasons for these proceedings lay not only in the offence committed, but in the simple fact of being without hearth or home. The vagabond was a criminal, on the one hand because he refused to work as God had ordained, and on the other, because vagabonds, as a group, committed crimes, since it was from their ranks that thieves, bandits and other villains were recruited. (Geremek 2006, p. 42)

Appropriate institutions therefore had to be created to cure these wrongdoers by giving them work (by coercion), while keeping them under constant watch. This was the idea behind workhouses, houses of correction, reformatories and general hospitals. Anyone who refused to work for reasonable remuneration or profit and squandered his time in inns was placed in such an establishment (Ostrihanska and Rzeplińska 1988, p. 6). The first such institutions appeared in London in 1550 (Bridewell) but quickly spread throughout Europe (albeit under different names). These places were essentially factory prisons where poor people were condemned to forced labour. Some institutions had daily regulations that had to be followed to the letter to avoid being punished with hunger and imprisonment (Raś 2011, pp. 18–19; Kalinowski and Pełka 1996). The basic function of the English Poor Relief Act of 1601 was to ensure social discipline – helpless and vulnerable people were taken care of (albeit while being made to observe a strict regimen), and anyone capable of working was made to work, so as to prevent them from begging and to disqualify them from receiving charitable assistance.

> Conditional assistance, limited to essential support, and endeavouring to get people to secure their own destiny through their own labour were the underlying policies and principles … of the English Crown at the time and remained so for the next hundred years. (Frysztacki 2009, p. 200)

This trend was also apparent in Poland. Serfs fleeing feudal estates were punished from the fifteenth century. These runaways were to be returned post-haste to their feudal masters and harbouring and/or hiding them was strictly forbidden. It was likewise forbidden to employ servants 'without attestation', i.e. without a reference from their previous employer. It was further ordered, however, that servants or retainers be employed for a period of not less than a year (Diakowska 2009, pp. 128, 135). An individual who could not produce proof a least a year's employment was deemed to be a rogue, and it was acceptable to 'seize [and] … force him to work until such time as his lord hears of this and inquires about him' (Kamler 2010, p. 31). In the eighteenth-century, however, workhouses were comparatively empty and regulations in Poland concerning vagabonds were not enforced (Frančić 1967, p. 125).

Vagabonds were treated in two different ways in the cities. If they were caught committing minor offences (usually theft), they were subjected to torture, during which they would confess to all sorts of acts (even ones they could not possibly have committed) and then severely punished by the municipal courts. There were two standards of administering punishment in Poland in the sixteenth to the eighteenth century: one for residents and another for vagabonds (Salmonowicz 2011, p. 23). Another way to treat vagabonds was to remove them from the city. In the Polish society of this period vagabonds were considered a threat to the economic wellbeing of both cities (where 'tinkers' took income away from merchants and artisan guilds) and the countryside (by virtue of running away from feudal estates). In the Constitution of the Polish Parliament of 1611 they were also regarded as 'committing murders and rapes, and taking chattels and other supellectilia'[2] (Kamler 2010, p. 32).

A certain Andrzej Frycz Modrzewski, in his *O poprawie Rzeczypospolitej* (On the Reform of the Commonwealth), even went so far as to recommend establishing a special office of 'custodians of the poor' that would take care of people unable to find work. He did stress, however, 'the necessity of distinguishing genuine poverty from laziness, trickery and ingrained idleness' (Raś 2011, p. 23). Two hundred years later, Józef Wybicki, realising that one way to develop the Polish economy was to increase the number of hands available for work, planned to set up, on the one hand, institutions for orphans (which he named hospitals) to teach them trades, and on the other, correctional institutions for criminals. 'These should be maintained by the state and people shut up there for minor offences would have to contribute to the prosperity of the country through useful work' (Kurdybacha 1951, p. 65). In 1818 these ideas found their way into the draft regulations of the Penal Code of the Kingdom of Poland (Arts 310–13) prepared by the Council of State. To a large extent, these were modelled on the French legislature. Vagrancy and beggary were deemed offences punishable by incarceration in a reformatory for from eight days to three months (and for from three months to a year for group begging). A vagrant (vagabond) was defined as a person who 'has no fixed address, no visible means of support and … does not practise any trade or profession' (Śliwowski 1958, pp. 150–51). These regulations, however, did not find their way into the final version of the code.[3]

The nineteenth century saw a huge increase in the number of prisons and considerable development in the institution itself. Prisons ceased to be simply places where criminals were held in difficult conditions,[4] and the Enlightenment idea of rehabilitation began to influence the way they functioned. This approach aimed, on the one hand, to improve living conditions in prisons,[5] and on the other, to educate inmates by improving their morality, learning and work. Despite these lofty sentiments, the system has been anything but a success: authority is commonly abused in prisons and the places themselves tend to produce criminals rather then 'cure' them of their criminality. This is primarily because the prison system was designed to isolate prisoners and to make them perform unpaid work. The inordinately cruel conditions were also a huge problem, one that drove prisoners to riot and made them feel wronged and humiliated.[6] This may describe the thinking of the 1830s but much of it could have been written about the present situation. The result of these measures is that, once they regain their freedom, former prisoners are still strongly stigmatised – they are required to carry documents certifying their imprisonment and are subjected to special police inspections. This prevents them from finding work, so they become vagabonds and are often driven to steal out of necessity. Of further concern (and again, this is still topical) is the fact that imprisoning the main breadwinner of a family causes poverty and compounds the destitution of the entire family, as it cannot support itself unaided. This condemns children to vagabondage and beggary, from where, it is easy to drift into petty crime (see Foucault 1978).

Vagabondage remained a problem throughout the twentieth century. George Orwell brilliantly described the way the English poor were managed by the state in the 1920s and 1930s, which basically amounted to

2 'Supellectilia' denotes various kinds of household furnishings.

3 It is worth mentioning, however, that this code provided for a variety of punishments and even statutorily defined crimes according to social position. Theft, generally regarded a misdemeanour, was elevated to a felony when committed by servants or retainers to the detriment of their employers (Śliwowski 1958, p. 281).

4 As was the case at the end of the Middle Ages, when prison conditions were cruel and inmates were made to pay for their keep, including food, bunks and even straw. If they lacked the means, because they came from poor families, their only recourse lay in passers-by taking pity on them and tossing them something to eat (see Geremek 2006, pp. 17–18).

5 Ksawery Potocki has pointed out, however, that at the same time 'Prisons should not be instituted so as to be furnished with more comforts than the poorest class of people living in a state of innocence and freedom have available for use, as they would then become refuges offering a better existence to poor people, encourage more crime, and lose their main penal character to wit deterring crime' (quoted in Raś 2011, pp. 30–31).

6 Makarewicz (1922, pp. 146–8) also pointed out the problem of penal institutions releasing more recidivists, who might have succumbed to a 'moral infection as a result of breathing in the unhealthy ethical miasma of prison air'. He did not, however, call for restricting the use of incarceration, but rather for providing more and better support for people released from penal institutions.

legislation engineered to produce vagabonds. The state prevented people from starving to death but the whole system was set up in such a way as to make it virtually impossible for them to break free and lead autonomous lives. Orwell wrote:

> A tramp tramps, not because he likes it, but ... because there happens to be a law compelling him to do so. A destitute man, if he is not supported by the parish, can only get relief at the casual wards, and as each casual ward will only admit him for one night, he is automatically kept moving. He is a vagrant because, in the state of the law, it is that or starve. (Orwell 1933, p. 239)

Orwell's description of how the system worked and how the poor were extensively controlled is very instructive.

The communist authorities also managed vagrants, whom they referred to as social parasites. Apart from ideological considerations, their approach was driven by economic factors. Forced labour was introduced after the October Revolution to meet the needs of industrial development in the face of a manpower shortage. Avoiding work was considered a crime and was duly punished. Another purpose of this mandate to work was obviously to exercise greater control over society. In Poland these trends lasted until the 1980s, with the *ustawę o postępowaniu wobec osób uchylających się od pracy* (Act on Proceedings Against Persons Evading Work) being passed in 1982. This Act made special registration compulsory for men who had been out of work for more than three months. Employment bureaux would then put them to work on public works or oblige them to take up studies. Avoiding work or failing to register within the time limit was punishable by a fine or a two-year restriction of liberty. The purpose of introducing regulations on social parasitism, apart from a desire to control certain groups in society (mostly the poor, who were often former inmates of penal institutions, but also 'swingers' and 'speculators'), seems to have been to divert attention from the real problems of the People's Republic of Poland. The idea might also have been to stigmatise the leading figures of undesirable groups (the mere designation 'social parasite' had an especially negative connotation at the time), so that the economic ills besetting the country could be blamed on these manufactured enemies (Ostrihanska and Rzeplińska 1988, pp. 6–7, 72–7, 27–31).

The foregoing considerations indicate that constant attempts have been made over the centuries to mark out a specific area and place to isolate both poor people and people who choose to live their lives in ways that are not acceptable to most of society. The purpose of this has been to cordon off the poor and to enable the public authorities to manage their conduct by, for example, defining them and their activities as criminal or quasi-criminal and thus taking measures against them, placing them in isolating institutions of various kinds and forcing them to work. That this situation has prevailed since the Middle Ages is due to society being convinced that there is a link between criminality and poverty.

Contemporary Definitions of Poverty and Social Exclusion

The term 'social exclusion', as understood today, has many different meanings and can be analysed in both material and social terms. Exclusion is most commonly associated with poverty or membership of a minority group, although this need not always be the case. Many people consider the terms 'poverty' and 'social exclusion' to be synonymous and use them interchangeably. Indeed, delimiting the boundaries between them is extremely difficult and depends on which definitions are accepted.

Social exclusion is a result of individuals or groups being socially disadvantaged in various ways, leading to them being denied full participation in the economic, social and political life of their communities. Szarfenberg (2010, pp. 132–3), having analysed various definitions of the term, distinguishes four concepts that are accepted in the literature by different researchers. First, exclusion is associated with a lack of participation (or with partial participation) in several spheres of social life. According to other definitions, exclusion is associated with discrimination against certain social groups and a refusal to recognise their entitlement to certain rights – especially social rights. Another concept focuses on the refusal of certain resources – mainly goods or welfare from social institutions but also labour market access. The final group of definitions concentrates on linking social exclusion with material deprivation, i.e. poverty.

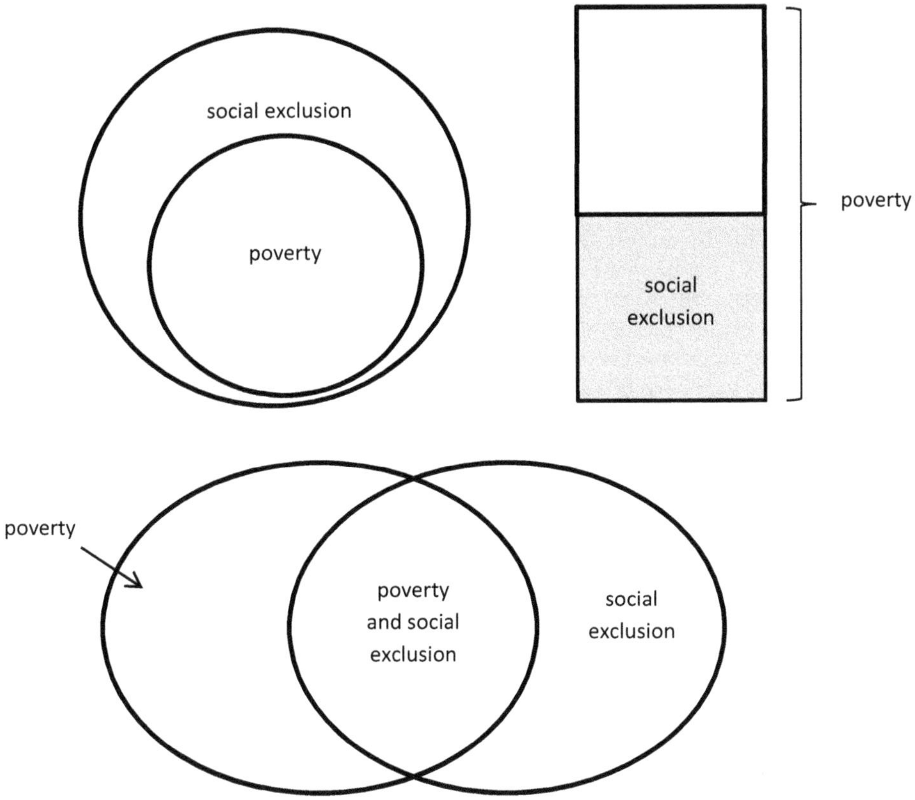

Figure 4.1 Poverty and social exclusion – interpenetration of the two terms

Words like 'poverty' and 'destitution' can also have many different meanings. The most standard definitions define 'destitution' in the survival sense, i.e. possessing the bare minimum for subsistence. Poverty is identified with a lack of sufficient material resources. The more recent interpretation, however, is much broader and embraces not being able to satisfy social needs that go beyond material issues and includes adopting different social roles and being involved in various social relationships that, in a manner, are commonly or sufficiently broadly accepted in the given society and that bring about a certain degree of social acceptance. Poor people are therefore excluded from the minimum acceptable lifestyle of the country in which they live (relative destitution is important here, i.e. destitution is always relative to the time and place in which the person lives). This definition, it is worth emphasising once more, concerns not only income, but also participation in social, cultural and political life. Destitution often hinders or prevents an appropriate level of human resources (social capital) from being created and renders people incapable of taking part in public and cultural activities. This imposes additional barriers, as it is often difficult for people to draw on their own resources, which, it should be added, are usually modest enough, when they are worn out from trying to make ends meet and are overwhelmed, as a result of their state of poverty, with feelings of despondency, hopelessness, helplessness and lack of control (Lister 2004, pp. 135–7). This leads to the next definition of destitution, which views poverty as a substantial restriction of a person's options to choose who he/she wants to be, what he/she wants to do and what kind of life he/she would like to lead (Lister 2004, pp. 12–36; Szarfenberg and Kurowska 2010).

Armed with such broad and diverse definitions of these two terms, researchers argue about the various relationships between them. Some note the progress and dependencies of the two states, but while some write about how poverty leads to social exclusion, others see a reverse relationship. Some researchers focus on the layers of meaning and present these two notions as aggregations (as shown in Figure 4.1). This, however, opens up a whole gamut of possibilities – from the term 'exclusion' encapsulating the idea of poverty, to the two terms overlapping in meaning, to the term 'poverty' encapsulating the notion of exclusion (in this case, excluded people are definitely the most destitute) (see Lister 2004, pp. 81–5).

This study adopts an intermediate conception that focuses on both perspectives, seeing the cause and effect relationship between destitution and social exclusion as being able to work in either direction – poverty usually contributes to social exclusion, while social exclusion (especially when substantially intensified, e.g. ostracism) can lead to poverty. These terms definitely share a common semantic domain as well – at least in part – although there are few cases of poor people who are not also socially excluded. Some excluded social groups, however, are not necessarily poor – here we are mostly dealing with minority groups, i.e. people of different ethnicities, sexual orientations or religions, but also members of, for instance, youth subcultures. It should be borne in mind that the extent of exclusion from society can be as varied as its cause. Some members of a group may also decide to behave in a highly distinct and autonomous manner and choose to remain outside the society of the country in which they live.

Kazimierz Frieske points out that conflicting interests between different social groups is one of the operating elements of contemporary society. It is necessary 'to come to terms with the fact that the various mechanisms of social exclusion comprise one of the institutional forms in which this conflict is expressed. These are therefore processes that you can try to stop or slow down but this must be accompanied by public intervention in the multi-faceted fabric of culturally conflicting interests' (Frieske 2004b, p. 23). This intervention should be guaranteed by adequately developed legal institutions. These would embody the principles of justice that, according to Tadeusz Kotarbiński, call for 'providing according to some equal measure, fulfilling that which was promised (explicitly or implicitly), and defending those that have been harmed or who are threatened with harm in the accessible domain of our intervention' (Kotarbiński 1987, p. 182).

Meanwhile, a number of legal philosophers, led by Ronald Dworkin, observe that the law intrinsically excludes and discriminates between certain groups. Indeed, the recently-coined term 'legal exclusion' is defined as 'social exclusion effected by law with the assistance of legislation and legal measures' (Kwaśniewski 2010, p. 190). Staśkiewicz (2010), however, points out that there is more to legal exclusion than simply refusing to grant specific entitlements to a certain group or ignoring their interests when applying the law (this corresponds to the concepts of being equal before and against the law). No less important in this regard is that certain groups are denied rights they have been granted by virtue of insurmountable barriers (e.g. high court costs, unintelligible laws, regulations that are not widely available or easy to access, illiteracy and lack of Internet access) or their own deliberate retreat to the margins of society. Not participating in public or political life (including elections) is another factor that will result in the needs or stated opinions of certain social groups not being taken into consideration by politicians when drafting legislation. This leads to a vicious circle whereby the law excludes certain groups because it is deaf to their needs and opinions and cannot hear them in any case because those excluded have neither the power nor the possibility to make their voices heard, articulate their expectations or influence any changes made to the law. The result is that the law, by its very nature, excludes the already excluded. By this interpretation, legal exclusion is partly identical to the state of affairs described by Ruth Lister.

This is another reason why some people require systematic support to enable them to participate fully in the different dimensions of social life. Indeed, simply acknowledging specific rights is often not enough because some people may not have the appropriate social competencies to take advantage of them. Thus the state and its institutions must play a major role in the process of inclusion. It is also worth noting that the very idea of social exclusion carries with it the imperative of inclusion (Young 2002, p. 457).

Does Poverty Cause Theft?

Does poverty cause theft? What is the relationship between destitution, exclusion and criminality? These are questions well worth asking. There are many theoretical conceptions on this topic but fewer studies that would unambiguously confirm them. The dependencies between these phenomena are apparent in some studies. What is not apparent, however, is their direction of causality, i.e. it is difficult to say whether poverty and/or social exclusion give rise to criminal conduct or whether the cause and effect relationship works in the opposite direction. One or the other situation can probably hold true depending on specific instances. The indefiniteness of the concepts with which we are working (as discussed above) is another cause of difficulty in studies on these relationships. Just as there are many definitions of social exclusion, the terms 'poverty' and 'criminality' are also subjective and are interpreted differently by different researchers (Kossowska 2013). This chapter discusses the results of studies that allow this topic to be better understood, albeit only slightly, both from a theoretical perspective and on the basis of cases taken from Polish studies.

The relationships between poverty and criminality: a theoretical glance

Ulrich Beck refers to contemporary societies as risk societies. It is risk that brings anxiety to the foreground and conditions the other activities of the individual, the authorities and the entire community. Beck writes:

> The movement set in motion by the risk society … is expressed in the statement: *I am afraid.* The *commonality of anxiety* takes the places of the *commonality of need.* The type of the risk society marks in this sense a social epoch in which *solidarity of anxiety* arises and becomes a political force. (Beck 2005, p. 49, emphasis in the original)

We are therefore dealing with a collection of defensive actions against various (actual or potential) threats, including criminality. This state is referred to as safety utopia.

David Garland claims that criminality is now generally accepted as a naturally occurring phenomenon in society. Leon Radzinowicz had observed this characteristic as a certain derivative of an increase in criminality as early as the 1930s. Radzinowicz (1969, p. 157) wrote that the overall growth of various types of crime meant that crime became an everyday occurrence and was greeted with indifference.[7]

These two academics both formulated their theses in situations that experienced significant increases in criminality: the Great Depression of the 1930s and the 1990s. It would seem, however, that once this feeling appears in society, it tends to linger. We therefore slowly stop thinking about the fruits of criminality and simply accept its existence. We reconcile ourselves to its existence. This acceptance, however, is accompanied by changes in our everyday behaviour – we start to factor in the risk of becoming a victim of crime as we do other dangers that may befall us and we try to avoid it by adopting various adaptive strategies. This 'ordinariness' assumption about criminality results in perpetrators being perceived differently.

> In contrast to earlier criminologies, which began from the premise that crime was a deviation from normal civilized conduct and was explicable in terms of individual pathology or fault of socialization, the new criminologies see crime as *continuous* with normal social interaction and explicable by reference to *standard* motivation patterns. (Garland 2009, p. 128, emphasis in the original)

These motivational patterns are nothing more than weighing the pros and cons of a decision to commit a crime. The perpetrator is therefore assumed to be completely rational and to analyse every act thoroughly before committing it. This assumption may well be justified in the case of crimes against property,[8] but it

7 It is interesting to note that Radzinowicz also pointed out that this approach to criminality often leads to a statistical decline, that is, in the number of reported crimes, because those harmed neither have the inclination nor see the need to notify the police (in any case, they seldom have any confidence in the effectiveness or efficiency of the police).

8 Studies on the profitably of burglary in Pennsylvania in the 1960s conducted by Michael Sesnowitz in the 1970s, however, contradict this theory as the results showed that the perpetrator statistically lost USD 197 per burglary. When analysing these costs, the gains of the burglary were weighed against the risk and probability of being convicted and the cost of imprisonment (Kiersztyn 2008, p. 48).

is difficult to explain in the case of aggressive crimes, especially those committed in the heat of passion. Theories that explain criminal acts as routine or lifestyle-associated activities (i.e. lifestyle theories) offer a much better approach. According to these theories, three elements need to be present simultaneously:

1. a suitably motivated perpetrator (e.g. by destitution);
2. a worthwhile goal or object (this may be e.g. an object that can be sold at a high price or which the perpetrator simply desires for whatever reason), which should additionally be left somewhere from where it can easily be stolen without undue risk of getting caught;
3. a lack of supervision or security in the form of a person (e.g. a state official, but also family members and others in a position to exercise control) or security devices.

Given enough opportunities, then, criminality will ensue (i.e. a thief will be made) and opportunities present themselves in the everyday lives the perpetrators and their potential victims lead. This is about, for example, increasing the number of small luxury items we possess or finding another way to guard property (instead of a multi-generational family in which there is always someone at home, we now rely on security firms and automatic alarms) (Newburn 2007, pp. 286–90).

Consequently, situational prevention is more and more frequently used to prevent crime. The object here is to eliminate one of the necessary preconditions to committing a crime, as mentioned above, by adequately safeguarding property from potential perpetrators. This is not so much a desire to change people (i.e. to implement measures to rehabilitate criminals) as to change the environment, and thereby the situation in which a prohibited act can potentially be committed, by installing security devices, surveillance equipment (e.g. cameras) and restricting the movement of certain people (e.g. football supporters during matches) (Sochacka 2010). This creates a higher level of feeling secure, or rather, what some authors refer to as an 'illusion of order'. This feeling of wellbeing is paid for by the poor and socially excluded, who are subjected to more and more control by the authorities (Garland 2009, p. 129; Coleman 2009, p. 68).

This increased control over potential perpetrators, which the lower classes, without exception, are held to be, may bring about the opposite result to that intended. According to the control balance theory of Charles R. Tittle, the huge imbalance between external control (exercised by society or government departments) and internal control (self-control or rather lack thereof) can make a person subjected to these actions feel a need to balance these levels of control by, for example, committing a crime. This is a rebellion against the excessive expansion of the rules and regulations to which the perpetrator is expected to submit (Schneider 1997–1998, pp. 29–30). This corresponds to deprivation theory, according to which a high degree of social inequality will lead members of excluded groups to feel animosity, jealousy and resentment towards people higher up the social ladder. This mostly causes an increase in the number of violent crimes (Bircan et al. 2011, p. 3).

At the same time, according to Robert Merton, everyone has to measure up against the entire spectrum of social expectations and culturally determined goals (in contemporary consumer society, this mostly means possessing certain specified objects, which often determine the status of individuals). It is clear, however, that a portion of society will not be able to achieve an adequate position as determined by possessing certain specified goods. This especially concerns destitute people, who not only cannot afford to purchase many of the goods, but have no prospects of being able to do so in future, as they lack the necessary education, skills and social contacts. It is worth bearing in mind that this does not concern objective poverty, but rather relative poverty, i.e. relative to the rest of society. The state in which destitute people find themselves may (again, as with deprivation theory) engender feelings of frustration and injustice and a desire (and sometimes a need) to acquire certain goods some other way, i.e. illegally, since they cannot be obtained by legal means.[9] They may also feel humiliated by the low social position in which they find themselves, i.e. their destitution and often the disdainful attitude that members of other social groups, including aid institution workers, display towards

9 One young Londoner beautifully explained this in his own words: 'Although, I'm not saying that I commit crimes, if you just look at some of the flash cars that can be seen in this area, you can see why crimes are committed. People need money, clothes and food. They are bored and even if there are things to do, you still need money and the dole does not pay that much. When we leave school we can only look forward to unemployment. … Sometimes, it is exciting to commit crimes, especially when you get away with it' (Mooney 2002, p. 219).

them.[10] Some socially excluded people will find that they do not have much to lose when they weigh up the risks of doing something illegal. This is a result of the weakening of social relationships and a stratifying society, so that those at the top willingly dissociate themselves from those at the bottom (whom they refer to as the underclass) (Grover 2008, pp. 42–7).

The most conspicuous expression of social differences is the carving up, prevalent in most Western cities, of areas and the creation of entire precincts (sometimes even ghettos) of socially excluded people. The result of this division is the isolation in the same territory of people with different issues and social dysfunctions.

> As a result of these processes, people living in the districts of large cities and poorly educated members of ethnic minorities have become cut off from their workplaces, and unemployment and destitution have assumed catastrophic proportions. … Those who have remained have a very slim chance of finding work and improving their lot – chronic unemployment and remaining on welfare have therefore become part of their way of life. A consequence of this has been an accumulation of social pathologies, such as family breakdown, dependence on social security benefits, and criminality. (Kiersztyn 2008, p. 57)

Living in an area like this also induces young people to mimic the behaviour they observe in their immediate environment (including criminal behaviour).[11] As no other benchmarks are available, whatever chance they might have had to lead different lives is eliminated.

Studies show that more social disruption can be observed in communities inhabited by people of low socioeconomic status. Economic deprivation and marginalisation therefore have a negative impact on the degree of social organisation and lead to a lack of solidarity and mutual trust. At the very least, this results in a significant decrease in the number of contacts between neighbours, and from there a weakening in the exercise of social control. It is not surprising, then, that a low degree of social interaction is correlated with an increase in the incidence of burglaries and robberies (Bircan et al. 2011, p. 4; Kiersztyn 2008, p. 68). The level of support the residents of these degraded communities can expect to receive from each other or from relatives in similar straits is likewise low. While people can usually count on family or friends during difficult times or crises, the families of destitute people often find themselves in the same situation and are therefore in no position to offer either material or moral support (Currie 2002, p. 137).

It is also worth noting that not everyone has benefitted from the general economic growth of recent years. These changes have gone hand in hand with changes in the structure of employment – especially with dismissing people with poor qualifications, perhaps cutting their wages and changing their terms of employment (from permanent employment contracts to 'junk contracts', i.e. temporary and low-paying ones). This has brought about the creation of an unemployed and a working poor class. The question then is whether unemployment is correlated with crime and here the data are ambiguous. Although there is a link between unemployment and crime, it is difficult to determine the causality between them.

Catherine Hakim has observed that unemployment increases the level of recidivism and the prison population, while parents being unemployed increases the probability of their minor children committing crimes as well. Most studies confirm that there is a link between unemployment and an increase in the number of crimes against property (Grover 2008, pp. 37–8; Bircan et al. 2011, pp. 3–4). When it comes to resorting to violence, however, the results are no longer unambiguous. Studies conducted by Ming-Jen Lin (2008) in the United States do not generally support such a connection (although a definite relationship between male unemployment and rape can be shown to exist by introducing additional variables). Belgian studies, however, show that there is a definite connection, although violent crime in certain regions of the country may have other causes than their high unemployment levels (Bircan et al. 2011, pp. 12–14).

US studies conducted in the 1980s showed that while an increase in unemployment among the white population brought about an increase in the burglary and robbery rates, this correspondence was not observed

10 This attitude among social aid workers and politicians is described in this volume in Chapter 5: 'Preventing Criminality: The Social Policy of Preventing Social Exclusion'.

11 At least this is what Canadian studies of homeless youths indicate – many of those surveyed resort to violence (although they are occasionally perpetrators, 40 per cent of respondents had been beaten). This can be explained by their way of life and by the aggressive patterns of behaviour they picked up at home (Gaetz 2004, pp. 425–7, 436–8).

among the black population.[12] The reason for this may be that the mere fact of having or not having work is relevant, as is the type of work the person does and how stable his/her employment is. Steady, secure and fairly remunerated employment definitely prevents crime, and conversely, long-term unemployment following its loss can lead to crime. Casual, boring and poorly-paid jobs ('junk jobs') do not have the same consequences. They simply do not offer enough to make anyone feel obliged to behave in a conformist manner (Kiersztyn 2008, pp. 60–63).

Studies also show that there is a connection between remuneration and criminality. Crime in the UK has fallen with the introduction of a minimum wage, which is interesting given that the major beneficiaries of this measure have been women, who comprise a small percentage of perpetrators (Grover 2008, p. 36). Causes underlying the weakening of the institution of the family may help explain this phenomenon. For example, the spread of work that is too lowly paid to decently support a family and which forces both parents to work, and sometimes even hold down more than one job, can result in growing children being inadequately supervised or cared for. If these children additionally grow up in a deprived area, as described above, then they can easily start to commit prohibited acts. The minimum wage has at least ensured that parents need only work one job (and do not have to work overtime to earn enough to maintain a decent living) and are able to devote more time and effort to raising their children (Currie 2002, pp. 138–9). The most difficult situation, however, is that facing single parents, most often single mothers, on whom society makes extraordinarily high demands. Single mothers are expected to be economically self-sufficient, i.e. to work so as to support themselves and their children, while at the same time be model parents who ensure that their children are raised properly, even though this is said to be impossible without the support of the father. In the case of destitute people, however, this is not possible without public support (which is presently restricted in most countries). These women simply cannot adequately provide for their children unless this support is forthcoming (Grover 2008, pp. 4–5; Taylor 2002, p. 245).

This issue takes us to the role of the state, its institutions and the social policies it pursues to counteract crime. Research conducted by Savolainen (2000) demonstrates a strong statistical correlation between a social policy based on welfare principles and designed to even out economic inequalities and the number of homicides. Criminality increases in countries with greater social stratification and a lack of adequate protection for the socially excluded (this is a general principle and is not limited to homicides). This thesis has been confirmed by other studies: for example, a decrease in financial support for older youth in the UK at the end of the 1980s brought about an increase in criminality among this group (this was connected with being shut out of the education system, which had nothing suitable to offer them). Contemporary British studies also reveal a link between impeded or limited access to social benefits and an increase in criminality (Taylor 2002, pp. 239, 243; Grover 2008, pp. 36–7).

Finally, whether theft is even a crime when committed by an extremely destitute person is an open question. At the beginning of the twentieth century, Zygmunt Bartkiewicz wrote: 'Someone floundering in the mud, driven by cold and worry, and mercilessly whipped by life cannot be either good or bad, because he is cold and hungry above all else' (Kaczyńska 1994, p. 56). Different standards have to be applied to such a person by virtue of the specific circumstances in which he/she finds himself/herself. This is not about relativising theft, or more generally speaking, criminality, but rather a consideration of how the concept of 'crime' can vary depending on time and place[13] and how the weight and significance of the term 'social harm of an act', which exists in Polish criminal law, is constitutive for the very recognition of a given act as a crime. There is obviously no space here to pursue these deliberations further – we can only acknowledge that the problem exists.

Poverty and criminality in Polish studies

The relationship between poverty and criminality can also be observed in Polish sources. These generally confirm the theories presented above. The oldest studies based on statistical data date back to the nineteenth

12 Ming-Jen Lin's studies, however, which were conducted at the same time, did not claim similar dependencies (Lin 2008, p. 431).

13 For more on this topic, see Chapter 1: 'Criminality Today and Tomorrow: Structural Stability and Variability'.

century and reveal a strong correlation between destitution and the incidence of crimes against property. For example, the incidence of theft (and vagrancy and beggary) increased with the price of bread. This is accurate for data from both the middle and the end of the nineteenth century. This correlation, however, is not confirmed in the case of violent crimes – indeed, no correlation was found between their increase or decrease and the prevailing economic situation in Poland during the period in question (Kaczyńska 1994, pp. 199–200).

Correlations between the makeup of convicted people and that of the general population in the nineteenth century, as drawn by Kaczyńska (1994, pp. 269–77), also reveal certain interdependencies, although they are no longer so obvious. According to Kaczyńska's studies, labourers were the most likely to commit theft (or to be more precise, to be convicted of theft), followed by peasants and domestic servants. The 'proletariat', i.e. the most destitute people in the city, only came fourth. This means that the poorest were not the most inclined to improve their material circumstances by taking other people's property.

These trends changed at the turn of the twentieth century, a period which saw an increase in the number of both violent acts and thefts. This was probably due to the deteriorating economic situation at the time (which followed an earlier period of economic development and improved material conditions). Unemployment appeared as a social problem, causing large-scale poverty and a significant deterioration in living conditions (a problem that persisted due to an incessant influx of people from the countryside to the cities). The increase in violent acts alongside crimes against property might be attributed to the widening social contrasts between those who were getting richer and the increasing number of destitute people.[14] Examples of deprivation theory (described above) and social tensions can therefore be observed in the Polish experience.

That there are links between destitution and crimes against property is once more confirmed by analysing the data of the Great Depression of the 1930s. The advent and persistence of the Great Depression resulted in a massive increase in unemployment and thence widespread poverty.[15] This in turn caused an upsurge in theft (which was associated with destitution and intensified as this problem worsened and the Depression wore on), burglary, robbery and fraud. Again, however, similarly to the mid-nineteenth century, this increase was not accompanied by an increase in the number of crimes against the person. If anything, the opposite trend could be observed – these crimes fell as the Depression worsened and increased after it was over. Leon Radzinowicz has noted that criminality (although it should be emphasised that this only applies to some acts) does not increase when societies are predominantly destitute, but when the standard of living drops suddenly and precipitously. The hostility of excluded people to the social order, and especially to the justice system, can be observed during a recession, as can a change in attitude, i.e. there is greater acceptance of marginalised people committing prohibited acts (Radzinowicz 1969). At this point, it may be profitable to return to the issue of relative poverty and social inequality as causes of criminality.

Polish data on the relationship between lack of work and criminality are sparse, and studies in which such dependencies are noted are mostly limited to the post-war period. It is worth noting, however, that unemployment, as the term is generally understood, did not exist in Poland at the time. A lack of work did not imply destitution and was often one of the symptoms of general social maladjustment. Research conducted by Stanisław Szelhaus on juvenile recidivists stands as an outstanding example of the work that was done in this area. Szelhaus (1969) found that a large portion of these adolescents (over 83 per cent) had either never worked at all or had only worked casually for short periods (7–10 days on average) with long intervals between them. This situation did not arise out of any lack of available work but was rather the result of the educational methodologies of the day and the world in which these youngsters had grown up. They had never been accustomed to work since they were small children, many of them had left school early (so they had no formal education and had not been taught any trade), they became quickly bored at work and they could not stand the constant discipline. One 20-year-old summed up their attitude to work beautifully:

14 It is possible, however, that the increase in the number of violent acts was due to other causes and not the increase in destitution and social contrasts (Kaczyńska 1994, p. 219).

15 Teofil Łaciak described poverty as being the norm in Katowice in the 1930s. Łaciak demonstrated that 13 per cent of working-class families went hungry and a further 40 per cent were undernourished through lack of money. The people he surveyed were living in appalling conditions. Every third family surveyed had experienced theft, alcohol abuse and other signs of demoralisation (Raś 2011, pp. 99–101). It is interesting to note that the living conditions of destitute families did not substantially change throughout the twentieth century (Kossowska 1978, pp. 174–5; Kossowska 1982, pp. 297–309).

> Maybe I could work, but nobody could ever make me get used to it. I don't have a trade either. It's too late now and I don't feel like it any more. (Szelhaus 1969, p. 117)

In those days, being unemployed was often more the result than the cause of criminal conduct, e.g. being imprisoned made it nigh on impossible to find work later.

A correlation between unemployment and criminality was revealed in statistical research conducted in Rzeszów in the 1990s. The proportion of confirmed crimes perpetrated by unemployed people doubled between 1992 and 1993. This was especially true of people who were not entitled to receive unemployment benefits. The greatest increases were recorded for economic crimes (from 1.7 to 14.5 per cent), crimes against the family (from 6.1 to 21.4 per cent) and crimes against life and health (from 3.4 to 15 per cent). These growth trends in the percentages of unemployed people perpetrating given types of crimes continued over the following years. In 1995 this share grew to 22 per cent for assault and affray, 21.5 per cent for robbery and 26.4 per cent for crimes against the family (mainly domestic violence). It is worth pointing out, however, that unemployed people did not make up the majority of perpetrators in a single one of these categories and the absolute numbers (from which these percentages were calculated) were relatively small. It is therefore difficult to unequivocally confirm the thesis that there is a link between unemployment and criminality (Tuziak 1996, pp. 159–62).

Nationwide research carried out by Anna Kiersztyn (also conducted on statistical data) does not confirm the thesis that there is a correlation between unemployment and criminality – either crimes against property or violent crimes. Detailed examinations of four places revealed the opposite trend, i.e. a positive economic situation brought about an increase, not a decrease, in criminality. Kiersztyn merely posited a definite hypothesis that referred to the possibility of a certain congruence between quality of employment and prohibited acts committed 'for gain' (there are more of these in societies in which the quality of work is generally low) (Kiersztyn 2008, pp. 171–3, 221–2, 249–50). The lack of any connection between poverty and criminality is also apparent in the aggregated nationwide data. Maps comparing areas that are home to the most destitute people with areas reporting the highest incidences of criminality indicate that no regularity is apparent (see Bieńkuńska 2012, p. 15 and Siemaszko et al. 2009, p. 246).

Criminality is generally a marginal consideration in Polish research on destitute people and the environments in which they live. It is merely one of the many pathological behaviours that can be observed in these communities, along with abuse of alcohol and other means of intoxication. It also appears as a background factor in family breakdown or the neglect of children and failing to teach them how to behave properly. The combination of alcohol and various forms of criminality, including violence towards other family members, is especially relevant. Alcohol is also associated with homelessness, but again it is hard to tell which is the cause and which is the effect – a way of coping with an extraordinarily difficult situation, viz. being constantly stressed and never feeling secure (Jaroszewska 2010, pp. 282–3).

Alcohol abuse is found everywhere in every generation and often spans many generations. Parents pass on their habits and way of life, in which alcohol is their constant companion, to their children. People who work in such environments have described them as follows: 'you can count the number of people who don't drink on one hand' and 'the only people who don't drink are children and old women, and even then not all of them' (Grotowska-Leder 1998, p. 104). Children are introduced to alcohol at a younger age and the problem drinker is their model consumer, so they frequently abuse it and become addicted, like their parents. As this is the only model of manhood and fatherhood that young boys ever come to know, it is the one they adopt when they start their own families. They also pass it on to their daughters, who become involved with boys in whose lives alcohol plays a part. That is because it is also hard to find anyone who lives any differently in these environments.

Many people therefore follow in their parents' footsteps. They come from homes where everybody drinks, where there is no emotional warmth, and where parents are not interested in children and do not take care of them. Drinking bouts are often accompanied by violence, so children often want to leave this environment as soon as possible and start their own families. Girls leave school early, run away from home, have casual relationships with boys and very soon become mothers. Their partners (sometimes de jure, sometimes de facto) are unemployed, poorly educated, sometimes already have some criminal experience behind them and are not shy of alcohol. Young boys follow a similar path. Lack of family ties often means they have stayed at various educational establishments seeking a home and some emotional warmth. They leave school early and start working to help their mothers, who receive no support from their fathers (who drink their entire earnings). Often, however, they are unable to hold down a job for long. They start their own families in the belief, shared by their partners, that they can manage a different life for themselves – all the while replicating the one their parents led. They soon become disillusioned with married life and find it difficult to make ends meet. The most interesting thing about these stories is that they have gone on for so many years and are based on the same formula. Even though they were described, along with their causes, with perfect accuracy at the end of the 1990s, the same scenarios were still being played out in the same families and in the same places in 2009. Absolutely nothing changed in all those years (Warzywoda-Kruszyńska 1999, pp. 83–5; Grotowska-Leder 1998, pp. 132–3, 142–3; Jankowski 2010, pp. 68–9; Bunio-Mroczek 2010, pp. 110–13).

Violence – both mental and physical – is an alcohol-related problem that affects many marginalised families. Researches are mindful of the role that addiction plays in cultivating violence. Alcohol is ever present in destitute families – sporadically at first, occasionally as it were – but little by little, it appears more frequently, bringing addiction in its wake. Problem drinking is more and more accompanied by the onset, and then the escalation, of violence. After all, alcohol brings about changes in the nervous system, resulting in emotional disorders and frequent outbursts of temper, and making it difficult to control aggressive behaviour. This affects both sexes, although men obviously abuse alcohol and resort to physical violence more often.

A huge problem is that, as one doctor said, 'young women seldom admit to violence in their families, although their mental state gives them away, they simply hide the causes and effects of their mistreatment' (Grotowska-Leder 1998, p. 109). It is not just the women who cover up this problem, but also the neighbours. Violence is a taboo subject. Nobody notices it and nobody talks about it. Besides, women do not want to leave husbands who beat them, as they are dominated by them, financially dependent on them, often have nowhere to go and, in any case, have never considered the possibility of leaving. They also fear exposing their children to greater discomfort (such as poverty) than a life with a violent father. Meanwhile, the accounts of children growing up in families like this are frightening. One respondent, speaking of her childhood said:

> I used to have nightmares all the time until I was seventeen. I'd wake up crying at night. … I used to wet the bed all the time until I was thirteen. I simply didn't feel it. If I woke up, I'd lie in it all wet, because I was scared that if I got up, I'd get a kick up the arse from my father. (Warzywoda-Kruszyńska 1999, p. 83)

Many of those surveyed spoke about experiences like this. It has to be borne in mind that violence affects every member of the family. It is most often spoken of in the context of women and children, although elderly people, whose grandchildren rob them of their superannuation or pensions to buy alcohol, are victims too (Michałowska 1999, pp. 161–2; Grotowska-Leder 1998, pp. 108–9).

When parents abuse alcohol, they leave their children unminded and take no interest in how they spend their spare time. The youngsters therefore go looking for acceptance among their peers, who are doing the same thing for the same reason, and join groups in which everyone tries to carve out a suitable position for themselves and impress the others.[16] To a large extent, however, these young people replicate the behaviour they see at home in that they drink together and then start brawling. They also have a lot of free time on their hands and are often absent from school. Even if they do not play truant, they have no additional classes, interests or hobbies once school is over for the day. For young people, having fun often means destroying property – smashing windows, damaging cars and vandalising stairwells, housing blocks and school property (Warzywoda-Kruszyńska 1999, p. 91; Grotowska-Leder 1998, pp. 114–15). They are said to want to make their presence felt. This conspicuous behaviour (i.e. talking loudly, using bad language and provoking and intimidating people) is intended to subdue and possibly even to appropriate the area. They take over the street and the courtyard because they have no place of their own. This is where they want to feel good and be at home. One recently surveyed street worker described the behaviour and motives of young people as follows:

16 Robert J. Sampson and W. Byron Groves noticed, after conducting studies for many years, that a community that manages to care for its young does not produce youth gangs whose behaviour gets out of control and who start to commit crimes. A close-knit community, with a high degree of social control, can therefore live in safety because it does not have dangerous youth gangs in its area (Sampson and Groves 1989, p. 778).

> They appropriate this area for themselves by displaying e.g. loud behaviour, acts of vandalism and even noisy football games. This is their turf. They look for areas like this where they can feel free – not with impunity, because they are aware that they will have to reckon with the police. But they feel free. They feel at home. They do not feel free anywhere else. (Frysztacki et al. 2011, p. 154)

Theft is also an element of group behaviour. Anna Pawełczyńska demonstrated the differences in thefts committed by groups comprised of younger and older children (up to and over 14). Pawełczyńska (1964, pp. 104–5) observed that if the younger children she studied mostly stole spontaneously, i.e. more for fun than for consumption, then the older ones more often than not planned to do so. In general, juveniles presently carry out a lot of other prohibited acts in groups (Klaus 2009a, pp. 176–80; Woźniakowska-Fajst 2010, p. 292). Apart from group pressure, poverty is a motivation to steal, especially among children. One person working in this area has described it as follows:

> The parents do not have anything to give. He's young. He doesn't want to study, so he steals. As it happens, it's easy and tempting, because he apparently has nothing to lose and everything to gain … he can make a reasonably intelligent living this way. (Grotowska-Leder 1998, p. 116)

Another person, describing children hanging around a nearby McDonald's, said:

> They don't have any money to eat, so they hang around in order to take advantage of any opportunity to filch something from somebody … These children seem to have no problem picking up e.g. a pencil or an eyeliner, because apparently nobody watches them there. (Warzywoda-Kruszyńska 1999, p. 91)

The research of Dagmara Woźniakowska-Fajst on juvenile girls may confirm destitution as a motive for theft. As many as two thirds of girls who stole came from families in which the per capita monthly income did not exceed PLN 400, i.e. from families that were definitely poor. What they misappropriated most were food, cosmetics and clothes – and usually cheap items (65 per cent less than PLN 100) (Woźniakowska-Fajst 2010, pp. 282–8, 293).[17]

People who work in environments with destitute people observe, however, the hazardous situation in which children are exploited by adults, sometimes even by their own parents, who encourage them to commit a variety of petty crimes (or at least tacitly condone such behaviour), because as juveniles, they are generally not punishable (to them, that means that at least they cannot go to prison, but other criminological research reveals that sentencing juveniles to closed institutions is also rare).[18] They therefore break into cars, commit petty thefts, including picking pockets, and break into cellars (where bikes are kept in winter). However, larceny is obviously not the preserve of the young. People of all ages commit theft and alcohol often accompanies or motivates it. Stealing non-ferrous metals to sell for scrap is something of a novelty (along with stealing wood from forests). The metal is taken from abandoned houses and post-industrial areas, and is also stripped from telephone and electricity poles. This activity has increased in recent years in line with scrap metal prices. It does not require a great deal of skill and is a relatively easy way of making a fairly good living. Handling stolen goods has also become more developed in these environments, as stolen goods have to be exchanged for money or traded for other things (Grotowska-Leder 1998, pp. 110–12; Kiersztyn 2008, pp. 233–35). Fraud and obtaining by deception are also new phenomena. Common examples involve taking out loans on the basis of forged or falsified documents (e.g. certificates of earnings) and, also in connection with taking out loans, using destitute people to commit financial or taxation fraud by having them pose as 'dummies', i.e. substitute or fictitious parties to contracts (Kiersztyn 2008, p. 358; Jankowski 2010).

Poverty is also generally associated with a specific kind of criminality, viz. misleading social workers (e.g. by giving false information on earnings, which are often paid cash in hand) or simply falsifying certain

17 NB: the author also acknowledges that some of the theft is 'for sport' or adventure (Woźniakowska-Fajst 2010, p. 284).

18 The Family Court did not take any action in 70 per cent of cases concerning young children, not even non-isolation preventive measures. 2.2 per cent of young offenders were placed in an institution (Klaus 2009a, pp. 298–304) as were 5 per cent of juvenile girls (Woźniakowska-Fajst 2010, pp. 353–5).

documents to get more assistance. This is a survival strategy employed by excluded people and is learnt from parents or neighbours (Grotowska-Leder 1998, p. 113). It is worth considering whether the destitute are solely to blame for this, or whether the system – which on the one hand permits such behaviour, while on the other, is not in a position to guarantee that beneficiaries will have their needs met (sometimes even their most basic needs) and so, to some extent, forces people to play these games – is guilty as well.

Another problem is a social policy that groups socially excluded people into certain areas. This excessive accumulation in one place causes the problems described above to escalate and intensify. This comes about through creating public housing in socially and geographically run-down areas of the city and continuously lodging destitute people (e.g. people evicted from other flats for non-payment of debts) or people who come from problem families there. This influx of poor residents is accompanied by an outflow of affluent people, who do not want to live in the same neighbourhood.

> Along with this exchange of residents, there was less neighbourly control, including watching over young people, who found themselves behavioural patterns among the newcomers. Buildings wrecked by tenants and not renovated by the city increasingly became places for housing poor people, who could not afford the higher rentals to live anywhere else, who were unemployed, addicted and without social roots. Spatial segregation was accompanied by social isolation, as evidenced by the progressive homogenisation of the socio-economic status of the residents. This led to a lack of examples of a better life or social advancement, either in the family or in the immediate vicinity. (Warzywoda-Kruszyńska and Kruszyński 2011, p. 53)

This has led to ghettos of a sort springing up in Poland. These urban areas have been best described by Łódź sociologists, who call them (and they are more city blocks than city areas) enclaves of poverty. That is how those parts of the city that consist of old, run-down tenement buildings (often unsewered) have come to be seen. These enclaves can be found on the fringes of the Łódź city centre and are inhabited by unemployed or working poor people, who are poorly educated and often rely on social assistance (Grotowska-Leder 2006, pp. 314–17). Such a concentration of poverty is a source of social stigmatisation (e.g. some employers are reluctant to take on people from 'thief districts') and breeds any number of objectionable social phenomena, including: deteriorating public health connected with widespread alcohol consumption; living in run-down premises and having insufficient means to ensure adequate sustenance (combined with an inability to prepare nutritious meals) especially for children; and, more broadly, an inability to take proper care of children (Jankowski 2010, p. 76; Grotowska-Leder 2006, pp. 318–19).

The problem of raising children properly and ensuring that they have access to education, when their parents (or the civil service in the case of substitute parents) do not support them in this endeavour, and there are no opportunities to develop their skills or passions, is especially exacerbated. Children in enclaves of poverty cannot count on having suitable developmental stimuli among their peers, who are being similarly raised. They therefore have no competing behavioural patterns. The result is failure at school and seeking out the self-realisation alternatives described above on or beyond the boundaries of the community, including an increase in criminal conduct. School, which should be a bond between people from different families and equalise opportunities, does not fulfil this function. That is because, as one teacher puts it:

> Poor and very poor children are often shunned by their classmates. … if it is dirty at home, … their [the children's] clothes are permeated with the smell of mould … or damp. … [the other children] have a sort of intuition. It's as if they can actually sense something like that and sometimes even … from a child like that, who seriously has no pleasant odours, and they pass on information to each other such as 'don't sit next to him' or 'hey you, don't stand near him' … and so these children are perceived as different by the rest of the class. (Warzywoda-Kruszyńska 1999, pp. 89–90)

The school environment itself therefore stigmatises children and compounds their segregation.

All this leads to the formation of a new (or newly named) phenomenon known as 'street children', i.e. young people who spend a fair portion of their time away from home, with their peers, far from their parents and other adults, and exhibiting behaviour that is abnormal for people their age. Falling into this state results in a variety of problems in the family home (not least problems associated with dysfunctional child raising).

The experts judge this phase to begin around the age of nine, although some cite examples of children as young as five who qualify as street children. A street child is someone who has gradually become emotionally and existentially independent from his/her parents or guardians. These children break free of family ties (although some occasionally live – or, more precisely, sleep – at home, others run away from home) and depend on their own resources. Older children sometimes start to take care of their younger siblings in loco parentis – even financially (via different methods of fundraising, e.g. begging, swindling and working). They thus cease to engage in any behaviour considered normal for their age.

Street children often join peer groups in which it is easier for them to operate. One result of being a street child is becoming a 'drunken down and out' or a 'bedraggled bum', i.e. suffering serious psychological, social and economic degradation that leads to being excluded from society. Most young people soon get into trouble with the law as well, as they very often resort to violence. Engaging in violent behaviour is a natural way of functioning to them and is even a way of life for some. The consummate degradation of these children was bluntly described by one of them examined by the police:

> Those who start early go to the dogs. They don't even get into any sensible crime. If they start drinking, smoking and doing drugs when they're 12, then they're not even fit for crime. Even there they don't cut it. (Frysztacki et al. 2011, p. 162)

Chronic criminals exhibit antisocial behaviour early (i.e. during childhood) and continue to do so for the rest of their lives. Criminals who have only committed prohibited acts from adolescence start to break the law somewhat later. This behaviour is very strongly reinforced in early adolescence but becomes increasingly rare after the age of 18. Therefore, small children who commit crimes or act in an asocial manner and exhibit symptoms of moral corruption should be given special care and support to prevent them from embarking on a criminal career (Batawia 1958; Klaus 2009a).

Studies on Kraków street children reveal a different kind of pathological behaviour. These differ, however, depending on where these children concentrate their main activities. The researchers divided street children into three groups: those who operate in the city centre; those who mainly stay around peripheral districts; and those who spend their time in supermarkets and shopping centres. The three groups obviously share certain behavioural patterns, viz. drinking alcohol, smoking cigarettes, using drugs, acting loudly and obnoxiously, frequently using foul language, and displaying a great deal of forceful aggression towards the other members of the groups to which they belong. Some behaviour, however, differs for each of the three types of place. Juvenile prostitution of both sexes is a problem that sets the centre of Kraków apart. This form of behaviour varies, however, between the two sexes, although the reasons for getting into it (even as young as 13) are primarily economic. Girls are induced into it by pimps, who later exercise control over them. This leads to association with criminal gangs, an inability to stop being a prostitute, and frequently remaining in that role for a long time. Boys (involved in homosexual prostitution), on the other hand, act for and by themselves. A lot of criminal activity (beatings, thefts, rapes etc.) can be observed in this environment. Some people therefore try to find a patron to maintain them. Some are uncertain as to their sexual orientation and their desire to make money is by no means their only motive for entering into sexual relations with other men (their earnings may be a bonus of sorts). Young people who focus their activities on the edges of urban settlements typically sit around in groups under stairwells, wander the streets aimlessly and sell drugs (older youths). By contrast, stealing CDs, clothes and cosmetics from shops, especially supermarkets, is characteristically observed for street children in shopping centres (Sierocka and Drewniak 2006, pp. 36–64).

This leads to a new phenomenon associated with children and young people in shopping centres – the problem of the 'galerianki' (mall girls), i.e. girls who offer sexual services in exchange for money or a promise to purchase something (NB: this phenomenon only concerns girls). Beata Sierocka and Marcin Drewniak have described this as follows:

> Provocatively dressed girls with a lot of makeup can be observed walking around the mall either alone or in groups. It is they who most often initiate contact with their 'sugar daddies'. 'Sugar daddy hunting' takes place in boutique stores – an expert sizing up of a man, most often middle-aged, is the first phase in the selection. Suitably expensive clothes, shoes and mobile phone reflect the depth of his pockets. The value of the

> merchandise the man is purchasing and the card he is using to pay for it are similarly scrutinised. … Sex is a cash transaction, although it can also be paid for with goods from a store of the girl's choosing. (Sierocka and Drewniak 2006, p. 48)[19]

Research on youth who spent their time in a Kraków shopping centre conducted barely a year later, however, failed to confirm their observations. The conclusion was that many young people do in fact spend time in shopping centres after school (and sometimes during lessons), but these merely seem to be substitutes for other meeting places at present. Adolescents prefer to spend their time in shopping centres than sitting around housing blocks or roaming the streets. There they have comfortable sofas, can listen to popular music, watch displays and eat at fast food outlets or buy something on special at the supermarket. The researchers did not notice any young people from problem families among those they observed in the shopping centre either. Most of them actually came from families of moderate means (Smagacz 2007). It is therefore difficult to determine unequivocally the extent to which 'mall girls' are a real social problem on a significant scale and the extent to which the whole thing is a media creation based on isolated and fairly exceptional cases. The authors of a study conducted in Warsaw shopping centres claim in the summary:

> The conclusion of the study is that the 'mall girls' are not such a common problem in shopping centres as the media would have us believe. There are, however, a large number of young people of high school or junior high school age who spend their free time – and even their school time – there. (Bielecka 2010, pp. 129–30)

It is additionally worth noting a specific kind of activity that takes place among youth on the western border. This is known as 'juma' (slang for 'theft') and involves going to Germany to commit petty larceny and then pawning the stolen goods in Poland. In the mid-1990s, as many as 30 per cent of young people living on the border admitted to having engaged in this activity. Moreover, this is regarded as an acceptable way of making a living by many (a third of those surveyed) young people, especially those from poor families. Prostitution is another fairly acceptable way of earning money – both by women and men (approximately 15 per cent). Furthermore, the young people surveyed argued that it was a legitimate way to make a living and considered it a good way to make money (including while travelling abroad) (Kurzępa 2010, pp. 99–112).[20]

In summary, it is worth stressing yet again that creating ghettos in which a lot of people with social problems are concentrated in a small area is not only not conducive to social integration but actually achieves the opposite effect, i.e. it increases and intensifies negative social phenomena. These regions of the city are often notorious for having a high incidence of common crime (e.g. vandalism and theft), although they are mainly places where perpetrators come from – not where they ply their principal activities. A resident of one of these areas appositely described what they are like: 'Such poverty that there's nothing to steal. The area breeds criminals but not crime – that all goes on outside … here, you can only steal old people's pensions' (Grotowska-Leder 1998, p. 110). This is, however, a place where poverty and pathology are preserved. Louis Wirth described the ghetto as 'not so much a physical fact as it is a state of mind' (Wirth 1929, p. 286). It is therefore difficult for people to escape, change their lives and avoid reliving those of their parents. Polish studies of these areas definitely confirm this thesis.

The Other Side of the Coin – the Effect of Poverty on Victimisation

There is, however, another side to poverty. Destitution increases the risk of becoming a victim of crime. Beck (2005, pp. 35–6) points out this relationship when describing what he terms risk society. He noticed that the

19 Observation was the primary research methodology (Sierocka and Drewniak 2006, pp. 28–32). This raises the question as to whether such behaviour can be diagnosed this way.

20 Polish nationwide studies on youth over junior high school age conducted in 2004 indicate, however, that the problem of youth prostitution is not highly visible. Only 1.4 per cent of those surveyed admitted to ever having provided such services. A further 2.4 per cent would have been prepared to engage in such activity but had not done so (Izdebski 2008, pp. 64–5).

risk he was describing was not evenly spread throughout society and affected destitute people to a greater extent, as more affluent people could afford to purchase security. In the context of being protected from criminality, this means that the wealthy in society have the means to at least ensure that they can live in better areas with more protection, that their houses or apartments are equipped with extra security, and that they can travel around the city after dark in taxis or their own cars instead of having to rely on public transport.

Research indicates that the risk of victimisation is greater for those who belong to any of the following categories: people who have already experienced victimisation, young people, single parents and people who come from lower socioeconomic environments (Grove et al. 2012, p. 183).[21] The widest study of the relationship between destitution and victimisation was conducted in England and Wales and made use of the results of the British Crime Survey, which has been conducted regularly since 1982. The most recent data reveal that while a general, and sometimes fairly substantial, crime drop can be observed over many years, this is not evenly distributed among all members of society. Some groups have significantly improved their security over the last few years (the study covers the period from the mid-1990s to 2010), while it is clearly apparent that the security of others has improved substantially less. This means that differences in the levels of security between different social groups are currently increasing.

The most destitute are those most vulnerable to the risk of victimisation. These are the people who earn the lowest incomes, who live in rental flats (often owned by the local government) and who are single parents. This rule applies to different kinds of crimes. Theft with burglary, car theft and crimes against the person (these were taken to mean robbery, crimes using violence, and theft) were analysed in the studies discussed above. In contrast with the Polish research results given above, a clear distinction can be seen here in that it is generally destitute people who most frequently fall victim to crimes against property (Grove et al. 2012, pp. 187–94).

Criminological theory can help explain this phenomenon. According to the routine activities theory, which is mainly concerned with crimes against property, an individual's risk of victimisation depends on the degree to which his/her daily activity and lifestyle (i.e. everyday, routine activity, such as going to work, going shopping and spending leisure time) match that of a potential victim and create an opportunity for a perpetrator to commit a crime (Newburn 2007, pp. 286–90). With respect to car theft, destitute people have cheaper and inferior vehicles that are potentially less appealing to perpetrators. At the same time, however, these vehicles have substantially inferior anti-theft security and are left in poorly guarded places (Grove et al. 2012, p. 195). A cheaper car is also easier to sell, either as is or as spare parts. Wealthy people generally insure their cars, so they will almost certainly report a car theft. A victim of a theft of a cheap, uninsured car will frequently not bother with the inconvenience of reporting the crime, as there is nothing to be gained from doing so (assuming that such a person has little faith in the effectiveness of the police in such matters). For this reason, stealing a cheap, old car poses significantly less risk to the perpetrator.

Similar principles apply to breaking into flats, although the richest are at risk here as well as the most destitute (the middle class is actually the safest social group). It should be stressed, however, that the risk for destitute people is twice that for the richest. Moreover, although there has been an overall decrease in the number of burglaries, security for the poorest has improved the least (Tilley et al. 2011, pp. 305–6). These data are confirmed by the following conclusion of the International Crime Victim Survey (ICVS): 'on average burglary rates between 1988 and 2004 decreased by 30 per cent among the upper income quartile and by 10 per cent among the lowest quartile' (Grove et al. 2012, p. 196). This trend might be explained by differences in the possession of various systems to improve the security of flats and houses. Although it is the most destitute who have invested the most in improving security – the growth in the number of flats equipped with security devices is greatest among this group – this is still the group with the largest percentage of people without any security whatsoever.

The perpetrators of these two kinds of burglaries obviously have completely different profiles – as different as the kinds of residences they burgle. Well-equipped houses and flats are burgled by professionals, who know how to get past sophisticated security. The flats of the most destitute, on the other hand, are burgled by

21 I would like to thank Prof. Andromachi Tseloni for her inspiration and support while I was writing this section, and for providing valuable materials.

people in the (often rundown and crime ridden) neighbourhood.[22] What is more, they are burgled incidentally, i.e. when the perpetrators see an opportunity while doing something else – to put it simply, whenever the opportunity presents itself (Tilley et al. 2011, pp. 310–11).[23]

Quality research conducted by Anna Kiersztyn can reliably confirm that the situation is similar in Poland and that a lot of criminal activity (most of it not reported to anybody anywhere) is spontaneous and occurs in those same communities. One of Kierszytn's respondents describes a typical burglary with theft (usually of a cellar) in her locality:

> There might be 'people from the den' around here, who, let's just say, eagerly, as if they're off to earn money to consume that alcohol, go down into the cellars, often in their own vicinity, and steal from each other. (Kiersztyn 2008, pp. 229–30)

People being interviewed pointed out the link between low income and lack of physical home security and the frequency with which flats are burgled. They also noted that destitute people are not as well protected and are consequently more vulnerable to this type of act (Kiersztyn 2008, p. 236).

Magdalena Goldschneider came to similar conclusions while researching criminality in the Warsaw district of Praga. A great many (almost 90 per cent) of the acts there were committed on the spur of the moment and by taking advantage of opportunities that presented themselves, were often committed under the influence of alcohol or other intoxicants, and were committed in the immediate vicinity. The perpetrators broke into poorly guarded premises (mainly flats) that often lacked even minimal security. This excerpt from testimony given by an accused person in court says it beautifully:

> D said that they were drinking alcohol at his friend Danuta's place and that we could go there. We mainly drank vodka there. In the end, everyone went to sleep except me and D. We went out onto the balcony and kept drinking alcohol. That's where we got the idea to walk around the balconies. So we went onto the neighbouring balcony and from that balcony we wanted to go onto the next balcony. When we stepped onto the first balcony, we noticed the door was open, so we went inside the flat. (Goldschneider 2010, p. 216)

The British results are again corroborated by an examination of statistics of car burglaries. As many as 40 per cent of the vehicles broken into are very old cars, e.g. Polonezes and 125p and 126p model Fiats. Of particular note is the distance between the place of residence of the perpetrator and the place of commission of the act. While the average distance between the place of residence of the perpetrator and that of the victim was 2.5 km in the case of home burglaries, it was 500 m in almost 50 per cent of cases. Similarly, one in three car burglaries and two in three street crimes, including robberies, were committed no more than 1 km from the place of residence of the perpetrator (Goldschneider 2010, pp. 216–26, 296–309).

The British research on crimes against the person concludes that single parents are the most vulnerable group (twice as vulnerable as people from other kinds of families), followed by people in rental accommodation (whether from public or private owners). The links between income level and vulnerability to this type of crime, however, are not so clear-cut – the highest earning people are those most at risk (Grove et al. 2012, pp. 187–8).

A relationship between income level and vulnerability to violence can likewise be discerned in Polish studies on violence against women. A woman's material situation may not affect the risk of her becoming a victim of physical or sexual violence inflicted by a strange man, but it definitely does so in the case of domestic violence.[24]

---

22 There is a significant correlation between income level and living in a 'bad' district. In the case of burglary, we can speak of the influence of both income level and place of residence – in a rundown and crime-ridden part of the city (Grove et al. 2012, p. 196).

23 Research shows that state intervention, in tandem with a higher level of physical security in flats, is the most effective way to combat burglary among the destitute.

24 It should, however, be emphasised as strongly as possible that this does not mean that the problem of family violence only concerns the most destitute environments and not the most wealthy. Statistical differences in the occurrence of violence in these types of household are not significant. Moreover, the impression painted by these results might also be skewed by the fact that wealthier and better educated people might be more embarrassed at finding themselves in situations like this and not admit it to researchers.

Women earning less than PLN 1,100 per month were victims of both physical and sexual violence at the hands of their partners twice as often on average (Gruszczyńska 2007, p. 87). Research conducted by the Polish market research firm TNS OBOP concludes that households in a poor material situation are more often affected by domestic violence and that victims are subjected to higher incidences of many kinds of violence (psychological, physical, economic and sexual) (TNS OBOP 2007).

Anna Kiersztyn's research also shows a definite link between destitution and poverty. Intoxicated people are the most regular victims of frequent robberies and muggings. As one of her respondents described it: 'he's a bit short for wine there, so they fleece a drunk or they get a something there, they take something from him there, some ten złotys, and things are of that sort' (Kiersztyn 2008, p. 238). Most of these incidents occur around bars and discotheques; most are not planned – they simply occur to the perpetrators as the opportunity presents itself. Incidents of assault and affray take place among the same group of people in discotheques. The situations described here indicate that perpetrators and victims come from the same environment and are not wealthy.

A special category of victims should be mentioned here, viz. the homeless. These people are particularly at risk of victimisation. British research shows that they have a risk of becoming crime victims and suffering bodily harm as a result of being assaulted that is 15 per cent and 3,400 per cent greater, respectively, than the average member of society. Almost 82 per cent of the homeless young Torontonians surveyed by Stephen Gaetz had been victims of crime in the preceding year and this was not a one-off experience for 79.4 per cent of them. The overwhelming majority of perpetrators of these assaults are not other homeless people but 'respectable citizens'. Other homeless people are only in the majority when it comes to committing crimes against property. Being insulted and abused is so common that it is difficult to keep count. It could even be said that homeless people are victims of hate crimes (or prejudice) and that the reason for this is their extremely low financial status. The difficulty in counteracting the victimisation of this group is that most of the community believes that they are on the streets through their own fault, i.e. they must have done something to bring about their present situation and do not therefore require any extra protection (Gaetz 2004, p. 434; Grover 2008, pp. 156–8).[25] This is in line with Zygmunt Bauman's observation:

> There is a constant temptation, then, to burden the poor with guilt for their own misery, strictly speaking, to shift the blame for their condition from the failure of the socially accepted norms where those who find themselves poverty stricken are looked upon with aversion to the observance of those norms. (Bauman 1998, p. 3)

The increased risk of victimisation of homeless people is also closely tied to their straitened economic circumstances and the means they use to try to earn money. Given their illnesses, addictions, paucity of education and lack of fixed address, most of the work they take on consists of short-term, menial cash-in-hand jobs. Being shut out of the legal labour market forces them to accept illegal work, such as providing sexual services, begging, cleaning car windscreens at intersections and even committing crimes, such as theft and drug dealing. These activities are risky in turn, especially seeing as homeless people have a significantly lower status and are in a considerably weaker position than the experienced criminals who 'employ' them, e.g. pimps and suppliers of minor drug dealers (Gaetz 2004, p. 430).

Unfortunately, there are no Polish studies to analyse broadly the links between wealth status and victimisation. Information on this subject only appears in the side notes of studies on victimisation. In his presentation of the findings of the ICVS from 1992 and 1996–1998, Andrzej Siemaszko found a positive correlation between achieving higher income levels and susceptibility to victimisation. Siemaszko (2001, p. 137) stated that 'the risk of becoming a victim is very strongly correlated with social position indices'. This observation refers both to criminality in general and to its division into particular kinds of crime (although the income level of the respondents was only one of the factors in analysing some of the acts).[26]

---

25 It is worth noting, however, that homeless people use a different kind of security to prevent or reduce the risk of being victimised, viz. sleeping in places that are well lit or where there are people (usually other homeless people) about, keeping dogs and devising other strategies to respond to violence from the community (Grover 2008, p. 159).

26 This is lacking, for example, in the case of theft and assault.

Conclusion

In conclusion, it is worth reiterating that the 'socially excluded' do not comprise a homogenous group. Exclusion covers many areas and can assume different forms and affect people from very different social groups. Those who have no home, have been cut off social security, have no legal right to be in the country they are in are among the most excluded. Victimisation may also be the primary cause of such deep-seated social exclusion, e.g. young people on the streets after fleeing domestic violence and neglect, victims of totalitarian regimes and people who have escaped from extremely poor countries in the hope of finding shelter and a better life. In the case of homeless people, this concerns the bare basics, e.g. personal shelter, which offers minimal security. Being relegated to the margins of society makes them more prone than anybody to commit prohibited acts and more vulnerable than anybody to be harmed by them.

It is vital that action be taken to prevent social exclusion and to bring people living on (or beyond) the margins of society back inside its framework. This will have to be scrupulously planned and should draw on the experience of other countries while avoiding their mistakes. One such mistake would be to create a market society by introducing too many market mechanisms into social policy. Elliott Currie defines this to be a society in which all activity, including social activity, is reduced or subjected to the imperative of making a profit. This was the approach implemented in the United States in the 1980s. This led to destitution, homelessness, drug addition and a variety of illnesses becoming more widespread and to an increase in the number of violent crimes being committed (Currie 2002, pp. 134, 131).

It is also important that we free ourselves from stereotypical thinking about the poor. First, there are those who are responsible for the situation in which they find themselves and whose destitution is primarily the result of their own actions. What is needed here is more empathy to see that their problems are often the end product of the social and economic changes currently taking place. People who have lost out as a result of these changes are in no position to help each other and need the support of those who have benefitted from these transformations. Second, we need to cease fearing the destitute as a group, to stop seeing them as 'the Other', to stop seeing them as threatening and as nothing more than people who create problems, because this leads to the creation of assistance programmes whose actual purpose is not to offer this group assistance or support but simply and solely to monitor them as a dangerous element (Jones and Novak 2009, pp. 247–9). Only a rejection of these two erroneous assumptions will enable us to draw up an action plan that offers any realistic chance of success in curtailing the problem of destitution and in bringing socially excluded people into society.

Chapter 5
Preventing Criminality: The Social Policy of Preventing Social Exclusion

Witold Klaus

Introduction

This chapter is a continuation of the discussion in the previous chapter.[1] Chapter 4 demonstrated that there is no direct link between poverty and criminality. In other words, poverty (when associated with unemployment) is not the main factor that drives people to crime. On the other hand, most of the people who show up in police statistics (and against whom one or more agencies in the justice system have therefore officially taken action) belong to the most destitute groups in society. It is therefore worth considering the sort of support and assistance the poor are given and to what extent a change in government policy in this area could be perceived as one way of preventing crime.

With respect to preventing crime, three theoretical perspectives, which have changed over the years, can be distinguished (it is worth noting, however, that all these approaches continue to be adopted in parallel, although they vary in strength and effectiveness in different countries). The first approach can be defined as isolation and is predicated on segregating people who commit crimes (or are perceived as capable of doing so) from the rest of society. Appropriate institutions, such as prisons, juvenile detention centres, rehabilitation institutions and – in days of yore – homes for vagrants, have been established and offenders (or potential offenders) locked away in them. The second approach can be labelled supervision. This recognises that community interaction is indispensable to effective rehabilitation and that offenders should therefore be kept in their own surroundings but placed under special supervision. As part of this idea, probation institutions have been set up and sponsored by social organisations or people of proven trustworthiness. Monitoring the offender by means of various kinds of electronic devices is another trend in this movement. A person under supervision will often remain inactive, i.e. the main thing expected of him/her is that he/she does not commit more prohibited acts. The third approach involves implementing preventive activities in groups threatened with social exclusion, i.e. in environments where people might potentially be recruited to commit prohibited acts in the future. The key to this approach lies in the people being assisted and the people providing the assistance working together to resolve the issues affecting the former (Wójcik 2008).

Research shows that the 'strategies which only target the perpetrators and victims of crime and the high crime areas in which both groups live, will not achieve a significant reduction in crime unless they are accompanied by measures to reduce income inequality and promote social cohesion' (Acheson 1998). As this kind of approach to preventive activities makes the most sense, this chapter accepts the assumption that it is worth presenting the problem of counteracting criminality within the broader context of implementing social service activities intended to counteract poverty and social exclusion.

Juliusz Makarewicz, the outstanding Polish criminal law specialist and one of the drafters of the Criminal Code of 1932, stressed the validity of this approach. Makarewicz wrote:

> The truth has to be faced squarely. The *modern penalty* is *a blunt and clumsy instrument* with which to fight criminality. … Criminal policy has to cry in a loud voice: 'If you do not want crime, try to remove the foundations of crime'. … not only is it necessary to correct those who have already shown an inclination towards crime, but we have to build social relationships which will ensure, as far as possible, that this inclination does not occur. This is not yet part of criminal policy as such. To work out the details of a complete preventive program,

1 See Chapter 4: 'The Relationship between Poverty, Social Exclusion and Criminality'.

> this study has to turn to *social policy*, to this expertise that has taken upon itself the task of implementing, if possible, the best organised social life. … We know that *misery*, and thus an overall lack of quality of life, is a poor advisor. The task of social policy is therefore to devise a just distribution of social income, to see to it that anyone looking for work can easily find it, and that anyone unable to work does not have to be relegated to the ranks of the criminal proletariat or hold his hand out for charity. (Makarewicz 1922, pp. 137, 148–9)

Social Crime Prevention versus Penal Social Policy

The views of the founders of the Chicago School on the causes of criminality are a cornerstone of criminology. These were sought by researching communities that were excluded and degraded both socially and geographically. Various criminological theories claim that growing up in a place where it is difficult for young people to find positive behavioural patterns, combined with the growth of particular subcultures specific to those communities, is conducive to deviant, including criminal, behaviour. Moreover, the poor are subject to antipathy and are excluded by the rest of society, especially by the more affluent, who in many ways dissociate themselves from the poor and treat them paternalistically.

It was these theories that underpinned the idea of social crime prevention, which sets itself the goal of reducing criminality and its causes through the implementation of extensively planned social programmes. This approach does not concentrate on working with isolated cases of potential criminals. Nor is it focused solely on individual shortcomings. Rather, it sets out to create a welfare policy that embraces every member of society and whose implementation is the responsibility of several government departments. Social policy understood this way therefore includes activities in the realms of housing policy, spatial harmony, healthcare, education, the labour market, integration and social assistance. The focus here is on working in specific communities – not just those where there is a real risk of deviation or criminality, but also those whose members are particularly vulnerable to falling victim to criminal behaviour. This sort of policy is meant to support specific groups that are at risk by offering various forms of assistance and support. It is not meant to focus exclusively on counteracting criminality. This last function is to some extent incidental and occurs as a result of other activities inclusive to the community (Melossi and Selmini 2009, pp. 167–8).

This approach comes close to Jock Young's conception of social exclusion, its causes and ways of counteracting it (Young 2002, pp. 457–8). Young points out that exclusion is more of a social than an individual problem. It is caused by changes in society that occur as a result of global transformations, including those in the labour market, and not through individual factors. He therefore rejects those modern and widely held liberal explanations of poverty and exclusion which shift the blame for this state of affairs onto the individual and which attribute to him/her a desire for self-exclusion through laziness or lack of motivation (e.g. to take up 'available' work) and for an easy life that involves 'foraging' in the public welfare system. Neoliberal ideologies are critical of the welfare state precisely for 'creating' categories of people who want neither to work nor to take responsibility for their own lives, as they can live quite well courtesy of the public purse.

Loïc Wacquant observes that statements disparaging the poor by labelling them a social problem are made quite frequently whenever criminality is discussed. Some politicians claim that these are the most dangerous people in society. Rich and poor are contrasted and only the former have a recognised right to security and protection. The initiatives of William Bratton, the legendary New York City Police Commissioner, provide an example of this kind of thinking and acting. For Bratton,

> the enemy is the subproletariat that mars the scenery and menaces or annoys consumers of urban space. It is this group, castigated under the catchall pseudo-scholarly category of 'underclass', that has been the priority target of the policy of 'zero tolerance', whose avowed objective is to restore the 'quality of life' for those New Yorkers who know how to behave in public, that is, the predominantly white middle and upper classes. (Wacquant 2009, p. 16)

A restriction of social rights is a result of this way of thinking, as, according to some politicians and academics, the welfare state is responsible for the rise in criminality.

Zygmunt Bauman claims that 'it is formed this way and substantiates the conviction that the problem of destitution is mostly a problem of harmony and order and that it is necessary to begin with this in the same way as fighting crime and reacting to law breaking' (Bauman 1998, p. 13). This means utilising police, administrative and often penal resources to combat (this is the exact wording used) poor people and not poverty as such. Paternalistic treatment of socially excluded people is becoming increasingly widespread, as is the conviction that they should be subject to greater control by the state. Wacquant, citing the views of Lawrence Mead, notes that paternalistic programmes emphasise obligations. The main idea is to ensure that the state provides the poor and socially excluded with organisational structures (read: controls) rather than assistance and support. The lives of the poor should therefore be managed by public authorities (Wacquant 2009, pp. 48, 52). On this view, severe punishment and criminalising subcriminal behaviours, e.g. littering, insulting language and graffiti, are considered to be the only effective means of preventing criminality. In this way, the welfare state is giving way to the penal state, where society is regulated by the instruments of the criminal law.

An 'economy of fear' is therefore built on the pervasive fear and feeling of being threatened by crime, the perpetrators of which are destitute or generally 'other' (e.g. members of ethnic or religious minorities, the latter also being potential perpetrators of terrorist acts).[2] This is driven by the public being induced to feel that they need to have the government control social groups that make them feel threatened. Increased supervision is supposed to reduce the threat posed by these groups or eliminate it altogether (in reality and/or in the mind of the public). To this end, the rest of society will accede to having their freedom curtailed and will readily submit to increased control on the part of the state. This control is for their own good and their own safety. Most people do not realise (or want to realise), however, that this control is most of the time merely ostensible, as it is wielded over actions that ultimately cannot be completely controlled (or controlled at all).

We can therefore speak of two parallel, ongoing and complementary processes that focus on the poor and excluded, and aim to have government departments exercise more and more control over them. Together, they make up a process that can be called the penalisation of social policy. On the one hand, as mentioned above, this has to do with the criminal law being extended into areas where it has never been applied. Punishing subcriminal conduct leads to greater control over this kind of perpetrator (through e.g. assigning a curator or some other supervisory official), who will be held in further breach of the law if he/she breaks his/her probationary conditions. On the other hand, increasing control is also being introduced into the social assistance sphere in the strict sense. More and more of the conduct of its 'charges' is being subjected to control, and more and more obligations are being imposed on them, resulting in them being denied their benefits if they fail to carry said obligations.

An example of this sort of practice is the Anti-Social Behaviour Order (ASBO) introduced in the UK. While an ASBO can theoretically be made against any member of the public, in practice it is used against poor families, now known as problem families, who disturb the peace and whose children either do not go to school or demand more attention from the teaching staff on account of their inappropriate behaviour (Grover 2008, pp. 83–4). The UK Home Office acknowledges that 'antisocial' behaviour means different things to different people – drunken youngsters 'roaming' around town, begging, vandalism and littering. Those who drafted the Order, however, believe that it is precisely this sort of behaviour that leads to serious criminality.[3] The idea behind the ASBO, then, is that it 'promotes a "quality of life" unhindered by degenerate forces: the criminal, the unruly and the nuisance. A presumption exists that the "blighting" of peoples' lives should be understood primarily as a problem of street behaviour – particularly the behaviour of the poor, usually young' (Coleman 2009, p. 67).

The ASBO can be supplemented with a Parenting Order. This can be made whenever parents, in the opinion of a magistrate, fail to take proper care of their children. Parents can be penalised when, for example, their child is found in a public place during school hours (it should be borne in mind that the child needs to have been absent for several days for this to apply). These penalties are most frequently imposed on single mothers, who are thereby condemned for the behaviour of teenage children over whom they often have no control (Grover 2008, pp. 89, 98).

2 For more on the topic of feeling frightened and threatened by crime, see Chapter 9: 'The Social Perception of Criminality'.

3 In this case one can invoke the 'broken windows' theory (Kelling and Coles 1996).

An approach based on penalties and employing penal measures to resolve other issues can also be observed in 'zero tolerance' education programmes. Schools are making increasingly greater use of the instruments of the criminal law to control their pupils and counteract some mythical proliferation of violence and criminality on their premises. Schools have therefore installed security systems (inspection cameras, metal detectors etc.) and employed additional security (Poland has security firms; the US has special school police units). Penal responses are employed instead of educational interaction and government institutions such as the police and the Children's Court are often within reach. Pupils begin to be treated like potential criminals – this is even what these 'problem causers' are called by their teachers (Hirschfield 2008).

All the above activities combine a variety of social security, police and criminal law mechanisms to exercise greater control over the behaviour of poor people, who are shunted from one institution to another and placed under increasing supervision by the state. Penal sanctions are used against them in case of failure or disobedience (i.e. not complying with the rules and prohibitions laid down). The state regards these as potentially dangerous people whose behaviour needs to be duly controlled and not as people in need of assistance or support (Mary and Nagels 2012; Garland 2009). The poor are a special kind of scapegoat, who, as deviants, can be penalised whenever the need arises. In this way, they are contrasted with 'healthy' society. Nobody speaks up for them when politicians portray them as being responsible for their own destitution – they are, after all, lazy and depraved.

> The constant temptation is to … encumber the poor with the blame for their own misfortune, strictly speaking, to shift the blame for their state from the failure of socially recognised standards to a reluctance to adhere to those standards on the part of those who find themselves poverty stricken. It is not the standards that are riddled with flaws: misery is the outcome of the deficiencies of those who have fallen into it. (Bauman 1998, p. 3)

The rest of society can therefore maintain the belief that being unemployed is a huge threat that can lead to corruption, and from there to criminality, and finally to criminal liability. This strong attachment to the idea of work and the requirement from government departments that all citizens be employed (or perform some other compulsory tasks) in one way or another has come to be known as workfare. This term was coined by Wacquant and denotes state coercion of people enjoying various forms of social assistance to perform specific kinds of work under pain of losing their benefits.[4] This work is mainly overseen by public administration officials. These techniques are also used in probationary activities. In some US states, it is necessary to work to remain on conditional early release, a consequence of which is that, in some cases, people who cannot find work are returned to prison (Wacquant 2011).

This idealisation of work and the portrayal of employment as a cure-all for both destitution and criminality is reminiscent of the nineteenth-century rehabilitation theorists. Antoine Édouard Ducpétiaux wrote at the time that work in penal establishments should not be considered a supplement or tightening, so to speak, of the penalty, but an alleviation, and this privilege cannot be taken away (Foucault 1978, p. 270). As a result, prisoners are obliged to work (for their own good, of course). We seem to have come full circle and to be once more presenting work in exactly the same way (although destitute people can be discussed more broadly here), i.e. as something of benefit to them. Meanwhile, the institutions (public and private) that run prisons largely benefit from the inmates' work. It is worth noting that forced labour is legally permitted in US prisons and while there is no official 'compulsion' to work in most of them, those who do not work are denied various rights (family visits, entertainment and other activities etc.) (Browne 1996; Wacquant 2010).

It is worth asking, therefore, whether, because of all the different methods employed to combat the poor, they are really, as Zygmunt Bauman claims, redundant to society? Are they merely a burden or can some social functionality be attributed to them? It seems that, in many cases, the destitute (or destitution) are perceived as Christie's 'suitable enemy', with whom the struggle is unceasing and who manage to destroy

4 It is worth noting that, according to the regulations in force in Poland, unemployed people also have a duty to perform public works. Refusing to do so disqualifies them from being unemployed, which means they lose the right to unemployment benefits and health insurance (Art. 33 § 4(3) *ustawa o promocji zatrudnienia i instytucjach rynku pracy* [Act on Promoting Employment and Labour Market Institutions]). This therefore carries serious consequences. Job creation programmes most often involve hard manual labour.

themselves but never completely (Christie 1986). They can be depicted as a social threat or they can be offered assistance in a show of compassion, as the need arises. Herbert Gans, however, has shown that the poor are very useful to society in various situations. First, they do the hard, low-paid work that nobody else wants to do but which is indispensable to the running of society, especially the more affluent part of it, as they make the lives of the affluent easier and, for instance, allow women to take up paid employment.[5] Poor, unemployed people also make up a reserve army that can be put to work in times of prosperity. Moreover, the exploitation of people deprived of freedom as a hidden 'forced labour', as occurs in the US private prison system, is also observable. Furthermore, simply by existing, the poor generate employment positions for those who either help them or try to protect society from them (police officers, social workers, public prosecutors, probation officers [curators] etc.). Destitute people also buy products that nobody else buys, e.g. low quality or 'second freshness' food and second-hand clothes. This group is also needed as a baseline against which the better endowed can favourably compare themselves and feel better in the knowledge that there are people worse off. The poor make it possible to engage in the occasional charitable activities that assuage the conscience and improve self-esteem and self-satisfaction. Finally, they help consolidate certain desirable qualities in society (industriousness, thrift etc.). They can thus be said to serve as an example that should not be followed (Gans 1976; Gans 1994).

Polish Social Policy as an Instrument to Counteract Poverty and Prevent Criminality

Poverty has always existed in society and is unlikely ever to be eradicated, no matter what public institutions do. What is worth doing, and what should be done, however, are to limit this state of affairs and to try to eliminate the negative consequences associated with it. The government's responsibility is to endeavour to ensure a minimal livelihood to everyone within their jurisdiction and to create opportunities for people, especially children and young people, to realise their potential.

Preventing criminality is not the direct goal of social policy. The effectiveness of social policy cannot therefore be directly correlated with the level of criminality, which is dependent on numerous factors. What the social services do needs to be perceived from a different standpoint. Using social assistance as a means to control destitute people is obviously a very bad proposition. Moreover, the mechanisms employed in criminal policy should not be introduced into social policy. Unfortunately, both occur at present.

It has to be remembered that what social workers do has an impact on destitute people and thus on their prospects for building new lives or preventing themselves from falling deeper into poverty or social exclusion. Government policy and official discourse can also bring the poor and excluded to the attention of society in general and thus influence social exclusion and inclusion. Social attitudes, however, remain likely to affect political views and social policy for the foreseeable future. This is why the opinions of Polish people, including national decision makers, on poverty, its causes and on destitute people are analysed here before going on to look at what the social services do in Poland.

Poverty as perceived in Poland

Before going on to describe what the Polish social services do in order to reduce poverty and destitution, it is important to look at how socially excluded people are perceived in Poland by the general public, politicians and the people who work directly with them. This attitude subsequently determines both the need and the desire to devise preventive programmes and implement them as appropriate.

Poor people are generally perceived as being the dregs of society – dirty, slovenly and shabby – and as people who draw attention to themselves and arouse aversion. Many people perceive the poor as being alcoholics, beggars and homeless. At the same time, Polish people see little support from public institutions in counteracting poverty (34 per cent of all respondents and 43 per cent of poor people) (Falkowska 2000; Lepianka 2002b). In a 2012 survey people who could not afford food or rent were generally considered poor (more than 95 per cent) as were those who had nowhere to live (80 per cent). One in three respondents

5 This is now defined as 3D work, i.e. dirty, dangerous and demeaning (or difficult).

Table 5.1 Polish opinions on the causes of remaining in poverty

In your opinion, what is the main reason why some people cannot escape poverty?	1997	1999	2000	2004	2007	2012
Lack of work, unemployment	58	67	79	79	53	53
Powerlessness, unable to arrange affairs	40	33	27	31	37	46
Alcoholism	35	39	31	31	40	43
Laziness, aversion to work	31	25	20	18	35	42
Illness, invalidity	41	37	27	23	27	34
Lack of education and/or professional or trade qualifications	26	32	35	38	39	21
Lack of state support or care	20	20	34	35	24	15
Low pension	29	31	32	27	22	14
Lack of family support or care, lack of family	6	5	3	4	3	5
Fate or misfortune	5	5	5	5	5	2

Note: Percentages do not add up to 100 because respondents could choose three factors.
Source: Kowalczuk (2012a, p. 8).

regarded a person who could not manage to go away on holiday once a year as poor. More than half (54 per cent) of the respondents regarded the poverty line as an income of PLN 800 or less per family member per month. The average value of the poverty line in these surveys was PLN 695, which was significantly more than the amount that would have entitled someone to receive social support (Kowalczuk 2012a).[6]

Polish people believe that the poor are mostly unemployed (67 per cent), retired on a pension (22 per cent), or victims of fate or misfortune (elderly, disabled, sick etc.) (11 per cent). Respondents in 2000 mostly identified internal factors as the cause of poverty, e.g. unemployment, constitutional and legal changes and low earnings. Relatively few people put the blame on the poor for being in that state. Only 12 per cent of those surveyed singled out alcoholism, laziness, stupidity or other pathologies as the source of poverty, and only 9 per cent selected helplessness or inability to adapt to change (Falkowska 2000, pp. 27–30). This picture changes when people are asked about the causes of remaining in poverty. An examination of the changes in Polish attitudes on this issue leads to some interesting observations (see Table 5.1). There has been considerable fluctuation over the past 15 years but people currently claim to hold views similar to those of the mid-1990s. Polish people are beginning to blame the poor for their own poverty to an increasingly greater extent. Although unemployment is still held to be a cause of poverty, more people link this with personal factors, such as powerlessness, alcoholism, aversion to work and laziness. The last two of these factors, which combine poverty with pathological behaviour, especially, are increasing noticeably rapidly. The structural problems of living in poverty (poor qualifications, lack of public support etc.) are becoming marginalised to an ever greater extent.

This raises the question of what caused these changes. The Global Financial Crisis does not seem to be the sole explanation, as the upward trend began in 2007, when the Polish economy was growing very rapidly. One explanation might then be the dissemination of increasingly liberal views in society, especially by politicians (there are generally no differences between political parties on this).

Politicians see poverty as extreme destitution, and the role of the state as supporting the weak, sick and disabled. Despite that, they downplay the issue of destitution and are oblivious to the poverty around them. One has even said 'I suspect that if this is really about poverty … if these statistics were real, there'd be

6 At the time, the income thresholds to qualify for social assistance were PLN 477 for a person living alone and PLN 351 for a person in a family of four. These were increased to PLN 542 and PLN 456 respectively in October 2012.

people lying around starving. But there aren't any' (Danecka 2007, p. 132). They also point out that people are 'cheating the system' on benefits: 'we turn a blind eye to the fact that some citizens (who say they're smarter than everyone else) are cheating the state out of certain benefits' (Woźniak 2012, p. 168). Politicians can obviously see the links between destitution and lack of work and are aware of the issue of poverty, especially in areas formerly occupied by state farms (although they often regard the people living there as a loss to society) (Woźniak 2012, p. 170). Unemployment often crops up in public debate but little if anything is actually done to reduce it. This could not be further from the approach of Swedish Prime Minister Olof Palme in the 1980s. Palme claimed that every minister in his government had been unemployed (Zalewski 2002, p. 125).

Politicians focus most of their attention on the causes of poverty. Unlike the general public, however, they usually lay the blame squarely on the socially excluded themselves (even when they can see that there are additional, external causes). They speak of a 'culture of helplessness and a culture of exploiting a lack of work' and say that 'a healthy person has to have the right conditions to earn money. There is nothing worse than people getting money for nothing. It warps their character.' They point out that welfare should not be given 'for nothing' and say some sort of community work should be demanded from those collecting it. They generally expect activity from the destitute and the unemployed: 'I have to improve my qualifications and get busy instead of looking for security'.[7] These remarks give rise to the expectation that the poor should be put to work instead of being given goods. A lone dissenting voice was heard in an address given by a member of the Samoobrona (Self-Defence) Party, who pointed out that the state has an obligation to support the poor by virtue of Art. 67 of the Constitution (especially Paragraph 2[8]) (Woźniak 2012, p. 173). Politicians also talk about the poor abusing their right to welfare, claiming they cheat the state by receiving benefits while working illegally.[9] It is telling that members of all political parties generally express these same views.

Preventing and alleviating poverty is not even a pressing issue for local politicians. Social Assistance Centre workers tell researchers that they and the people they assist feel ignored and barely noticed by local community leaders (Lepianka 2002a, p. 207; Racław 2011, p. 47). Their feelings are not surprising given local politicians' announcements. These local politicians do not see preventing or alleviating poverty as their job and charge local social assistance services with full responsibility for dealing with the problem, while blaming destitution on those afflicted with it. It is also evident that what little they know about the problem of social exclusion comes from their own experience, anecdotes or the media (Woźniak 2012, pp. 197–8).

Most intriguing of all, however, is the way social workers view their charges. After all, the extent to which they support them and integrate them into society depends on it. On the one hand, social workers, when describing those in their care, point out the objective characteristics that people who turn to social assistance typically possess. They stress their 'limited social and cultural capacity, their inability to manage their lives and a "social assistance" lifestyle handed down from generation to generation' (Racław 2011, p. 36). They point out their passivity and their need to be constantly monitored and cared for. On the other hand, however, the 'clients in these stories [from social workers] often appear as hostile, demanding people who threaten the life and health of the worker' (Racław 2011, p. 36). Social workers, when surveyed, also frequently use pejorative notions when describing their clients (cesspit, reveller, demoralisation, pathology etc.) and refer to them as being passive, lazy, not concerned about anything and bereft of moral principles.[10] They describe them as conmen out to exploit the system. This is not just about submitting false data to obtain some form of assistance, but deliberate manipulation in the form of mistreating their own children so as to obtain the disability assistance to which they are entitled (this is known as 'breeding sickness') (Golczyńska-Grondas 2002, pp. 153–7; Woźniak 2012, pp. 182–3). A certain ambivalence, and a strange mixture of a paternalistic and contemptuous approach bolstered by a fear of their clients, can be discerned in the above remarks. What

7 Quotes taken from Danecka (2007, pp. 129, 139, 137).

8 'A citizen who is involuntarily without work and has no other means of support, shall have the right to social security, the scope of which shall be specified by statute.'

9 Research shows that one in three people are working cash in hand while receiving state benefits such as pensions and unemployment benefits, and that one in four do so because social support is not enough to live on (Bednarski et al. 2008, pp. 121–2).

10 It is symptomatic that social service workers took the term pathology to mean nothing more than destitution or poverty, without any additional characteristics, such as addiction, criminality or violence (Woźniak 2012, pp. 189–90).

is lacking here is a subjective approach with respect for those being assisted. It is necessary, however, to emphasise that this is not specific to Poland. Family Court judges in the UK likewise refer to the parties for whom they adjudicate condescendingly. They even permit themselves to conduct (and express) indiscriminate assessments of their behaviour and attitudes (Grover 2008, p. 97).

Another common charge levelled by social workers towards their clients is their demanding attitude. Meanwhile, psychological tests reveal that this kind of attitude is typical of the poor and socially excluded. Difficult experiences inculcate feelings of hurt and dissatisfaction that find their outlet in demanding attitudes. These comprise a fitting emotional response to social exclusion and are most often combined with passivity and resignation from satisfying personal needs (Żemojtel-Piotrowska and Piotrowski 2011). It would seem that professionals should be familiar with and understand these mechanisms and be able to work with such a client in a way that counteracts this process and leads to activity.

Social workers also have feelings of powerlessness. They feel that many of those in their care are beyond help and take advantage of the resources available to them. This is due to both excessive bureaucracy and the small de facto armoury of readily available options. One social worker described this as follows: 'We social workers have no way of making, or influencing, any change in the lives of these people. We are limited to filling in and checking paperwork' (Golczyńska-Grondas 1999, p. 175).

Two thirds of social workers also consider that anyone capable of working should enjoy social assistance benefits for the shortest possible time, i.e. just long enough to obtain qualifications, and then quickly return to the labour market. In their understanding 'Social assistance is there to serve people, who because of e.g. age, disability or accident, cannot cope with a difficult life situation. Anyone who can work should be prevented from being able to get social assistance benefits.' Another added firmly: 'Nothing for nothing. Those days, thank goodness, are over' (Danecka 2008, pp. 127, 131). Social workers must have adopted this worship of work as the ultimate social value from politicians, who, as quoted above, place the greatest stress on the necessity of work combined with a lack of public monetary benefits. Nor should it be forgotten that there are currently a large number of people out of work and, in a peculiarly modern twist, unemployment affects not just the old and the unqualified but also the well-educated. Many people, therefore, have suffered this experience to some degree. It is therefore necessary to come to grips with the fact that some people, especially the most socially excluded and the least qualified, cannot return to the labour market and that this is generally no fault of their own.

This also raises the question of whether being employed is really a way out of poverty. This is precisely what the exponents of neoliberalism claim. According to these theses, the point of working is not just to earn money. Work becomes a way of life, helps satisfy our ambitions and aspirations, supports our development and is the key to independence and self-respect. This approach, however, seems overly idealistic.[11] Would this mean that every job is like this? What about 'junk jobs'? Do they support the development of the worker in any way? Do they build self-esteem? Not necessarily. Having analysed this issue, Young (2002, p. 473) claimed: 'to suggest that any work is better than no work, and that work has this essential redeeming quality, is bizarre in the extreme'. Moreover, not every unemployed person is actually failing to perform socially important work. At the very least, women who raise children or take care of elderly family members are worth mentioning here. Their labour, however, is not normally regarded as work (Bauman 1998, p. 16).

Furthermore, studies show that working people can also sink into poverty. In Britain it has been demonstrated that half the poor children in the country are raised in families in which at least one parent works (Grover 2008, pp. 29–30). In Poland too, almost 14 per cent of working people earn so little (up to PLN 640 per month for a person in a family) as to qualify as poor. This category of person is defined as the working poor. Any attempt to characterise the working poor in Poland would find that almost half of them are middle-aged (40–55 years old), 70 per cent of them live in the country or small cities (up to 20,000 inhabitants)

11 Orwell maintained that an order to work is often dictated with a desire of the rich to control the poor: 'A slave … should be working when he is not sleeping. It does not matter whether his work is needed or not, he must work, because work in itself is good – for slaves, at least. This sentiment still survives, and it has piled up mountains of useless drudgery. … this instinct to perpetuate useless work is, at bottom, simply fear of the mob. The mob (the thought runs) are such low animals that they would be dangerous if they had leisure; it is safer to keep them too busy to think' (Orwell 1933, pp. 141–2).

and most of them live in Poland ‘B’.[12] It should be added that 89 per cent of them work full-time and 40 per cent of families only have one breadwinner (Kuźmicz and Stasiowski 2008). These people are most likely employed on ‘junk contracts’, which are characterised by low wages (most often the minimum wage) and are often based on civil law agreements (or without any written contract, i.e. ‘on the side’) instead of employment contracts. This mode of employment therefore deprives the worker of any feeling of stability as well as certain entitlements, e.g. paid sick leave and recreation leave. Studies show that the scale of the working poor phenomenon does not depend so much on economic development as on the policy of the given country and its employment profitability and remuneration policy tools (Duszczyk 2010, pp. 313–14).

A second important issue that has to be considered, because it recurs in the citations above, is the problematic aspects of the connection between the obligation to work and the social assistance system, i.e. only receiving monetary benefits in exchange for work. This issue is also ambivalent. It should be noted that ‘inclusion through work can permanently mark assistance recipients and exclude them from society’ (Babińska-Górecka 2009, p. 509). Work in exchange for benefits mainly involves performing simple, physical labour. These sorts of tasks, when undertaken for too long, can make it impossible to find other work that is better and more suited to the qualifications and/or preferences of the unemployed. They should therefore be used with caution and a decision should be made as to whether this is the best way to help the poor person in question in each individual case.

And finally it is necessary to consider the connection between poverty and criminality among those surveyed. It is worth emphasising that this rhetoric does not as a rule appear in the responses. Kurowska makes use of this, although she writes in relatively general terms that ‘people in extreme poverty are beset with various kinds of pathologies such as alcoholism and drug addiction more often than other social groups’ (Kurowska 2008, p. 17). This concurs with what politicians and social workers say. Criminality generally only appears in a single context, viz. petty theft and others acts committed by juveniles. This reminded one police officer of the dilemma he had in deciding whether, knowing about these acts, he should have reported them and initiated proceedings. ‘The general problem from our side lies in whether to punish these children for this [petty larceny] as this would bring us full circle. We know these children have nothing to eat at home. They simply don’t have the money’ (Golczyńska-Grondas 1999, p. 178) This is a really serious dilemma which requires combining social and penal policy and which is hampered by the extremely restricted effectiveness of the latter in the cases described. It is just as well then that there appears to be some degree of reflection on this issue on the part of those employed in the services responsible for public order.[13]

The efforts of the Polish social services in combating poverty and social exclusion

According to the Act of 12 March 2004 on Social Assistance, the social services are required to assist citizens and their families in overcoming difficult circumstances in life. They are meant to guide them in obtaining full independence and facilitate their participation in social life. This perception of need, not just to satisfy the ongoing and minimal material requirements of an individual, but to bring about his/her inclusion (in the sense of being the opposite of social exclusion) and incorporation into society and to counteract his/her renewed marginalisation, first appeared in Polish social policy thinking at the beginning of the twenty-first century, no doubt as a result of working with the countries of Western Europe, where this concept has long been widespread.[14] Taking preventive measures, and not just offering immediate assistance in difficult circumstances, therefore became accentuated as well.

---

12 Poland ‘B’ is a widely-acknowledged term describing what is generally considered the poorer, less economically developed part of Poland, mostly in the east part of the country, where people tend to be more traditional, religious and inward-looking. The term Poland ‘A’ is used to refer to the more economically developed and cosmopolitan west part of the country.

13 Especially given that surveys present such a picture of thieving juveniles. The reason some young people steal certain things (e.g. deodorants) is a social expectation among peers that they have them. However, their parents earn too little to provide them (Klaus 2009a, pp. 153–7; Woźniakowska-Fajst 2010, pp. 282–8).

14 During the 1990s, social assistance was most visible in its efforts to shield people from the political and economic transformations that were taking place, i.e. it focused on ensuring temporary assistance was given to people who could not cope with the new situations (Rymsza 2012, pp. 353–6).

This approach implies a single key assumption: that it is based on the subjective evaluation of the person being given support. All the social services are therefore required to see that the people they assist maintain their dignity, and to ensure necessary and adequate support is given in a manner that does not affront that dignity. Dignity is invoked in the Act on Social Assistance as well: according to Art. 3 § 1, government support should satisfy the essential needs of people who need to call on assistance and make it possible for them to live in conditions befitting human dignity. These conditions are to be construed as:

> life above the biological minimum (i.e. bare subsistence), at a level corresponding to the basic standard of living of an average person in a given society. Moreover, human dignity, which also applies to the psychological sphere, is expressed in a guarantee of autonomy, freedom and equality, and this includes the domains of economic and social rights. (Babińska-Górecka 2009, p. 510)

This obviously raises the question as to whether this objective, which underpins the new legislation and which is formally presented by decision makers, is achieved in practice. A clear majority of academics who work on social policy would answer in the negative. Joanna Staręga-Piasek makes this point forcefully:

> Social assistance in Poland does not combat destitution. Social assistance only assists certain categories of destitute people in mitigating the effects of their destitution. The right tools have to be used to combat destitution. The tools available to social assistance neutralise some of its effects. … Social assistance does not counteract social exclusion. It helps a certain category of person deemed socially excluded subsist on a low standard of living. (Staręga-Piasek 2005, pp. 317, 319)

These are very strong words. The research results presented below allow some assessment to be made of the extent to which they remain justified.

Staręga-Piasek considers a minimum guaranteed income to be a tool to fight poverty. In Poland, this concept is only discussed by political scientists and has not entered the general political or public debate. Meanwhile, it is commonly applied in EU countries. A minimum guaranteed income depends on the authorities ensuring the citizenry has the minimum resources to survive and earn a living (Kłos 2003). This means that every citizen can count on receiving a minimum sum from the government to help him/her survive. This is paid without any prerequisites or additional obligations on the part of those who need it. It is generally the amount comprising the 'subsistence minimum' (or 'biological minimum'), i.e. the means considered essential to survive in a given society.[15] In 2012, this was PLN 521.11 per month for a single-person household and almost PLN 443 per person per month in a four-person household. The fact that the subsistence minimum was higher than the income threshold above which there was no entitlement to social assistance (PLN 477 and PLN 351 respectively) is worth noting. This means that there were people who, despite earning too little to live on according to these calculations (i.e. too little to ensure a dignified existence), could not receive any support from the government.[16] The situation has not changed much since the income thresholds were revised in October 2012. The amounts that now entitle people to draw social assistance benefits were increased slightly (to PLN 542 and PLN 456 respectively) but they are not much higher than the subsistence minimum (Kurowski 2013). This forces social assistance recipients to earn extra income, as the welfare they receive is too little to live on.[17] As they cannot legally earn income (because it leads to a corresponding reduction in social assistance benefits), they take up employment 'on the side'. Research reveals that one in three people working without a contract are additionally receiving public benefits, such as a pension or some form of welfare, and that the reason for this is that the benefits are simply insufficient (Bednarski et al. 2008, pp.

15 In Poland, this is calculated by the Institute of Labour and Social Studies – the research institute of the Ministry of Labour and Social Policy.

16 It is worth stressing that only the minimum survival costs, i.e. food and payments connected with housing, were taken into consideration when calculating the amount of welfare. Medicine, heating and energy were not included, nor were any other costs connected with education or culture. Nor was any provision made for people who could not live in council flats and had to rent on the open market (Staręga-Piasek and Wóycicka 2011, p. 188).

17 Destitute people even stress this in surveys. One woman said: 'As I'm writing [to social assistance], they give us a couple of groszy, a hundred, a hundred and fifty złoty, but it's a drop in the ocean' (Gawlicz and Starnawski 2011, p. 32).

121–2; Zalewski 2002, p. 119). Statistics also show that fewer and fewer people are receiving social assistance benefits (between 2004 and 2009 the percentage decreased from 1.45 to 0.48 per cent) and that the number of people living below the subsistence minimum fluctuates between 5.5 and 8.0 per cent of Polish society (these people constituted 6.7 per cent of society in 2011) (Staręga-Piasek and Wóycicka 2011; Kurowski 2013).

These data justify the claim that social assistance benefits are too little to satisfy basic human needs and to enable people to lead dignified lives. Thus the aims of the Act on Social Assistance, mentioned above, have not been realised. The social minimum would have to be paid for welfare to satisfy the requirements of the Act. This is calculated in such a way as not only to ensure biological survival but to allow for recreation, education and culture as well. This is obviously considerably higher than the subsistence minimum and in 2012 averaged PLN 1026.94 per month for a single-person household and PLN 844.75 per person per month in a household of four (Kurowski 2013). This was clearly higher than the income threshold above which there was no entitlement to public assistance.

These calculations show that in practice Polish social policy has adopted a model of absolute poverty as the public assistance threshold. Therefore, contrary to the assumptions and the aims of the Act on Social Assistance, bare survival is the sole aim of public support. 'The borderline of absolute poverty is set at the level of physical viability. Life satisfaction, intellectual development and social capacities are ignored. … The model of absolute poverty takes no account of social or cultural context. The poor are abstracted from society' (Babińska-Górecka 2009, p. 505). To include them would necessitate carrying out social work of a high quality. This is a basic obligation, and, at the same time, a work tool for social service workers. Social work is predicated on promoting social change and aims to empower recipients so as to bring about their wellbeing, and to intercede in their relations with the local community with which they are in contact. Increasing the social capital of people on welfare, and not just supporting them economically is one of the objectives of social work. A social worker should therefore work in parallel with his/her client and the environment (including the institutional environment) in which that client lives and with which he/she is in contact. The idea is to make socially excluded people more active and to work with the entire local society so as to include everyone in the community (Kaźmierczak 2006). The important role played by the local community in ensuring the wellbeing of all its members is apparent here. This is why social assistance has been transferred to the commune level. The local authorities are more familiar with local issues and can plan ways of including socially excluded people. Unfortunately, research shows that these idealistic assumptions have not been successfully put into practice. The reason for this is the weakness of local government and the lack of any real local community in Poland. Commune authorities do not support social assistance establishments but rather see them as mainly a source of problems and budgetary expenditure.

This therefore raises the question of how effective the Polish social services are. This applies not just to social assistance establishments, but to employment services as well. Social assistance has to be broadly understood. It has to transcend the strictly social. Studies on social assistance centres show that only 9 per cent of their clients ceased to avail themselves of their support within 18 months. The remainder made use of the assistance they provided for the entire period. When they did cease to draw benefits, it was never for more than a month at a time. Moreover, the reasons for this dependence had nothing to do with the operations or activities of the centres (Zub 2011, pp. 126, 187). These results confirm the findings of earlier studies conducted in Łódź, where it transpired that poor people likewise found government assistance insufficient to become financially self-sufficient and frequently came back for assistance. The researchers claimed at the time that it was possible to speak of transmission of poverty in Poland, i.e. poverty induced by unemployment and/or low incomes or social assistance payments (poor qualifications and large, single-parent families are most often at the bottom of this) (Grotowska-Leder 1999, pp. 48–9).

One reason for the persistence of poverty and social exclusion, i.e. the ineffectiveness of social assistance, might be that no actual social work is done with the clients.

> That social workers devote most of their time to 'following the necessary procedures in helping their clients with material assistance and services' and 'giving their clients direct support (e.g. with material assistance and services)' to a large degree bureaucratises their work and relegates the provision of qualified assistance to the margins. (Kaźmierczak 2012, p. 176)

Social workers are aware of this. They are critical of this working paradigm and complain about the excessive formalities associated with welfare payments and the lack of time available to spend on real work with clients. On the other hand, however, they do nothing to change this state of affairs. As one of them stated in an interview, 'They do as they're told' (Granosik 2012, pp. 195, 198–9; Racław 2012, pp. 242–3).

Job centres were similarly ineffective. Whatever assistance they provided did not translate into any occupational activity on the part of their clients whatsoever (statistically). Their clients generally found work independently of any help they might have received from the centre. The clients deemed the work of the 'employment agencies' moderately useful. Their lowest assessment was reserved for assistance in looking for work (fewer than half of those registered received any offer of employment from the centre). Job placement, which – it would seem – should be the main task of job centres, is rated poorly on surveys. Professional advisers generally do not know their clients. Almost 80 per cent of initial interviews with advisers take less than 15 minutes and subsequent visits are even shorter. Long-term unemployed people are seldom contacted by officials – just half of them once a month and a third of them once every two months. This may be why 31 per cent of unemployed people do not avail themselves of the assistance of these institutions at all (Zub 2011, pp. 184–92; Kryńska 2009, pp. 59–61).

These findings do not give cause for optimism. The social services do not seem to prevent either poverty or social exclusion. Nor do they realise the goals of social assistance inscribed in the regulations. Most of the problems are systemic (this is often a hangover from the socialist period – even today) and pinning them all on those who work directly with the destitute is overly harsh. This is because

> a bureaucratised system cannot cope with challenges as they arise, but focuses on the meticulously observed rituals of clerical propriety – (budgetary) resources are consumed, (social) problems remain unresolved, and the durability of the system can be seen as a sort of fig leaf with which decision makers cover themselves when they declare that a certain budgetary amount has been allocated to social assistance in a given year. (Raźniewski 2009, p. 78)

What is most lacking is a Polish policy conception, i.e. there is no desire to tackle the problems of poverty and social exclusion, to turn declarations into practical actions that would prevent them from arising. Such measures would obviously be costly but well worthwhile in the long run.

Education as a Means of Counteracting Social Exclusion and Criminality

Education is one of the planks of social policy that can and should be employed to prevent social problems becoming entrenched. Applied judiciously, this could serve to even the odds between children from different backgrounds. The education system should be designed to counteract negative social phenomena (e.g. committing prohibited acts at a young age) or prevent them from arising. Education should be appropriate to these ends (levelling educational inequalities and giving developmental prospects to children and youth), the school environment should be conducive to learning and teach correct social behaviour, and children and youth should be shown ways of using their free time profitably. As Stanisława Golinowska correctly puts it,

> fully participating in a good, customised education is the basis of success in later life. That is why not being able to go to school, learning difficulties, and dropping out of school are a fundamental threat in this area. They make people's path in life more difficult and even lead to them dropping out of mainstream society, i.e. to social exclusion. (Golinowska 2010, pp. 43–4)

The role of education and schools in preventing social exclusion: equalising educational opportunities

It would be a truism to say that children beginning their education experience highly unequal opportunities as soon as they enter the system. These opportunities depend on the family environment in which they are brought up. Children from intellectual families bring numerous skills and experiences from home, which increases the odds of them succeeding at school. Similarly, people from poor backgrounds are not free of baggage either. It is just that their baggage is different, and happens to be more of a burden than a bonus. Evening out these educational inequalities so as to put every child on an equal footing is therefore one of the tasks confronting educational institutions (Zahorska 2009, pp. 51–2; Dolata 2008, p. 15).

The education system should therefore aim to counteract social exclusion and poverty, as higher and better education is correlated with a lower probability of sinking into poverty. Research indicates that a basic and/or basic vocational education more than doubles the likelihood of later poverty while higher education reduces it three times. A low level of education is also conducive to feeling socially excluded.[18] A third of those who feel like second-class citizens and almost half those counted as lower class possess this sort of education (Kozarzewski 2008, pp. 161, 158–9). Equalising educational opportunity and giving all children an education that corresponds to their potential therefore acquires a great deal of importance. The education system has a major role to play here, as children generally inherit their parents' level of education. Children whose parents are intellectuals therefore have a significantly greater chance of acquiring higher education than do children whose parents belong to other social groups (e.g. more than 100 times more than children whose parents are farmers) (Kołaczek 2004, p. 43; Dolata 2008, p. 40).

There are obviously strong links between education and income level and approach to education, i.e. perceiving it as something valuable. As mentioned above, poorly educated people are usually poor and thus cannot normally afford to invest in the education of their children. Economic factors are thus crucial in the case of educational inequality. They are even more important than the educational aspirations of parents. More than half the parents from the poorest social groups mention lack of money as the major obstacle to educating their children. Additional classes or private lessons are out of the question. Place of residence is also part of the problem. People living in rural areas have greater difficulty in getting access to education. This is compounded by the necessity of incurring additional expenses, such as driving children to school (Kołaczek 2004, pp. 89–95). One mother living on a farm describes the problem thus:

> There are no problems with them [the children] in school, because they want to learn … and they even learn well … But when it comes to finances, things don't look so rosy. When they want to go somewhere further, you know yourself, that those journeys, that monthly ticket, or, for example, to that dormitory … and those expensive textbooks and everything. (Tarkowska 2002, p. 180)

Poverty also makes it necessary for children to go to work. This is especially significant in the country, where children have always performed many farm chores (and unfortunately still do) to help their parents. They sometimes earn money from a young age to support the family budget by collecting groundcover or scrap metal. Moreover, older children are responsible for minding their younger siblings while their parents are at work (Zahorska 2009, p. 54; Tarkowska 2002, pp. 165–71). This affects large rural families but the issue often arises in poor urban families as well, especially multi-problem families. The problem of maintaining a home when parents are not in any condition to do so is not uncommon either (Frysztacki et al. 2011, p. 167).

Furthermore, many young people do not continue their studies. The most frequently cited reasons for discontinuing education (dropping out) had to do with material problems – 53 per cent of respondents in the case of vocational school and 37 per cent in the case of middle school. Further down the list was taking up employment (approx. 32 per cent of cases) and an aversion to education (26 per cent). Very different reasons are put forward in the case of not continuing education past junior school, viz. aversion to learning (60 per cent) and learning problems and inability to get into school (52 per cent combined) (Kołaczek 2004, pp. 87–9). The reason for this last situation may be the low level of scholarships in country schools, where no additional extracurricular classes or any after-school activities to develop children's skills and talents are available (Kozarzewski 2008, pp. 150–51, 153). Not wishing to continue studies may be a result of a lack of achievement in this area.

The problem, however, is not merely that people are discontinuing their studies, but that they are dropping out of the education system. While the official statistics are extraordinarily optimistic (Poland's 5.5 per cent of school dropouts places it at the forefront of the EU), the reality is very different. Studies show that school principals do not exercise any real control over compulsory education and do not therefore have any reliable

18 A 'low level of education' means junior high school (or lower) and vocational.

data on youth who are not learning. Nor do school principals have any interest in revealing how many pupils have left school (as they would then receive less in subsidies, as these are calculated based on head counts). A practice of automatically promoting pupils to the next year, even if they do not attend school, is also in evidence. This is because an active policy is in place against repeating a year under which detailed explanations have to be given for keeping anyone down. It is therefore much simpler to promote everyone. The covering up of truancy is sometimes termed 'hidden waste' and results in social exclusion and semi-literates completing their education at the high school level (Zahorska 2009; Golinowska 2010).

It is extremely important that truancy and dropout rates be monitored, as criminological studies conducted over the years show that they are linked to illegal behaviour on the part of children and youth. In studies of girls conducted by Dagmara Woźniakowska-Fajst, it was found that 7.4 per cent of them neither studied nor worked, although they were legally obliged to go to school. Most of the girls who made trouble and ended up in the Family Court were not good pupils (this percentage is even higher in the case of perpetrators of violence). More than half of them skipped classes, two thirds did so regularly, and 15.4 per cent of them had been kept down (despite the reluctance of teachers to resort to this measure) (Woźniakowska-Fajst 2010, pp. 243–9, 310). This information seems analogous to that regarding the commission of prohibited acts by juveniles under the age of 13. One in five had to repeat years, even though they were still in junior school, 25 per cent were regarded negatively by their teachers (for causing educational problems), and three quarters only achieved the bare minimum to pass. The links between an early departure from the education system and a later career in crime are strong and are demonstrated in several studies (Klaus 2009a, pp. 206–10; Esterle-Hedibel 2005, pp. 16–19).

Parental attitudes to education are another factor in determining whether children continue with their schooling. Parental support for education has been shown to be a vital component in preventing children from starting to commit prohibited acts (Salmi and Kivivuori 2006, pp. 126–8, 140–41). Poland has witnessed significant change in its appreciation of the role of education in recent years. Parents in post-communist villages are seeing education as something increasingly valuable. They are interpreting it as success for their children later in life and make comments such as, 'Education is a necessity these days', 'I tell my children to go to school now, so that they finish some sort of schooling. It's really hard without a trade or profession nowadays', 'Learn, definitely just learn, now just learn. You're lost without learning ... It's always been hard to get a job without education', 'I've got a hard life. You make sure you study, so you can have a better future' (Tarkowska 2002, pp. 174–5). The people surveyed, however, do not see education as something valuable in its own right. They associate education with their children having a better position in the labour market and value it solely from a utilitarian perspective. This approach, however, carries its own risks. This motivation loses a lot of its rationale in the face of the high rates of unemployment prevailing at present, even among the best educated. Those surveyed, therefore, do not value higher education and prefer to have a specific trade or profession. Some of them dismiss 'sitting at a desk' as not really working.

Fighting educational inequality was one of the goals of the educational reforms of 1999 and the creation of high schools. It is not easy to say whether this has been achieved. Research conducted by Roman Dolata suggests that these measures have been partly successful in equalising opportunities. Dolata (2008, pp. 98–145; see also Post 2007, pp. 160–62) went to villages where high school pupils exhibited more apparent diversity in terms of socio-economic characteristics than did the pupils in the more homogeneous rural junior schools. The children thus learn in a mixed and varied environment.[19] On the other hand, the very opposite occurs in large cities. High schools have made the students more segregated. Even when pupils from different backgrounds attend the same school, they often sit in different classes, i.e. for bright and not so bright pupils. This division is a result of the rivalry between schools (their rankings depending on the grades attained) and of parents (for whom school ratings are very important) being given the option of choosing high schools. Transfers are rarer in villages and children generally attend regional high schools. This occurs considerably more often in the cities (where 25 per cent of children do not attend regional high schools). Changing school is particularly pronounced in the case of children of upper-class parents (place of residence is immaterial here). A process of 'improving' the social makeup of the student body by drawing 'better' children from outside the region can be observed in the cities. Moreover, rural and urban high school principals evince significant differences in

19 Different conclusions are reached by Górniak and Kalbarczyk (2007, pp. 97–8).

the way they separate children into classes. While the former are more in favour of egalitarianism and place students in a variety of surroundings in a classroom (and see a great deal of value in this), the latter are more elitist and consequently segregate children according to the grades they have achieved.

It is therefore worth asking whether mixing children from different backgrounds in the one classroom is really conducive to raising educational achievements. Pedagogical studies show that the answer is not clear-cut. There is no doubt that teaching gifted and not-so-gifted children (and perhaps those from 'good' and 'not-so-good' families) together dramatically improves the grades of the latter. For the former, however, the reverse is the case. Gifted children taught in mixed classrooms achieve lower grades than their peers in elite classrooms. These processes are not equal in strength. Poor students obtain considerably more than gifted students lose as a result of their being taught together (this obviously only looks at the issue in terms of scholarly achievements and ignores social skills and values). Such are the findings of Polish studies, which conclude: 'with segregation, the better gain while the weaker lose; with desegregation, the reverse holds true' (Dolata 2008, pp. 218, 174–5, 204).

One last important aspect of evening out educational inequalities needs to be addressed. This concerns the earliest period of education, i.e. the value of having children attend kindergarten. Once again, a huge disparity exists between urban and rural children. The latter have fewer opportunities and possibilities of being placed in this type of institution, even though they would get the most out of it. In fact, studies show that boys and girls with low cultural potential living in large, destitute families benefit most from attending kindergarten. Kindergarten does not exert that much of an influence on children whose parents are well educated. The time spent in kindergarten (optimally, this should be three to four years) is rewarded with considerably greater success in mathematics and, later, Polish (this was the only issue examined). But kindergarten brings other values to socially excluded children: it generally prepares them for the responsibilities of school, it teaches hygienic habits, how to play with crayons and improves their vocabulary (including use of appropriate language) (Zahorska 2009, pp. 52–3; Matyjas 2008, pp. 192–3; Górniak and Kalbarczyk 2007, pp. 22–4).

How then should the Polish school system operate? Many experts are convinced beyond doubt that evening out inequalities of opportunity and fostering and developing the interests of the pupils should be among its primary goals. One of the ministers surveyed provides a potent image to conclude a description of the ideal school:

> which should not restrict itself to giving the same lesson to everyone, which has a whole other sphere of activity where it tutors, does revision and makes homework easier. ... It has to start to be an afternoon school – to put it as simple as possible – that actively equalises opportunities. For the first, it helps him do his homework, for the second, it makes it possible to develop interests of various sorts, for the third, who is going to hang around tower blocks, it suggests a match on the oval after lunch. For the fourth, it additionally explains what a computer is, because he has a drunk for a father and he's never seen a computer in his life. (Post 2007, pp. 168–9)

Unfortunately, it seems that, at present, children with deficiencies do not find at school what they need to overcome them. This is because schools do not implement any inclusion strategies (Golinowska 2010, p. 48).

Schools' educational activity in counteracting violence, and 'Zero tolerance' programmes

'The attitudes of socially maladjusted pupils to teachers, school and learning, and their conduct on school grounds are ... prognostic factors in their punishability' (Ostrihanska and Wójcik 1984, p. 166). At the same time only 13–14 per cent of Polish 15-year-olds like their school (Golinowska 2010, p. 49). This fact is not surprising, given the substantial impotence of teachers to maintain discipline at school. So much so, that they often resort to improper means. Students claim that teachers have used offensive language towards them (15 per cent), that they have been intimidated by them (10 per cent), have had their ears pulled (11.6 per cent) and had their knuckles rapped (4 per cent) (Ostrowska and Surzykiewicz 2005, pp. 61–4). The fact that the spiral of violence in schools has grown to the point that, as Jacek Pyżalski's studies reveal, one in four teachers claims that his/her school has a place to administer corporal punishment and one in three believes this to be the only method of instruction for certain students must give cause for concern (Grabek 2007). On the other hand, students claim that teachers frequently fail to respond to aggression between their peers. Only one third of junior school pupils stated in surveys that teachers always broke up displays of violence, while 11 per cent thought they were completely passive towards it. Students also say that teachers know little if anything about the scale and frequency of violence in school. This view was shared by more than half those surveyed (Krajewski 2001, pp. 175–6; Nowakowska 2004, pp. 163–6). According to a third of students, schools do not cope particularly well with the violence that takes place on their grounds (one in 10 teachers share this view). Importantly, this information was obtained at the schools taking part in the 'School Without Violence' campaign, i.e. in establishments that were conducting various kinds of preventive measures (Czapiński 2009, p. 103).

There are so many programmes in place to prevent violence in various schools that it would be difficult to describe them all. Every school is required to have an applicable document describing ways of dealing with this problem. What they lack, however, is a general analysis and some attempt at evaluation. The best known such document is the national 'Zero Tolerance for Violence in School' programme approved by the Cabinet in 2007 (Ministerstwo Edukacji Narodowej 2007). Those who drafted it wrote that it was devised and implemented to meet an ever more pressing need to make schools safer for children and the youth. Although the foundations were properly laid, the proposed preventive measures have to be adjudged negatively. The whole document was written in a prescriptive and distributive spirit, with educational activities relegated to the sidelines – they were mentioned, but only in a fairly general way (Siellawa-Kolbowska 2007). A great deal of stress, however, was placed on implementing surveillance in schools and on pointing out the legal and administrative liability of youth for engaging in socially undesirable behaviour. It was also proposed that difficult students be removed from school and placed in special purpose institutions.

This programme was modelled on similar initiatives pursued in Western countries. These were likewise premised on fitting schools with technical security equipment (CCTV, metal detectors, security guards etc.) and on tightening discipline. Evaluative studies of these programmes, however, have conclusively demonstrated the ineffectiveness of these measures. These programmes have not raised the level of discipline in schools, but have worsened the prevailing atmosphere and the way the schools are run. Nor have they guaranteed any improvement in the level of safety in schools, even though the worst behaved people have been removed. Some schools actually became less safe after introducing a programme of this sort and witnessed an increase in aggressive behaviour (e.g. fighting) compared with other schools. A correlation between introducing technical measures and students experiencing violence and becoming more fearful of violence has also been observed. Some students, especially potential victims of violence, actually felt less safe (Skiba et al. 2006, pp. 4, 72–4; Morrison 2007, p. 52). These findings should come as no surprise. Michael Rutter confirmed the correlation between criminality and a high level of punishment and a low level of praise for children and youth in schools as early as 1979 (Farrington and Welsh 2007, p. 83). Similar results could be observed in Poland. Implementing a 'zero tolerance' programme did nothing to reduce peer violence. If anything, it had the opposite effect. Within the space of a year, teachers and students became visibly more aggressive towards each other and the number of young people who stated that they liked going to school fell significantly (even by as much as 10 per cent) (Żakowski 2007, p. 6).

Furthermore, 'zero tolerance' programmes have brought further, unforeseen negative consequences. They have led more students to leave school and have brought about a considerable worsening of learning conditions and a lowering of educational results among problem students. Teachers more frequently administer different kinds of strict disciplinary measures towards more difficult students (in the US these were often members of ethnic minorities), who have emotional and/or behavioural problems. These are punished for less serious offences than their classmates, who are not deemed 'difficult students', e.g. once a student is suspended, he will be given this punishment significantly more often in future, regardless of the seriousness of the transgression (Skiba et al. 2006, pp. 4–8). Labelling theory, according to which someone who has been deemed a troublemaker once will be perceived as one later, is eminently applicable here. This has led people already on the margins of society to become even more deeply excluded from it. These actions definitely cannot be said to be aimed at limiting criminality, as excluding young people from school with abnormal frequency sets them on the road to crime.[20] Polish studies further show that alienation and labelling result in a higher level of aggression and a tendency towards manifestations of violence (Kulesza 2008, p. 79).

20 The links between being excluded from school and criminality are confirmed by several studies that have been conducted over many years. Teachers cannot cope with children who are overly lively or hyperactive, or who receive

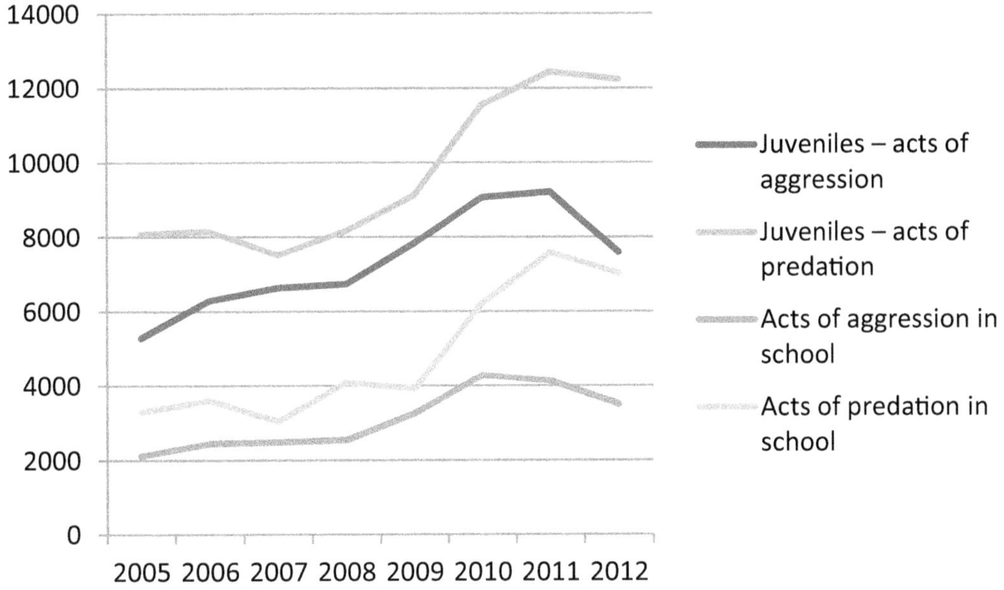

Figure 5.1 The total number of reported acts of aggression committed by juveniles and the number committed on school grounds. Based on police statistics 2005–2012

Note: The data on acts committed on school grounds only include junior schools and junior high schools. By 'act of aggression' is meant homicide, damage to health, taking part in fighting or assaults and rape. By 'act of predation' is meant mugging, robbery and extortion. Police statistics adopt this division. Statistical data on juvenile crime are available online at http://statystyka.policja.pl/portal/st/942/50256/ and data on crime in schools are available at http://statystyka.policja.pl/portal/st/950/50868/Przestepczosc_w_szkole_i_i_innych_placowkach_oswiatowych.html (accessed 29 April 2013).

The number of teenagers whose cases were heard in the Juvenile Courts also increased after the implementation of a 'zero tolerance' programme. This is hardly surprising in view of the concept behind the intervention being implemented (which leads to young people being held responsible for the non-application of educational methodologies) and the measures being applied (mainly technical and repressive) (Skiba et al. 2006, pp. 8–9). It is worth noting that a similar effect can be observed in Poland, where this has also led to a statistical increase in the number of juveniles taking part in committing crimes against the person (see Figure 5.1 for details). The number of crimes committed on school grounds is similarly considerable. This trend only changed in 2012 and it is difficult to pinpoint the reasons for it. The change might have followed the substantial fall in the number of acts of aggression in schools, although it is difficult to say what might have caused this, i.e. an actual decrease in aggressive behaviour or a drop in the number of children and youth attending school as well. There might also have been a change in school policy that led to fewer cases of fighting and assault being reported to the police, although the incidence of such behaviour remained unchanged (i.e. the fall was statistical, not real).

The key factor in preventative programmes is the consequences of improper behaviour. As Stanisław Mika (1969, pp. 248–9, 258–60) pointed out, the effectiveness of punishment depends on several factors, the most important of which is whether the person being punished agrees with the rules that have been laid down, the extent to which he/she internalises them and whether he/she has a positive relationship with the person

poor grades, even when they have a relatively high degree of intelligence. Badly behaved children are more often given unsatisfactory grades (Batawia 1958, pp. 74–82; Ostrihanska 1980, p. 73; Klaus 2009a, pp. 202–11; Hirschfield 2008, pp. 92–3; Esterle-Hedibel 2005, pp. 17–18).

administering the punishment (here the teacher). The punishment cannot successfully change the behaviour of the young person until all these conditions have been met. School rules therefore have to be drawn up jointly and teachers have to enjoy the respect of their students if they are not to treat punishment as a display of aggression or retaliation.[21]

It should be borne in mind, however, that punishment administered in a manner that deprives the person being punished of respect, even when the punishment is justified, causes defiance and rejection and perhaps an increase in undesirable behaviour (Morrison 2007, p. 60). Apart from that, frequent punishment is ineffective. It does not deliver the expected change in the behaviour of the person being punished, but merely causes the person meting out the punishment to be perceived as someone inimical and vindictive. Educators therefore caution against responding frequently and severely to minor transgressions (Surzykiewicz 2000, pp. 655, 661; Mika 1969, pp. 209–14).

Studies show that students have nothing against teachers administering punishment, so long as it fits the transgression. According to them, however, the main thing is that discipline can be maintained in the classroom through cordial relations between teacher and students, and not sophisticated educational methodologies. One student described it as follows: 'Don't expect students to treat you well if you treat them badly' (Pyżalski 2007, pp. 32–3). Educators, when writing about the effectiveness of punishment, point out the necessity of refraining from repressive measures, such as ridicule, shouting, threatening, assigning extra work and, obviously, corporal punishment. An educative approach should be characterised by explanations, clarifications, exhortations to behave positively, expressions of sadness, disillusionment or disapproval (for the act, not the perpetrator), but most of all, by rectifying any harm and repairing damaged relations. With this aim in mind, clearly stated rules of behaviour have to be jointly established and accepted by everyone in the school (Pilch 2009, pp. 92–3; Mika 1969, p. 204; Pring 2009, p. 110). This sort of approach to students is vital. In junior schools, violence increases whenever teachers treat their pupils unequally (favouring some and humiliating and insulting others). In secondary schools, it is crucial that the students have confidence in their teachers, i.e. that they will have someone they can turn to for help in the event of violence. It is also important that they feel that the teachers know what is going on between the students (Komendant-Brodowska et al. 2011, pp. 30–32).

The 'School Without Violence' campaign, launched in 2006 and widely publicised in the media, is based on similar premises, i.e. a desire to introduce clearly stated rules and make schools part of their local community. Some 4,500 schools (approx. 15 per cent of all schools) took part in the 2012/2013 school year. Under the 'School Without Violence Code' programme, which was widely advertised in educational establishments, a website was launched, social research was conducted on violence in schools, competitions for students and teachers were held, and teachers were sent to various meetings and were given training to improve their qualifications on counteracting peer violence. Apart from general guidelines, however, no detailed description is provided of what activities teachers should introduce into their schools or classrooms. Interventions consequently vary considerably in number and kind. This might explain why it has not brought about a decrease in violence in the schools that implemented it, according to an evaluation programme conducted in 2009. On the other hand, alcohol consumption, narcotics use and cigarette smoking by students all decreased in those establishments that conducted more of the educational activities recommended in the programme. Activities delivered significantly more positive results in establishments that worked together with parents. The better this cooperation, the lower the incidence of aggressive behaviour among students (*Program społeczny 'Szkoła bez przemocy'* 2009, pp. 10–20; Czapiński 2009, pp. 115–16).

A 2011 report of 150 surveyed 'Schools Without Violence' provides some fascinating insights. One result is that there is no difference in the incidence or intensity of violence between the city and the country. Another is that the size of the school has no bearing on the scale of violence. The most effective way to limit violence is to improve the atmosphere in the school and raise the level of democratisation (active self-government). Improving the school atmosphere is considerably more conducive to safety than any technical measures (including monitoring and security) and incomparably cheaper (Komendant-Brodowska et al. 2011).

21 Meanwhile, studies reveal that students are holding their teachers in lower and lower esteem. Only half believe their teachers try to teach them to think for themselves and only 40 per cent believe that they are fair towards students. At the same time, one in five students believes that teachers merely want to 'rattle off' their lessons and not to teach them anything, and 37 per cent think they show more interest in students with good grades and neglect the weaker ones (Kalka 2011, pp. 27–8).

A new strategic document was drawn up when the governing coalition changed in 2008, viz. the governmental programme for 2008–2013, 'Friendly and Safe School'. The drafters were at pains to distance themselves from the 'Zero Tolerance' programme, pointing out that a school should

> ... teach social values, alternative behaviour and important life skills. Rebuilding interpersonal relationships and creating a friendly, supportive social atmosphere in school, however, are the most important tasks in countering aggression and violence in schools. Punishment, discipline and restrictive measures are not to be employed until the available corrective, educational actions have been exhausted. (Ministerstwo Edukacji Narodowej 2008, pp. 3–4)

Setting up this programme thus placed educational activities ahead of repressive ones. The drafters also pointed out the need for cooperation between all the stakeholders in a school (parents, teachers and students), being open to student needs and preparing an accurate diagnosis before planning any preventive activities. Unfortunately apart from these lofty objectives, the programme did not indicate any new activities for schools to adopt and its provisions remain largely general. The only specific measure envisaged was to place more visual surveillance equipment in educational establishments – a measure taken from the 'Zero Tolerance' programme.

Conclusion

The issue, which becomes apparent when social policy discourse in analysed, is that socially excluded people are depicted as a 'problem to be fixed'. Rhetoric discrediting the poor recurs in the discourse of politicians and even of people working in these environments. They compare the poor with the middle class without noting that the two groups do not have the same opportunities or capabilities. The fact that these shortcomings are not the result of any deliberate fault on the part of the socially excluded but of the entire complex social mechanism that causes and/or reinforces poverty and exclusion is overlooked (Hancock 2009, p. 169).

Piotr Żuk writes that this sort of approach brings about a change in the policy and functioning of the government

> ... which, under the impact of economic globalisation, abdicates its social obligations towards the citizenry smoothly and without opposition, i.e. it ignores demands to ensure that everyone receives fair remuneration and it has discarded society security, full employment and equal participation in public life. It does, however, wish to justify its existence, so it willingly assumes the role of a sheriff, who merely protects us from gangsters, terrorists, unwanted guests from other parts of the world, and 'foreigners', who threaten to spoil our special home-grown ambiance. In this way, by abandoning any aspirations of planning for the common good in the socio-economic sphere, the government eagerly reshuffles its 'public security' concerns and activities to once more give pride of place to 'law and order'. The upshot of this rearrangement of priorities is that issues such as 'fighting crime', 'ensuring public safety' and 'putting the Criminal Code in order' have assumed increasing importance in political discourse and election campaigns as well as in the activities of government departments. (Żuk 2010, p. 127)

This description generally applies to every post-modern society but is particularly appropriate to the Polish situation.

Chapter 6
Justice and Its Many Faces

Beata Czarnecka-Dzialuk and Paulina Wiktorska

How Should a Criminal Be Treated? Fundamental Criminological Paradigms

> There are few social phenomena that resist academic study as much as crime and punishment. Our knowledge … is still not far removed from the earliest human reflections of crime being the product of a defective nature and an ill will and of punishment being retribution for inflicting wrong. This simple philosophy of crime and punishment has proven to be quite durable in the history of social thought. (Falandysz 1986, p. 5)

The classical approach to the meaning and substance of criminal punishment and to the need to treat criminals in a specified manner, likewise present in contemporary criminological thinking, does not exhaust the broad spectrum of solutions that have been proposed to date. It is possible to be more or less a supporter of the assumptions underlying individual conceptions, but due credit has to be paid to their contribution to the development of criminology as an academic discipline and to the importance they have for the methods now being proposed to treat individuals who violate legal norms.

The primary dichotomy in the approach to a perpetrator of crime has its origins in the dispute over the deterministic and non-deterministic conceptions of the individual (Krajewski 1994). The first posits that a human being is a free individual fully responsible for the choices he/she makes. The second, per contra, is predicated on the assumption that nothing a person does is ever exclusively an expression of his/her individual will, as his/her actions are determined by certain factors to varying degrees. Some of these are inherent and others are to be found in the world around the individual. This controversy is now considered to be essentially outmoded and no longer valid. This is not to say, however, that adherents of one or the other approach have completely given up raking over extreme argumentation. Non-determinists are mostly identified with supporters of the classical school of criminal law, as opposed to the exponents of the positive school, who subscribe to the deterministic conception of the human individual.

The classical approach on treating perpetrators of crime was based on the conception of a person as a free and rational individual, who makes fully conscious and completely unfettered choices. As a result, a choice between good and evil, or obeying the law and crime, is not determined by anything other than the decision of the individual, who should therefore take full responsibility for the consequences of his/her choice.

> The classical approach practically never considered the possibility that crime could be conditioned, either socially or individually. This would have implied various kinds of nuances to do with degree of liability and diversity of treatment. … It was assumed that every criminal had the same capability to resist temptation as anyone else and that they therefore all deserved the same penalty. … Everyone was to endure a punishment that would infringe his rights and freedoms to the same extent that the crime he committed infringed the rights and freedoms of others. (Radzinowicz 1966, pp. 8–10)

The fitting penalty for committing a crime should be retributive, just, commensurate with the crime and inescapable. It should effectively deter both the perpetrator and any potential members of the public from engaging in crime. Finally, the suffering it causes should exceed any benefits and advantages the perpetrator obtained through committing the crime.

The more progressive Enlightenment thinking of the mid-nineteenth century challenged this approach to crime and reacting to it. It was postulated that social problems should only be studied using the methodological accomplishments of the natural sciences. As a result, both the individual and the world began to be perceived in clear deterministic categories and every event in terms of cause and effect. The focus was on discovering and formulating the general laws that governed social phenomena (Szacki 1983, pp. 258–9). Perpetrators of crime could no longer be treated as free and rational individuals making unfettered choices in coming to specific decisions under this understanding of positivism. Rather, an individual had to be treated as a being whose conduct was driven by precisely defined causes that were beyond his/her control and even awareness. The spectrum of these possible causes had to be understood very broadly. The positivist school stressed the significance of determinants of biopsychological origin, such as anthropological, genetic, genealogical and personality traits, as well as characteristics having their source in the social world, such as social structure, cultural diversity, the strength of social control, and the mechanisms of learning social behaviour (Błachut et al. 1999, p. 91). The foregoing assumptions imply that the scope for burdening individuals with responsibility for actions that are not the outcome of conscious choice but to a greater or lesser extent determined are severely restricted. In this light, applying criminal sanctions, as classically understood, would not only be mistaken but harmful to individuals. Retributive punishment should therefore be replaced with interaction and correction, and this in turn should be as individualised as possible and tailored to the perpetrator of the crime, not commensurate with the crime itself.

The classical and positivist theory on approaching perpetrators of crime and establishing penalties is sometimes simplified and brought into the dispute between criminal law and criminology. 'The fundamental criminal law principle that criminal liability only enters the picture when the perpetrator had the option of choosing to behave other than criminally is irreconcilable with the criminological conception of a criminal as an individual whose behaviour is in some way conditioned' (Krajewski 1994, p. 26).

It has to be borne in mind, however, that the two conceptions of treating perpetrators of crime presented here are the oldest but by no means the only ones. The third criminological paradigm, which attempts to explain the phenomenon of criminality and suggest the most appropriate means of responding to its prevalence in society, is a movement, and perhaps a direction, known as antinaturalism. This had played itself out (as had classicism earlier) as a way of analysing criminality by the middle of the twentieth century. Advanced social labelling and social conflict theories, and radical, critical, phenomenological and even extreme abolitionist theories have begun to assume a leading role in explaining this phenomenon (Błachut et al. 1999, p. 50). All these positions are linked by neutrality towards values, an adoption of the research methodology of humanistic psychology and a preference for qualitative analysis over quantitative measurements. Antinaturalist criminology grew out of a conflicting vision of society. It was built on an interactionist genesis of crime and attempts to determine how to 'reactively' answer the questions of why some actions, but not others, are considered criminal and why some people, but not others, merit the appellation 'criminal'. This has led to a complete upheaval in criminological concerns. Attention has been drawn away from the perpetrator and the act itself to the 'social auditorium' and the control mechanisms it applies, and the labelling of nonconformists, among whom it has been seen fit to include criminals.

The mechanisms for shaping human personality (including the personality of the criminal perpetrator) are based on the 'looking-glass self', which the antinaturalists have borrowed from Charles Horton Cooley (Cooley 1964). From here, rejecting the basis of correction, which aims to reintroduce the criminal perpetrator into society, is only a couple of steps away. 'Deviation and deviant should be appreciated, i.e. accepted for what they are … they have the right to be different and to radical non-intervention' (Błachut et al. 1999, p. 143). It is worth recalling three names at this juncture. The first is Ken Kesey, who wrote *One Flew Over the Cuckoo's Nest* (1962), a novel that affirms 'differentness' or, to put it better perhaps, 'exceptionalness'. The second is Erving Goffman and his term 'total institution', which brilliantly describes the penal institution, which until then had constituted the basic remedy in combating criminals (Goffman 2006). It was, however, ineffective. This is because the totality of prison undermines its correctional impact, mainly by breaking down the barriers that partition the fundamental areas of human life and lead to the deterioration of the personalities of its 'wards'. Finally, the third name is Michel Foucault, who ventured to state that the postulates of humanising the management of a perpetrator of crime and subjecting him/her to correctional supervision in a closed institution were nothing more than a cover for the modern 'microphysics' of power. The only new thing that would dissociate twentieth-century communities from mediaeval methods of approaching perpetrators of crime is the fact that from being an art of unbearable sensations punishment has become an economy of suspended rights (Foucault 1978, p. 11).

New ideas on treating criminal perpetrators that were consistent with these intellectual trends had to make their appearance in criminology. Nils Christie has called for a response to crime that would assume a more consensual character, based on negotiating, mediating, repairing damage and remedying harm (Christie 2004a). This is based on the hypothesis that crime is a particular form of social conflict that the government has appropriated without reason or justification. Christie's abolitionist views (subscribed to uncritically by some, criticised resolutely by others) have led to new ways of responding to the conduct of a criminal perpetrator in many systems of criminal law. Jim Consedine next proposed a 'compensatory' rather than a 'retributive' response to crime. The central question in a retributive system is how the offender should be punished. In a compensatory system, the question becomes how to remedy the loss or damage inflicted by the offender (Consedine 2004).

Martin Wright in turn demanded that justice should restore loss of respect (Wright 2005). Wright pointed to the general approval of inflicting violence in the name of justice and enforcing respect for the law, and stressed that repeated recidivism on the part of so many individuals belies the assertion that the law is respected and obeyed.

It is worth mentioning here that the repercussions of a remedial approach to crime and responding to its perpetrators remains clearly etched in modern criminological thinking, although it has obviously come in for some strong criticism from the founders of various neoclassical theories. The originators of these theories hark back, more or less directly, to non-deterministic conceptions of the individual, following the thinking of Cesare Beccaria and Jeremy Bentham.

The critical trend towards criminality in the antinaturalistic paradigm incorporated the concept of just retribution, the economic theory of criminality and the routine activities perspective (Błachut et al. 1999, pp. 171–88). Andrew von Hirsch's concept of just retribution mostly criticised the different treatment of perpetrators of similar acts, i.e. that the size of the penalty does not depend on what was done but on who did it. The originator of the theory also criticised resocialisation as forcing criminals to be happy, which contravenes the autonomy of the individual. The economic theory of criminality made use of ideas employed in economics to analyse market behaviour, the assumption being that all behaviour, including criminal behaviour, could be analysed in terms of supply and demand. The individual was held to be rational by nature and would therefore only commit a crime if he/she had determined that the expected gains outweighed the losses incurred beforehand. This restored the idea that punishment should mostly be a deterrent and be sufficiently severe to convey the message that 'crime does not pay'. The routine activities perspective, on the other hand, explained the occurrence and extent of criminality through the prism of the 'supply of opportunities for crime'. This is constantly changing, depending on all sorts of circumstances. The dwindling informal social control mechanisms have caused more and more activities to be transferred to institutions exercising formal control, thereby overloading and weakening them. Fighting and preventing crime in this sense would seem to be possible with the support of revitalised informal social control mechanisms (Błachut et al. 1999, pp. 174–87).

Theories closely connected to the idea of retributive justice were likewise fairly popular at the turn of the twenty-first century (and remain so). The phrase 'just retribution' has replaced the milder 'principle of proportionality' with no concessions to advanced modern society (Królikowski 2005, p. 7). This actually concerns the same assumptions about penalisation, but interpreted in the light of new social conditions, i.e. abandoning correctional measures in favour of punitive ones, which are understood to be completely legitimate and appropriate methods of responding to criminality. The penal suffering meted out to the perpetrator should be retrospective and correspond to the degree of culpability of the crime. Contemporary retributivism was borne of an unrelenting criticism of restorative justice, deeming it justice denied in that it is 'ultimately tantamount to the satisfaction of the individual, subject to particularisms, and divorced from any general rules or laws' (Królikowski 2006, p. 123).

The current controversy between the adherents of restorative justice and contemporary 'advanced' retributivism seems to have replaced the erstwhile dispute between determinists and non-determinists. This is a hard fought contest but perhaps one that does not require resolution. The claims that the contemporary penal system cannot rely on the assumptions of only one of these opposed theories of punishment, especially the concept of retribution (or, as some prefer, the principle of proportionality), seem convincing (Daly 2000, pp. 35–8). Modern punishment should be understood as a holistic reaction. It cannot be exclusively respective, but must also, perhaps most importantly, be directed towards the future. Only a future perspective can make development – social, legal and any other – possible. Contemporary societies seem unable to return to the traditional retributive approach to the penal system, just as they seem unable to bring back capital punishment or mutilation (Tonry 2011).

David Garland argues that the penal system should be treated in a multifaceted and holistic manner, as it is definitely one of the most import aspects of the social structure (Garland 1990). The concept of criminal punishment can be understood as a consequence of social solidarity combined with various interdependencies between individuals striving to ensure mutual safety and order. Punishment is simultaneously a tool of power and dominion, a certain technique to exercise supervision and control over the observance of generally approved rules and principles. It is also deeply rooted in culture and customs and often assumes an added mystical and religious dimension. It is a peculiar expression of social sensitivity, punitiveness and tolerance. Finally, it is a certain form of social assistance offered to, or forced on, individuals who refuse to behave in a socially appropriate manner (Garland 1990).

The once sharp academic divisions on the issue of how to approach and react to crime have become blurred. The most topical issues related to the functioning of the justice system at present are those connected with current and future criminal policy, to which penal populism poses a serious threat (Warylewski 2010, pp. 97–8).

> There is currently no agreement to what populism actually is – an ideology, a political movement or perhaps a manner of pursuing a policy or a normal political strategy. Populism, as generally understood, has most often been seen pejoratively as a simplified way of depicting social reality in order to garner the support of the less educated part of society or marginalised social groups. (Przyłęcki 2012, p. 14)

There can be no doubt, however, that penal populism is manifested in

> unthinking and ad hoc legislative initiatives that completely ignore the experience of practitioners and scholarly works on what is known about how legal rules function in this area. Rules created in this manner are incompatible with the fundamental human rights standards grounded in the civilisational attainments of our culture. They are based on the populist assumption that there is a simple relationship between the severity of the criminal law and its social effectiveness, which displays a complete ignorance of both academic findings and the experience of other countries.[1]

Penal populism is especially dangerous when it creeps into the political area and 'fighting crime' becomes a basic electoral tool (Rzeplińska 2010, pp. 195–201). Certainly a postmodern society, or perhaps its would be better put nowadays as a society subject to rapid change or a 'society in the era of liquid modernity' (Bauman 2007b) (even the term 'postmodernity' is starting to sound a little dated), makes us once more (and this will certainly not be the last time) examine our approach to the perpetrator of crime, our reaction to it, and the reinstating of a disturbed harmony and order, or social 'cleanness', the striving for which presupposes 'displacing things, settling them somewhere other than where they would have nestled themselves, without the intervention of human volition – without pushing, pulling, prodding, coaxing, encouraging or compelling …' (Bauman 2007a, p. 120). Where are we today in this 'displacement' of difficulties that do not fit the Baumanesque cleanness, i.e. when it comes to criminality, for which our contemporaries are striving? What stage are we at? Between punitiveness and prevention? Between retribution and restorative justice? Will we be able to formulate a rational vision of how to resolve the social problems associated with criminality for a society subject to rapid social change in which we have come to function?

Justice as Understood in the Criminal Law

Continuing the topic 'what shall we do with criminals' or how to 'judge them justly' we cannot find an easy answer. The concept of justice is not at all clear and obvious. Nor is it immutable, even though this is a

1 Resolution of the National Convention of the Department of Substantive Criminal Law, Szklarska Poręba, 24–27 September 2008.

fundamental ethical and legal concept. The evolution of justice has come to be seen as a natural occurrence connected with social changes and ethical systems (more on this below). Dictionary definitions are not all that clear and satisfactory, when they claim that justice is 'fairness, integrity, detachment, objectivism' (Doroszewski 1996–1997). Justice denotes a quality attributed to individuals, activities or social institutions, and is most often associated with ethnical virtues (Plato considered justice one of the most important ethical virtues (Plato, *The Republic*), an equitable distribution of goods or a levelling of 'accounts' – punishing or compensating losses (Aristotle distinguished between distributive and redistributive justice) and/or fairness (developed by John Rawls 1971). Justice is generally taken to mean applying the same moral yardstick to everyone and treating everyone equally, fairly and in accordance with the ethical norms to which the judges subscribe. Herman Bianchi demonstrates that justice is an ethical and legal concept and that law should not be separated from ethics, as abuses would easily follow (Bianchi 1994).

Justice is therefore secondary to ethics and the primitiveness of ethics affects the variability in the comprehension of justice. The reference point changes – there are different ethical systems and these are likewise subject to change. Fattah points to the lack of a universal definition and presents a series of questions: is there any such thing as absolute or divine justice? Is it a biological instinct, a psychological imperative, an internal need or an innate longing? Is justice a timeless and universal concept? Do different cultures share common elements in their understanding of what justice is? Is justice a teleological concept, a philosophical idea or simply a legal concept? Is it abstract or concrete? Is it an existing and measurable thing? (Fattah 2012, pp. 11–12).

John Rawls distinguishes the idea of justice, understood as the right balance of competing claims, and the concept of justice, i.e. the set of related principles that indicate the considerations that define this balance. The idea of justice is defined by the role its principles play in assigning attributes to laws and obligations and in specifying an equitable distribution of social benefits. The concept of justice is the interpretation of this role (Rawls 1971).

Justice can also be interpreted as the negation of injustice, a concept that seems to precede the notion of justice. Primitive societies had no conception of crime and their response to an act that offended generally accepted mores was more an answer to injustice (not yet to crime) (Bauman 2000, p. 88 discussing views of Barrington Moore Jr).

The following words of Leszek Kołakowski are worth pondering:

> Writing on these topics ... they pointed out that justice is often understood simply as a general term for moral good; a just person is a respectable person, a just deed is something that has to be done in that situation according to moral rules, and to proceed justly is to proceed according to a binding moral code. The notion of justice, however, is of little use within such an all-encompassing meaning. There is also a variety of moral codes: here there is the demand for retribution, there a call for forgiveness .... Some say that progressive taxation is unjust, others that banning the ownership of firearms is .... According to the ancient expression, it would be just to give everyone their due. But how are we to know what everyone is due .... But what the spirit of the world actually expects from us is not so much justice but kindness to our fellow human beings, friendship and compassion, i.e. those qualities that cannot be derived from justice. (Kołakowski 2003, pp. 260–66)

There are many and varied definitions of generic justice in the legal philosophical literature. Justice can be identified with the legitimacy of actions in the context of positive rights, with proceedings determined by natural law and with actions undertaken for the general good (Ziembiński 1996, p. 11 citing Bird 1967, pp. 3–5 and 33–5). Various categories of justice have been differentiated, in particular substantive, formal and procedural (Gmurzyńska 2011, pp. 1669 ff. and the views of Majka quoted there). The discourse on the proper allocation of goods, i.e. distributive justice, has dominated the debate for centuries. This has led to the development of philosophical theories that reflect particular societies and political systems. Nowadays, more weight is placed on the role of fair procedure, i.e. the idea of procedural fairness, in achieving justice. John Rawls, who developed the idea of procedural justice defines justice as 'the first virtue of social institutions' and the main idea is justice as fairness (Rawls 1971, p. 3).

Borucka-Arctowa (1988, p. 19) believes that isolating procedural justice is apt, given the lack of a uniform theory of justice, and the numerous conceptions and criteria for a just and equitable distribution of goods: 'as it is easier to agree on procedure than on the notion of distribution'. Apart from that, studies show that procedural justice has an enormous influence on how justice is generally perceived. Proper procedures and the just treatment of litigants have more influence than the outcomes of cases (Lind and Tyler 1988, p. 42; Deutsch et al. 2006, p. 47). In law, the concept of justice helps shape the legal response, including the penalty, and the way it is assessed, i.e. whether a determination was fair and equitable (Peno 2009, p. 152). The fundamental issues for the penal system (how crime is to be construed, how far the boundaries of criminality are to extend, and to whom, for what purpose, and in whose name punishment is to be administered) are determined by the prevailing views on society, the individual and the state in a given society, as is the form of the relationship between the citizenry and the authorities (Królikowski 2005, p. 155). This is a two-way process. The penalty is shaped by a variety of cultural patterns, and at the same time shapes how it is interpreted locally and affects the values and sensitivities that contribute to the emergence of the dominant culture (Garland 1990, p. 249).

It has to be admitted that there is no absolute justice, e.g. when only one of the apprehended joint perpetrators is punished or only the perpetrator of a detected crime. Innocent people are sometimes punished as well. Punishment additionally depends on a subjective evaluation and may be considered too severe or too lenient.

Anna Markwart has shown that in a rapidly changing world, where the issue of condign punishment for criminals is a constantly recurring theme in the media, we have to ask ourselves repeatedly: What is a just punishment? What are its most important aims? What values should be paramount? Justifying punishment is not a trivial issue either. The question of what the aims of punishment are and what makes it just, and whether this justice can be reconciled with other values that should be taken into account when deciding punishment remains open. Do we have to ask ourselves this in every judgement and in every discussion on whether to make penalties more severe or more lenient? (Markwart 2010, p. 704).

Applying the norms of the criminal law should satisfy the community's sense of justice, although it does not always do so. The idea of a 'sense of justice', as with justice itself, is complicated and evolving. Wojciech Załuski defines it as one of the innate, natural cognitive dispositions that make up the motivating factor to behave in accordance with legal rules. He distinguishes two forms of the sense of justice: rudimentary, i.e. biological adaptation; and authentic, arising as a result of social study. Załuski shows that jealousy and the instinct for retribution demonstrated by Sigmund Freud and Frans de Waal lie at the bottom of our primal sense of justice (Załuski 2009, pp. 137, 148 ff.). The rudimentary sense of justice determines not only the expectation of what portion of goods we should receive but also motivates us to punish those who frustrate these expectations. It therefore functions on a corrective as well as a material level. According to Załuski, this instinct for revenge seems to be a product of natural selection. Administering punishment to the perpetrators of immoral treatment is evolutionarily beneficial to their victim, as this retributive behaviour sends a clear signal to these and other potential perpetrators that this victim will not be so easily exploited in future (Załuski 2009, p. 149).

A sense of justice shared by the members of a community plays a fundamental role in the strength of the social system (Rawls 1971, p. 462). The presence or absence of an ability to possess a sense of justice is a key consideration in Rawls's theory of justice as fairness (1971, p. 513).

It is shown that justice is one of the roles fulfilled by the criminal law (Marek 2010b, p. 8). This was historically the first of its functions and its essence lies in satisfying the sense of justice of the person wronged by a crime, as well as his/her family and various social groups, by punishing the perpetrator. The classical and neo-classical schools of criminal law, which hold that criminal punishment should be above all a just payment for committing a crime, especially refer to the justice function, whose primacy was also argued for by Immanuel Kant and Georg Wilhelm Hegel. Kant claimed that punishment for crime was the result of a categorical (moral) imperative, whereas for Hegel, punishment was a logical consequence of crime, which was an absolute negation of the idea of law – punishment, by negating the crime, reinstated the idea of law (Budyn-Kulik et al. 2009, p. 26).

The question of how to take the social dimension of crime into account therefore arises when considering a just response to crime. This is a political tool, a prerogative of the state and an instrument for the protection of the common good. A hundred and twenty years ago, Imre von Liszt claimed that we should examine crime as a social phenomenon and punishment as a social function, so that we can predict the effectiveness of punishment with scientific precision in order to protect legal interests and prevent criminality. Punishment has to be useful to society but it is not the creation of an individual, extra-social consciousness and has no application outside society. Everything that concerns it, including who punishes whom, for what, to what extent, in what form and also the intentions and aims of inflicting the punishment, has a predominant social dimension (quoted by Bałandynowicz 2000, p. 19). Punishment has to compensate society for damage sustained but it also contributes to its welfare, both by rehabilitating the convicted person and by indirectly educating others and even deterring them from committing crimes. Claus Roxin claimed that criminal policy is obviously a social strategy when, over 20 years ago, he presented the clash between the theory of retribution (according to which punishment should be limited to suffering and its social effects disregarded) and criminal law concept of rehabilitation (Roxin 1990, p. 101). He cited inter alia the view of Hans Jescheck that the criminal justice system should be treated solely as a social assignment and the foundation of criminal policy should be a readiness to deal actively with a criminal perpetrator (Jescheck 1979, p. 1050).

Michał Królikowski believes that proportionality is the means to ensure the criminal justice system has a just purpose. This requirement is relatively independent of the generally accepted view on social order. Proportionality of punishment, as an ethical condition and one that arises from a specific philosophy of the individual and society, is essential in a contemporary democratic state, where an 'ethical discourse between free moral subjects' is assured. Proportionality makes administering punishment a stable procedure. At the same time, it requires the changing social judgement that actually accompanies social transformations to be taken into account when judging the seriousness of a crime (Królikowski 2005, p. 164). David Garland has shown that there is more to creating a penal policy than deciding how to deal with a group of people on the margins of society (whether to deter, correct or neutralise them) or simply using the authorities or economic resources for punishment. In this manner and at the same time, we define ourselves and our society, so that it can even be the central issue for our culture and political identity (Garland 1990, p. 276).

A constant return to the issue of proportionality and retribution has been observed for many years. Fattah is strongly opposed to retribution and regrets that it is still the key sentencing principle, and that judges are persisting in their futile efforts to make the punishment fit the crime. He illustrated this by saying that if Beccaria could be brought back to life, he would be amazed to see how little had changed since his day. The criminal justice system has become archaic, both philosophically and as a tool, and has remained insulated from all the progress and changes of modern society. For whatever reason, he resisted all attempts of change and modernisation, and was loathe to reject the idea of atonement and repentance for sins in favour of reconciliation and compensation (Fattah 2012, p. 15). The penal response is based on imprecise, abstract and subjective ideas such as justice (as discussed above). Fattah enumerates over 30 'types of justice' mentioned in the criminological and penal literature (Fattah 2012, p. 11). Analysing them (curiously, the accompanying adjectives are explained; it is as if the concept of justice is self-explanatory), however, is not the most important thing (Fattah 2002, p. 312). There is a desperate need to move from philosophical abstraction to remedial action, from senseless retribution to meaningful restitution, and from just retribution to restorative justice, although in view of its limitations, the last-mentioned is no panacea for the problems of administering justice (Fattah 2012, p. 71).

It is worth recalling one of the formulations of Kant's categorical imperative: 'Act in such a way as to treat the humanity whether in your own person or in that of anyone else, always as an end and never merely as a means' (Kant 1785, p. 29). When this injunction is applied to the administration of justice, it is clear that it should be humane and should be worthy of human dignity – that of the giver and receiver of the punishment. The slogan could be then 'judge humanely and punish humanely'.

As already mentioned, in the beginning, compensation of damages was the major component of any response to acts that now qualify as crimes, although vengeance was a basic factor as well. In Europe, the punitive system of controlling crime began to take shape in the early twelfth century and was a fully formed system of 'severe public repression' based on a philosophy of suffering by the mid-eighteenth century (Bianchi 1994, p. 15). This still invokes a sense of anomie, which Herman Bianchi has shown to be understood as a lack of rules to underpin social interactions. Here, this would mean a feeling of not being involved in personally experiencing the law. The law is applied mechanically, through the agency of institutions, and without the involvement of the parties concerned. This increases feelings of powerlessness and dissatisfaction. In a punitive system, the legitimacy of the rules is made known through frightening examples of the consequences of breaking the law. Meanwhile, psychologists argue that punishment most often breeds defiance, not repentance. People exhibit a natural tendency to avoid conflict as quickly as possible. The punitive system, however, makes that impossible. Bianchi proposes an alternative, consensus system, based on eunomy (conscious participation), which would have rules that would let people resolve their conflicts and overcome the feelings of alienation they invoke. In contrast to a repressive system, this does not view criminals as enemies that have to be fought and ostracised, but seeks to find resolutions with them. A eunomic system does not ignore the interests of those wronged but seeks opportunities for reconciliation. This is an educational system, that is persuasive about the legitimacy of reason and that gives the perpetrator an opportunity to expiate his/her guilt permanently in a manner that does not strip him/her of his/her dignity (Bianchi 1994, pp. 49–69), aimed to respond positively to the harm caused by the crime, remedy the wrong inflicted, reconcile the perpetrator and the victim, and achieve a consensus (Zalewski 2006, p. 181). The importance of the community and its participation in the integration or reintegration of social norms has to be taken into consideration.

John Braithwaite points out that the psychological literature demonstrates that people do not behave in accordance with the law out of fear of punishment or even shame but simply because criminal conduct is repugnant to them. Most serious crimes are unthinkable to most people by dint of the consciousness of evil they acquire as they grow up. This restrains adults from doing wrong far better than any punishment. Braithwaite writes that for most people the punishment of their own mind is more painful than that of the criminal justice system. The sanctions imposed by their friends, family and community also seem to have a greater effect on criminal behaviour than those of faceless legal authorities (Braithwaite 1989, p. 72).

The punitive model of responding to crime has been developed over a period of centuries. It has been supported by any number of theories, streamlined in terms of effectiveness and profitability, and covered in rules and regulations. But it has become increasingly divorced from the real problem. Crimes have become breaches of legal rules and not acts inflicted on specific people in specific social settings, and the response of the justice system has overlooked the interests of those actually affected. Victims of crime are the biggest losers in punitive justice systems. Personal conflicts have been moulded into public crimes and punitive measures have been substituted for restitution and dispute resolution at the expense of the interests of the victims, who have been assigned a peripheral role in judicial processes (Fattah 2011, p. 729). The crime victims' movement has become a powerful pressure group since the latter half of the twentieth century. It is active in many countries and has led to certain changes, e.g. the creation of government compensation programmes. These, however, are mostly modest as they are chronically underfunded and offer little more than token support to small groups of victims. As studies conducted abroad have shown, this sort of compensation is 'too little too late'. Even worse, those who completed government compensation programmes felt even less satisfied than those who did not (Fattah 2011, p. 724; Fattah 1999). Similar results have appeared in studies conducted in Poland over recent years.

On the basis of her studies, Lidia Mazowiecka claims that people potentially entitled to government compensation are often not aware of this option. This is attested by the small number of finalised compensation cases – only 481 in 2005–2009. The applications were returned or rejected in 65 of them and compensation granted in 152, i.e. roughly one in three. The judgements are very inconsistent in that different sums of damages are awarded for similar suffering, e.g. PLN 137–10,100 for an implant of a knocked-out tooth. Mazowiecka considers that obtaining compensation on the basis of the regulations in force not only fails to mitigate the original victimisation but is a source of secondary victimisation (Mazowiecka 2012, pp. 319 ff., 323, 335). There is, however, much more to the crime victims' movement than obtaining money. There are also efforts to obtain practical and emotional support, and especially to improve their position in criminal proceedings. A number of changes have been made to the regulations of several countries, and many of the recommendations concerning victims of crime formulated by international organisations, which were laid out in detail in the literature, have been implemented (for further details, see Bieńkowska and Mazowiecka 2009). Even if many countries, including Poland, have a series of regulations designed to strengthen the position of the victim, the main thing, however, is that these regulations are, and shall continue to be, availed of in practice, as nowadays they are not being used by victims entitled to them (Dudka 2006, pp. 288 ff.; Mazowiecka 2012, pp. 137–40). As Mazowiecka writes,

> state compensation, similarly with criminal law institutions that give the option of remedying the harm done to someone, is very seldom made use of. The explanation for this state of affairs might especially be the lack of appropriate information for victims on the possibilities of taking advantage of this institution.

And earlier:

> Studies demonstrate that, in practice, legal institutions that provide for remedying harm either do not work properly or are not made use of at all. The solutions that have been adopted are too numerous and too inconsistent for any but a few people to take advantage of them. It is not just victims who are confused, but also the bodies that administer these institutions, which get lost in a frequently changing law that does not create a consistent and coordinated system. (Mazowiecka 2012, pp. 335 and 334)

Despite the theoretical progress that has been made and the practical work that has been done, it remains extraordinarily difficult to change the perception of someone who has been harmed from a troublesome applicant wishing to exercise his/her rights to one of the central figures in the trial, whose interests require more care than statistics on finalised cases.

This would require a paradigm shift in the social response to crime, based on a different philosophy; one propounded by restorative justice, that was born of taking the views of the crime victims' movement into consideration. The basis is that interactions in society should as much as possible be voluntary. The moral, and not the punitive, aspect is what counts when responding to crime. Evil actions are to be 'paid for', not through suffering but reparation. This would show that criminals have positive attributes, help them build self-respect and facilitate their being accepted into society once more (Wright 2010, p. 17). Lawrence W. Sherman and Heather Strang state that 'while such neoclassical theory therefore centres on punishment, RJ [restorative justice] centres on persuasion. The aim of punishment is to enhance fear of further punishment; the aim of persuasion is to enhance moral support for voluntary obedience of the law' (Sherman and Strang 2007, p. 15).

Earlier publications on restorative justice readily employ the stark contrast between this and conventional penal justice. Penal (or retributive or conventional) justice is said to have viewed crime as a breach of the rights of the state, whose task was to confirm guilt and dispense suffering (i.e. penalties) by focusing on what the perpetrator deserved. Restorative justice understands crime as a breach of the rights of people and relationships. Victims, perpetrators and society are all involved in making an effort to rectify the problems by focusing on what the victim requires, and what the perpetrator needs to pay and do to make amends. In recent years, authors such as Howard Zehr have suggested that retributive and restorative justice are not polar opposites but have a great deal in common. They only differ in the way that equilibrium should be restored. They should be regarded as a continuum along which we try to advance as far as we can towards restorative practices (Zehr and Gohar 2002, p. 61).

How is justice understood in criminal cases in the Polish criminal justice system as it functions at present? How should proceedings be conducted and punishment administered in order to be 'just'? It is first necessary to examine the Criminal Procedure Act (Art. 2 § 1 Pt 1) as it is here that the aims of administering justice are laid out. This includes not only what is mentioned in CPA Art. 2 § 1 Pt 1 of this regulation/article, i.e. that 'the perpetrator of a criminal offence shall be detected and called to penal responsibility and no innocent person shall be so called', but also what is included in CPA Art. 2 § 1 Pts 2 and 3, i.e. that the aim is 'by a correct application of measures provided for by criminal law, and by the disclosure of the circumstances which favoured the commission of the offence [e.g. conflicts], the tasks of criminal procedure shall be fulfilled not only in combating the offences, but also in preventing them as well as in consolidating the rule of law and the principles of community life' and that the 'legally protected interests of the injured party shall be secured'. It can be seen that these aims coincide with those of restorative justice – finding a positive, constructive resolution to conflicts which are at the bottom and/or the result of crime is more important than punishment – i.e. administering suffering – getting all interested parties to come to an agreement on this issue. In contrast to the conventional, formalised manner of hearing cases, it has to be consensual, give a sense of affecting the situation and the settlement. Restorative justice should not then be treated as something alien to our system of administering justice. Practitioners would do well to think with restorative justice categories – broader than justice directed at retribution or mainly on rehabilitation (Czarnecka-Dzialuk 2013, p. 119).

It is becoming increasingly obvious that responding to crime is an issue that cannot be left to the various branches of the justice system so that these can later be charged with full responsibility for not having made the phenomenon disappear. Responding to criminality involves a variety of activities related to pre-emptive and diagnostic prevention, i.e. all forms of social control or activities aimed at subordinating the members of society to group norms (Błachut et al. 1999, p. 460).

It is a truism, albeit apropos here, that prevention is better than cure. Criminological works, however, still seem to be too seldom consulted in practice. This particularly concerns formulated postulates and prevention strategies, especially at the initial actions stage (Błachut et al. 1999, pp. 459 ff.). The literature has a great deal of information on different crime prevention strategies. The classification itself, however, introduces problems (Kołakowska-Przełomiec 1984, pp. 44 ff.). It is worth looking at the destructive and creative strategies. The destructive strategy takes direct action against crime in order to destroy it. This stems from a derogatory view, which holds that crime can be expunged from social life. Repressive measures are employed to wholly or partially prevent certain conduct, and to muffle it, i.e. to respond to crime with negative sanctions or the threat of them. The creative strategy stems from the view that criminality is inextricably bound with society and advocates using methods to help build the desired attitudes, aspirations and motivations, e.g. training, persuasion, instructing and transforming the environment to make it conducive to appropriate behaviour. Strategic creativity also embraces responding to criminal perpetrators in line with the above. Therefore empirical findings on the moral impact of the criminal law are interesting (Szamota-Saeki 2007–2008, pp. 203–14).

A combination of the creative and destructive strategy, where the advantages and limitations of both have been considered, is deployed in practice. It is impossible not to accede to the view that the rational solution would be to stress the creative strategy with an ancillary use of the destructive strategy, although this sometimes works out differently in practice, when the destructive strategy is shown to work more conspicuously – which does not mean more effectively – than the creative one (Błachut et al. 1999, p. 472). The most important conclusion to be drawn from analysing the advantages and limitations of each is the need to consider which combination of the two strategies is likely to yield the best result.

There is, however, a distinct dearth of preventive measures and a lack of any coherent and effective system of counteracting criminality and adverse social phenomena, including in Poland. In the end 'alternative reactions' may happen, such as the lynching of a recidivist who threatened the residents of a village with a machete. The residents, who could not wait for police assistance, despite having called several times, beat him to death.

Although the formulated response to criminality on the part of the authorities has increasingly superseded the unformulated response of individuals or groups of people (the victim, his/her or the perpetrator's family, neighbours, acquaintances etc.) over the centuries, the boundaries of these types of response remain blurred. Certain categories of problem have remained within the responsibility of extra-legal control agencies (e.g. peer courts and religious institutions), but the development of social control figures connecting local communities organising themselves in order to prevent criminality should be noted as they approximate formalised agencies of legal control (e.g. 'neighbourhood watch' groups). New forms of social control are appearing, e.g. the municipal guard. This was set up based on local government bodies and its authority is increasingly approaching that of the police force. Various kinds of uniformed services and institutions to protect property or personal safety are becoming increasingly visible. Their personnel often wear distinguishing clothes marked with words like 'security' or 'guard'.

Public places have more cameras and control gates. There are also more walled housing estates. It has becoming increasingly easy to have our freedom restricted in various ways under the banner of preventing crime and/or rendering it impossible.

Of all the different ways of responding to criminality, the formalised response of the criminal law still has the greatest application. It has been set a variety of goals, with several of them differently emphasised, depending on the views, assumptions and preferences of theories of punishment. Justice (satisfying the social sense of justice) alternates with prevention (acting on society), special prevention (acting on the perpetrator) and compensation (redress and mitigation of wrong) (Cieślak 1994, pp. 14–16).

There are, however, more and more critical voices being raised against the conventional criminal law response, especially in relation to imprisonment, which was once considered progress over cruel corporal punishments and mutilation. As mentioned above, however, nervous, and often immediate and near hysterical reactions to criminality have returned with a vengeance. The picture is distorted and ripe for manipulation at the hands of politicians.

This raises a whole series of questions. What can be done to make our reaction to crime as apposite, sensible and rational as possible? How to counter this so that it does not come down to 'punishment therapy' for a neurotic society? What social changes are necessary to make responses favouring freedom prevail? How is society to be educated on penal policy if the desired changes in attitude towards criminality are to be made and alternatives sought and accepted? In particular, how are those who administer justice to be educated?

'Ethics is a core value of the justice system. There can be no talk of justice if legal practitioners are not up to the challenges posed by professional ethics' (Dziurnikowska-Stefańska 2011, p. 59). Unfortunately, there is an apparent crisis in this area. The decline in adhesion to corporate community values on the part of people practising professions of public trust is one sign of this. This feeling has been supplanted by the idea of a professional body as a group of people with common interests (Dziurnikowska-Stefańska 2011, quoting Łabieniec 2008, p. 54). Furthermore, effectiveness and refusal to compromise have become the core values of a good lawyer and the basic criterion on which people have been selecting attorneys over recent years. Lawyers used to be referred to as knights in robes and apostles of the law. This image of a lawyer honouring the profession's good name and code of ethics, honouring parties to the proceedings, has been replaced by that of the 'aggressive lawyer', i.e. a calculating player who does not baulk at anything, not even bribery or producing fake witnesses (Dziurnikowska-Stefańska 2011, pp. 242 ff.). A study on ethical and moral attitudes towards practising law conducted among future lawyers, viz. students at the Faculty of Law and Administration at the University of Warsaw, is especially interesting. These studies were first conducted in the latter half of the 1990s and again in 2008, and comprised beginning, intermediate and finishing students. Candidates for the legal profession surveyed in the 1990s said that pragmatic effectiveness took precedence over ethical considerations in professional practice. This sparked a social and community debate on the moral fibre of lawyers. Several steps were taken to change the awareness of society and law students as a result. The 2008 studies showed that approval of a lawyer paying a bribe, at the behest of a client, to fix a case, fell from around 40 per cent to less than 10 per cent of the students surveyed. The percentage of students in favour of perjury likewise fell, although not so dramatically. This is due to more intensive operations against corruption and economic crimes by law enforcement agencies, greater stigmatisation of unethical behaviour by professional bodies representing lawyers, and the introduction of professional ethics classes in law courses. The longer these future legal practitioners had been studying, the fewer of them approved of this sort of conduct (Dziurnikowska-Stefańska 2011, pp. 244–5).

The next issue to consider is the views of the judiciary and public prosecutors on core values and ways of responding to criminality. Is the current view, that they are disinclined to accept and apply new ideas and measures, justified? Unfortunately, some findings appear to confirm this by occasionally showing the daily routine of some practitioners, their reluctance to reach out and try new ways of doing things, and their presupposition that they are not even worth investigating. Studies conducted by the Justice Institute in 2010 showed that almost 70 per cent of a group of Family Court judges who did not see any need for mediation to be more broadly applied had no personal experience in referring cases to mediation. Conversely, almost 70 per cent of those who did have mediation experience would have liked to have seen it applied more broadly. It is striking that respondents value mediation in juvenile cases and yet few of them actually use it. More than half the Family Court judges and as many as 95 per cent of curators saw a need for mediation to be more frequently used, but only 46 per cent of judges had ever referred a case to mediation and fewer than one in three curators had ever suggested it. It is worth adding that fewer than half the Family Court judges surveyed had ever referred a case to mediation (questionnaires were sent to all judges and 311 were completed, i.e. the participation rate was 26 per cent) (Czarnecka-Dzialuk and Wójcik 2011, pp. 912–16; and 2012, pp. 63–8).

Unfortunately, stating that new views and measures have been accepted does not mean they are used in practice. Apart from that, official statistics indicate that victim-offender mediation is used extraordinarily rarely. That is certainly the case with measures such as the obligation to compensate for damages or perform community work. This was ordered in a small percentage of cases, although there are convincing examples of their being used effectively, e.g. by the Family Court in Mikołów, where almost a quarter of juvenile offenders were ordered to perform social work. Around 80 per cent of these obligations were discharged and there was a noticeable educational impact (Mańka 2010; Buszko 2010, pp. 131 ff.). Most judges participating in these surveys did not declare any need to change the list of measures available against juveniles. Nor did they suggest any overly innovative proposals. The findings of other studies on Family Court judges, which attest to the perfunctory and schematic nature of sentencing, likewise give pause for thought (Woźniakowska-Fajst 2010, pp. 359 ff.; Klaus 2009a, pp. 288 ff.).

The next issue is how far society is prepared to accept new ways of reacting to criminality, especially given that consensual interactions are voluntary by nature. As already mentioned, the new paradigm is about persuading people to obey the law voluntarily. This is why it is important to acknowledge not only the views of practitioners, academics and politicians on responding to criminality, but also those of ordinary people. Opinion polls and attitude surveys conducted over the past couple of decades give some cause for hope that these new means of response might be more broadly accepted in certain situations than the current majority view in favour of severe punishment, or as Teodor Szymanowski puts it 'the myth of an allegedly severely repressive attitude towards criminal offenders on the part of society', would lead us to assume. Prior and current studies in this area have been subjected to synthetic analyses (Kaczmarek 2009, pp. 33–40; Szymanowski 2012, pp. 179–89, 301–12). Zofia Ostrihanska and Dobrochna Wójcik surveyed breaking and entering victims in two Warsaw suburbs in the 1990s and found that some respondents were more interested in having the perpetrators compensate them than seeing them put in a penal institution, and 40 per cent were capable of forgiveness, provided their possessions were recovered and they could be sure the perpetrator was not going to reoffend. More than half the respondents were of the view that the penalty could be waived so long as the damage was rectified, the stolen items were returned, and the perpetrator expressed remorse, understood the harm he/she has inflicted and promised to change (especially in the case of young people) (Ostrihanska and Wójcik 1993, p. 129). Another study in the same area has proved that 46.4 per cent of the surveyed Warsaw residents advocated waiving penalties for petty larceny, and 41 per cent for misappropriating property of little value, so long as the victims are recompensed (Bieńkowska and Wojciechowska 1993, pp. 34 ff.). After studying the issue for a couple of years, Aleksandra and Teodor Szymanowski confirmed the tendency towards a broader acceptance of the possibility of abandoning judging and punishing perpetrators who have come to an arrangement with their victims in the case of such offenses as failing to pay alimony (73 per cent), defamation in the mass media (70 per cent) and battery that only causes slight bodily harm (56 per cent) (Szymanowska and Szymanowski 1996, pp. 120 ff.).

After comparing OBOP (Centre for Public Opinion Research) studies conducted in 2002 and 2006, Teodor Szymanowski confirmed that societal attitudes in Poland on criminality and the penal response to it are becoming increasingly moderate and rational (Szymanowski 2007, p. 19). Aleksandra Szymanowska analysed the suggestions of the 2006 survey respondents on punishing the perpetrators of a variety of crimes and noted a 'distinct preference for non-isolation punishments, such as fines and community sentences, as well as mediation for the perpetrators of certain crimes'. The respondents suggested mediation instead of punishment in the case of such crimes as theft causing little damage (30 per cent), euthanasia (30 per cent), failure to pay alimony (25 per cent), robbery with little damage (23 per cent), abortion (16 per cent), bribing police officers (16 per cent) and bribing government officials (12 per cent) (Szymanowska 2008, p. 303).

Surveys on mediation conducted in Silesia a few years ago, although admittedly unrepresentative, questioned respondents on their possible inclination towards settlement in three different categories of case. 56 per cent of those surveyed were inclined to settle cases of burglary and 18 per cent to waive punishment altogether. Just over 49 per cent would have done so in the case of maliciously violating legal rights. Only 27 per cent saw any possibility of settlement in the case of causing damage to health and a mere 8 per cent would have waived punishment. These results come as no surprise. The strongest retaliatory response was for infringements of personal property rights, especially since health (just after life) was indicated as the most valuable good (Sitarz et al. 2012).

To recapitulate: it can be assumed (and cautiously hoped), that restorative measures are going to be increasingly more widely accepted in society in certain categories of case, so long as people are not persuaded by harshness and repressive attitudes to conceal their reluctance for non-routine proceedings. Monika Płatek cites the expression 'Why don't bananas grow in Kazakhstan? Because the nation is not yet ripe for it' in the context of tracking the development of mediation in Poland (Płatek 2009, p. 171).

Fattah believes that social changes in the twenty-first century will usher in a new era of politics and governance that will reveal an urgent need for a new paradigm for the criminal law and the justice system. Replacing an archaic, punitive system with a system of restorative justice will require much willpower and determination if it is going to '… reduce the pain and suffering that is being inflicted on millions of people in your name and the name of a pseudo justice' (Fattah 2012, pp. 11–12). It is going to take time to change the paradigm. It is in this context that Martin Wright declared, after receiving the Restorative Justice Prize at the 7th International Conference of the European Forum for Restorative Justice in Helsinki, 14–16 June 2012, that it took a century to abolish slavery. The new paradigm in the administration of justice has only just begun.

Chapter 7
Controlling Criminality

Irena Rzeplińska and Paulina Wiktorska

Criminal Policy, Penal Policy and Crime Control Policy

> Combating crime and its forms and methods can be understood and deliberately expanded upon once information has been obtained on the essence of the activity being fought, its causes, and perpetrators and their manner of fighting. (Wróblewski 1922, p. 1)

Criminal policy based on examining the possible ways of organising institutions charged with combating crime in order to achieve the greatest moral and material progress on behalf of the public is a new discipline that grapples with the issues involved in deliberately and rationally combating crime. So said penologist and criminal policy specialist Bronisław Wróblewski in 1922 (Wróblewski 1922, pp. 3, 11). Leszek Lernell wrote that criminal policy is a component of social policy and embraces three spheres of activity: the types of negative human behaviour it is intended to restrain; the entities charged with pursuing such activities; and the forms of activities undertaken with a view to limiting criminal occurrences (Lernell 1978, pp. 19–27).

The current criminal law textbook by Andrzej Marek defines criminal policy as the totality of actions undertaken by the state and the public with a view to either preventing or combating criminality. Part of criminal policy is penal policy, 'which is concerned with programming the fight against criminality with the assistance of penalties and other legal measures' (Marek 2007, p. 36). This encompasses the penalisation and depenalisation of human conduct, the application of penalties and other penal measures and the scheduling of their execution (Marek 2007, pp. 36–7).

Teodor Szymanowski defines criminal policy as everything that state and social entities do to prevent and counteract criminality. Penal policy is a distinct component of criminal policy that Szymanowski defines as what the courts do to counteract and curb criminality through the application of the provisions of the criminal law. This is put into effect through the decisions (sentences and judicial orders) handed down by the courts (Szymanowski 2010b, pp. 214–15).

Jerzy Jasiński, whose analyses of penal policy are classics in the annals of Polish criminology, wrote that the objective of the penal policy of the courts (and in one passage, public prosecutors as well) are the decisions, which have legal ramifications, pronouncing specific people as perpetrators of crime (Jasiński 1982, p. 26).

In criminology, social stigma was considered an important problem in the way society (including criminal law circles) responded to criminality and the institutions that formulated social control. The object of research, it made a sociological analysis of the criminal law, penalties, penal measures (i.e. the criminal law response) and institutions broadly understood as the justice system (i.e. investigative bodies and the courts) (Błachut et al. 1999, p. 22). Criminal policy fits into this analysis as the action taken by the state in shaping the criminal law (i.e. the criminalisation and decriminalisation of certain conduct) and establishing specified categories of penalties and penal measures, together with rules for administering them to perpetrators of crime, in criminal legislation. This is also where penal policy fits in. This is understood as making decisions that have legal consequences, including ordering the imposition of penalties and penal measures, and pronouncing given people as criminal perpetrators. The makeup of penal policy depends on the types of penalty (e.g. isolative or non-isolative) that are preferred in a given society at a given time. Long-term analyses of penal policy reveal that it varies considerably, as do its justifications.

Other definitions, apart from criminal policy and penal policy, have appeared in the literature over recent years, e.g. crime control policy, penal culture, crime control policy culture and the culture of control (Garland 1990, pp. ix–xii, 120, 167–92; Tonry 2007, pp. 95–6). The broadest category, which embraces the concept of criminal policy and penal policy, is criminal control policy. This describes state policy towards criminality. If the incarceration rate is used as a yardstick, this can be seen to have varied from severe to lenient over the years. Why is this? Why is it that penal policy is made harsher in some countries but not others? What do changes to penal policy tell us about the societies in which they occur? Michael Tonry writes that a harsh policy that is rationalised, justified and properly executed 'deadens us to whatever it was that made us initially perceive it as repressive and makes it easier to introduce even more repressive regulations the next time controversial issues associated with crime control policy arise' (Tonry 2007, pp. 95–6). The changes currently taking place in the area defined as the social response to criminality are being shaped by social, cultural and political factors, some of which are international (EU criminal law, European and international human rights law, UN conventions etc.), which together influence political choices and administrative decisions in societies, thereby creating a culture of crime control (Garland 1990, pp. 193–5).

How Are Criminal Policy and Penal Policy Formed in Contemporary Poland?

The main subject of this part of the chapter is penal policy in the sense of 'what the courts do to counteract and limit criminality when they apply the provisions of the criminal law' (Szymanowski 2010b, p. 215). To put it simply, this discourse can be regarded as concerning a policy of administering the respective penalties available to the perpetrators of prohibited acts deemed to be crimes. The idea of punishment is here taken to mean personal suffering inflicted on the perpetrator of a crime. It is a direct response to the commission of the crime, expresses condemnation of the crime and is administered by the state body constitutionally empowered to do so (Wróbel and Zoll 2010, p. 413). The law states that the penalty should meet the objectives of general and individual prevention and satisfy the need to shape the legal consciousness of society. Contemporary criminal law also stresses that the objective of a penalty, and in particular penal measures ordered in addition to or instead of a penalty, should be to repair the damage and compensate the person wronged by the crime (Wróbel and Zoll 2010, p. 417).

The Criminal Code of 1997 currently in force has been subjected to more than 60 amendments concerning, inter alia, the degree of punitiveness of the penal sanctions, the criminalisation or (exceptionally) decriminalisation of specified actions and the necessity of adjusting domestic legislation to meet the requirements of EU law. However, the fundamental principles on which its prescriptive content is based and which enable the application of predefined methods of responding to criminality have remained intact. The following are especially worthy of mention:

- protecting particular individuals and society as a whole from crime
- protecting the constitutional system of the state
- observing the dignity of both the perpetrators and victims of crime and abiding by humanitarian principles
- recognising that the criminal law is an ancillary measure in combating crime
- rejecting the assumption that the severity of penal repression is a precondition for effectively combating crime
- treating punishment – and especially imprisonment – as a last resort
- giving priority to non-custodial penalties and penal measures over imprisonment (*in dubio pro libertate*)
- endeavouring to redress damage in summary offences
- desisting from imposing severe penal repression of recidivists and enabling them to benefit from conditional early release
- using remand exclusively as a procedural remedy to prevent the evasion of justice
- adhering to European standards on criminal law and counteracting criminality (Szymanowski 2010b, p. 229).

Table 7.1 Crime detection rate

Year	Proceedings initiated	Confirmed crimes	Number of suspects	Detection rate (%)
2012	950,834	1,119,803	500,539	67.8
2011	981,480	1,159,554	521,942	68.7
2010	964,614	1,138,523	516,152	67.9
2009	994,959	1,129,577	521,699	67.1
2008	968,620	1,082,057	516,626	65.9
2007	1,014,695	1,152,993	540,604	64.6
2006	1,156,031	1,287,918	587,959	62.4
2005	1,235,239	1,379,962	594,088	58.6
2004	1,296,356	1,461,217	578,059	56.2
2003	1,248,082	1,466,643	557,224	55.2
2002	1,277,420	1,404,229	552,301	54.9
2001	1,275,418	1,390,089	533,943	53.8
2000	1,169,185	1,266,910	405,275	47.8
1999	1,075,869	1,121,545	364,272	45.0

Source: Police Headquarters official website, http://www.statystyka.policja.pl (accessed 10 March 2013).

The Criminal Code of 1997 did away with additional penalties, instead dividing its penal provisions into penalties and penal measures, and evincing a preference for non-custodial penalties. It is explicitly stated (CC Art. 58) that imprisonment is only to be ordered when the applicable penalty or penal measure is unable to fulfil the objective of the punishment. This principle is reflected in the new

> ... philosophy of punishment, in accordance with which the option of applying a more lenient kind of penalty should be considered in the case of being able to select the kind of penalty to be imposed. A harsher penalty should only be imposed after establishing that the penalty is not sufficient to fulfil the objectives of the punishment as specified in Article 53 of the Criminal Code. (Melezini 2010a, pp. 36–7)

The number of convictions per 100,000 people is one of the fundamental indicators that can tell us something about penal policy. This is the number of finalised court cases in which penalties or penal measures were imposed. On the eve of the constitutional and political transformation in 1989, the number of convictions was a little over 90,000 p.a. This figure rose slowly until 2000, shot up to 429,000 p.a. in 2001–2006 and then slowly began to fall once more. The number of convictions reached its highest level in 2006. At this time, there were more than four times as many male convicts and six times as many female convicts as there had been in the early 1990s (Siemaszko et al. 2009, p. 88). The strong statistical increase in criminality in 2001 is mostly explained by the penalisation of driving a motorised vehicle while under the influence of alcohol. This was upgraded from a summary offence to an indictable offence in the Criminal Code (Art. 178). The increase in the number of convictions among women compared with men might partly be explained by the changing position of women in contemporary society, assuming that this increase in the criminality of women is nothing more than the 'dark side of their liberation'.[1] Since they participate more broadly in social, economic and political life, they naturally end up being convicted of committing crimes more frequently too. An increase in recorded convictions obviously cannot be automatically translated as an increase in criminality. If the numbers

1 http://forum.gazeta.pl/forum/ (accessed 12 September 2012).

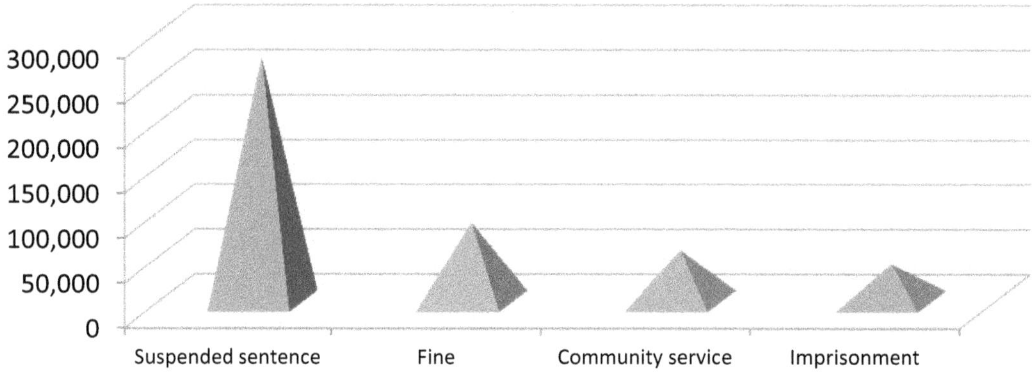

Figure 7.1 Composition of penalties imposed in Poland

of convictions for 1990, 1997 and 2008 are compared, and then crimes under Article 178a of the Criminal Code and crimes connected with drug possession under Articles 48 and 62 of the Act of 29 July 2005 on Countering Drug Addiction are removed from the 2008 convictions (categories of crime not considered in the 1990 and 1997 statistics), it turns out that criminality did not increase four times but just under three times during this period and the difference between the number of convictions in 1997 and 2008 was therefore only approximately 70,000 (Szymanowski 2010b, pp. 245–6). Add to this the fact that the crime detection rate systematically increased (see Table 7.1), and the conclusion to be drawn is that, in general, crime has clearly been falling since 2005 (Siemaszko et al. 2009, p. 12).

The most recent statistics from Police Headquarters show that a slight increase in criminality was recorded in 2011 but that it started to fall again in 2012.[2] It is worth noting that the number of the most serious crimes – i.e. homicides, rapes, robberies, burglaries – has continued its downward trend while growth has been most evident in such categories as economic crime, traffic offences, theft and damaging health. In 2012, there was a visible decrease in every category of crime and only a slight increase in theft.

It is interesting to analyse the statistical data on the specific kinds of penalties imposed. This enables certain conclusions to be drawn on penal policy as applied in Poland in the first decade of the twenty-first century. The penalties most frequently imposed were suspended sentences (272,653), then, relatively infrequently, fines (88,407) and community sentences (57,918). The courts least frequently imposed imprisonment (42,549). These data are illustrated in Figure 7.1.[3]

This composition of penalties imposed by contemporary courts essentially follows the principle of giving preference to non-custodial sentences expressed in the Code. Unfortunately, when the share of imprisonment in the makeup of every kind of penalty is examined, it turns out that it has been steadily increasing in percentage terms over the last 10–20 years. One of the consequences of this is a growing prison population. This has been exacerbated by an escalation in the practice of applying temporary detention in the early 2000s, as well as the ever restrictive rules on granting conditional early release. This criminal policy has resulted in Poland having one of the highest incarceration rates in Europe (Melezini 2007, p. 491). The number of convicts serving or waiting to serve prison terms now exceeds 45,000 per year (Lelental 2009, pp. 339–50).

There is currently a slight downward trend in the policy on degree of penalty – at least when it comes to imprisonment. It is not certain, however, whether this is due to the sentencing policy of the courts, which still adheres to the principle of giving priority to non-custodial sentences, whether prison is not a viable option in light of the overcrowding of penal institutions, or whether it is part of the general decline in criminality over recent years. The last two arguments would seem more convincing, as imprisonment has only given way to suspended sentences, not community sentences or fines (Siemaszko et al. 2009, p. 96).

2 http://www.statystyka.policja.pl/portal/st/918/Wybrane_statystyki.html (accessed 10 February 2013).

3 Statistical data for 2006 (Siemaszko et al. 2009, p. 95).

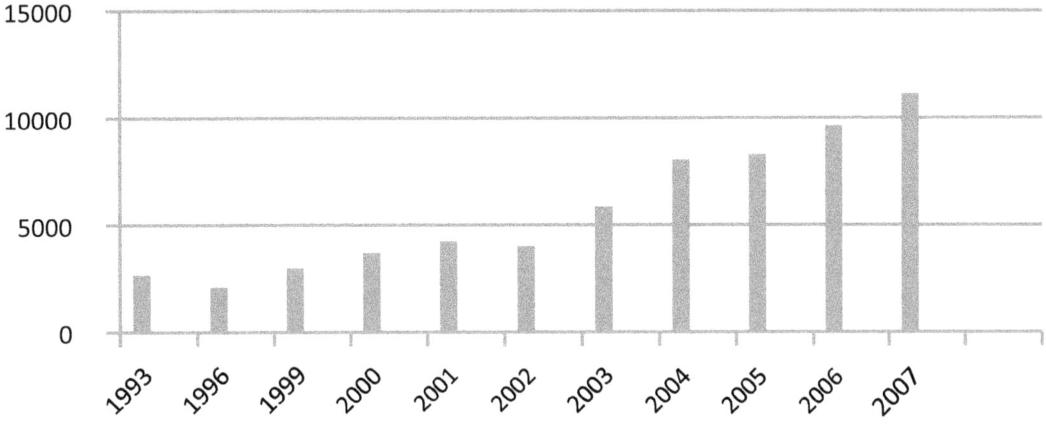

Figure 7.2 Number of prison sentences of six months or less

It is worth examining the composition of the specific penalties currently being imposed by Polish courts. To take imprisonment first, it has to be stated that the number of short sentences (six months or less) has been increasing gradually since the early 1990s. This is shown in Figure 7.2.

This increase in short sentences is probably due to the courts deciding that these are appropriate for perpetrators of crimes associated with driving a motor vehicle while under the influence of alcohol. There would be no point in ordering longer sentences with considerably more isolation, although any term of imprisonment is problematic in these sorts of cases.

The remaining sentences continued at pretty much the same level until 2004, when they increased abruptly, before starting to fall once more. This decrease is most evident in long-term sentences, i.e. over 10 years. This is shown in Figure 7.3 (Skupiński 2009b, p. 15).

Examining the harshest sentences, it can be observed that there has been an increase in sentences of 25 years or more (from 20 in 1990 to 133 in 2005) and life imprisonment (from one case in 1996 to 34 in 2005)

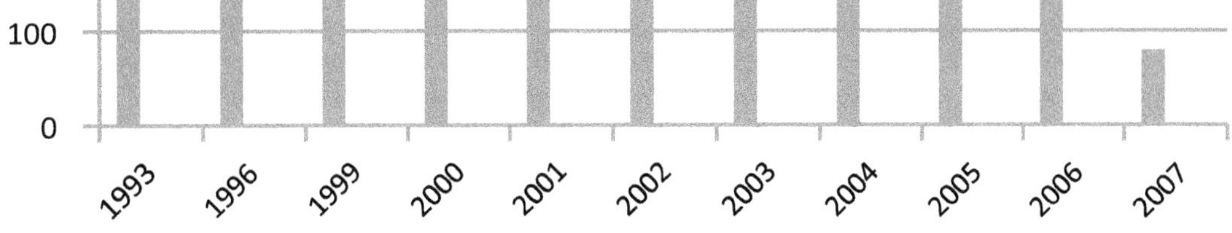

Figure 7.3 Number of prison terms of over 10 years

Table 7.2 The average length of finalised unconditional prison terms imposed on convicted adults (in months)

Year	Unconditional sentences	Suspended sentences
2003	19.4	10.3
2004	19.3	10.5
2005	18.3	10.2
2006	17.9	10.0
2007	15.8	9.8

since the 1990s. The harshest sentences are currently exhibiting a slight downward trend (Siemaszko et al. 2009, p. 97). The average prison term has gradually decreased, although not significantly. This is especially evident in the case of immediate custodial sentences. This is shown in Table 7.2 (Skupiński 2009b, p. 16).

Shortening the length of prison terms should be viewed positively, in view of everything that has so far been written about the degrading effects that serving time in prison has on the individual concerned (Goffman 2006, pp. 316–36; Ciosek 2001; Szymanowska 2003; Niełaczna 2011). On the other hand, the policy of granting conditional early release from some of the sentences has been surprising. Studies show that there was a marked drop in the number of applications for conditional early release lodged by penal establishments, and consequently the number of conditional releases being granted, in the first few years of the criminal legislation of 1997 coming into force (Wiktorska 2010). This was caused by prison administrations, not the penitentiary court, which, being legally authorised to do so, continues to decide whether, and if so how, to apply this measure. The number of conditional releases granted since 2002 has maintained an overall upward trend. This is shown in Figure 7.4. The percentage of applications given positive consideration, however, continued at a similar level of around 40 per cent.[4]

The main thing to note is that the tightening of the policy of granting conditional early release from prison observed at the turn of the twenty-first century did nothing to make this institution more effective, according to any formal legal assessment. This is because the return to crime of those conditionally released continued to remain at a similar level, according to the National Crime Record. On the other hand, the lack of appeal proceedings against decisions on granting conditional release is disturbing, as is the disparity in the few appeals court decisions that have been handed down. Unfortunately, it also happens that in justifying their 'facade' decisions, the penitentiary courts invoke arguments unsupported by the Code, e.g. general preventive considerations, too distant an end of the sentence, disproportionality between the sentence imposed and that served, the particular nature of the crime, and even the non-fulfilment of the punitive function of the sentence. The individual criminological prognoses of candidates for early release authorised by the Criminal Code of 1997 have been largely ignored for some inexplicable reason. Even more problematic is that the Central Prison Service Board, in an announcement on the population of penal establishments dated 27 July 2012, proudly stressed that penitentiary establishments were starting to become 'unquartered', because their 'occupancy rates' had fallen to an average of 98.6 per cent.[5] When the detailed statistics for particular penitentiary establishments are examined, however, it turns out that many of them are still overpopulated and that free places are often in remand centres, women's establishments and diagnostic centres. Moreover, the Minister of Justice gave assurances that, as a result of capital expenditure, the country had obtained 1,318 new cells and that it had to be borne in mind that, by any statistical measure, crime had been falling continuously over the previous few years.[6] What we see here might not be so much the product of a rational criminal policy as the result of what Loïc Wacquant has courageously described as the 'growth of the prison industry'

4 http://sw.gov.pl/pl/o-sluzbie-wieziennej/statystyka/statystyka-roczna/ (accessed 14 March 2013).

5 Announcement available on the official website of the Central Prison Service Board at www.sw.gov.pl.

6 Interview with Justice Minister Krzysztof Kwiatkowski (2009–2011), in *Forum Penitencjarne*, vol. 14, no. 153 (February 2011).

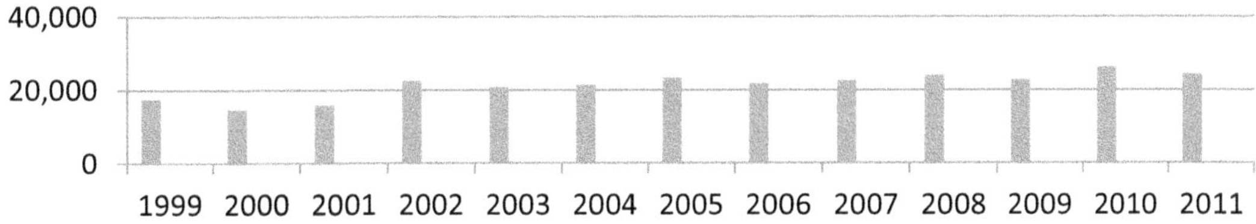

Figure 7.4 Number of conditional early releases granted in absolute figures

(Wacquant 2009). In view of the foregoing, further restricting the conditions for early release does not appear to be the best idea for the additional reason that this institution is one of the most essential regulators of the still sizeable prison population. The fewer the inmates, the greater the possibility of meeting international standards on implementing imprisonment, the more effective the work on socially readapting convicts and, finally, the greater the chance of ensuring adequate working conditions for prison service personnel.[7] These last complain about e.g. staff shortages, performing tasks outside the scope of their duties, excessive bureaucracy, feeling a sense of injustice from managerial sensitivity to the rights of inmates with no regard to the realities of the service or the conditions inside penitentiary establishments, and the inadequacy of the classes and training programmes proposed for convicts in meeting the very real requirements associated with their social readaptation (Pomiankiewicz 2011). The necessity for a radical change to penal policy in this area is emphasised.

> There are people in prison today who did not have to end up there. It should be reserved for really dangerous people who have committed serious crimes and need to be isolated. Drunken cyclists, of which there are several thousand, do not necessarily have to finish up in prison. This is the pathology of our system.[8]

Prison sentences can be served under the normal system, with a planned activity programme, or with a therapeutic programme, but in general, only the last two enable any sort of rehabilitative work with the convict. Statistics from December 2011 show that most convicted inmates in closed penal establishments serve their sentences under the normal system, somewhat fewer with a planned activity programme and fewest of all with a therapeutic programme.[9] A planned activity programme was ordered for virtually all adolescents, a little less than 50 per cent of first-time offenders and around 50 per cent of recidivists.[10] An average of 10 per cent in each of these groups was given a therapeutic interaction programme when serving their sentences. Inmates of half-open penal institutions in December 2011 were most often serving their sentences with a planned activity programme, slightly less often under the normal system and most rarely with a therapeutic programme. Adolescents are definitely put in a planned activity programme most frequently, with first-time offenders and recidivists somewhat less frequently. However, in view of the specificity of open establishments, most convicts are included in planned activities. This tendency is even more noticeable in open penal establishments, where virtually all the inmates serve their sentences with a planned activity programme, very few of them under the normal system, and hardly anyone with a therapeutic interaction programme. All adolescent inmates, and a decided majority of the rest, are given a planned activity programme when serving their sentences. It might be assumed, then, that rehabilitative work and preparing inmates for freedom would be most effective in these establishments. When that is contrasted with what the convicts say about the benefits of serving time with a planned activity programme, however, it turns out that only a negligible percentage mention being

---

7 This especially concerns Recommendation Rec (2006) 2 of the Committee of Ministers to the Member States of the Council of Europe on European Prison Regulations (adopted by the Council of Ministers on 11 January 2006 in a session of 952 delegates).

8 A. Zoll in conversation with A. Łukaszewicz, 'Sady zbyt często zawieszają wyroki', *Rzeczpospolita*, 11 March 2013.

9 Statistics available on the Central Prison Service Broad webpage www.sw.gov.pl (accessed 4 June 2012).

10 Pursuant to Art. 95 of the Criminal Code, adolescents obligatorily serve their prison sentences with a planned activity programme.

prepared for freedom. The majority see this way of serving their sentences as completely lacking in any benefits except as a means to obtaining passes, conditional early release or employment (Szymanowska 2003, p. 189). It should be added that the social and living conditions in parts of penitentiary establishments are still very difficult (Niełaczna 2011). It has to be said that representatives from the European Committee for the Prevention of Torture and Inhuman or Degrading Treatment or Punishment (CPT) have been visiting Polish penal establishments for the past 10–20 years, and while there are still problems, every inspection has resulted in a higher assessment of the way imprisonment is administered (Wągiel-Linder 2011, p. 20). Some of the more serious issues include overpopulation and, as previously mentioned, the inadequacy of the occupational courses and training sessions that are offered to meet the demands of the contemporary labour market. This comes very close to stating that prison unfortunately does more to isolate and unteach responsibilities than it does to enable conduct to be improved, raise social capital and help people released from isolation with the difficulties of readapting to a society subject to constant change. The lack of ideas on how to administer imprisonment effectively, which may not have any future, has prompted a search for alternatives.

If not imprisonment, then what? A simple solution that automatically suggests itself is to 'threaten' imprisonment, i.e. applying a penal sanction in the form of a custodial sentence that is conditionally suspended. This is the most popular penal measure in Polish penal policy, although it is not necessarily the best (Jakubowska-Hara 2009b, p. 12). This penalty comprises close to 60 per cent of all ordered and served sentences and this percentage has been gradually but steadily increasing at the expense of immediate imprisonment. This raises the question as to whether this has been due to observing the principle enunciated in the Code that preference be given to non-custodial sentences, or rather a forced side-effect of overcrowding in penal establishments, or, to go even further, a lack of ideas for a rational penal policy. Conditional sentences consume the least financial resources, require the least involvement on the part of the services responsible for enforcing penalties, and cause the least suffering to the offender while giving the public at large the impression that he/she has been punished. It appears to be the 'Weber ideal type' of avoiding responsibility in imposing penal sanctions, however, still enjoys the greatest approval among the Polish judiciary (Szacki 2002, p. 458) Pursuant to Art. 72 of the Criminal Code, the court may order the offender to comply with certain obligations envisioned in this regulation when suspending a custodial sentence. However, this option is seldom exercised in practice – only in 30 per cent of cases in recent years (Skupiński 2009a, p. 47). Fines can also be imposed in addition to conditional sentences.[11] The courts, however, only exercise this option in approximately 40 per cent of cases. Moreover, the relatively modest size of this sort of fine (most do not exceed PLN 500), renders it nothing more than a token addition to the discomfort occasioned by a conditionally suspended sentence (Jakubowska-Hara 2009a, p. 58). The essence of conditionally suspending the enforcement of this penalty is to put the offender on probation. During the probationary period, the offender may be placed under the supervision of a curator, a person worthy of trust or a social association, institution or organisation responsible for taking care of educating convicts, preventing them from being corrupted and assisting them. This supervision is mandatory for adolescent perpetrators of premeditated crimes and perpetrators convicted in cases involving repeat recidivism. It is therefore probable that supervision is mainly ordered for these groups of offenders because they do not exceed 30 per cent of cases (Skupiński 2009a, p. 50). If the offender is left without support or supervised control during the probationary period, there is little chance of him/her finding employment or taking other steps to improve his/her position, and whether the period ends on a positive note will predominantly be left to chance. The conditionally suspended sentence most often only affects the offender 'on paper'. Neither supervision nor obligations nor fines are ordered in most cases, and when such a remedy is ordered, it is very small. This creates a situation where crime goes unpunished. The only thing demanded of the offender is that he/she refrains from reoffending, which is obviously expected of all citizens, regardless of whether they have ever violated the provisions of the criminal law. It is therefore difficult to state that this penalty fulfils any individual or general preventive aims.

In this context, a suspended sentence does not seem to be an alternative to immediate imprisonment, but merely a consequence of not being able to impose it. What then might constitute a genuine alternative to imprisoning a perpetrator of a crime? Logic would suggest a community sentence. While this imposes a certain degree of discomfort on the offender by way of obligations and restrictions, it is still a non-custodial

11 Art. 71 of the Criminal Code.

sentence. For all that, however, it has been the least frequently applied penalty in Polish criminal policy over the last few years, accounting for just over 10 per cent of all penalties ordered (Jakubowska-Hara 2009a, p. 12). The essence of a community sentence is that it prohibits the offender from changing his/her permanent residence without the permission of the court, and imposes an obligation to furnish explanations during the course of the sentence and perform unpaid, supervised community work or, in the case of an employed person, have a predetermined amount deducted from his/her remuneration. As with a suspended sentence, a community sentence may be combined with the imposition of supervision and specific obligations.

The few community sentences imposed in Poland are generally limited to the shortest terms, i.e. those that do not exceed six months, and most often take the form of mandatory community work. Only very occasionally (approximately 1 per cent of cases) do they take the form of remuneration deductions. This is obviously because convicted people seldom have stable employment or the regular income that goes with it. Community sentences are most often imposed without any additional obligations (Kunicka-Michalska 2009, pp. 100–140). This sporadic imposition of community sentences is hard to reconcile with the directive in the Code that preference be given to non-custodial sentences. Claims to the effect that this penalty should be an alternative to short-term custodial sentences dominate theoretical texts (Szewczyk 2010, p. 240). This position has meanwhile been taken over by the suspended sentence in penal policy. There is still a good deal of wariness regarding community sentences on the part of the Polish judiciary and a disinclination to impose them. The excessive workload of social and court-appointed curators, which considerably exceeds the limits stipulated in the Court Appointed Curators Act, may be an indirect cause of this state of affairs, as curators really cannot be any more broadly engaged in administering this penalty (Gruszczyńska 2010, p. 119).

The legislators who passed the Criminal Code of 1997 wanted to make the fine the basic penalty unit to be applied whenever that would suffice. When the percentage of penalties in which fines are imposed is examined, it turns out that fines are actually imposed quite frequently, although somewhat less frequently than suspended sentences.[12] The Criminal Code of 1997 anticipated the possibility of fines being imposed as a standalone, i.e. sole, penalty and as an 'extra penalty' imposed in addition to imprisonment. When these two situations are differentiated, it can be seen that a standalone fine is handed down in barely 20 per cent of cases. This is significantly less than the average of nearly 40 per cent of cases in which a fine is ordered in addition to imprisonment (mainly conditionally suspended) (Jakubowska-Hara 2009b, p. 12). A fine, as a standalone penalty, is preferred on legislative grounds but is not especially popular in practice. This can be explained by the many disadvantages of this form of penal response, which is shown in the defects in legal regulation, intensified by their improper application in practice. The lack of options in paying a fine, and in collecting it by having the prosecution enforce payment from a convict who does not have the means to pay, render this penalty virtually inapplicable. Handing down a fine that exceeds the convict's ability to pay makes it necessary to apply an alternative penalty, which defeats the whole idea of a financial penalty (Jakubowska-Hara 2009a, pp. 59–60).

There are two rules governing the size of a fine in Polish criminal law, viz. establishing the number of day fine units and determining the amount of a single day fine unit. Article 33 of the Criminal Code anticipates that the lowest number of day-fine units is 10 and the highest 540 and that the amount of a single day-fine unit varies between PLN 10 and PLN 2,000.[13] After analysing penal policy in applying fines, it can be said that fines handed down as standalone penalties come to a slightly higher amount than those handed down with prison sentences. Half the fines ordered as standalone penalties were between PLN 500 and PLN 1,000, fines up to PLN 500 were ordered slightly less often, and fines between PLN 1,000 and PLN 2,000 least often of all. Fines in excess of PLN 2,000 were for isolated cases. Fines ordered in addition to imprisonment were for amounts up to PLN 500 more than half the time, between PLN 500 and PLN 1,000 slightly less often, and PLN 1,000 or more least often (Jakubowska-Hara 2009a, p. 85). The amount of any fine meted out must be adjusted to the financial means of the offender. This is probably what determines this particular schedule of amounts and not some other criterion. Polish people are not affluent and most of those who commit crimes come from the poorest and most marginalised sectors of society. Large fines, to have any chance of being paid,

12 19.1 per cent of penalties imposed were fines and 38.1 per cent were suspended sentences in 2006 (Jakubowska-Hara 2009a, p. 12).

13 This was the legal status of the Criminal Code as at 20 April 2011.

can only be imposed on perpetrators of some crimes, mostly economic ones. Even with this policy of deciding the amount of a fine, however, it loses its essence as a financial penalty in a fair number of cases. Almost 30 per cent of fines ordered in addition to imprisonment, and 20 per cent of standalone fines, are commuted to imprisonment (Jakubowska-Hara 2009a, p. 91).

To recapitulate, it needs to be stressed that around half the fines handed down by the courts are imposed on perpetrators who are either not able to pay them or who simply prefer to have them commuted to short prison sentences. The average amount of a fine handed down by a court in Poland is frequently less than a traffic ticket, which can often be considerably more than PLN 500 but which can be collected with no additional effort.[14] This gives rise to the incongruous situation where someone who has committed a summary offence sometimes incurs a more severe penalty for his/her transgression than someone who has committed a crime enumerated in the Criminal Code.

Contemporary penal policy is not only based on the principle of seeking out alternative solutions to immediate imprisonment, but goes much further in that it also tries to introduce extra-curial methods of resolving disputes where the law has been broken. In some situations, approaching a crime as if it were a dispute that can be resolved through conciliation can be highly effective. In others, this might even be the only correct approach. Contemporary legal systems are in a state of constant flux. They are subjected to social and functional changes and a diversity of value systems by dint of the ever increasing complexity and volatility of social arrangements and by the law being used as an instrument of policy and control. One consequence of this is that the justice system has to diversify as well (Zienkiewicz 2007, p. 13). This is the spirit in which the institution of mediation began to operate in Polish criminal law.[15] For over 20 years, mediation has been added to penal policy with varying degrees of success. Mediation proceedings can be initiated by the court, the public prosecutor and the police department at the preliminary proceedings stage. Data from the Ministry of Justice illustrate the difficult beginnings of this institution, which had to work very hard to win over judges and prosecutors, to say nothing of the police.[16] 2006 saw the greatest number of criminal cases in the common courts referred to mediation – 5,052 cases were referred to mediation that year, of which 3,062 ended in a settlement being reached. The number of cases referred to mediation began to fall over the next few years. In 2009, there were only 3,714 cases, of which 2,505 ended in a settlement. In the first half of 2010, the number of cases referred to mediation was 1,756. This would seem to justify the prognosis of a further decline in the frequency of this remedy. It should be noted, however, that although the number of cases being referred to mediation has fallen, the effectiveness of mediation has continued to increase since 2002. This is shown in Table 7.3. A slight decline in its effectiveness can be seen in 2010–2011.

The decline in the number of cases referred to mediation cannot therefore be viewed as a result of its ineffectiveness or pointlessness. Nor can it be regarded as part of the tendency in the penal policy of the last few years to prefer retributive over remedial measures. The ever increasing proportion of mediations ending in settlement indicates that cases referred to mediation are probably on a higher level and concern matters better suited to this remedy. While considerably fewer cases are referred to mediation by prosecutors during preliminary proceedings than by the courts, over 70 per cent of them result in a settlement being reached. Mediation is used even less frequently in juvenile (family) proceedings. On average, however, 90 per cent of cases successfully end in a settlement. This may attest to the particular effectiveness and purposefulness of this remedy in juvenile matters. The use of mediation in the Polish justice system is part of the policy of the EU, which has consequently published many recommendations and promoted good practices on this subject.

No description of Polish criminal policy can limit itself to the problems associated exclusively with applying penalties. This is because the Criminal Code of 1997 introduced a certain amount of duplication in this area, by anticipating a broad catalogue of penal measures instead of the additional penalties in force on the basis of the Criminal Code of 1969. Article 39 of the Code enumerates the following penal measures: deprivation of civil rights; prohibition on occupying a specific position, practising a specific profession and/or running a specific type of business; prohibition on raising, treating, educating or caring for minors; obligation

14 http://bip.kgp.policja.gov.pl/ (accessed 7 November 2012).

15 Institution regulated by Art. 23a of the *ustawy z dnia 6 czerwca 1997 r. Kodeks postępowania karnego* (Criminal Procedure Code [Journal of Laws No. 89, Pos. 555 as amended]).

16 http://bip.ms.gov.pl/pl/dzialalnosc/statystyki/ (accessed 7 November 2012).

Table 7.3 **Number of cases ending in settlement in absolute numbers and as proportions of all cases referred to mediation**

Year	Number of cases referred to mediation in court proceedings	Number of cases ending in settlement	Percentage of cases referred to mediation that ended in settlement
2002	1,021	997	58
2003	1,858	1,108	59
2004	3,569	2,123	59
2005	4,440	2,755	62
2006	5,052	3,062	60
2007	4,178	2,753	65
2008	3,891	2,551	65
2009	3,714	2,505	67
2010	3,480	2,274	65
2011	3,251	2,071	64
2012	3,252	2,251	69

to not enter or remain on specified environments and/or places; prohibition on contacting specified persons; prohibition on approaching specified persons; prohibition on vacating a specified place of residence without the consent of the court; prohibition on attending a mass event; prohibition on entering a gaming centre and participating in games of chance; order to vacate premises jointly occupied with an aggrieved person; prohibition on driving vehicles; confiscation; obligation to repair damage or redress a wrong; exemplary damages; payment of money; and having the verdict and sentence published.

The objective that motivated those who compiled the catalogue was to increase the role of this kind of measure so as to rationalise penal policy and better adapt the penal response to particular types of crimes (Zoll 1998, pp. 8–11). In abandoning the construction of additional penalties, which could only have been ordered along with the main penalty, fairly broadly envisaged options of exclusively penal measures, which were to be confined to the judgement against the perpetrator, were anticipated (Melezini 2010b, pp. 410–11). It has to be stressed that penal measures are not possessed of a homogeneity through which they can fulfil a variety of penal functions and ensure that the principle of individual penal liability is put into practice. Most fulfil preventive functions, e.g. the prohibition on driving vehicles and the prohibition on occupying a specific position. The repressive function of increasing the hardship of the penalty is uppermost in some, e.g. deprivation of civil rights, while others fulfil a compensatory role, e.g. repairing damage or redressing a wrong. Most penal measures are discretionary, although a fairly large group are applied mandatorily. This is regarded as an unnecessary restriction on the freedom of the judiciary by some theoretical texts (Melezini 2010b, pp. 414–15). The Code anticipates a wide range of options in applying penal measures. These may be ordered cumulatively – either standalone or in addition to the sentence – as a supplement to probationary measures and as designated preventive measures. An aggregate sentence with several penal measures is an additional possibility. Some have a 'one-off' character, e.g. confiscation, publishing the verdict and the sentence, others are of limited duration, and still others can be ordered for ever. Some penal measures appear in response to events being publicised in the media. The prohibition on engaging in any activities connected with raising, treating, educating or caring for children was inserted into the Criminal Code after several 'affairs' in which the main protagonists had been sexually exploiting children. The prohibition on attending mass events was instituted in response to the publicised behaviour of hooligan football supporters, and the order to vacate premises jointly occupied with an aggrieved person was instituted after a prominent social campaign on preventing and counteracting domestic violence.[17] These changes to the catalogue of penal measures brilliantly illustrate the instrumental use to which politicians put the criminal law as their most effective remedy to mend social ills. This may be regarded as disturbing and as contravening the theoretically espoused principle of the need for subsidiarity in criminal law (Gardocki 2008). On the other hand, however, it can be argued that these changes have left the criminal law flexible in the face of new challenges. Social changes make it necessary to introduce new penal measures and place a question mark over those that have become outdated. Deprivation of civil rights might serve as an example. This was a reasonably popular sentence when the Civil Code of 1969 was in force but has become increasingly rare since the adoption of Criminal Code of 1997. By 2010, it only accounted for a marginal share of penal measures ordered by the courts.[18]

The statistics on the prohibition of occupying a specified position, practising a specific profession and/or running a specific type of business paint a similar picture. This measure has been ordered 360 times a year on average since the Criminal Code of 1997 has come into force. This compares with over 3,000 during the time of the previous Code (Kulesza 2010, p. 528). The prohibition on attending a mass event was a measure that generated a great deal of excitement. This penal provision was enacted in haste and it quickly became difficult to apply. A prohibition on attending a mass event could not be effectively enforced until the administrative regulations under the Act on Safety at Mass Events were adopted (Sakowicz 2010, p. 564). Police Headquarters figures indicate that the number of disturbances involving football hooligans is falling.[19] Moreover, the Euro 2012 Championships, which were held in Poland, showed that, apart from a few violent incidents, which almost always occur at mass gatherings, football hooligans did not make any trouble, contrary to what some media pundits had been predicting. It should be stressed here, however, that Euro matches attract a somewhat different set of spectators from those who attend club matches, where aggressive football supporters usually go looking for trouble.

The prohibition on driving a vehicle has likewise had an interesting history. The number of such prohibitions more than doubled in 1991 (Sienkiewicz 2010b, p. 564). This can be explained by the huge increase in road safety offences that followed the socio-economic changes and the accompanying increase in the number of cars being purchased and registered. In 2000, driving a motor vehicle while under the influence of alcohol or drugs was upgraded from a summary offence to a crime that carried a mandatory prohibition on driving a vehicle. The number of prohibitions has consequently increased 10 times since mid-2000 and 20 times since 2004. A slight decrease in the number of prohibitions on driving a vehicle has been discernible since 2006, although the overall level has remained high.

Unfortunately, there are no available statistical data that would illustrate the growth rates of all penal measures. It can be assumed, however, that expanding and upgrading the catalogue of these measures has achieved the aspiration of rationalising criminal policy (Zoll 1998, p. 9). It is worth considering here whether making non-compliance of the criminal measures a separate type of crime pursuant to Articles 244 and 244a of the Criminal Code is part of the general trend towards rationalisation.[20] This regulation shows that the legislature reasonably assumed that penal measures ordered in finalised judgements would not actually be performed. Consequently, additional sanctions in the form of three years' imprisonment (except in the case of the prohibition on attending a mass event which carries two years' imprisonment), a community sentence or a fine have been provided for non-compliance. Adopting this solution therefore seems disturbing, mainly in that it assumes a certain debasement of penal sanctions and endeavours to force obedience to court decisions through the threat of additional penal sanctions.

Some attention should also be devoted to that part of criminal policy that deals with juveniles who break the law. For years, there have been announcements, especially in political debates and the media, to the

17 See, inter alia, http://www.kochamniebije.pl (accessed 4 June 2013).

18 When the Criminal Code of 1969 was in force, the numbers of convicted people deprived of their civil rights were as follows: 1970 – 8,141, 1975 – 5,841, 1980 – 4,651, 1985 – 5,244, 1989 – 2,681, 1991 – 4,432 and 1995 – 5,050. The numbers since the Criminal Code of 1997 has been in force are: 1999 – 724, 2000 – 340, 2001 – 193, 2002 – 81, 2003 – 60, 2004 – 71, 2005 – 59, 2006 – 35, 2007 – 26 and 2008 – 34 (Kulesza 2010, p. 492).

19 http://www.statystyka.policja.pl/portal/st/943/50862/Nietrzezwi_sprawcy_przestepstw.html (accessed 4 June 2013).

20 Art. 244 in the wording of the Act of 10 June 2010 (Journal of Laws No. 125, Pos. 842) and Art. 244a in the wording of the Act of 22 July 2010 (Journal of Laws No. 152, Pos. 1021).

effect that juvenile criminality is on the rise and that juveniles are committing increasingly aggressive and dangerous crimes. However,

> … contrary to media reports, the number of most serious crimes committed by young people is not very high at all. While there has been a noticeable increase in aggressive crimes, especially brawling and assault, it would appear from self-report studies that crimes that technically qualify as such on the basis of these regulations are not really all that serious, and their numerical increase may be caused by a change in societal response to this kind of behaviour, i.e. by schools and parents shifting the responsibility for resolving it onto the state. (Klaus 2009a, p. 145)

Theft, robbery, extortion, causing damage to health and participating in assaults and brawls are the crimes most often committed by juvenile offenders. An examination of the judicial response to punishable acts perpetrated by juveniles shows that nothing has changed for many years. The main penal measure continues to be standalone supervision by a probation officer, which is only a correctional measure. This is partly explained by wariness to impose preventive measures, of which there are quite a few in the law currently in force, on the part of Family Court judges, a lack of consideration being given to the effectiveness of the sentences being passed, and little if any interest in the new options now available, even when these are offered by NGOs (Klaus 2009a, p. 352). A good deal more attention needs to be devoted to the methods of responding to juvenile behaviour when formulating criminal policy. This is because the majority of adult offenders are recruited from the ranks of those who had their first brushes with the law as juveniles.

This fragmentary sketch of contemporary criminal policy in Poland is based on various data supplied by statisticians, criminologists, academics, politicians and representatives of social control bodies. It should be borne in mind, however, that 'The information received is to a significant extent dependent on the opinions and objectives of those who provided it' (Lem 2006, p. 224). Obtaining information this way only allows a rough sketch to be drawn of the contemporary resolutions, or rather lack thereof, to social problems associated with criminality. The causes of the inconsistency – and oftentimes irrationality – of our penal policy are too numerous to mention, let alone describe, here. In concluding these considerations on the resolutions to the social problems associated with criminality, it should suffice to say that despite the unquestioned progress and the advances in democracy and the rule of law, Poland still lacks genuine political elites. Nor does it yet have an abundance of organisational, social and economic associations. This situation will not be improved by statutes and injunctions. Family, social and public life is shaped by people's attitudes (Lem 2006, p. 224).

Should the progressive expansion and politicisation of the criminal law be curbed in this context? Should it be conceded that the criminal law is not the best remedy for societal ills, including criminality? Perhaps a society in a state of constant flux should concur with Jim Consedine that it is necessary to believe that family members and representatives of the community in which the offence was committed and the loss or damage inflicted have to be involved in the administration of justice (Consedine 2004). This just might allow the existing means of social control to be rationalised as they are almost certainly no longer adequate to confront the challenges posed by post-modernism.

Chapter 8
Supervised Freedom

Dobrochna Wójcik

Probation

Introduction

Seeking alternatives to imprisonment as a means of punishment in carrying out legislative and judicial functions and in implementing criminal policy has a longstanding tradition. On the one hand, there seems to be an increasing number of people in favour of restricting the use of imprisonment, treating offenders humanely and respecting their dignity. On the other hand, however, a periodic (cyclic) strengthening of a punitive,[1] or even populist (Czapska and Waltoś 2007, pp. 404–7 and 410–12; Zalewski 2008, p. 130) tendency has long been observed and the feeling of being threatened by criminality has always been reasonably high.[2]

The beginnings of probation: origins, organisational and legal basis, concepts, aims and methods of action

Among the various alternatives to imprisonment, the importance of probation cannot be overstated. The institution of probation has always played a vital role here and continues to do so. Nancy J. King (2007, p. 5) accurately expressed this when she said, 'The great contribution of the probation service has been to the humanization of justice'. This institution has undergone many changes and has developed differently in different countries in the hundred years or more that it has been in operation.[3] This has made it part of the legal system, culture and customs of those countries. Probation has come into existence on the basis of two primary legal systems, viz. the common law system that prevails in countries such as the UK, the United States and Canada (where this institution has evolved through praxis) and the system of continental law that prevails in most countries in Europe, including France, Belgium and Poland.[4]

Probation essentially consists of:

1. recognising that the offender is guilty of committing a crime;
2. suspending the execution of the sentence or penalty imposed;
3. imposing obligations on the offender during the probation period;
4. placing the offender under the care of a probation officer (Marek 2010a).

---

1 This concerns both changes to the law and a more harsh criminal policy. See Jasiński (1993, pp. 128–31) and Melezini (2003); Sienkiewicz (2010a); Płatek and Fajst (2005, p. 86) write: 'The pendulum of the justice system therefore only touches the state and the offender as it swings between the two extremes of retribution and rehabilitation'.

2 The most recent ICVS findings indicate, however, that anxiety about criminality is waning in Poland (Siemaszko 2010, p. 187).

3 The authors are not certain as to where and when the institution of probation first came into being. The general consensus is that probation was devised in Massachusetts, USA and that the prototype of the probation officer was a tailor named Augustus. For a discussion on the probation system as previously developed in mid-nineteenth-century England and authorized by legislation in 1879 and 1887 before being adopted by Massachusetts (and considerably later by other US states) on the basis of this experience, see Marek (1999); Veillard-Cybulsky (1968, p. 147); Marek (1978, p. 290). The author distinguishes three probation systems in Europe: Anglo-American, Franco-Belgian and Norwegian-Danish-Dutch (Skupiński 1992, pp. 24, 147).

4 According to Marek (2010a), the principal difference in the structure of legal probation in the two systems is that in the common law system, probation is a form of conditionally suspended sentence while in the continental system it is a conditionally suspended execution of a sentence already handed down by the court.

Many authors consider the 'cornerstone' of probation to be the last of these four elements, while others say it is the probationary period (Stępniak 2009b).

The development of the institution of probation has ushered in some very diverse legal results. It can be employed at various stages of criminal proceedings and in connection with diverse penalties and penal measures. Overall, however, the essence of probation, viz. supervised freedom and compliance with specific conditions laid down by the court, remained virtually unchanged until the 1980s. Did the reasonably fundamental modifications introduced in the US, England and Wales – and proclaimed as 'the end or the death of probation' by some academics and practitioners – actually change its essence and purpose? (Raynor 2012a, p. 945). If so, how great an influence did they have on changing the way this institution functioned? These questions shall be discussed at the end of the chapter.

The concept of probation came out of the Police Court Mission that existed in England at the end of the nineteenth century. The idea behind this institution was to help people in difficult situations and give them a chance to improve (Wright 2005, p. 59). The stated philosophy of giving the ward advice, assistance and a show of friendship informed the design of this institution from the moment of its inception and remained in effect until the end of the twentieth century (Raynor 2002, p. 1172; Wright 2005, p. 56). It was then that the British Home Secretary Michael Howard introduced changes to the National Probation Service. These included limiting what was generally considered the great achievement of probation in the UK, viz. including distinct social work components in the work of probation officers (Raynor 2012a, p. 936). The literature mentions a variety of purposes that the institution of probation is meant to serve (Ostrihanska and Greczuszkin 1999, p. 11). In practice, these are treated and realised in different ways depending on the country. As a general rule, the fundamental goal of this institution has now been changed to rehabilitation, although probationary measures are applied to people who do not require rehabilitation. Another goal is to extend assistance to offenders so as to facilitate their integration into society and enable them to function properly socially. Motivating offenders to change their behaviour and encouraging them to become active and work to this end with their probation officers or other persons or institutions charged with supervising convicted people is likewise deliberate. Another goal of probation is to control the behaviour of offenders and to ensure they comply with the conditions and commitments stipulated by the court.

The conviction that correctional work and rehabilitation are more effective is predominant among practitioners, as is the belief in their worth and moral strength. The work of the probation officer, especially in the beginning, was treated as missionary activity. The main approach was working one-on-one. This was the basis of rehabilitation. The task of the probation officer was to assess the circumstances of the offender, diagnose his/her personality, supervise and control him/her and make decisions about subjecting the person being supervised to specific interactions (Ostrihanska 2008, pp. 165 ff.), The probation officer was given a great deal of autonomy in assessing the behaviour of the criminal and deciding what sort of intervention should be taken. The functions of the probation officer depended on his/her own experience, knowledge and sensitivity and his/her skill in forming an appropriate relationship with the supervised person, assessing that person's requirements and winning his/her trust.

It is worth noting the dualism of probation emphasised in the literature, i.e. the dual functions of punishment and assistance (Cartledge et al. 1981, pp. 20–21). Probation gives the offender a chance to change his/her behaviour and leaves him/her at liberty but at the same time reserves the option of executing the sentence in the case of committing another crime or even failing to observe the obligations laid down by the court. These two approaches are difficult to reconcile – and not just theoretically. The option of punishment accounts for the place of probation in the system when the judiciary can respond to any failure to respect the rules of the criminal law. The element of assistance afforded by probation, on the other hand, is an expression of the humanitarian approach. It is a component of the social policy administered by the state and an expression of human solidarity granted to support psychologically those who have difficulty in functioning properly in society. The possibility of remaining at liberty is an incentive that encourages many criminals to accept their probation conditions. At the same time, it is an enormous challenge and creates difficulties in meeting them. More will be said about how offenders take advantage of this opportunity in practice in the section on the Polish probation system.

Those who supported probation adduced the following arguments in favour of its justness and which testified to the benefits of introducing it:

1. probation is better suited to some categories of crimes and perpetrators than isolating measures (e.g. incarceration);
2. probation avoids the negative consequences of prison, promotes rehabilitation and social integration, and is more humane;
3. probation is less costly than imprisonment;[5]
4. probation lowers the prison population, 'lightens the load' of penal institutions and makes it easier for those establishments to administer rehabilitation work on the convicts who remain there (Ville et al. 1997, p. 23).

The evolution of probation – the era of rehabilitation

The longstanding tradition associated with the function of probation invites investigation as to how the philosophy of this institution has been shaped during the time it has been in effect and what influences have been exerted on its operation by various ideas and theoretical concepts, legislative changes, new trends in specifying the aims of the justice system, the functionality and results of criminal sanctions, and tendencies in criminal policy.

In this context, certain stages can be distinguished in the development of probation. These facilitate investigation into how the changing socio-economic and political situation has shaped the different approaches to the problem of criminality, the different ways of treating offenders subjected to supervision, and the extent to which this has changed practice.

The review and appraisal of these ideas and trends is chiefly based on changes observed in England and Wales and the United States. This raises the question as to their repercussions in Europe, and especially in Poland. It is worth saying at the outset that the influence of these concepts has been moderate in Europe (and especially in Poland) (Marek 2009a). In the positivist school of criminality, probation was dominated by a rehabilitative approach known as the treatment model. This depended on individual intervention towards the offender that was educational and therapeutic. The basic methodology of working with criminals (as already mentioned) was case work based on individual contact and a close relationship between the probation officer and the person being supervised. This built an emotional bond and mutual trust between them (Ostrihanska and Greczuszkin 1999, pp. 61 ff.).

Some fairly sudden and radical changes in the way probation functioned occurred at the turn of the twenty-first century. These are a subject for analysis in a subsequent part of this chapter.

The effectiveness of the practice of probation is therefore often assessed critically. This leads to further searching for suitable and effective ways of responding to crime and often results in a change of approach in dealing with offenders.

The greatest development in rehabilitation in the United States occurred during the 1950s and 1960s. The prevailing view at the time was that penalties should be tailored to the individual requirements of the offender so as to ensure his/her rehabilitation and that this depended on his/her criminal prognosis and personality traits. The priority given to rehabilitation, both in the legislative sphere and in determining criminal policy, brought about an almost complete rejection of such classical criminal law principles and standards as proportionality to the seriousness of the act and guilt of the perpetrator. The judges were given a lot of discretion and judgements often failed to specify a time period, as it was argued that the time required for rehabilitation could not be determined in advance.[6] (This did not happen to the same extent in Europe.) The uncertainty of the judgements is worth mentioning as it is typical of protective and paternalistic systems.

---

5 Some writers point out that the programmes currently being used for criminals are very expensive (i.e. to develop and execute), although this argument might only be applicable in some cases. See Raynor (2006).

6 The Model Sentencing Act 1963 has references on criminal procedures in the United States: 'convicted persons should be treated according to the possibilities for rehabilitating them' and 'dangerous criminals need to be identified and placed under long-term rehabilitation' (cited in Marek 1980, p. 100; Stańdo-Kawecka 2007, p. 69).

The decline and fall of the rehabilitation age

From the middle of the twentieth century, various changes were made to the functions of probation as it developed. This resulted in the scope of its services being considerably extended. Apart from supervising and rehabilitating offenders, probation officers have been entrusted with monitoring people released from prison. For a while now, they have also assisted in organising and supervising community service orders, and have liaised with victims and informed them of when the convicts who have harmed them will be released from prison. Furthermore, more rigorous probation officer supervision began to be ordered – primarily against dangerous criminals and perpetrators of serious crimes (e.g. those involving sex or violence). Changes were also made to the way probation officers worked and were recruited and trained, and the probation and social services worked closely together.[7] Some countries (e.g. England and Wales) have done away with a unified juvenile court system. Protective cases are heard by the civil courts while criminal cases are heard by the former juvenile as they are 'similar to the criminal courts' (Stańdo-Kawecka 2007, pp. 200 ff.; Stępniak 1998, pp. 247 ff.)

All these changes, and the inordinate burden of added responsibilities they have placed on probation officers, have had negative effects and repercussions in assessing their work.[8] The excessive autonomy of probation officers and the difficulty of reliably controlling the quality of their services (or even the inability to control them) were criticised. Furthermore, the excessive freedom of probation officers in making decisions on supervised people was rated negatively as it made their work too diverse, disjointed and inconsistent. It was stressed that their work had not changed in a hundred years and had not adapted to changing conditions (Burnett et al. 2007, pp. 2010 ff.). They were criticised for their discretion in selecting methods and for employing programmes whose effectiveness had not been confirmed. They were also reproached for focusing too much on the problems of the criminals and devoting too little time to the victims as well as for failing to perceive the need to work to protect society (Ostrihanska 2006 quoting Lacey 2002). It could be said that what was once considered the advantage of having probation officers was now considered their drawback.

The changing social situation at the end of the twentieth century was also highly significant. This included such negative phenomena as an increase in criminality and a heightened feeling of being threatened by it, and a hardening of attitudes and demands from the public that the state do more to protect it from criminality. Changes in moral and social awareness also played an important part. The result was a demand that the authorities exhibit more transparency and justify the decisions they make that affect ordinary people, as well as an acquisition of more influence over them. The idea of penal populism (Zalewski 2008, p. 10), which included disavowing criminological knowledge, dismissing the opinions of experts (with the exception of government criminologists), and changing laws according to the diktat of social expectations and demands, often led to adverse changes in criminal procedures manifested in increased harshness.

At the same time, some studies questioned the effectiveness of rehabilitation programmes.[9] This brought about an abrupt collapse in the conception of rehabilitation in the US in the mid-1970s. This was chosen by Robert Martinson as the date to release the findings of his 1974 meta-analyses in which he proved that programmes designed to counteract recidivism were ineffective and that criminals who did not participate in them were just as likely to return to crime as offenders subjected to the influences of rehabilitation.

Opponents of rehabilitation proposed suspending sanctions with indeterminate or relatively indeterminate durations, restricting the discretionary power of judges and making the penalty proportional to the seriousness of the crime, arguing that excessively individualising rehabilitation led to a huge range of penalties for similar crimes. The views of Martinson, encapsulated in slogans like 'Nothing Works', became the basis for the moral, ethical and philosophical arguments deployed by opponents of rehabilitation and constituted the

7 For an understanding of social work in the work of probation officers, see Raynor (2012a).

8 M. Maguire is critical about parole, which in the 1980s and 1990s led to a considerable increase in the number of people freed and a huge increase in the workload of the probation services (Maguire 2007).

9 Marek (2009a, p. 102) cites 1973 research by Kennedy and Kerber, which was published earlier than that of Martinson (1974) and which denied the effectiveness of rehabilitation. Brody obtained similar results to Martinson in 1976. Moreover, as the findings of the Home Office IMPACT study (Folkard et al. 1976) did not confirm the proposition that the 'more probation', the better the 'treatment' results, treatment is acknowledged as not being particularly effective, especially in the case of serious crimes. The conclusion was a negative assessment of the purpose of probation (Raynor 2012a, p. 932).

official pretext for the authorities ceasing to use rehabilitation policy on a large scale, especially in the US and England (all the more so as it was very costly).[10] This decision and the then reigning climate of undermining the desirability of administering programmes for criminals helped dampen the interest of some scholars in studying the effectiveness of rehabilitation, even though Martinson, who had triggered all the confusion, recanted his argument and published a statement to that effect.[11]

This raises the question as to what influence, if any, the collapse of the idea of rehabilitation in the US had on other countries. Opinion is divided. Some authors, e.g. Andrzej Marek, consider that none of this has significantly influenced probation practice in Europe, which has never shared the US's enthusiasm for rehabilitation and has never renounced it so abruptly.[12] Krzysztof Krajewski has expressed a similar view, stating that 'in no European country, apart from some Scandinavian states, has there ever been such a profound departure from the classical conceptions of criminal law (free will, liability, guilt and retributive punishment) as occurred in the US, and to a significant extent, in the UK as well' (Krajewski 1992, p. 85)

After the collapse of the idea of rehabilitation in the US there was a marked return to the neoclassical approach towards treating criminals, and an acceptance of the concept of just deserts and the principle that the punishment be proportional to the seriousness of the crime. Proponents of harsher punishments added their voices as well (Stańdo-Kawecka 2010b, pp. 900 ff.). This resulted in several changes, including a harsher criminal policy, an increase in the prison population and, despite saving on the costs of rehabilitation, a more expensive criminal justice system. In Marek's view 'dismissing rehabilitation is an expression of impotence in fighting crime and always ushers in a return to harshness and severe penalties with reason giving way to emotion. And harshness is even less effective' (Marek 1980, p. 100), or, in a more literary vein, 'when reason sleeps, phantoms awaken'.

The diversion movement

During this time, the diversion movement constituted a certain remedy to the growth in the prison population (Kołakowska-Przełomiec and Wójcik 1990, pp. 13 ff.). This was derived from the labelling concept of Howard Becker and Kai Erikson in the US in the late 1960s and early 1970s (Siemaszko 1993, p. 262). Diversion depends on being able to exclude the offender from the criminal justice system and direct him/her to specific programmes in which he/she could participate while remaining at liberty (Merrington and Stanley 2007, p. 432).[13] Labelling theory contributed to modifying the formal reaction to criminality, especially towards juveniles, and fostered the development of such forms as redressing damage and mediation (Błachut et al. 1999, p. 141; Czarnecka-Dzialuk and Walczak-Żochowska 1995, pp. 127 ff.). The stated aims of diversion include avoiding stigmatisation, diminishing the role of force and control on the part of official agencies and limiting recidivism (Palmer and Levis 1980). It is worth emphasising, however, that 'net widening', which involved increasing the number of people under social control, was an unintentional side effect of diversion (Falck 1992, p. 32).

The diversion movement, through promoting the ideas of avoiding the negative appraisal of a stay in prison and achieving a significant cost reduction, became very popular, not just in the US but in other countries as well (e.g. Germany, the Netherlands, Belgium and Norway). In practice, the principles of diversion were mainly applied to juveniles, although sometimes to adults as well. The concept was not implemented in Poland, although as a substitute of sorts, the Family Court could hand over juveniles to the schools they attended or the social organisations to which they belonged (Klaus 2009a, pp. 71 ff.). However, there were no special programmes for juveniles at the time.

---

10 Raynor (2012a, p. 932) stresses that Martinson's findings were consistent with what he wanted to find and what the government, which was interested in reducing spending on rehabilitation programmes, was expecting.

11 Another analysis of Martinson's findings (including his contribution) led to the conclusion that the results were not all that unfavourable to the argument of the effectiveness of rehabilitation. Martinson also resiled from such radical conclusions in a separate statement. Similarly, Blackburry, after analysing Martinson's results, claimed in 1980 that some limited recidivism nevertheless did occur (Raynor 2002, p. 1176; Ostrihanska 2006, p. 613).

12 Marek (2009a, p. 68) intended most European countries, but he particularly mentioned the Scandinavian countries as having had a heightened reaction against rehabilitation (see also Stańdo-Kawecka 2007, p. 71).

13 The suspended sentence and the community service order were also introduced at this time. These served to keep offenders out of prison using a kind of 'diversion' concept.

Probation reform: a change in philosophy from care and assistance to 'case' management

Abandoning the rehabilitation approach also had repercussions for evaluating the performance of probation, and redoubled the determination of the authorities (especially in England and Wales) to radically reform the whole probation system with a view to making it more effective. A thorough reform began in the 1990s and is ongoing. This has been characterised by rapid and radical measures that have often been modified due to political changes and which have not been accepted by all practitioners. These changes were intended to ensure better organisation, and a streamlining and centralisation of the work of probation officers. The result was the creation of the National Probation Service, financed by and completely dependent on the Crown. This severed the probation service from its former connections with local government, which had guaranteed the service greater independence. Currently, however, the independence of probation officers is not seen as a desirable.

These changes had a mixed reception. Everyone, however, agreed that they were very radical and that they were adopted very hastily but were not necessarily well thought out or well prepared.[14] Some scholars, however, have emphasised their positive aspects, pointing out that they have enabled procedures to be standardised, made probation officers more disciplined, laid down clearly defined and detailed standards (sometimes a little too detailed) and improved work practices. Establishing more transparent supervisory regulations and conditions (e.g. disciplinary discipline, consistently administered and involving redress of damage) helped too, as did administering tried and proven programmes to criminals (Ostrihanska 2006, p. 614, quoting Lacey). Subsequent changes involved building closer cooperation between the prison and probation services through a single administrative body, the National Offender Manager Service (NOMS).[15]

All these radical changes and sharp criticisms of probation officers were met with distinct aversion and resistance from a significant proportion of probation practitioners and theoreticians. Many scholars (and especially practitioners) were quite critical in their appraisal of the reforms, fearing that probation would become a hierarchised and bureaucratised institution, that the nature of the work of the probation officer would be completely changed, and that the many positive features and values of probation would be lost. The changes, which were not merely organisational, were introduced over a period of several years and completely transformed the philosophy and functioning of the institution of probation and transformed the model that had been in force. In the traditional model (Maguire 2007, p. 406):

1. the offender can choose whether to take part in probation;
2. the probation officer assists and supports people under supervision;
3. the probation officer responds to the needs of people under supervision;
4. the probation officer and the offender build a relationship based on mutual trust;
5. the offender is not subject to excessive pressure to amend his/her behaviour.

Since 1990, probation officer's tasks have been re-formulated. Nowadays it is stressed, that:

1. the basic task of a probation officer is curbing criminality;
2. the probation officer's duty is to assess systematically the needs of the offender and the risk that he/she will reoffend;
3. the probation officer needs to focus on those needs of the offender that are bounded with his/her criminality (these are considered criminogenic or high risk);
4. the probation officer can apply a certain amount of pressure or force in his/her educational and rehabilitation work (Maguire 2007, p. 407).

14 Raynor (2012a, p. 941), for example, taking a stand against the introduction of the National Offender Manager Service (NOMS), writes, with a fair amount of passion, that combining the prison and probation services came as a 'shock' to probation workers.

15 A critical report by Carter contributed to the organisational changes in the probationary services. This alleged that there was a lack of coordination between the probation and prison services, that their operations were inconsistent, and that unverified rehabilitation programmes were being administered. See the Carter Report, 11 December 2003, Home Office, http://www.cabinetoffice.gov.uk/strategy/downloads/files/managingoffenders.pdf (accessed 1 June 2013).

The priorities in the probation officer's tasks were reordered, i.e. assessing the risk that the person under supervision would reoffend, determining criminogenic needs associated with criminality, focusing on curbing the criminality of people under supervision by monitoring changes in attitudes and behaviour, and protecting the community. All these changes are called 'the case management' (Kemshall and Wood 2007, p. 384).[16] The priority in case management is the attitude to 'high risk' criminals, i.e. dangerous offenders (Kemshall and Wood 2007, p. 385). The rehabilitation that was previously commonly promoted is no longer crucial. Applying pressure to reduce criminality and protect the community modifies the relationship between the probation officer and the offender. The probation officer does not focus on individual relations with the offender. He/she has neither the time nor the skill. He/she is supposed to identify offenders and manage them. To a large extent, the tasks connected with limiting and managing criminality used to fall on the state. They have now been transferred to local communities and governments (which have not always been provided with adequate funding). The state is increasingly reneging on its responsibility to control criminality and it is now the local community that will bear the consequences of negative behaviour on the part of the citizenry. It is expected that society 'will learn' to tolerate such behaviour. This raises the question of whether people are really ready for this.

The rebirth of rehabilitation

Those who support rehabilitation (especially in English Common Law countries) did not lay down arms but continued their research, fine tuning their methods of predicting whether someone would return to crime. By the 1980s, a movement known as 'What Works', consisting of practitioners and scholarly opponents of Martinson, had sprung up. Canadian academics obtained significant results in empirical studies that were of a decidedly higher methodological standard than those of their British and American colleagues (Hedderman 2007, p. 468). The results of these studies demonstrated that properly planned corrective intervention could significantly restrict any return to criminality provided specified conditions were observed (Cullen and Gendreau 2001, pp. 330 ff.; Andrews et al. 2006).

In 1990, Don Andrews, James Bonta and Richard Hoge (1990, pp. 468 ff.), devised the risk-need-responsivity (RNR) model. This very quickly became the best known model for assessing the risk that someone would return to criminality as well as the possibilities of limiting this risk and rehabilitating criminals in Canada, the US and many other countries.[17] The basic theoretical model for RNR was the social theory of learning, problems with the general theory of psychology, and selected elements of cognitive psychology (Andrews et al. 2006; Bonta and Andrews 2007; Bonta 2002). The basic principles of RNR are risk, need and responsivity. Risk refers to estimating the risk of a return to criminality and states that intervention should apply to high-risk offenders and correspond in intensity to the degree of risk. The second principle draws attention to the significance of the criminogenic needs of the offender (combined with his/her criminality) while directing him/her towards appropriate programmes. The third involves employing the methodology of the social theory of learning to build programmes that will most effectively influence the behaviour of the offender, e.g. through social modelling, applying reinforcement and disapproval techniques, teaching problem solving skills, taking into consideration the learning styles and strengths, personalities, intelligence of offenders, as well as any favourable biosocial factors in their development, when motivating them to change their behaviour.

Evaluating the risk of reoffending during a structured interview, and then utilising specially formulated diagnostic and prognostic tools to this end has become standard correctional practice (Andrews et al. 2006).[18] This is not to say that the evaluation is always a good one or that practitioners fully utilise the

16 The concept of case management and the categorisation of offenders according to risk assessment leads to the practical work of the probation officer becoming 'fragmented'. The offender is 'referred' from one specialist to another. This makes it impossible to build a relationship between the probation officer and the offender (Burnett et al. 2007; Burnett and McNeil 2005, pp. 229–35; Wright 2005, pp. 58 ff.).

17 In 1980–1990, the results of their research were ignored in both the UK and the US. Later, however, they became 'noticed' when the increasing influence of conservative governments in those countries legitimised limiting public expenditure on prisons (Raynor 2012a, p. 935; Raynor 2012b, pp. 173–89).

18 The literature stresses that the RNR model, along with the 'Good Lives' model of T. Ward and the Desistance Theory of S. Maruna and T. LeBel, is one of the three major theoretical approaches to managing criminality (McNeill et al. 2010).

'prognostic power' of the tools they use. Don Andrews, James Bonta and Richard Hoge claim that their tools (Level of Service Inventory Revised LSI-R) not only predict the likelihood of reoffending but also enable changes in the degree of risk to be evaluated as they occur during supervision through the impact of the correctional programmes being employed. This enables the rehabilitative interactions to be modified and their effectiveness enhanced. They therefore recommend repeated (even several times) use of these tools, i.e. to repeat the evaluations during the rehabilitation and intervention programmes or while treating an addiction.

This sounds very promising, since although there are numerous studies affirming the effectiveness of certain programmes in generally limiting criminality fall, empirically substantiating the changes taking place during the course of rehabilitative interaction is more difficult (Losel 2012). Mariusz Sztuka cites examples from some of these studies (Sztuka 2007). These studies also showed that different tools should be used with different categories of offender and that they should be verified (Kemshall and Wood 2007, p. 388). There are currently very diverse instruments available to evaluate the risk of reoffending for different categories of offender (Wójcik 2014)

Community sentences

The beginnings of community sentences in England and Wales were associated with the diversion movement. The 1990s were a period of intensive development. While the term 'community sentence' is widely used, Raynor (2002, p. 1168) believes it is difficult to cover its semantic domain. A variety of penalties and measures have been incorporated into this concept (e.g. fine, supervision, probation, electronic supervision) as the law has changed. Legal changes to community service have generally involved either adding to the conditions binding on offenders, or making them more stringent. This has also been associated with nomenclature changes. The Criminal Justice Act (1991) changed the legal status of probation. This had previously been applied on the basis of a court order, and not a sentence, and which from that time has been ordered precisely on the basis of a sentence.

Raynor (2012a, pp. 931–5) considers that, although probation has always contained a certain element restricting freedom, this underscores the fact that community punishments are not generally of an exclusively punitive nature (like, say, a fine) or are not based solely on a compulsory deprivation of freedom (like imprisonment).[19] To begin at the beginning, the now defunct 'probation order' and the current 'punishment in community' have given offenders the possibility, in principle, of remaining at liberty, of taking responsibility for themselves, of accepting imposed obligations and of submitting to supervision, which is a combination of control and assistance from their supervisors, who should possess the motivational skills to inspire their charges to make positive changes. This also concerns the means applied to juveniles. In reality, however, community sentences are still probation in the opinion of this writer, despite being complemented with the various means of supervision ordered for adult criminals and being served in the community (Raynor 2002a, pp. 1169 ff.). On the other hand, Merrington and Stanley (2007, p. 434) consider that restricting the freedom of the offender is still a penalty in the same sense as a fine or a term of imprisonment. These authors also stress that imposing severe limitations and conditions on the criminal and sending him/her back to court, when he/she does not adhere to these demands, is meant to convince society that the sanctions are effective and sufficiently severe.

A further tendency to make the law on ordering community sentences harsher can also be observed. The Criminal Justice Act (2003) introduced the option of a custody plus sentence. This combines a brief term of imprisonment followed by a longer term of community supervision (Maguire 2007, pp. 412 ff.). Raynor ends his treatise on community penalties by saying that if current trends in England and Wales continue, 'we can expect to see more diversity and variation in the provision of community sentences, with both good and bad results. These developments, however, seem likely to be driven more by political ideologies and expediency than by needs of courts, victims, or offenders' (Raynor 2012a, p. 949).

---

19 The author stresses the merits of the Criminal Justice Act (1991) a little too consistently, perhaps, while simultaneously adjudging it detrimental to probation.

Instead of a summary

The UK recently celebrated the centennial of the passing of the Probation of Offenders Act (1907). For many years, probation in England and Wales has served as the model of how this institution should be regulated and should function for many other countries, and the probation officer has been the archetypical upright and competent social worker, who has helped supervise criminals in resolving their problems in life, maintained contact, including emotional contact, with them, accepted them and won their trust. The philosophy and axiology on which probation was based (viz. advise, assist, befriend) has become known and accepted internationally.

The major social, economical, political and cultural changes that took place at the end of the twentieth century, however, cannot be ignored. These have influenced our approach to criminality and the way we react to it. They have also contributed to the growth in the punitiveness of criminal policy in many countries. David Garland (2009, pp. 106 ff.) has expressed the view that we have to accept that we live in a 'high crime society' where a high crime rate is 'a normal social fact'. Hence the basic rules of the justice system have undergone change. The current priority is to reduce crime, contain the damage it causes and protect the public from it. The evolution of probation presented here, and especially the somewhat abrupt departure from its operative ideas, and the initiation of reforms that may have been essential but were too radical and which neither practitioners nor scholars were prepared for and generally have not accepted, shows how serious the problems are. The changes of the past three decades are deeply thought provoking and raise questions about the subsequent development of this institution.[20] David Garland took a stand for the changes in approach to criminality in many criminal law systems in Western countries. According to his conception, these were linked with the social and cultural metamorphoses in late-modern societies; he also drew attention to the effects of globalisation, e.g. capital accumulation, economic changes, an increasing tendency to interfere in private life, the commercialisation of social activity (including the probation service) and an excessive focus on evaluating the risk of criminality and dangerous cases (Raynor 2012a, p. 944).

Of all the reforms discussed, the most difficult to accept is the change involving the conjoining of probation and imprisonment in a single organisation (NOMS) where the prison service plays the leading role and probation has lost its significance.[21] Comments such as 'there is no longer a probation order or a community service order', 'everything is managed by NOMS' and 'probation officers are just going to write reports and become nothing more than controllers and supervisors' recur when speaking with probation officers. The tendencies to apply marketing principles to probation and to privatise activities that were once the responsibility of probation officers are unwelcome. The argument, adduced by the authorities, that creating a variety of probation services makes them more effective and more likely to propose innovative ideas by promoting competition between them is not convincing. Initiatives for privatising rehabilitation programmes and entrusting their management to commercial firms, remunerated for 'getting results', as well as public interest establishments, likewise raise doubts. Practitioners seem to regard these projects as doing nothing to rehabilitate criminals or curb their recidivism. This merely fits in with the 'ideological' biases of the authorities while constituting a threat to the institution of probation and those who work in it.

Another change was the sentence of probation, which was introduced as a penalty in 1991. This was also connected with the revocation of the practice where the accused had to agree to be placed under supervision, even though this principle still applies in many European countries. Raynor (2012a, p. 929) has commented enough on this fact, claiming that according to EU standards, probation is not habitually treated as a penalty. There are also minor changes, which do not always appear to be comprehensible or necessary, and which are not accepted by the community. For example, it is worth mentioning that the term 'offender manager' has

20 The symptoms of these transformations could have been accurately discerned earlier, during the collapse of rehabilitation. The tendency towards a more punitive approach to criminals, labelled 'just deserts', was already evident in many countries. D. Garland believes that these changes began even earlier – during the welfare state era (1890–1970) (Owen 2007).

21 The concept of creating a single organisation responsible for both community and prison sentences was devised by P. Carter, in line with 'end-to-end offender management' – one of the three fundamental changes recommended in his report (see footnote 15).

relatively recently been introduced alongside the commonly understood 'probation officer' (a highly qualified professional). This new term denotes someone who supposedly 'manages' a criminal and who is trained only to do this. Some researchers even suspect that this was a prelude to dropping the traditional term altogether, although this has not happened. Both terms are currently in use but English probation officers when asked what they are, answer 'probation officer'.

There are many similar examples, only some of which have been cited above. All these changes have led to the British probation model losing significance and no longer occupying the position it once did. In the rest of the EU, with the possible exception of France, which has also evinced a tendency to make probation conditions more stringent, the rehabilitation approach is still in effect. Great British friends of Poland, having sympathetically observed the changes and achievements Poland has made in probation and mediation, e.g. Martin Wright and Robert Canton, have warned strongly against going down the same road. Does the Polish probation system draw on English Common Law models? If so, to what extent does it do so? If not, should it do so? In what direction is it developing? We shall attempt to answer these questions in the following sections.

Probation in Poland

Before presenting the current state of the probation service in Poland, a brief description of how it evolved is in order. The focus, however, is on its actual configuration following the ongoing reforms introduced by the passing of the Court Appointed Probation Officers Act (2001).

The political situation in Poland at the beginning of the twentieth century was such that court appointed probation service was not implemented until after the country had regained independence in 1919, and after other European countries (Gromek 2002, pp. 16 ff.; Bachmat 2010, pp. 22 ff.). Four stages can be identified in the development of this institution in Poland: (1) the period from 1919 to 1965 was one in which a suitable probation model, whose social nature had been established in 1935, was sought; (2) conceptual work and debate on transforming this social model into a professional one lasted from 1965 until 1992; (3) the period 1992–2001 was one of reform and of drafting and passing the Court Appointed Probation Officers Act (2001) (with the same social and professional model); (4) since the Act was passed, it has been a topic of ongoing discussion and amendments have been made to the system of probation defined therein (Stasiak 2010, pp. 45 ff.).

Probation service for juveniles did not start to progress until 1951, although it had been introduced as early as 1919, albeit only in three cities (Stasiak 2008, p. 23). Probation service was introduced for adults in 1958 and a professional probation officer service was set up for both juveniles and adults in 1959 and 1965 respectively.

There were various substantial, political and organisational reasons why work on reform took so long. It is worth emphasising that probation officers themselves took the initiative in this area in the early 1970s by arranging discussions, together with judges, practitioners and academics, on the need for changes to the probation system (Martuszewicz and Rzepniewski 2003; Sawicka 2010, p. 130). The agenda included theoretical problems and comprehensive solutions, e.g. the position of the probation officer in the justice system, the range of activities performed by probation officers, their status and relationship with the judiciary, and the rights, responsibilities of probation officers, as well as their liability (Stasiak 2008; Sawicka 2010, p. 130). According to Tyszkiewicz (2003, p. 444), the major reform issues were the relationship between the judiciary and probation officers, the official status of the probation officer, and specifying his/her qualifications and duties.

One major reform was the creation of the Family Courts in 1978 (Kubiak and Kasprzycki 1977, pp. 1045–8; Bańkowska 1999, pp. 131–2). This made it possible for all family cases to be heard in the one court and even by a single judge. This did not eventuate in practice as these courts were given too wide a jurisdiction and certain limitations had to be imposed (Strzembosz 1984, pp. 167 ff.).

The Ministry of Justice (MoJ) launched two fundamental projects to reform the Court Appointed Probation Service. This affected both juveniles and adults. In the project concerning juveniles, which generally involved expanding on the ideas of Stojanowska and Strzembosz (1978, p. 255), probation officers were given greater autonomy and were made senior workers of the court, becoming equal partners with judges.[22] The following were mentioned as the three major probation reforms: (1) transforming the social-professional probation model into a professional-social one; (2) abandoning control-repression probation service in favour of educational probation service; and (3) changing the status of the probation officer from administrative worker to senior employee and defining the position as a profession of public trust (Sawicka 2010, p. 126). This last point was an essential component of the reform. It was emphasised in the doctrine that granting a probation officer the status of senior employee was a precondition for a good relationship with the judge – a relationship based on partnership and cooperation (Ostrihanska 1986, pp. 11 ff.).

The ideas behind these changes presupposed that probation officers, as senior employees, would form standalone groups within the framework of the courts and that probation officers and judges would form functional and informational ties rather than official and supervisory ones.[23] Ideas were also proposed (curiously, by the judges themselves) concerning transferring some of the jurisdictional competencies of the judges for juveniles and the judges for adults to probation officers, although these were not included in the final draft (Sawicka 2010, p. 133).

The regional probation officer, as a specialist in prevention and rehabilitation, should be the direct superior of the professional probation officer. Subordination has always been multilevel. The probation officer answered to the Chairperson of the Department, the Chief Justice of the Regional Court, the Voivodeship Probation Officer and the Chief Justice of the Voivodeship Court. Most of these superiors were not professionally prepared to manage the educational and rehabilitative activities that fall under the probation officer's care (Sawicka 2010, p. 129). Here, it is worth mentioning that the changes proposed by the act, which encroached on the subordinate relations between probation officers, judges and the chief justice, constituted one of the factors that made the departmental authorities eager to reinstall the ancien régime after a couple of years. The fact that the probation officer essentially answered before the Regional Probation Officer and was only formally subordinate to the Chief Justice of the Regional Court was impugned. The latter was responsible for the probation officer's work, yet had no say in staff selection, and thereby quality, and no influence in implementing probation policy (Mycka 2008, pp. 157–8). This was one of the reasons, although not the major one, for attempting to amend the Court Appointed Probation Officers Act. This has not as yet been done.[24]

The position of probation officers in the justice system

The Court Appointed Probation Service has been thought of as an institution answerable to the courts (Juvenile/Family and Criminal) since its inception, as it has performed various tasks during court proceedings and in executing judgements (Sawicka 2010, p. 130). The distinct lineage of the Polish probation service (which, unlike in other countries, was not organised through initiatives of local communities, social services or charitable institutions) has resulted in a somewhat different development. This is also the source of the court system's strong authority.

This close link between probation service and courts has long been critically regarded by some, albeit not overly many, Polish academics and practitioners. It is argued that this is a departure from the model generally adopted in Europe, where the probation system is independent of the court system and has a great deal of autonomy (Stępniak 1992, pp. 25–39). As a result, critics say that probation officers mainly, if not exclusively, perform tasks for the courts, and are less occupied with people under supervision in their community and with offenders lodged in various kinds of open and closed institutions. Moreover, they work less often with

22 The authors considered that subordinating probation officers to the judiciary and the courts would stifle their initiative, motivation and autonomy and could even cause demarcation disputes over rehabilitation methodologies, where probation officers believe themselves to be experts.

23 Probation officer teams began to be created in 1994 (Jedynak and Martuszewicz 2007).

24 Another of the Department's reservations was the excessive influence of the Regional Probation Officer Assembly on the selection of Regional Probation Officers (Art. 36 Act on Court Appointed Probation Officers) (Mycka 2008; Stępniak 2009a). The author analyses the proposed amendments to the Act on Court Appointed Probation Officers, calls attention to the inconsistency of some of the proposed regulations to increase the authority of the Chief Justices of the Regional Courts at the expense of the Regional Probation Officers, and points out their incompatibility with the EU Regulations on Sentences and Alternative Measures.

the local community than do their counterparts in, for example, the English and Wales probation system (Moczydłowski 2006).[25] It is also difficult to predict whether there will be any revolutionary changes in this area in the next few years, although the Ministry of Justice has indicated there might be.[26] Similar discussions on placing probation within or without the justice system can be found in the literature around the world. Jehle (1996) states that having observed practices and legal changes in this area in several countries, there is no close link between the effectiveness of the probation services and their inclusion in, or exclusion from, the justice system, or their dependency on government agencies, local government bodies or private institutions.

Those who favour following other Western European countries and placing the probation service outside the courts have proposed several solutions. The one put forth by Paweł Moczydłowski is fairly controversial. Moczydłowski (2006, p. 114) proposes making the Polish probation system part of the organisation that executes judgements and combining it, as does the UK, with the prison system by creating a separate Department of Probation and Prisons under the MoJ.[27] The author justifies this idea by stressing that the primary task of probation officers is executing court judgements and they therefore should come under the execution authorities. He also points out that educators in penal institutions perform de facto probation functions.[28] This point is unarguable.

A solution that aimed to make the court appointed probation officers independent of the courts was proposed by Stępniak (1992, pp. 117 ff.),[29] who presented two versions to the MoJ. Both assumed that the probation officers for juveniles and adults would be separated. These plans did not win the approval of the Ministry of Justice, especially on account of the proposal to 'exclude' the probation service from the courts. There was also thought to be no justification for splitting the two types of probation officer.

Plans for such fundamental organisational changes to the probation system, especially coming after a relatively recent reform, did not win the approval of probation officers. In studies conducted by the Institute of Justice, professional probation officers were asked whether the probation services should remain with the courts and the MoJ or whether they should be disconnected from them. Most did not question the current arrangement and were for maintaining the status quo (Buczkowski et al. 2010, pp. 163, 189).

Professional-social vs social-professional model

Arguments in favour of the longstanding tradition of maintaining a social-professional model are inevitably raised when discussing the best probation model for Poland. This model is still in operation, despite proclamations and attempted changes, although nobody has denied the need for a model that is exclusively professional or at least professional-social (Gromek 2001, pp. 231 ff.).

Ministry of Justice declarations on changing the probation model over the years have come to nothing. We therefore still have a social-professional system as evidenced by there being considerably more social than professional probation officers (see Figures 8.1 and 8.2) and by the fact that more than two-thirds of probation officers' educational tasks, such as supervision – even in difficult cases – are submitted by professional probation officers to social probation officers. There is also a consensus that professional probation officers should take the 'most difficult cases'.[30] This raises the question of why this has not been achieved and what

25 This inclines the author to the radical view that such a close connection between probation officers and judges prevents the Polish system from meeting the conditions that would qualify it as probation.

26 Mycka (2008, p. 167) suggests the possibility of creating a distinct probation officer service organisation in the future.

27 As far as I know, this has never been accepted as an official project but has remained a 'certain vision'.

28 Utrat-Milecki (2007, p. 66) has firmly opposed combining the probation officer and prison services, claiming that penology treats the probation officer services in family and criminal cases as a homogeneous professional group and that this would contradict educational studies that have defined the essence and mission of probationary institutions.

29 During this time, P. Stępniak was a member of the expert team (with J. Jasiński and P. Moczydłowski), convened on the initiative of P. Moczydłowski from the MoJ, that supported the project. He also obtained provisional acceptance from the Department but a change of government prevented it from coming to fruition (Stępniak 2005–2006).

30 This is borne out by empirical studies conducted twice by Stępniak (1992 pp. 115 ff.). The results show that the ratio between the two classes of probation officer has remained roughly constant for approximately 20 years, despite there being more social and professional probation officers. Social probation officers therefore continue to take on substantive and/or difficult cases, despite having less technical training and being principally focused on control. The social-professional model has thus remained unchanged.

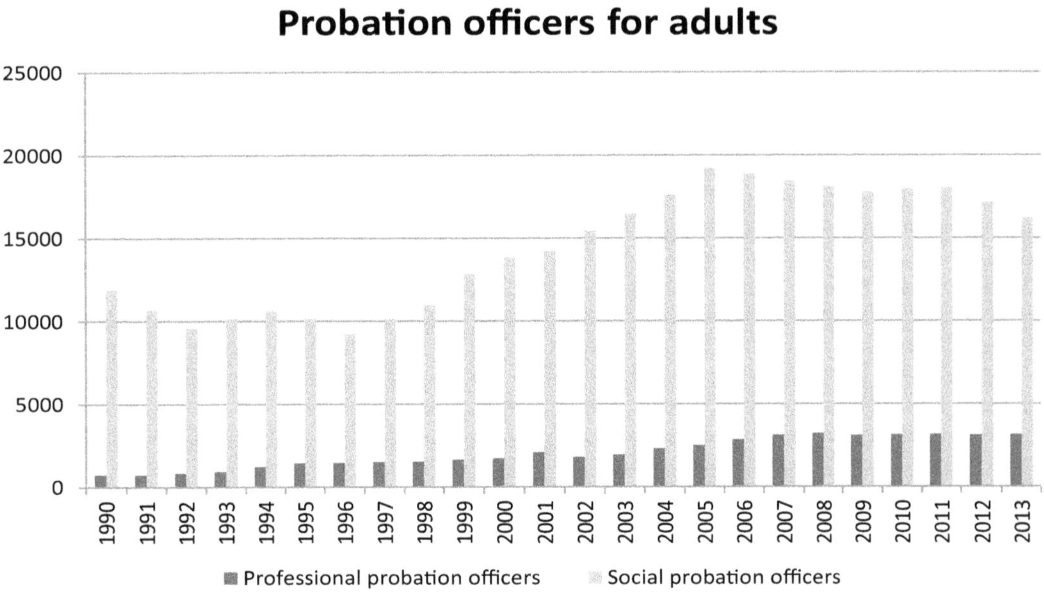

Figure 8.1 Number of professional and social adult probation officers 1990–2013

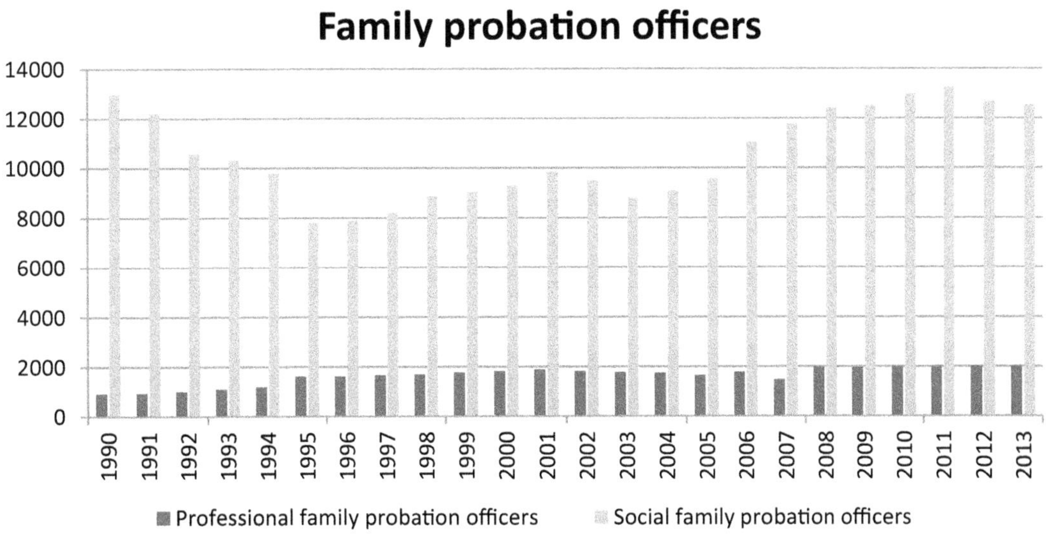

Figure 8.2 Number of professional and social family probation officers 1990–2013

needs to done. While this is frequently a result of there being too few professional probation officers, such officers are also clearly overburdened with administrative and bureaucratic work, which should not be the case. This is a vicious circle that has not yet been broken, despite periodic ministerial resolutions and proclamations to the effect that professional probation officers should constitute approximately 70–75 per cent.

Figures 8.1 and 8.2, depicting the numbers of professional and social probation officers, raise the question of whether the professional group should be increased by transforming the social-professional model into a professional-social one.

One of the more radical ideas to increase the number of professional probation officers was to cease paying lump sums to social probation officers and to have them fill vacancies in the professional staff. This was intended to increase considerably the number of better educated and more qualified professional probation officers as well as improve the quality and effectiveness of their work. Curiously, more than half of those asked for their opinion on professional probation officers (of which there were slightly more family than adult) accepted a decrease in the number of social probation officers, but did not advocate abolishing them completely (61 per cent and 54 per cent respectively) (Buczkowski et al. 2010, pp. 163 and 189).

Whenever the probation model is discussed, the merits of social probation officers are stressed. For example, their familiarity with the local environment, including their knowledge of the conditions and customs of a given area, enables them to be treated as 'locals' and not 'outsiders' (Kamiński 1997, pp. 1091 ff.). Living nearby facilitates means frequent contact with the person under supervision and better relations with the institutions that provide material assistance and offer various programmes and/or assistance in resolving issues. On the downside, social probation officers have a lower level of general or formal education, and less legal and socio-pathological knowledge.

Legal considerations on court appointed probation officers

Legislatively speaking, probation supervision or control can apply to both juveniles and adult criminal offenders. For juveniles, the Family Court can apply independent supervision by a probation officer or placement in a juvenile educational centre or correctional house. Placement in a correctional house may be suspended (Art. 6 and Art. 11 §§ 1 and 2 of the Act of 26 October 1982 on treatment of minors). Adult supervision can be applied by: a conditional stay of criminal proceedings (CC Arts 66–8); a conditionally suspended custodial sentence (CC Arts 69–76); and a conditional early release from prison (SC Art. 161 §§ 1–4). Pursuant to CC Art. 36 § 1, the court could order supervision as part of a community sentence. This was changed when the Criminal Code was amended on 5 November 2009. A professional adult probation officer performs extra tasks and activities connected with supervision, e.g. lodging various applications at the court, executing custodial sentences, assisting offenders preparing to be released from prison (CC Arts 77–84a), and performing specified activities in implementing electronic supervision and community sentences (Szymanowski 2010c, pp. 178–81).

Probation involves putting the offender's behaviour to the test, through the probation officer's supervision, when there are premises that allow a prediction, with a high degree of probability, that even if more severe measures are not applied, a perpetrator will obey the law and not reoffend. Probation may be combined with the imposition of specific obligations, which all too seldom occurs in practice (10–25 per cent of cases, according to some authors).[31] The view that there has been a failure to impose obligations is shared by almost every judge, prosecutor and probation officer. It is curious then that this consensus finds no correspondence either in the number of applications lodged by probation officers or in the sentences being imposed (Mycka 2008, p. 156).

The prevalent view in the literature is that probation of adults constitutes, perhaps rightly, an alternative to imprisonment, especially since the Criminal Code of 1997 gives priority to non-isolation measures by, for example, extending opportunities for probation and community sentences. It is evident from practice, however, that this view is incorrect. More and more authors, such as Skupiński (2009b, p. 314), Jakubowska-Hara (2009a, p. 8) and Melezini (2007, p. 493), are taking the view that probation is not an alternative to imprisonment. Jan Skupiński has emphatically stated that it is only a 'pseudo-alternative', from the standpoint of both legal solutions and sentencing practice. Probation is, as the doctrine stresses, more of an alternative to other non-isolation penalties, such as fines, community sentences and possibly short-term prison sentences (Szewczyk 2007, pp. 58 ff.).

31 The penalty most frequently imposed is the suspended sentence (60–70 per cent). The offender is subjected to probation supervision in approximately one third of these cases (Zagórski 2008, pp. 100 ff.).

Moreover, the belief that probation is too lenient, not very effective, indulges criminals and is an inappropriate sanction that is not commensurate with the act committed, is widely held among the public (Moczydłowski 2006, pp. 101 ff.). The prevalent view, even when the penalty is a suspended sentence, is that the offender 'has got off' and 'was not punished' (Siemaszko 2004, p. 119).[32] In practice, however, executions of suspended penalties are relatively rare. Probation officers do not often apply for it, even if circumstances warrant it, and even if they do, the courts do not always approve their applications.[33] The public is also considered insufficiently informed about the existence of probation service or its advantages or educational merits or about subjecting offenders to specific conditions and imposing obligations whose performance should be monitored. This all adds up to definite harshness for the offender and the option of applying the suspended penalty if he/she does not fulfil the conditions ordered by the court is always open. Belief in the effectiveness of severe and harsh penalties is fairly widespread among the public and it is difficult to debunk the 'myth of harshness', even when the findings of objective studies are brought to bear (Bałandynowicz 2010, p. 93).

It would appear that the era of academics and experts has passed and the mass media has almost completely taken over the role of explaining the complexity of the workings of social phenomena, especially those concerning criminality.[34] It could be, however, that supervision and/or control by a probation officer would be more socially accepted if the public and the judiciary believed that the hardship of a penalty did not solely depend on imprisoning the offender, but also on subjecting him/her to specific probationary conditions and obligations that restricted his/her freedom, which could be onerous for him/her, and which had to be consistently executed, and that a good, effective probation officer contributed to making society safer through his/her work (Szymanowski 2002, p. 24).

It is worth asking how many adults are placed under probationary supervision by the courts. Answering this has so far caused difficulty, as precisely determining how many people the courts have ordered placed under probationary supervision (e.g. suspended sentences) has proved to be reasonably complicated.[35] On the other hand, it has been easy to determine for juveniles and analyses have been conducted for that reason. Thanks to a new Council of Europe publication, we now have access to data on the number of people against whom the courts in EU member states have ordered alternative measures of various kinds (Aebi et al. 2010, pp. 18–19). The 2010 data for Poland show that, of an estimated population of 38,167,300, the total number of adults under probation officer supervision was 249,688, of whom 198,544 were being supervised as part of a suspended sentence, 3,845 as part of a community sentence, 43,724 as a result of a conditional early release from prison, with a number of remaining cases (Aebi et al. 2010, pp. 18–19). It can therefore be established that of the 432,891 people sentenced by the courts in 2010, according to the Krajowy Rejestr Skazanych (National Criminal Register), approximately 10 per cent were serving prison sentences and 57.7 per cent were under probation officer supervision (most of whom had been given suspended sentences). There were, however, very few community sentences ordered in 2010, with just under 4,000 people under supervision (it should be added that ordering supervision was suspended in 2009 following an amendment). By way of comparison, there are approximately 100,000 people sentenced to community service orders in Belgium.

Tables 8.1 and 8.2 show the kinds of basic tasks and activities performed by probation officers (this is obviously not an exhaustive list). It is worth observing that the number of controlled and supervised adults and juveniles has fallen. This is not something to celebrate. In the case of juveniles, this is associated with demographic changes. As can be seen in the case of adults, approximately one third of those given

32 The author believes that conditional penalties are not treated as penalties by the majority of offenders as they inflict no hardship and that almost 90 per cent of offenders incur no real liability. He further believes the probation model needs to be completely overhauled, and that probation officers should be more disciplinary towards juveniles who fail to observe their probationary conditions (e.g. not abusing alcohol and not inflicting violence on family members) and should not tolerate bad behaviour from them.

33 Judges are not concerned about this when ordering supervision. Nor are probation officers, who do not exhibit sufficient ingenuity and initiative to apply for the imposition of obligations that might contribute to a favourable course of supervision (Zagórski 2010, pp. 70 ff.; Mycka 2008, p. 157).

34 See Chapter 10: 'Criminality and the Media'.

35 It does not seem correct to count everyone given a suspended sentence, a community sentence, a stay of criminal proceedings or a conditional early release as being on 'probation as commonly understood'. This accounted for some 750,000 people in 2007 (Mycka 2008, p. 155). It is difficult to imagine that many people being put under supervision.

Table 8.1 Supervision and other activities performed by probation officers for adults 2007–2013 (number of people)

Activities performed by probation officers	2007	2008	2009	2010	2011	2012	2013
Supervision in suspended sentences	222,297	214,469	2010,378	198,544	194, 860	162,558	167,030
Supervision in stays of execution	3,560	3,584	3,572	3,429	3,545	3,243	3,486
Supervision in community sentences	5,255	4,980	5,659	3,845	787	–	–
Supervision in early release	39,832	41,560	42,575	43,724	44,774	36,269	37,608
Other supervision	647	113	150	146	125	7	15
All supervision	271,591	264,706	262,184	249,688	244,091	202,077	208,139

Source: Data from MS-40. Information on the number of cases as at the last day of the reporting period (Journal II, Table 1 Pos. 7).
Note: From 2012 supervision in community sentences ceased.

Table 8.2 Control exercised by family probation officers 2007–2013 (number of people)

Control by family probation officers	2007	2008	2009	2010	2011	2012	2013
Control in educational and protective cases	72,059	71,567	75,964	77,046	79,465	67,430	79,329
Control in juvenile cases	49,745	48,731	48,970	47,077	47,178	39,558	41,882
Including independent educational measures	47,764	46,869	47,008	45,069	45,277	37,935	40,304
Control (detoxification cases – adults)	26,150	27,496	27,604	25,064	23,899	18,520	23,291
All control	147,954	147,791	152,538	149,187	150,542	125,508	144,502

Source: Data from MS-40. Information on the number of cases as at the last day of the reporting period (Journal II, Table 1 Pos. 7).

suspended sentences are subject to supervision, which does not always guarantee control by the courts. It is worth adding that the amendments of 5 November 2009 restricted the options for granting conditional release.

Objectives and significance of court-appointed probation officer legislation

The Court Appointment Probation Officers Act (2001) was crucial to the development of probation. The profession had been waiting and preparing for this for years. The Act clearly defines the role and objectives of the probation officer and establishes preventive and educational activities as his/her overriding priority (Szymanowski 2005a, pp. 74–7; Szymanowski 2002, pp. 16–19). In order of importance in achieving these objectives, Art. 1 of the Act enumerates educational/rehabilitative, diagnostic, preventive and controlling tasks as those to be undertaken by probation officers in executing court orders. It is worth emphasising the difference in the approach of the Act in appraising and prioritising the tasks of Polish probation officers and that of the contemporary England and Wales act on probation (the Criminal Justice and Court Services Act [2000]) according to which the objectives of probation are, in descending order, limiting criminality, appropriately punishing offenders, making them aware of their responsibilities and finally, rehabilitating them. This reverse order of probation officer tasks in the two acts is symptomatic. This did not come about fortuitously and it illustrates the different approaches the two countries take in responding to criminality.

The Act stipulates the social-professional status of probation officers and the place, organisation and tasks of the court-appointed probation officer service within the framework of the justice system. The court-appointed probation officer service is recognised as an integral and substantial part of the machinery of the justice system and professional probation officers are defined as an independent body that executes court orders in executory proceedings (PEC Art. 2 Pt. 6).[36] According to the Act, the entitlements, as well as the tasks and obligations, of professional, and to a certain extent, social, probation officers have been significantly increased. The former gained the more prestigious status of a separate and autonomous service, at the same time becoming an expert service and a uniform professional formation through the imposition of certain conditions and requirements, e.g. having completed higher education and legal training.[37] Some theoreticians, however, say that probation officers are encumbered with tasks that are too onerous, incompatible with existing practice and even tradition, and that they alter the probation model and go beyond the regulations of the Punishment Execution Code (Szymanowski 2002).[38] Their three main reform objectives can be concisely expressed as:

1. permanent employment
2. professionalisation[39]
3. legislation

This means ensuring sufficient probation officers, especially professional ones, for the job, raising their qualifications (specialised training) and level of education, and making appropriate legal changes. Many essential organisational matters have become regulated and a local government probation officers framework has been created. These aims, however, remain unrealised (Stasiak 2010, p. 66).

Organisation and characteristics of the work of court-appointed probation officers

The work of the Polish probation officer is performed in a fairly traditional manner. Surveys on adult and family probation officers conducted by the Justice Institute reveal that a significant majority (80 per cent) of professional probation officers declare that they apply the case method in their communications with people under supervision (Wójcik 2010, pp. 149–50). They rely on influencing their charges, mainly through motivational, admonitory, supervisory and preventive talks, and where necessary and if possible, suggest

36 Some author/practitioners, however, have pointed out that only professional probation officers for adults have the status of an executory body. This does not apply to family probation officers, who remain an 'auxiliary body' of the court in contravention of the European rules on sanctions and alternative measures. Similarly disturbing are statistical data showing that the number of social family probation officers grew between 2000 and 2008, worsening the professional to social probation officer ratio (Jedynak 2010, pp. 203–6, 210 ff.). Lelental (2010, p. 186) presents the contrary view that all professional probation officers (including family probation officers) are executory bodies.

37 Gruszczyńska (2010, pp. 115–19) gives a detailed socio-demographic description of professional family and adult probation officers, and claims that almost all of them met these conditions in 2007. 93 per cent of professional probation officers have higher education, many of them have expert training and court work is their sole employment.

38 Szymanowski (2001, p. 71) also expresses the view in the Criminal Code of 1997 'the tasks and responsibilities of court-appointed probation officers increased prodigiously'.

39 This refers to probation officers applying contemporary methodologies of interaction with those under supervision (rehabilitation) (Jedynak and Martuszewicz 2007, p. 30).

taking treatment for alcohol or drug addiction or undergoing specific therapy. More rarely do probation officers, especially adult probation officers, apply relatively modern methods, e.g. the contract method.[40]

Professional adult probation officers spend the greater part of their time on exercising personal supervision and completing various administrative and bureaucratic chores. Professional family probation officers, by contrast, devote a lot of time to conducting environmental and supervisory interviews. Communications with the people under their supervision are not all that frequent. On average, around 70 per cent of both classes of professional probation officers visit their charges in their family homes once a month and the visits, going by the survey answers, vary from 10 minutes to one and a half hours (Wójcik 2010, pp. 150, 179). Should we not consider how often these meetings need to be held before we can speak about real interaction and effective use of the case method, and not just perfunctory inspections?[41] Because it can be argued that everything depends on specific cases. As to whether the effectiveness of probation is dependent on frequency of contact with the probation officer, this is subject to several interpretations in the literature and has not been settled (Ostrihanska and Greczuszkin 1999, p. 47). As the research cited above reveals, the biggest problems for a probation officer are trying to find those under his/her supervision at home, their unwillingness to work with him/her, their aggressive behaviour and their families' aversion to him/her. More than half the probation officers surveyed reported that their charges had exhibited negative behaviour towards them. This generally took the form of abusive language but it sometimes involved threats and even physical aggression.[42] Adult probation officers encounter their greatest difficulties in arranging the execution of community sentences. Almost 85 per cent of probation officers surveyed held that the greatest nuisance in executing this sentence lay in the convicts either abandoning the work assigned to them or not even taking it up (Wójcik 2010, p. 154; Zagórski 2010, p. 223). Disturbing data from the MoJ also reveal delays in the execution of community sentences of more than twice the sentence period caused by the tardiness of sentencing bodies, i.e. probation officers and judges ruling in executory matters (Wójcik 2010, p. 154; Szymanowski 2005a, p. 99; Zagórski 2008). These results indicate that urgent legislative and organisational changes are necessary to improve the functioning of this penalty and that practitioners need to take appropriate disciplinary action in executing it (Mycka 2008, p. 156).

It is also worth looking at those ordered to serve community sentences because, as is evident from some studies, this penalty is pointless for some people. For example, alcoholics and drug addicts require systematic treatment and no work can be expected of them (Ostrihanska and Rzeplińska 1988, pp. 18 ff.). A tendency to order fewer of these sentences has been observable for a couple of years (Skupiński 2009c, p. 21). Demands were also reported, especially by probation officers, to abolish probation officer supervision in community sentences (which were eventually met, although whether this was the right solution is an open question) (Lelental 2010; Zagórski 2008, p. 228).

Many scholars have been critical of the way probation service works in Poland. Various charges have been levelled at both the legislative nature of probation service and the practice of applying and performing probation officer control or supervision. Janusz Zagórski and his team at the Office of the Commissioner for Civil Rights Protection conducted extensive research on this topic.[43] This led to charges of both a material and an organisational nature being levelled at probation officers' practice, e.g. probation officers too infrequently applying to the courts to lay down, extend or alter specific obligations (and the courts complying in only approximately 10 per cent of cases), to say nothing of the other kinds of applications that lie within their responsibility. Other probation officers' activities also came in for criticism as did the insufficient supervision on the part of their superiors. Zagórski's team found that in approximately a third of the court files they

40 The pioneering research of Ostrihanska and Greczuszkin concerned the contract method deployed by probation officers in their educational work with juveniles. Contracts concluded by juveniles on specific matters of importance to them were studied. 37.4 per cent of juveniles completed all their assignments, 38.5 per cent completed some of them and only 18.1 per cent did not fulfil the contract. The contract method has proven very useful in the work of the court-appointed probation officer (Ostrihanska and Greczuszkin 1999, p. 222).

41 In England and Wales, for example, Nationwide Standards specify the number of meetings the probation officer is to have with the offender, who is sent back to prison if he/she twice violates his/her obligations (Ostrihanska 2006, p. 617).

42 For probation officers feeling threatened by aggression from those they supervise and reportedly requiring physical protection, see Zagórski (2010, p. 223).

43 This sort of accusation attests to a lack of control in the work of both judges and probation officers (Zagórski 2008; Szymanowski 2005a).

analysed, probation officers had taken no action against convicts and did not do so until after six months from the start of the trial period in roughly 40 per cent of cases. Moreover, decisions were handed down by the courts too late to be executed. This neglect seems fairly significant. More control over the execution of these sentences should be applied with a view to improving the situation.

Probation service: rehabilitation or social work?

The Court Appointed Probation Officers Act is a product of those schools of thought based on the educational/rehabilitative approach. This mode of thinking has guided the practical activities of probation officers in Poland since the inception of the institution in the country. Probation is meant to achieve several aims, according to the literature. The basic aim used to be to rehabilitate perpetrators of crime and the means of achieving it were mainly based on the case method. This idea also held sway in Poland but it was put into practice in a very different way from e.g. Western Europe and the US (there were no formal programmes to prevent recidivism; nor were there any formal training or therapeutic programmes; and it is not known whether probation officers commonly employed the case method) (Ostrihanska 1986, pp. 11 ff.).

Rehabilitation is no longer the most important component, having ceded first place to protecting the public and curbing criminality. Rehabilitating people under supervision has been put on the backburner.[44] It is thought that the work of the probation officer should consist of 'case management' and in assessing the behaviour of an offender in terms of the risk of reoffending, by considering his/her criminogenic needs, which may be conducive to such behaviour. The role of the probation officer lies in observing those under his/her supervision in order to understand what fosters their criminality and in motivating them to make an effort to alter their behaviour by showing them how they can learn to avoid situations that lead to breaking the law. Well organised supervision designed to achieve specific aims and linked with obligations is what makes the probation officer more effective, just so long as the people being supervised accept his/her assistance.

The probation officer is also supposed to suggest that the offender participate in various programmes that may aid his/her social integration and return to society and prevent further detrimental behaviour on his/her part. These ideas are modern, although they have been given some critical appraisal (Case and Haines 2009, pp. 309 ff.; Wójcik 2014, pp. 89 ff.). Although they have found supporters in Poland, the extent to which they have been put into practice is so far relatively limited.[45] The rehabilitative approach in dealing with criminals is generally accepted and reasonably well developed in Poland, at least in theory, by a sizeable group of academics and practitioners.

Sometimes attempts are made, mainly by practitioners in prisons and juvenile detention centres, to design and run rehabilitative and therapeutic programmes for criminal perpetrators and to adapt reputable programmes from abroad to Polish conditions (one of the successful adaptations was the Atlantis Program; one of the not so successful was the Aggression Replacement Program [ART]).[46] Data from the Central Prison Service Board reveal that some 30,000 convicts in penal institutions have participated in approximately 600 programmes of various kinds over the last few years. These data are both surprising and worrying. Not much is known about the type or quality of these programmes. Relatively few of them are described in the work of Monika Marczak; reading this reveals that most of these programmes have not been evaluated and that, in general, this was not an option (Marczak is, however, cognisant of the problems and the difficulties the need for such studies pose) (Marczak 2009, pp. 333–41). Henryk Machel has expressed a similar view, stating that the main shortcoming of these programmes (stressed by those who design and run them) is their lack of evaluation, as this makes

44 The Ministry of Justice officially takes the same view: 'the main aim of probation officers is to reduce criminality, and rehabilitation, education, control and electronic monitoring are merely means to that end' (Mycka 2008, p. 157).

45 Stańdo-Kawecka (2010a, pp. 114 ff.) writes that the 'what works movement', designed to curb criminality, was not a matter of interest for Polish writers.

46 The Atlantis Program was implemented in Poland by US therapist Bill Burgin in the mid-1990s at the behest of the Stefan Batory Foundation. Many therapists were trained at the time. The programme is still being run in some prisons (Zalikowska 2009). Majcherczyk (2008) writes that more than half the 200 educators trained so far no longer work in the prison system and that very few of the remainder are used to conduct classes with convicts. Can this programme therefore be considered a success? Dubiel (2009, p. 32) laconically adds that the ART program has been running in the prison system for almost 10 years without specifying, however, how many prisoners have participated or how the programme has been assessed.

it impossible to gauge their effectiveness and thereby their usefulness and cost-effectiveness (Machel 2009, pp. 58 ff.). Machel takes a positive view of the increase in the number of rehabilitative programmes and their development but he is critical of some of them in view of their poor quality and weak theoretical underpinnings. The situation in juvenile detention centres is similar. The fact that such measures are being taken at all has to be seen positively, but they should be planned, organised and controlled, and the programmes themselves should be assessed, reviewed and submitted for evaluation (Drapała 2012).

Another topic discussed in the literature is orienting probation officers more towards social work with offenders, e.g. by working more closely with social welfare institutions as happens in many other European countries where the traditional 'comprehensive care' model has been supplanted by multifaceted activities in the local environment in tandem with supporting people in need of assistance and integrating them into society (Stępniak 1998, pp. 46 ff.). The areas that social work covered have been considerably enlarged and their scope extended. This has altered the role of the social worker, who is now expected to stimulate social activity and to teach people how to solve their problems independently. Social workers therefore need to move away from being caring and protective and towards motivating their charges and organising and inspiring, spurring local communities into action. This is consistent with the idea of decentralising social policy and activating society (Kotlarska-Michalska 2004, pp. 212 ff.).

Reliable, expert social diagnosis, and the appropriate corrective action that results from it, became the basis of, and the precondition for, effective social activity (Matyjas 2004, pp. 235–6). The problem with these wonderful ideas, however, is that any attempt to put them into practice is invariably met with any number of almost insurmountable barriers (Kromolicka 2003, pp. 246 ff.). Krzysztof Krajewski (2007b) describes the work of probation officers, claiming that, probationary functions being part of the social system in the modern world, authentic social work by way of assisting those in their care solve their own problems in life should be the probation officer's basic aim. Given that the work of a probation officer in Poland mainly consists of (as it used to) controlling and monitoring their charges as well as checking whether they have fulfilled the obligations laid down by the courts and not committed any crimes, the Polish probation model should be amended accordingly.

Piotr Stępniak (1998, pp. 104 ff.; also Tyszkiewicz 2004, pp. 43 ff.) has long supported the idea of adding social work to the functions performed by probation officers. Stępniak became critical in his assessment of the significance of rehabilitation after tracing the evolution of social work from the time the idea of rehabilitation ceased to be part of the framework of treating criminals in Western Europe. At the same time, he stresses the difference between rehabilitation geared towards a difficult to assess and fairly abstractly defined change in an offender's personality, and social work, whose aims are generally reasonably specific and whose achievements can be relatively easily verified.

When looking at the relations between social work and educational/rehabilitative activities, many authors stress that these two fields have increasingly more areas in common in that they adopt similar axiological assumptions, and their workers are involved with the same people and have similar work principles (Pytka 2001; Mudrecka 2004, pp. 299–301). All this justifies the two professions working closely together but not becoming one and the same.

There is a great deal of significance in probation officers working with a specific local community. This may, after all, make the community more receptive to socially integrating convicted people by employing and housing them in a given environment and becoming more accepting of them.[47] Piotr Stępniak claims, however, that rehabilitation in Eastern Europe and social work in Western Europe 'do not constitute separate models of dealing with convicted people'. Differentiating these ideas, then, does not make a lot of sense (Stępniak 2001, pp. 77 ff.). Andrzej Rzepniewski considers that probation officers engage in activities of a social nature as part of their work but not in a strict, professional sense (2008, pp. 317 ff.).

The difficulty of probation officer work lies in fulfilling two disjointed roles, viz. someone who helps the offender (educational) and an officer of the court. Education needs to be based on trust, respect and acceptance, as does monitoring the behaviour of the offender during the trial period to make sure he/she fulfils the obligations ordered by the court and does not commit any crimes. As an officer of the court, on the other

47 Social workers who also work with criminals name people released from prison as one of the four most difficult categories they deal with and the one with whom they are least prepared to work (Olech 1998, pp. 303 ff.).

hand, the probation officer is duty bound to take predetermined action in the event that the offender does not comply with these conditions. The person being monitored should be made aware of this. The effectiveness of a probation officer lies in his/her skill in maintaining and balancing these two roles without bringing them into conflict (Ostrihanska and Greczuszkin 1999, pp. 48 ff.; Cartledge et al. 1981, pp. 20–21).

Effectiveness of probation

The high degree of effectiveness of the institution of probation is emphasised in criminological literature around the world (including Poland), although evaluative studies are inconsistent, making it difficult to make comparisons and draw definitive conclusions. The effectiveness of probation depends on a number of factors, e.g. criminal justice systems, legal regulations, categories and forms of supervision, the size and assortment of the group to be supervised, and the period for which such supervision has been ordered. It should also be borne in mind that probation officers have always worked under variable conditions. Other types of institutions and organisations (e.g. NGOs) that support what probation officers do have sprung up and the number of professional and social probation officers has increased considerably. There have also been substantial changes in the probation officers environment, viz. they have a distinctly higher level of education, have been given more responsibilities and have expert training. Only those who are really interested are going to try to improve their qualifications, especially, as is sometimes the case, in their own time and at their own expense. Many Polish researchers cite a publication by Andrzej Marek (1986, p. 202), who describes this institution in detail (mainly by drawing on works in English), when they refer to the effectiveness of probation. They also cite his data that recidivism, after probation, is 'only' around 10–20 per cent. Subsequent revivals of this position have always included the same data, cited as current by some academics, although it can be observed, using more up-to-date statistics and empirical research, that returning to crime after probation is definitely on the increase in Poland. Empirical research conducted in Poland over the last few years demonstrates this. It is first necessary to specify, however, how the effectiveness of probation is to be evaluated, i.e. what criteria of effectiveness should be adopted and what should be understood by a lack of effectiveness on the part of this institution. It needs to be clarified at the outset that the effectiveness of probation (as an institution) cannot be equated with the performance of probation officers. The latter is extraordinarily difficult to evaluate and is not the topic of this analysis.

Considering the criteria for gauging the effectiveness of probation and describing the policy of applying it in Poland is not an easy task. It is generally accepted in criminological literature that one of the main aims of probation is to prevent the offender from re-offending and to protect the public, obviously without forgetting about rehabilitation. Some criminologists may well take a negative view of the fact that the number of repeat offenders who appear during the course of the probation period (3–5 years) is an indicator of the effectiveness of probation, but other kinds of measures are difficult to establish and are even less precise. Professional probation officers surveyed by the Justice Institute were convinced of this when asked about the indicators that should be used to evaluate their own work (Marczewski 2010, p. 244). They had a lot of difficulty in establishing criteria against which this could be done. Primarily, however, they were at pains to point out that offenders reverting to crime cannot and should not be the only criterion for evaluating their work. They suggested considering the quality of what they did and not encumbering them with responsibility for failures that were not their fault and then assuming negligence on their part instead of e.g. bad regulations, excessive numbers of people to supervise, offenders avoiding contact with probation officers, and an inability to arrange basic needs for people under supervision (employment, housing, health care etc.).[48] They put forth other proposals as well, suggesting, for example, that the preparedness and competence of a probation officer be assessed by training courses completed, years of work experience, and workshops and specialist conferences attended. Another approach would be to conduct a workload survey based on e.g. the number of cases each probation officer in a team has to manage. One interesting proposition, although difficult to apply, was assessment that took account of (professional, social and emotional) changes in the way the offender functioned, and tasks and goals achieved by the charge (and/or his/her family in the case of family probation officers) (Marczewski 2010, p. 245). The difficulty of such an assessment lies in how to determine whether

48 Gruszczyńska (2010, p. 1100) remarks on the frequency with which probation supervision was ordered in 1990–2006.

and to what extent a change in the behaviour of someone being monitored can be attributed to the probation officer and to what extent it was due to any number of other variables, many of which are sometimes difficult to ascertain or evaluate.

Tadeusz Jedynak, Andrzej Rzepniewski and Henryk Pawlaczyk have proposed a test to determine the effectiveness of a probation officer based on the number of judged cases (analogous to the way prosecutors and judges are assessed). They suggest using the number of cases managed by the probation officer to calculate the number of people who have fulfilled their probationary conditions and whose supervision has been successfully completed – and of those, for whom execution of suspended penalty or a revocation of conditional early release has been ordered (Jedynak 2008, p. 5; also Jedynak 2008, pp. 9–17). This means of evaluation can also raise questions though. Assessments of recidivism based on statistics and file research are generally less reliable than the data on convicts recorded in the National Criminal Register. This would, nevertheless, be a partial solution.

Reverting to crime on the part of adults placed under various forms of supervision cannot, then, be accurately determined in practice. There are no general comprehensive statistical data available and empirical studies are relatively few involving small number of cases and touching just one kind of probation.[49] On the other hand court statistics on juveniles subjected to probation officer supervision will not suffice to establish the extent to which they reoffend as they do not contain all the data on minors over their entire probationary periods.

The fact that people do reoffend, however, has to be accepted as a measure of the ineffectiveness of probation (despite criticism of this view). It has to be clearly stated that the best, or even the only, means of assessing the effectiveness of this institution reliably and relatively quickly is to conduct applicable individual examinations. These consist of checking criminal records in the National Crime Record for the entire probationary period in the case of adults, and local family court register in the case of juveniles. There is no way of telling whether any given person (adult or juvenile) for whom probation control or supervision had been ordered was sentenced again during the probationary period using yearly statistics from the MoJ. Nor is there any way of determining how many such people there are.

It is, however, worth citing some of the empirical studies on reversion to criminality by category of perpetrator under probation supervision that have been conducted in Poland over the last few years.

In 2008, detailed studies to measure reversion to criminality on the part of people placed under various forms of probation supervision were conducted by the Office of the Commissioner for Civil Rights Protection under the direction of Janusz Zagórski. The first part of the studies examined probation supervision of people given suspended sentences. An analysis of the executory court files of 200 criminal cases has shown that execution of penalty was ordered in 33 per cent of cases. These were not data on individuals from the National Crime Record, however, but data from court executory files, so some information on crimes committed or cases in progress might not have been included in the files that were analysed and considered by the author (Zagórski 2008, pp. 69 ff.). The second part of these same studies – conducted on another group of convicts, viz. those given conditionally suspended sentences without supervision – shows that the recidivism rate was lower: 18.5 per cent (Mazur 2008, pp. 31 ff.). This result does not seem strange, as convicted people whom the courts saw no need to have supervised were probably a less demoralised population.

In 1996, the Institute of Justice conducted studies to establish the determinants of conditional early release and to measure its degree of effectiveness. The population comprised 1,430 men conditionally released early from prison in 1991. During a five-year follow-up, 41.7 per cent were sentenced again, according to the National Crime Record (Gruszczyńska and Marczewski 1997–1998, pp. 213–25). Studies on the effectiveness of probation supervision of people given suspended sentences were also conducted by the Institute of Justice relatively recently, with results very similar to the earlier ones cited. According to the National Crime Record, 45 per cent of convicts were repeat offenders. Various risk factors and their accumulation were analysed, as were protective factors.[50]

49 This work includes an examination of the documentation on reoffending on the part of people sentenced to various forms of probation supervision (Zagórski 2008, pp. 69 ff.).

50 Analysis of this group was justified by the fact that probation supervision is most often ordered as part of a suspended sentence, although it is applied in no more than 30 per cent of cases. It should be added that of the remaining

Szymanowski (2010b, pp. 273–82) re-examined the criminal records of offenders given suspended sentences, 184 of whom had been placed under supervision. Within five years of being sentenced, recidivism among those placed under supervision was 33.9 per cent compared with 22 per cent for the others. Recidivism among another group who were merely fined was 28 per cent. All these penalties were checked in the National Crime Record.

The extensive, mainly documentary, studies of juveniles conducted at the Department of Criminology, Institute of Law Studies, Polish Academy of Sciences, a few years ago are an example of research analysing the extent of juveniles reverting to criminality.

Irena Rzeplińska examined a representative sample of juvenile perpetrators (771 people comprising 692 boys and 79 girls) of punishable acts, aged 13–17, tried in the Polish Family Court in 2000. In October 2005, after checking their details in the National Crime Record, it turned out that 16.5 per cent of the now former juvenile girls and 46.2 per cent of the now former juvenile boys had committed repeat crimes tried in the criminal courts (Rzeplińska 2007–2008, p. 409).

Dagmara Woźniakowska-Fajst's study was concerned with the problem of criminality in girls. The study sample comprised 873 juveniles (girls) being tried in the Family Court in 2000. Follow-up studies that consisted of checking their criminal records in the National Crime Record were conducted in 2010 when the former juveniles were 23–27. It is worth noting the extraordinary length of the follow-up period. One hundred and eleven, i.e. 12.7 per cent, of the former juveniles had committed repeat crimes (Woźniakowska-Fajst 2011).

The third of these important studies concerned the youngest juveniles. These people were under 13 when their cases were being heard in the Family Court. Klaus (2009a, pp. 185 ff.) analysed their criminality and their subsequent fates in a four-year follow-up, i.e. while they were still juveniles. The result was that 38.1 per cent of them had been back in court, of whom two-thirds had committed three or more acts during the period (data on subsequent cases were taken from the Family Court Registers). The point was to validate the thesis, well known in criminology, that early criminality bodes ill for the future. The study completely confirmed this.

Percentages of recidivism were higher in studies that used data on repeat, officially registered punishment of specific people than in works based on less precise measures.

In summarising the results of the studies on adult and juvenile repeat crime presented here, it is worth stressing the importance and the value of longitudinal studies, where the subsequent fates of the people studied are tracked, in criminology. This characterises the studies conducted at the Department of Criminology, Institute of Law Studies, Polish Academy of Sciences.

Conclusion

It is probably no exaggeration to say that rehabilitation has been in a permanent state of crisis since Robert Martinson called its effectiveness into question. This challenged the ideas and philosophy behind rehabilitation, and, in many countries, led to a thorough critique of the institution of probation and fundamental changes being made to how it functions. It is therefore worth asking how rehabilitation in Poland appears in this context. Is it going through a crisis as well? If so, does this crisis affect the perception and assessment of court appointed probation in Poland?

There are many facts and signals to indicate that the idea of rehabilitation is generally accepted in Poland's probationary practice, although there are a few exceptions.[51] This is affirmed by the controversy that broke out at the Fourth Polish Penitentiary and Prison Conference in Kalisz in 2006. David Thomas from the UK presented a critical overview of the situation regarding probation in that country and stressed that academics and practitioners were pondering its future. This provoked pretty strong objections from some Polish prison reformers, who claimed that rehabilitation is seen as a necessary, good and reliable institution in Poland and that its continued development was not in any doubt (Stępniak 2007).

---

70 per cent, those on whom the courts impose no specific obligations (no more than 10 per cent) are virtually uncontrolled (Wójcik 2010, pp. 256–369).

51 Stępniak (2008, p. 96) writes on this topic critically and with unconcealed surprise and regret. He does not support rehabilitation in its present form (or perhaps at all) and has often made this clear in his many publications.

The problem, however, is that what is accepted as rehabilitation in Poland is not what is applied in practice. This is unambiguously demonstrated by academic studies and the statements of many judges, public prosecutors, police officers and probation officers. These people approve of: various obligations being imposed on offenders and seeing to it that they are performed; referring cases to mediation; and committing offenders in domestic violence cases to participate in corrective and educational sessions. And yet they do not do these things. Why not? The question of what this practice really is has to be asked.

The vast majority of probation officers, both for juveniles and for adult offenders, when asked about work methodology, declare that they use the individual case method. But when asked to describe exactly what this approach entails, and what meetings with people under their care – which are generally known from studies to happen no more often than once a month – look like, the answer is terse, stereotypical and vague. Some scholars are also sceptical about the possibility of probation officers applying this method more broadly, as they are not suitably trained, and, in any case, there are too few of them to be able to cope with more of these responsibilities (Szymanowski 2005a, p. 95). One should mention the difficulty in accessing the applicable literature, which describes how this methodology is employed and the benefits that can be derived by both the probation officer and the person under supervision.[52] The relationship between the probation officer and the person being monitored should essentially be based on joint participation and mutual respect and acceptance. A juvenile must not be placed in a situation of compulsion, but one of choice (Kępka 2006, p. 83).

However, do we know what the work of the probation officer involves? Zofia Ostrihanska and Aneta Greczuszkin write that knowledge of what the work of a probation officer with a juvenile entails in practice is very incomplete, even among experts. It is not known what actions the probation officer takes towards the juvenile, how the probation officer handles difficulties, what their meetings involve and what the atmosphere is like, what methods are being applied – whether they are correct, whether the probation officer has altered them, when they are ineffectual etc. This cannot be discovered from their reports as they are not detailed enough.

When probation service reforms were being introduced in the 1990s, the prevailing view was that the control approach outweighed the educational approach in probation officers' activities. Any attempt to change or redesign their work model proceeded under the banner of 'educational probation'. It is not so easy, however, to turn 'control' into 'education or rehabilitation'. For this reason, Katarzyna Sawicka, the originator of this idea, has recently acknowledged that implementing the educational (i.e. rehabilitative) model continues to run into difficulties and remains wishful thinking in practice, as probation officers are inadequately equipped in work methods, not enough interested in their own professional training, and overburdened with work (Sawicka 2010, p. 126).

The situation is a little different for adult probation officers. The need to rehabilitate offenders has never been all that prominent, especially during its initial stages. Nor has there been any urge to introduce rehabilitation in prisons. Some academics state point blank that in Poland 'the concept of rehabilitation, in the full sense of the word, has never existed in practice' (Ambrozik 2010, pp. 193–210). Changes only began after the period of transformation.[53] Over the last 10–20 years, definite, positive changes have manifested, along with a realisation that educational and therapeutic measures need to be taken towards convicted people. Rehabilitation has returned to grace, and working in prisons has started to attract psychologists and psychotherapists. Numerous varied interactive programmes for prisoners have appeared in a relatively short time, and having appeared reasonably spontaneously and impulsively, there are definitely too many of them. Moreover it is not always possible to state their origins or how or whether they have been verified. Indeed, there is little, if any, precise information on how they have been evaluated. All of this gives cause for concern. However, it is certainly worth checking whether any of them are practicable, and, if so, to what extent and under what conditions. Applying programmes that are ineffectual or of little use is a waste of effort on the part of many people who could be put to better use – but at least it makes it possible to 'keep inmates busy'.

52 Anossi-Sołtysiak (2007, pp. 334–6) shows, in an accessible way, how probation officers should relate to the people being monitored, how to motivate them, knowing what will make them independent, teaching them how to cope with their problems, giving them confidence in their capabilities, and making them aware of their needs as well as the factors and circumstances conducive to criminality.

53 Stępniak (2012, pp. 91 ff.) as has observed, however, by introducing three ways of serving prison sentences, the legislature has limited the option of rehabilitation to the programmed interaction system.

The choice between the educational model of probation (with the case method) or the control model of probation (or, to put it in more contemporary terms, case management model) is still open. The cited statements and facts warrant the assumption that the proclaimed model is not common in practice. It is therefore worth asking whether the traditional model of probation officers' activities can feasibly be maintained in the current environment of too few professional probation officers with too many responsibilities. This model is based on the case method, which consists of personal, relatively frequent contact between the probation officer and the supervised person, which often binds them with strong emotional bonds. Is not professing a desire and a need, or even an obligation, to maintain this model tantamount to endorsing a fiction and creating a make-believe model of probation? Would it not be better to abandon individual interaction with a portion (perhaps a significant one) of people under supervision and just focus on some of them?

1. Those who require intensive supervision, greater control or specialist programmes and therapy should be subjected to interactive work as it can be effectively applied to them.[54]
2. For those offenders who do not require such measures, probation officer supervision should not be ordered but rather specific obligations – with monitoring obviously being an option, either ad hoc by the probation officer or directly by the court.

This is not posited as a way of bringing on the 'twilight' of traditional probation but perhaps merely to put its current assessment and expectations on a realistic footing. Let us resign from building pretences where it is not mandatory (Beck 2002, p. 348). We will then be able to proceed more rationally and realistically.

54 These ideas were announced by the MoJ, following the example of Western countries, and consisted of, inter alia, building a means to evaluate the risk of reoffending and applying it during criminal proceedings. As far as I am aware, this is still at the discussion and analysis stage. For opinions on and evaluations of these sorts of tools, see Wójcik (2014).

Chapter 9
The Social Perception of Criminality[1]

Witold Klaus, Irena Rzeplińska and Dagmara Woźniakowska-Fajst

Introduction

This study broadly explains the social perception of criminality. This comprises several phenomena, of which the most important is anxiety about criminality on the part of the citizenry, followed by their assessment of the standard of Polish law, the operation and effectiveness of the justice system, and the services of public order. This apprehension is greatly influenced by the rhetoric used by politicians in public debates and the media. The influence these two fora exert on the social perception of criminality is a sufficiently broad and complex issue as to merit its own chapter in this publication.[2] The remaining phenomena, viz. the social feeling of being threatened by criminality and the corresponding degree of punitiveness on the part of Polish people, and the relationship between politicians and criminal policy, are described in this chapter.

Social Perception of Being Threatened by Criminality

Ulrich Beck, who has defined contemporary society as 'risk society', writes that it is based on science, media and information. Scientific advances and media reporting of scientific discoveries, often in a simple or simplified manner, have contributed to an increase in anxiety and a feeling of being under threat among the citizenry. Beck (2005, p. 97) says that anxiety and reassurance can have only one cause: not being able to imagine the danger with which it is necessary to live. As a society, we are constantly bombarded with all sorts of information about the dangers around us, showing us just what risky times we live in. These reports come at us from all sides – from the threat of crime and terrorism, to vulnerability to diseases (including lifestyle diseases) and epidemics, and on to those reports about the impending end of the world that crop up from time to time. There is also the observable phenomenon of one threat being replaced with another. This is not always because the threat is more real – sometimes it is simply more necessary (e.g. to achieve certain aims, including political ones), more easily understood or, for whatever reason, more convenient (e.g. because it obviates the need to think about a more real but more frightening threat). For these reasons, it is often easy for politicians to substitute anxiety about criminality for real fears.

Studies on social anxiety about criminality run into numerous methodological problems. Respondents can give extremely varied responses, depending on how questions are framed. Questions about the degree of safety is most often phrased in an exceptionally general way, e.g. 'Is Poland a safe country?' or 'Are you worried about crime?' Answers are also affected by when the study was conducted, as they can be conditioned by current events, e.g. a recently committed crime that was particularly brutal and is being widely reported in the media. This raises the question as to how many of these public opinion surveys are indicative of actual public attitudes and how many merely reflect current social moods (Kury 2002, pp. 135–6).

Poland did not just go through a period of rapid and extensive media development in the 1990s after censorship was lifted; the country also saw an enormous and very real increase in criminality following a profound social, political, economic and agricultural transformation. These factors, combined with an overwhelming tide of media information on criminality, gave rise to a lot of anxiety in society (in 1987, as

1 This chapter is a modified excerpt of the text: K. Buczkowski, W. Klaus, A. Kossowska, I. Rzeplińska and D. Woźniakowska-Fajst, 'Politicians, Media and Society's Perception of Crime', in A. Šelih and A. Završnik (eds) *Crime and Transition in Central and Eastern Europe*, New York-Heidelberg-Dordrecht-London: Springer, 2012.

2 See Chapter 10: 'Criminality and the Media'.

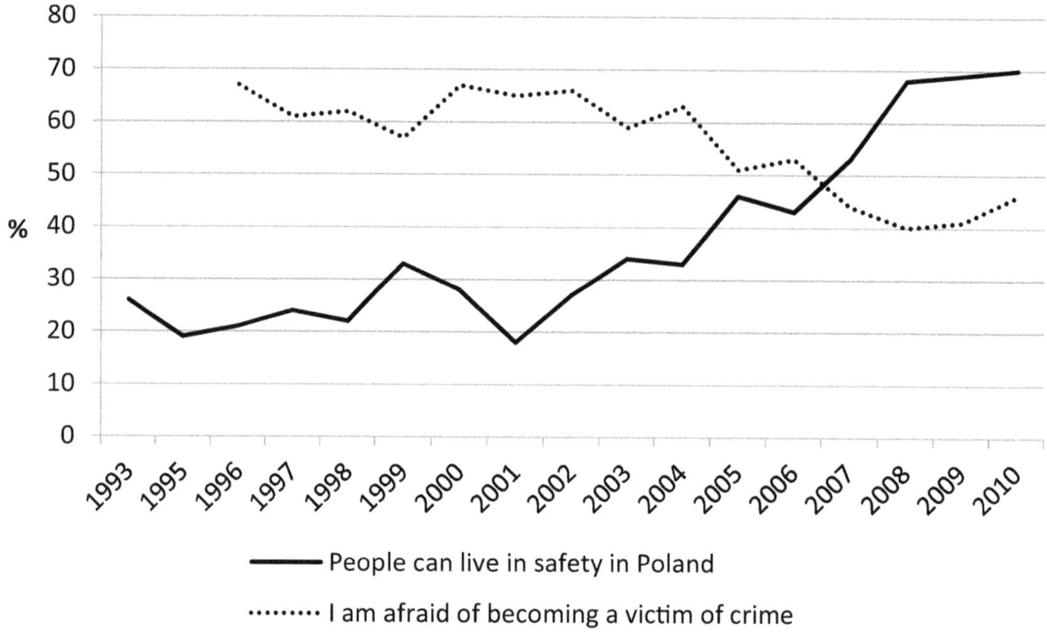

Figure 9.1 Anxiety about crime in Poland 1993–2010

Note: The question about feeling threatened by victimisation was first asked in 1996.

Source: Kowalczuk (2010b)

many as 74 per cent of those surveyed said that Poland was a safe country, in 1993, this figure fell to 26 per cent, and in 1995, to 19 per cent) (Klaus et al. 2008, pp. 378–9). On the other hand, however, this period witnessed increased confidence in the police. This led, inter alia, to more crimes being reported.

When we take an overall look at anxiety in Poland, it turns out that, what people fear most is loss of health (their own and that of those close to them). Next on the list, however, and ahead of unemployment, alcoholism, drug addiction, AIDS and hooliganism, is fear of becoming a victim of crime (Stankiewicz 2006). As for the threat of crime, when people were asked what they feared most in their own homes, they ranked theft and burglary first (46 per cent), then robbery (41 per cent) and reckless drivers (39 per cent). The ones that followed were not so much threatening as annoying: aggressive behaviour from people under the influence of drugs or alcohol (26 per cent), being accosted by aggressive youth (25 per cent), noise and boorish behaviour from neighbours (10 per cent) and vandalism (29 per cent) (Bieńkowska 2006). When speaking of 'anxiety about criminality', Poles seem to conflate serious criminality with this sort of unpleasant but less threatening behaviour.

While acknowledging all the caveats associated with comparing police reports and self-report studies over a period spanning several years, the following pattern, discussed in previous chapters, can nevertheless be observed: criminality first increased considerably between the 1980s and the turn of the twenty-first century, but, since then, there has been a marked stabilisation and even a slow decline. Moreover, even the type of criminality we fear most, viz. everyday crimes, has decreased. Self-report studies also reveal a clear trend towards a definite stabilisation in the number of crimes being committed, if not a distinct decline (Czapiński and Panek 2006, p. 179). As the level of criminality has stabilised, or even slightly decreased, the detection rate has increased, as has confidence in the police.[3] When the new police force was formed on 24 July 1990, a

3 See Police Headquarters Statistics: http://www.statystyka.policja.pl/portal/st/842/47682/Postepowania_wszczete_przestepstwa_stwierdzone_i_wykrywalnosc_w_latach_19992010.html (accessed 30 May 2011).

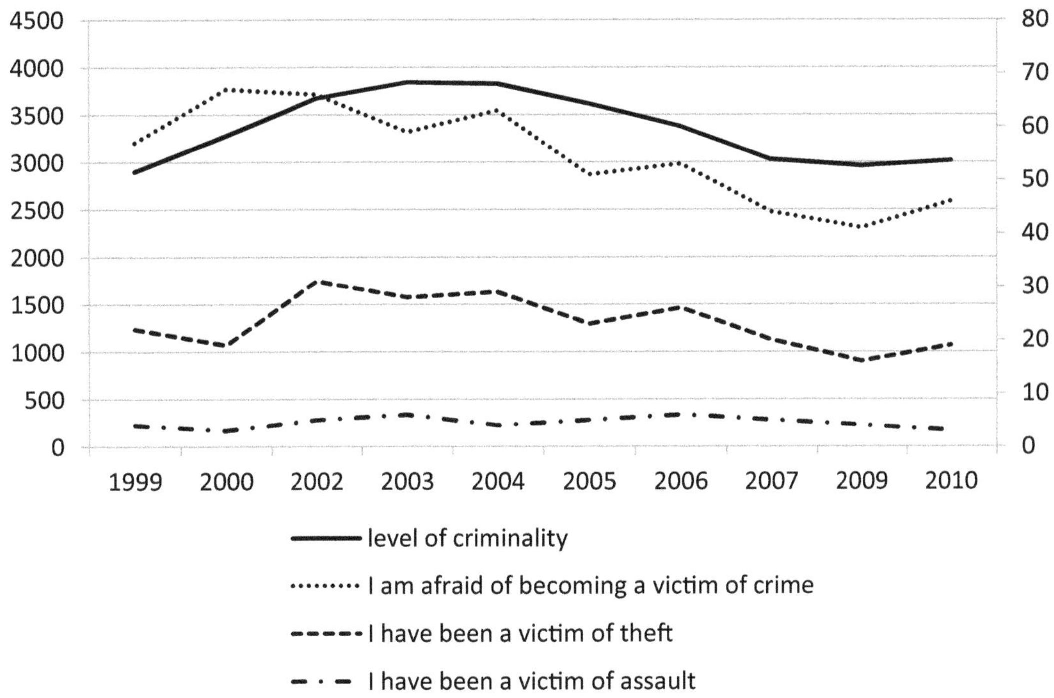

Figure 9.2 Feeling of being threatened by criminality in Poland as indicated by victimisation and statistical data 1999–2010

Note: Data for 2001 and 2008 not included as this kind of study was not conducted at the time. The level of confirmed criminality per 100,000 residents is presented on the basis of Police statistics (*Proceedings Commenced, Crimes Confirmed and Detection Rate 1999–2010*, available online at: http://www.statystyka.policja.pl/portal/st/842/47682/Postepowania_wszczete_przestepstwa_stwierdzone_i_wykrywalnosc_w_latach_19992010.html [accessed 30 May 2011]) and calculated on the basis of Główny Urząd Statystyczny (Central Statistical Office) data on the number of people. Victimisation data are given as percentages.

Source: Kowalczuk (2010b, pp. 4–6)

survey put the level of public trust at 56 per cent. By 2006, this had risen to 70 per cent,[4] and in 2011, 72 per cent gave a positive assessment of the work of the police force.[5]

Studies show that the public's overall assessment of safety in Poland has significantly improved over the last few years (see Figure 9.1). In the 1990s, around 25 per cent of respondents saw Poland as a country where people could live in safety, compared with almost 70 per cent at the time of writing. This increase in feeling safe corresponds to a decrease in fear of becoming a victim of crime, from 70 per cent to around 40 per cent. It could be said, then, that public opinion habituates itself in a peculiar way to criminality and adapts to life in a society in which this is a permanent and normal feature.

When the picture of criminality compiled from police statistics (i.e. information regarding confirmed crimes) is superimposed on this assessment by survey respondents, and the result is compared with the actual level of victimisation experienced by those surveyed, it turns out that public opinion is sensitive to the changing picture of criminality in Poland in a way that is surprisingly accurate. The trend illustrated by Figure

4 Police Headquarters Statistics: http://www.policja.pl/portal.php?serwis=pol&dzial=3&id=1 (accessed 30 May 2011).

5 Police Headquarters Statistics: http://www.statystyka.policja.pl/portal/st/905/70276/72_proc_Polakow_dobrze_ocenia_Policje_wrzesien_2011.html (accessed 30 May 2011).

9.2 shows that changes in the incidence of criminality (based on both statistical and victimisation data) over a period of several years accord surprisingly well with the feeling of being threatened by criminality. Similar relationships were observed in the Polish Criminality Studies (2007). Respondents living in voivodeships where the incidence of criminality was higher, generally felt anxious about it more often than did those in safer voivodeships. These relationships, however, have not been observed in International Crime Victims Surveys (ICVS) (Siemaszko 2008, p. 111; Siemaszko 2007–2008).

Criminological studies frequently measure the threat of criminology by inquiring as to how threatened people feel when taking a walk around the immediate neighbourhood after dark.[6] One in four respondents do not feel safe in this situation and one in three avoid certain places and streets out of fear for their safety. Those surveyed were most afraid of reckless drivers (36 per cent), being assaulted or robbed (24 per cent), provoked or attacked by a group of young people acting aggressively (24 per cent), burglary (23 per cent) and having their property damaged or destroyed by vandals (22 per cent) (Siemaszko 2008, pp. 110 ff.). Society therefore feels most anxious about crimes whose incidence is relatively rare. Victims of violent crimes fell 5.7 per cent, burglary 7.2 per cent and theft (other than car theft) 4.6 per cent (Siemaszko 2008, pp. 19–32).

Relative to other countries, Poland has an average level of criminality but an extraordinarily high level of anxiety about it (van Dijk et al. 2007). Kraków residents felt least safe compared with respondents in other countries according to comparative international studies conducted in 2002 (their level of anxiety was more than four times that of the residents of the other cities).[7] In this case, there was no correlation between the threat of criminality in the minds of those surveyed and actual danger, as criminality in Kraków (as measured on the basis of victimisation data) was only average compared with the other cities (Krajewski 2008a, pp. 125 ff.).

It is extraordinarily interesting that, despite the high subjective threat of criminality, Polish people do not go to any great lengths to try to protect themselves from the risk of falling victim to a prohibited act. The most commonly employed method of reducing this risk is to avoid certain places (i.e. places believed to be unsafe). Only a small percentage of respondents (both in comparison with their stated level of fear and the practice of the residents of other cities), however, decide to put extra locks on their doors (18 per cent compared with an international average of 45 per cent) or install alarms (3 per cent as against an average of 16 per cent) (van Dijk et al. 2007, pp. 135–9).[8] This fear has not gone unnoticed by residential developers. Virtually the only thing developers have had to offer over the past few years are apartments in gated communities (even though only around 20 per cent of purchasers cited the fact that an estate was walled as a decisive factor when choosing to purchase property within it). Warsaw especially has seen a significant increase in guarded estates. Studies comparing the level of anxiety about criminality on the part of residents of walled estates and residents of estates that are open to the street show that the former consider Warsaw a less safe place (the difference in the stated level of threat between these two groups can be as high as 50 per cent). By contrast, they felt perfectly safe 'behind their walls' on their estates (Waszkiewicz 2006).

Researchers studying the problem of anxiety about crime stress that the stated fear of becoming a victim of a prohibited act is a reflection of all the fears in society – the feeling that there is a lack of safety and stability, and uncertainty about the immediate future in a rapidly changing world.[9] People convinced that the

6 The question asked in the Polish Criminality Studies and the International Crime Victims Survey (ICVS).

7 Studies were conducted at the same time in Budapest, Amsterdam, Vienna and Hamburg.

8 These percentages were higher in large cities, although still lower than the international average. In Warsaw, 46 per cent of respondents in this same survey said they had extra locks and 5 per cent said they had alarms. Similar results were obtained for Kraków in 2002. Around half the respondents said they had extra locks or bars on their windows. Most often, however, respondents avoided specific places (80 per cent). A few enrolled in self-defence courses (12 per cent) or carried objects that could serve as weapons, e.g. tear gas, knives and sticks (8 per cent). It is interesting to note the lack of correlation between the victimisation experiences of those surveyed and the means of protection they chose (see Czapska 2008, pp. 155–8).

9 What stands out when looking at the anxieties of Polish people is their constant feeling of being threatened by criminality (although, this has decreased by 10 per cent when the 1993 and 2006 studies are compared). Respondents list unemployment (33 per cent), criminality (30 per cent), health (26 per cent) and bad government (22 per cent) as the factors that most threaten their personal security (see Szymanowska 2008, p. 54). Poles are generally pessimistic when asked about their overall mood. Most respondents in a survey conducted at the beginning of 2011 stated that the prevailing situation in the country was getting worse (approximately 60 per cent) and the economic situation was similarly negatively assessed (over 40 per cent). When asked specific questions about their own situation, however, very few rated the material conditions

threat of criminality is serious organise their lives so as to minimise the risk of victimisation. On the other hand, however, the phenomenon known as 'safety utopia', where a strong feeling of safety is accompanied by a desire to lead a free life, without being held back by prohibitions, is also evident (Kossowska 2006). This leads to a certain schizophrenia in that we want to be as free as possible, but, in order to achieve this, we strive to limit the freedom of others, who, for whatever reason, we regard as 'foreign' and who 'threaten' our community.

Anxiety about crime is not evenly distributed throughout society. Repeatedly being victimised is, not surprisingly, one of the factors that make people in Poland feel more threatened (Siemaszko 2001, p. 150). However, it is women and the elderly who most fear being harmed by crime, and yet, paradoxically, they relatively rarely become victims of crime (Goldschneider 2009, p. 13). Apart from such factors as living in large cities, having higher education, knowing someone who has been a victim of crime and experiencing emotional disorders, the feeling of being threatened is influenced by news about crime and criminality (Kuć 2007, pp. 114–15). Yvonne Jewkes has an interesting view of this. Jewkes cautions against being too hasty in drawing conclusions from the finding that anxiety about criminality is dependent on frequent contact with the media. She states:

> the findings that the readers of popular newspapers (that is, those that report crime in a sensationalized and salient fashion) have a highest level of fear of crime may simply reflect their actual risk of victimization. Readers of tabloid newspapers are concentrated in the lower socioeconomic strata of society, and are more likely to live in areas, and behave in ways, that expose them to greater level of risk of crime. (Jewkes 2010a, p. 142)

How Punitive Are Polish People?

The Polish media exhibits a high level of punitiveness.[10] They also convey the impression that they represent the entire community and speak on its behalf. Journalists often use phrases such as 'the public demands' and 'the public is appalled' without citing even the most cursory studies to support these assertions (Jones 2006, p. 99). The question as to whether this media stance is indicative of social attitudes, however, requires an answer. Poles exhibit a fairly high level of punitiveness compared to other European countries. In the 2004/2005 ICVS, where respondents were asked to specify the penalty that should be meted out to an adolescent criminal for breaking and entering a second time and stealing a colour TV set, Polish respondents, of whom almost 34 per cent answered 'mandatory imprisonment', came fourth in Europe (after the UK, Ireland and Greece) (Siemaszko 2007–2008, pp. 189–90). The mass media, however, seems to be partly responsible for the punitive attitudes of Polish people and especially for their frequent demands that offenders be imprisoned. The only 'fitting' punishment ever mentioned in a news report is mandatory imprisonment. The media invariably end reports on criminal occurrences with 'the perpetrator faces x years' imprisonment', where 'x' is the maximum penalty. The possibility of other penalties is never mentioned.

It is worth asking, however, whether this high punitiveness on the part of society reflects a severe legislature or whether the converse holds true, i.e. the country's restrictive criminal policy is shaped by social attitudes. Krzysztof Krajewski (2002, pp. 181–2) supports the latter contention. Krajewski argues that Polish society is highly punitive as a result of the totalitarian system that reigned in the country for years (as was the case elsewhere in Central and Eastern Europe). This shaped social attitudes that were conservative, inflexible and intolerant. The result is a very punitive body of criminal law, which has in turn meant frequent custodial sentences and a high prison population.[11] All this has led to imprisonment being devalued as a punishment. Indeed, imprisonment is now seen as the basic sanction in Poland and is the only fitting punishment in the eyes of public opinion. This is a natural tendency and occurs in many countries. In countries where the courts frequently hand down custodial sentences, people are generally in favour of imprisonment and see it as a

---

of their own households as poor (10–20 per cent), while approximately 40 per cent claimed that their families were doing well. Moreover, every second person on average rated their workplace situation as good (Feliksiak 2011).

10 For more on this topic, see Chapter 10: 'Criminality and the Media'.

11 For more on this topic, see Klaus et al. (2011).

natural and obvious consequence of committing crime.[12] The tendency of the media and politicians to shape opinions and promote certain types of conduct is not without significance.[13] In Poland, this means calling for imprisonment, the only 'fitting' punishment, as with a single voice (Kury 2002 pp. 123, 130–31).

Almost 100 per cent of Poles surveyed in 2006 strongly condemned serious crimes, such as homicide, rape and mistreatment of family members, and most frequently called for the imprisonment of the perpetrator. Nevertheless, once specific incidents were presented, their assessments were not only influenced by the nature of the act but also by the material circumstances, i.e. they would have treated a terrorist differently from a battered wife who had killed her husband (Szymanowska 2008, p. 299). The media, however, seldom bother to present a multifaceted picture of a crime. It is hardly surprising, then, that their simplified portrait of the criminal and the idealised victim should inevitably lead to calls for severe punishment. The media account of a crime often arouses such public condemnation and demands that its mandatory punishment be increased, that an acquittal (following a thorough examination by the court, a scrupulous analysis of the evidence and several consultations with experts) will provoke indignation and protest. Consequently, as many as 70 per cent of Poles asked for their assessment of the sentences handed down by the criminal courts in 2002 considered them too lenient. The public also believes that it is easy for criminals to escape punishment (a third of those surveyed thought this was true in homicide cases) and that the Polish penal system is too soft (Czapska 2003, pp. 46–7).

Survey results indicate that the media position is incontrovertible truth in the mind of the public. Respondents in one survey were divided into two groups and asked to assess the same case. The first group were required to give their verdict on the basis of what was in the media; the second from court records. The opinions of the two groups regarding the judgment of the court were diametrically opposed. While 61 per cent of the respondents in the first group considered the sentence too lenient, only 19 per cent of those in the second group held the same view (Kury 2002, pp. 139–40).

Politicians and Criminality

Poles asked about particular threats to social safety and security in 2002 named (by percentage of respondents): criminality (56 per cent), unemployment (55 per cent), alcoholism (22 per cent), drug addiction (21 per cent), child and youth aggression (20 per cent), poverty (19 per cent), bad government (17 per cent), economic abuses (16 per cent), corruption and graft (14 per cent) and mass emigration (11 per cent) (Szymanowska 2008, pp. 18–21). Fewer than 10 per cent indicated the economic situation, homelessness, abandonment of moral principles, poor health, bad jobs, laziness, apathy and indifference, populism, the poor environmental situation, rampant consumerism, easy access to weapons or the mass influx of foreigners. The concerns at the top of the list were similar to those expressed in Polish surveys conducted more than a decade previously (1993) (Szymanowska 2008, p. 20). At that time, respondents indicated the following as their major concerns: criminality (63 per cent), unemployment (52 per cent), alcoholism (24 per cent), bad government (21 per cent), economic recession (21 per cent), easy access to weapons (20 per cent), drug addiction (19 per cent), poverty (16 per cent), economic abuses (14 per cent), poor health (12 per cent) and mass influx of foreigners (10 per cent). Respondents were not asked about child and youth aggression, mass emigration or abandonment of moral principles as these were not distinctly noticeable in the early 1990s.

Polish people have consistently considered criminality to be especially threatening to social safety and security over the last 20 years. After that, they have indicated unemployment, although this primarily threatens individual economic security. At the same time, however, when a 2007 survey asked whether people thought Poland was a safe country, every second respondent answered in the affirmative (Szymanowska 2008, p. 18). In 2011, 75 per cent of Poles considered their country safe and 88 per cent thought likewise about their

12 For more on this topic, see the section in Chapter 7 ('Controlling Criminality') titled 'How Are Criminal Policy and Penal Policy Formed in Contemporary Poland?'

13 It should be stressed that the role of the media is merely ancillary in many cases. The media function as a catalyst that reinforces certain attitudes already present in society. Studies show that people choose media reports, articles, programmes etc. that are consistent with their own biases and view of the world (see Kury 2002, p. 113).

place of residence.[14] This positive assessment was an improvement on 1998, when only 25 per cent stated that Poland was a safe country (Szymanowska 2008, p. 18). Sociologists had predicted this identification of the social problems in Poland at the beginning of the transformation of the country. In line with these prognoses, the social situation in Poland was to be defined by three fundamental problems in the future, viz. unemployment, an increase in criminality[15] and young people entering adulthood finding it difficult to fit into society (Marody 2011, pp. 86–7).

Responsibility for ensuring social safety and security rests with the governing classes that organise the life of society. Protection from the threat of criminality, which includes managing an appropriate and effective legal response to criminal behaviour, is one of the main determinants of how effective their organisation is. The result is that the problem of criminality and the means of controlling it are always present in public debate and political discourse – in a word, in that part of the social sphere of democracy we define as political (as well as axiological, civil and economic) (Wnuk-Lipiński 2005, p. 183). It is here in the power struggle that politicians devise programmes and make election promises, and political parties and other groups, whose aim is to share power and at the same time assume responsibility for ensuring social safety and security, including organising protection from criminality, are active. During the 1989 election campaign for the Lower House of Parliament, every political party came up with slogans about improving public safety and doing more to protect the citizenry from crime. They also put forward the legal and penal means that would have to be deployed to achieve these aims. Criminality was and remains on the agenda of politicians striving for power and who try to win followers and elections with slogans such as 'fighting crime' (Widacki 2002, pp. 95 ff.; Bulenda 2005, pp. 41–64).

This does not only happen in democratic systems and it is not new to contemporary societies. Suffice it to recall the situation in the former People's Republic of Poland. The Polish United Workers' Party (PUWP) never failed to factor the necessity of 'fighting crime' into their political programmes. The Party even anticipated that victory in their 'struggle' would be assured and criminality reduced by a regimen of severe penal harshness. The issue of combating criminality was passed by special resolutions of the Central Committee (CC) of the PUWP. The Supreme Court (SC) then issued assessments and guidelines for law enforcement and jurisprudence. This is how, for example, the slogan 'struggle against recidivism', one of the major PUWP electoral campaign slogans in the 1960s, '70s and '80s, came to play such a central role. And again, victory in this struggle could only be assured by making the penalties for recidivism more severe. By coming up with slogans and formulating postulates like this, the ruling party intended to convince the public that it cared about protecting their safety, that it had the situation under control and that it was definitely 'struggling' with the phenomenon that was criminality.[16]

During the 20 years of the Third Polish Republic (i.e. since 1989) every party competing in elections (whether national or local) has made announcements about improving public safety and protecting the public from criminality. During the national parliamentary election campaign of 1997,[17] the Democratic Left Alliance declared that once it had won, it would 'fine-tune the law and make law enforcement agencies and the functioning of the justice system more efficient, mainly by simplifying and accelerating court procedures' (Widacki 2002, p. 95). The programme of the Freedom Union (a centre-liberal party) briefly stated that it would streamline the operations of the police and the justice system. Right-wing groups proclaimed the necessity of increasing penalties, reintroducing the death penalty and making prison conditions harsher. Solidarity Electoral Action, which won the 1997 national parliamentary elections, listed their duties in their electoral programme as ensuring that the state guaranteed public safety, fighting corruption and preventing the spread of mafia organisations (Widacki 2002; Bulenda 2005; Bulenda 2010, pp. 25–49).

---

14 Data available online at: www.kgp.gov.pl, in the section on crime statistics (accessed 30 May 2011).

15 This actually occurred for more than a decade until 2003.

16 Resolution of the Secretariat of the CC of the PUWP 20 September 1964 re: Criminal Policy, Law Enforcement and Jurisprudence Guidelines 19 January 1962, SC Judgement 1962 z. III., Pos. 37, Guidelines A/A 24 February 1967, SC Judgement 1967 No. 8, Pos. 48, Guidelines A/A 16 October 1967, SC Judgement 1968 No. 1, Pos. 1, cited in Rzeplińska (1985, pp. 10–11).

17 It should be noted that, with the exception of the Democratic Left Alliance, none of the parties that functioned at the time have sat in the parliament for years and most no longer exist.

In the national parliamentary elections of 2005, every political party voiced their position on the state of criminality, the threat it posed and their response to it. The Civic Platform programme decried a bad nation in which criminals went unpunished, the courts treated criminals better than their victims, and access to the courts was purely academic on account of proceedings being inordinately long. The Self Defence of the Republic of Poland (which currently has no seats in the national parliament) proclaimed the necessity of combating the inequality between the citizen and the law, corruption in the courts, and the fact that it was the poor, but never the rich or the politically well-connected, who were arrested. It was the Law and Justice programme, however, that contained the most sweeping statements on criminality and criminal policy. The party had decided that the level of criminality was high and that the public felt greatly threatened by it.[18] Law and Justice asserted that the authorities had failed to ensure that the public was appropriately protected and that the fault lay with a liberal criminal policy and poorly functioning courts, prosecutors and police. The Criminal Code in force at the time was described as liberal and, it was claimed, provided for sentences so light as to be contrary to the most basic sense of justice. By way of remedying these problems, Law and Justice proposed increasing maximum imprisonment to 25 years, introducing discretionary life imprisonment with no right of parole, reintroducing confiscation of property, and increasing the penalties for recidivism and crimes against life and body.

The Civic Platform programme of May 2011 (before the most recent parliamentary elections) stated that free citizens and a safe and secure nation were the two values on which the ideological postulates of the party rested and its operational basis. The state was meant to be friendly and efficient for the citizenry but severe on criminals.[19] It was asserted that Poles did not feel safe, that there was a high crime rate for offences, and that there was rampant corruption that posed a serious threat. It was planned to set up a coordinated system to fight threats to the safety of the state, including organised crime, corruption, espionage and terrorism, and to fight and prevent serious offences.

The Law and Justice programme had a similar diagnosis. It claimed,

> a safe Poland is a country where there is zero tolerance for breaking the law and where the courts work efficiently and pass just sentences; a country that occupies a worthy place in the community of nations by virtue of its politics being subordinate to the national interest and its having a modern army.[20]

Police statistical data show that criminality increased in Poland from 1989 to 2003. The number of reported crimes in 1990 was 883,346; in 2003 it was 1,446,643. Later, however, it fell (1,082,052 in 2008) before increasing slightly (1,159,554 in 2011). By contrast, victimisation studies, another type of data (i.e. apart from police statistics) used to indicate the nature and extent of criminality in Poland, show a successive decline in victimisation rates since 1992. Criminality has therefore fallen according to the information and assessments of crime victims. At the same time, the rate of reporting has gradually risen, which means that those wronged by crime are informing the police about criminal occurrences more often.

The feeling of being threatened by criminality has also diminished in society. Victimisation studies show that anxiety about criminality decreased by 40 percentage points between 1996 and 2008.[21] It should also be borne in mind that in the April 2011 surveys mentioned earlier 75 per cent of Poles rated their country as safe and 88 per cent thought likewise about their place of residence.[22]

What about the public debate on criminality in Poland today? What is the actual opinion about criminality and punishment for crime in contemporary society and what does it reveal?[23] Andrzej Kojder (1995, p. 269)

---

18 At the time (2005), criminality had actually declined significantly (for more on this topic, see Chapter 2: 'The Status of Criminality in Poland since 1918'), and the public had been feeling increasingly safe (as stated at the beginning of this chapter).

19 Data on the 2011 Civic Platform programme from a supplement to the Civic Platform political programme ('Civic Poland') entitled 'Free Citizens in a Safe and Secure Nation'.

20 Data on the Law and Justice Programme (in Polish) from: http://programpis.org.pl/ (accessed 27 May 2013).

21 The data on criminality, victimisation studies, data from studies on anxiety about criminality are taken from Siemaszko et al. (2009) and the criminality statistics available online at www.kgp.gov.pl.

22 Data available online at: www.kgp.gov.pl, in the section on *statystyki przestępczości* (criminality statistics).

23 These questions are posed in Tonry (2007, pp. 95–107).

considers that 'the law should be seen as one of the aspects of the overall culture of society' including the criminal law and the means of reacting to perpetrators of crime. If we examine the political programmes on the issues of public safety, criminality and policies towards punishing offenders analysed above, it becomes apparent that the slogans, opinions and proposals of political parties are at odds with the data on the nature and extent of criminality and about how fast, and by how much, the level of criminality has changed. The societal threat from criminality and the statistically increasing number of crimes loom large in the programmes. It would seem, however, that the politicians were not familiar with the data they were citing. The reality is that the inhabitants of Poland have been feeling increasingly safe (on the basis of victimisation studies), that crime has decreased, and that any statistical increase in criminality has been solely due to the actions of politicians themselves, namely in their criminalisation of more and more prohibited acts (more on this below). It is difficult for the public to verify the assertions of politicians as not many people are familiar with statistical data on criminality and the feeling of being threatened by it.

The conduct of political debate on the threat of criminality is one-dimensional and can be defined as characterised by a culture of punitiveness. The slogan 'fighting crime' is chanted the entire time and criminality itself is portrayed as a formidable phenomenon that unceasingly constitutes a serious threat to society. At the same time, a severe or very severe penal response, i.e. long prison sentences, restricting early releases and even reintroducing the death penalty, is deemed the only effective reaction. Politicians either cannot or will not speak any differently.

So how has the criminal law changed over the last 20 years? How do the changes in criminalisation and the severity of sanctions appear? What gains, if any, have politicians made in their 'war on crime'? How have they managed to cope with undesirable social phenomena? What legislative changes have been introduced?

The Criminal Code of 1997 had been amended 58 times, and the simultaneously enacted Criminal Procedure Code 60, by February 2012. Some of these changes were the result of using the criminal law as a 'political marketing tool' (Łukaszewicz 2012).[24] The rest have some sort of rational justification. It is perfectly normal to change the criminal law. Rationality, however, should be the only common standard to which any such changes have to conform.[25] As Andrzej Zoll (2011, p. 29) puts it, 'the need for rationality also applies to such radical social policy instruments as the criminal law'.

Examples of some of the amendments to the criminal law regulations over the last decade, along with references to the politicians who sponsored them, are presented below. The first to be considered will be those that have increased the severity of sanctions.

The concept of the 'hooligan nature of the act', in which special sentencing rules applied to crimes committed in these circumstances, was introduced in 2007.[26] This was an idea of the then governing Law and Justice party, which had successfully campaigned on the need to increase penalties for crime, and amounted to a return to the days of the People's Republic of Poland, i.e. severe penalties for 'hooligans' (for that matter, the definition of a 'hooligan act' was worded very similarly to the one in the Criminal Code of 1969). When sentencing for a summary offence legally deemed to be of a hooligan nature, the court was obliged to apply a penalty stipulated in the Code that was not less than the statutory penalty increased by one half.[27] Perpetrators of these types of acts were denied the possibility of a lighter sentence, e.g. a fine or a community sentence. After three years of relentlessly increasing penalties, the policy of punishing crimes of a hooligan nature was relaxed in 2010. Suspended custodial sentences were even allowed in exceptionally justifiable cases.[28]

Many of the changes to the Criminal Code were intended to extend the catalogue of penalties and increase the severity of penalties applicable to given offences. This was the case with paedophilia (defined as engaging in, or showing the performance of, a sexual act with a person under the age of 15 [CC Art. 200 § 1–2]), the penalty for which had been increased to two to 12 years' imprisonment in 2005 (prior to that, the penalty had

24 The phrase 'political marketing tool' is attributed to Marian Filar.

25 For more on this topic see Marek (2009b, pp. 89–119) and Wróbel (2009).

26 CC Art. 115 § 21 supplemented by the Act of 16 October 2006 (Journal of Laws 226, Pos. 1648), which came into effect 12 March 2007.

27 CC Art. 57a §1, which came into effect 12 March 2007.

28 CC Art. 69 § 4 Act of 12 February 2010 to amend the Criminal Code, the Sentencing Code and the Environmental Protection Law, which came into effect 1 July 2010.

been one to 10 years' imprisonment).[29] New punitive measures in the form of a prohibition on occupying any or certain specified positions or engaging in any or certain specified occupations or activities connected with raising, educating, medically treating or caring for minors were introduced, e.g. in the case of being convicted for a crime against sexual freedom or morality to the detriment of a minor. This measure can be ordered for life in the case of being sentenced to imprisonment for a crime against sexual freedom or morality to the detriment of a minor (CC Art. 39 Pt. 2a in conjunction with Art. 41 § 1a and 1b).[30]

Prohibitions on contacting or approaching specified persons, prohibitions on vacating places of residence, and orders to vacate premises jointly occupied with harmed persons are other new punitive measures. These can be ordered in the case of being convicted for a crime against sexual freedom or morality to the detriment of a minor or a premeditated crime using violence, including violence against a next of kin (CC Art. 39 Pt. 2b in conjunction with Art. 41 § 1 and § 2).[31] Prohibitions on appearing at mass events is another special punitive measure (CC Art. 39 Pt. 2c in conjunction with Art. 41b).[32] This was a reaction to what had been occurring at football stadiums during and after matches, viz. aggressive behaviour on the part of supporters, fighting between supporters of opposing teams and attacks on players. Both these punitive measures were introduced by Civic Platform governments.

Also during this period, and again as a reaction to specific occurrences – this time cases involving crimes committed by perpetrators with sexual pathologies – mandatory probation officer supervision during the probationary period of a suspended sentence was introduced as part of the sentence for any person convicted of a crime connected with a paraphilia (CC Art. 73 § 2).[33] Another way of responding to perpetrators of crimes against sexual freedom is a preventive measure that involves having the perpetrator placed in a secure institution or referred to ambulatory care after being released from prison (Art. 95a §1).[34] In either case, the aim is to administer pharmacological therapy or psychotherapy to the perpetrator.[35] The court is obliged to apply the foregoing measures where the accused has been convicted of raping a child under the age of 15 or of raping an ancestor, descendant, relative by adoption or sibling. In addition, convictions for sexual offences against persons under the age of 15 and punished by mandatory custodial sentences can no longer be spent.

Under Civic Platform governments, certain types of conduct have been criminalised and new types of crimes created, e.g.:[36]

- Capturing an image of a naked person or a person engaging in a sexual act that involves violence, unlawful threat or deception. Disseminating an image of a naked person or a person engaging in a sexual act without the permission of the subject is a crime (CC Art. 191a).
- Engaging in a new form of statutory rape where the victim is a child under the age of 15, an ancestor, descendant, relative by adoption or sibling; such an act is an indictable offence (CC Art. 197 § 3).
- Engaging in conduct that involves making contact with a child under the age of 15 via an ICT system or a telecommunications network with the intention of meeting him/her for the purpose of committing the crimes of rape or paedophilia, or producing or recording pornographic material (CC Art. 200a § 1).

29 CC Art. 200 amended by the Act of 27 July 2005 (Journal of Laws No. 163, Pos. 1363), which came into effect 26 September 2005.

30 Inserted by the Act of 27 July 2005 (Journal of Laws No. 163, Pos. 1363), binding as of 26 September 2005.

31 This is the wording of the Act of 10 October 2010 (Journal of Laws No. 125, Pos. 842), which came into effect 1 August 2010.

32 This regulation was inserted by the Act of 30 March 2009 on Safety at Public Events (Journal of Laws No. 62, Pos. 504), which came into effect 1 August 2009, and subsequently modified by the Act of 22 July 2010, which came into effect 4 September 2010. CC Art. 41b was then modified once more by Art. 5 Pt. 1 of the Act of 31 August 2011 to Modify the Act on Safety at Public Events and Certain Other Acts (Journal of Laws No. 217, Pos. 1280), which came into effect 1 January 2012.

33 This is the wording of the Act of 27 July 2005 (Journal of Laws No. 163, Pos. 1363), which came into effect 26 September 2005.

34 This is the wording of the Act of 5 November 2009 (Journal of Laws No. 206, Pos. 1589), which came into effect 8 June 2010.

35 Pharmacological therapy is not administered, however, if it poses any risk to the life or health of the convict.

36 All the acts enumerated below were added by the Act of 5 November 2009 (Journal of Laws No. 206, Pos. 1589), which came into effect 8 June 2010.

- Proposing to a child under the age of 15 via an ICT system of telecommunications network that he/she engage in sexual intercourse, perform or submit to some other sexual act, or participate in recording pornographic material (CC Art. 200a § 2).
- Publicly promoting or praising conduct that is paedophile in nature (CC Art. 200b).

Stalking is another new type of crime. The Polish Criminal Code defines stalking as persistent harassment of another person or his/her next of kin in such circumstances as to give him/her justification for feeling that he/she is under threat or that his/her privacy has been violated (CC Art. 190a).[37] Three years' imprisonment is the only sentence which can be passed. If aggravated (i.e. if an act defined in the Criminal Code [CC 190a § 1 or § 2] leads to a suicide attempt), the perpetrator is liable for up to ten years' imprisonment. Proposals for alternative punishments for this type of crime were abandoned, which is incomprehensible in light of criminological studies on different patterns of persistent harassment. This crime has such wide variations in pattern, duration and other circumstances that the argument for giving the judge the discretion to decide from a wide range of statutory punishments is compelling (Gruszczyńska et al. 2010, pp. 45–73).

The range of conduct prohibited by the criminal law was extended between 2004 and 2008 – and this is perfectly rational and justifiable – to cover conduct connected with the operation of computer systems, telephone networks and databases (CC Art. 268a, Art. 269 § 1, Art. 269a and Art. 269b).[38]

The issue of possessing small quantities of drugs for personal use is still being debated. One of the results of changing the Act on Countering Drug Addiction in 2000 was that drug addiction became a crime. The next revision was made in 2011. Since then, the public prosecutor and the courts have had the option of terminating the proceedings if the accused is being tried for possessing a small quantity of narcotics or psychotropic substances for personal use and there would be no point in passing sentence on the accused in view of the circumstances under which the prohibited act was committed and its small degree of social harm.[39]

Criminalising being in control of a motor vehicle while under the influence of alcohol or drugs was a reaction to a serious problem and to the fact that such behaviour was socially acceptable. This act was criminalised when Art. 178a was inserted into the Criminal Code in 2000 (it had previously been a summary offence). Being in control of a vehicle other than one defined in the Criminal Code (CC Art. 178a § 1) on a public road, in a residential zone or in a pedestrian precinct was criminalised in 2010 (CC Art. 178a § 2).[40] At the same time, in the face of people being convicted of this crime repeatedly, the option of a judgment banning the offender from driving a motor vehicle for life was introduced.[41] Further significant criminalisation and penalisation came 10 years later. Breaching an injunction was made a crime at this time (CC Art. 244). This included breaching a restraining order that prohibited the offender from driving a vehicle as well as the other injunctions mentioned in this Article.[42]

One noticeable phenomenon that has accompanied the political and economic transformations in Poland is corruption. The Criminal Code defines corruption as passive bribery (CC Art. 228 § 1), active bribery (CC Art. 229 §1), paid protection (CC Art. 230 §1) and granting or promising to grant a financial benefit in return

37 Added by the Act of 25 February 2011 (Journal of Laws No. 72, Pos. 381), which amended the Criminal Code of 6 June 2011.

38 Act of 18 March 2004 (Journal of Laws No. 69, Pos. 626), which came into effect 1 May 2004, Act of 4 September 2008 (Journal of Laws No. 171, Pos. 1056), which came into effect 8 October 2008, Act of 24 October 2008 (Journal of Laws No. 214, Pos. 1344), which came into effect 18 December 2008.

39 Art. 62a inserted by Art. 1 Pt. 15 of the Act of 1 April 2011 to amend the Act on Countering Drug Addition and Certain Other Acts (Journal of Laws No. 117, Pos. 678), which came into effect 9 December 2011.

40 CC Art. 178 § 2 as per the contents of the Act of 22 July 2010 (Journal of Laws No. 152, Pos. 1018), which came into effect 4 September 2010. Art. 178a was inserted into the Criminal Code by the Act of 14 April 2000 (Journal of Laws No. 48, Pos. 548), which came into effect 15 December 2000.

41 CC Art. 42 § 4 was inserted by the Act of 14 April 2000 (Journal of Laws No. 48, Pos. 548), which came into effect 15 July 2000. It was not until 2010 that the option of a conditionally suspended sentence for offenders already punished for a crime defined in the Criminal Code (CC Art. 178a and Art. 178a § 4) was exceptionally allowed in specially justified cases. This option was inserted by the Act of 12 February 2010 (Journal of Laws No. 40, Pos. 227), which came into effect 1 July 2010.

42 CC Art. 244 as per the contents of the Act of 10 June 2010 (Journal of Laws No. 125, Pos. 842), which came into effect 1 August 2010.

for arranging a matter (CC Art. 230a). These provisions were all added in 2003.[43] Public opinion was strongly in favour of 'fighting' corruption. The authorities therefore reached for the simplest solution and made use of the criminal law, even though it was apparent that this could not rectify the situation (i.e. curtailing corruption in society) on its own.

Changes made to court proceedings are no less worthy of mention. In 2006, the then governing Law and Justice party introduced special procedures, dubbed the '24-hour court' by the media, to speed up court proceedings. These regulations were justified by the need for a quick, efficient and appropriately severe response to perpetrators of summary offences involving hooliganism who were caught in the act or immediately afterwards, and apprehended and brought before the courts within 48 hours together with an application to have the matter heard according to the accelerated proceedings (CC 517b §1).[44] Law and Justice politicians were of the view that punishing perpetrators of summary offences quickly, decisively and severely was what the public was demanding.

As it turned out, the '24-hour courts' were used to punish people for being in control of vehicles while under the influence of alcohol (Marek 2009b, pp. 89–90). In 2008, after the Civic Platform party had come to power, an expert panel convened by the Minister for Justice opined that these specially designed accelerated proceedings were counterproductive, generated unnecessary costs and did not lead to accelerated proceedings (Wróbel 2009, p. 112). The Criminal Procedure Code now has a new Chapter 54a in which accelerated proceedings are regulated. There are no '24-hour court' regulations.[45]

The regulations on accelerated proceedings were soon utilised during the UEFA Euro 2012 European Football Championships. 'Pseudo' supporters apprehended during incidents after a match in Warsaw on 12 June 2012 were tried using accelerated proceedings. The accused were charged with being part of a crowd associated with a hooligan act and participating in an affray or being guilty of assault and battery. More than 50 judgements, in which some 80 people were convicted, were handed down.

The debate on in vitro fertilisation is the next example of the tendency of politicians to react harshly towards behaviour and social phenomena they would like to curtail. In July 2012, Law and Justice MPs announced that in vitro fertilisation should be banned completely and therefore proposed to employ the criminal law in this situation as well – by criminalising the behaviour and introducing an appropriate penal sanction. This is not likely to become binding law.[46] It does illustrate, however, just how easy it is for politicians to reach for the criminal law and repression. They do so automatically, as a kneejerk reaction, so long as the conduct they wish to influence can be controlled using the provisions of the criminal law.

A statement from a public prosecutor in June 2012 might well serve as a commentary on the foregoing considerations taken as a whole (the security for Euro 2012 was being discussed at the time): 'high profile political campaigns have to come to an end sometime; no matter how high up came the order to impose or even enforce it, sentencing policy has never been, nor will ever be, effective'.[47]

This tendency of politicians to react harshly to various types of deviant behaviour, including criminality, has been particularly noticeable in Europe over the last 20 years or so and has been given the name 'penal populism'. Politicians are naturally 'skewed' towards making sentencing policy more punitive (see Matthews 2005, pp. 188–96). As Jewkes writes after analysing the situation in the UK (in particular the 'moral panic' and the role of the authorities in reinforcing deviance), 'those in power label minority groups as subversive with a view to exploiting public fears, and then step in to provide a "popular" solution to a problem which, in the current rhetoric of populist punitiveness, usually amounts to getting tougher on crime' (Jewkes 2010a, p. 69).

Political scientists, assessing the situation in Poland after 1989, write that the development of populist movements has been fostered by the state's renunciation of its duties towards its citizens. This has been one of the results of economic globalisation. A change in the function and policy of the state can be seen at work

43 Act of 13 June 2003 (Journal of Laws No. 111, Pos. 1061), which came into effect 1 July 2003.

44 Chapter 54a inserted by Art. 2 Pt. 3 of the Act of 16 November 2006 to Change the Criminal Code and Certain Other Acts, which came into effect 12 March 2007.

45 Chapter 54a of the Criminal Procedure Code of 5 November 2009, which came into effect 8 June 2010.

46 Interview with PO MP Stefan Niesiołowski in *Gazeta Wyborcza*, 13 July 2012.

47 Statement from Ireneusz Kuna, Prosecutor at the Lublin District Prosecutor's Office in the article 'Temida musi być przede wszystkim skuteczna', in the supplement 'Prawnik' to the daily *Gazeta Prawna*, 27 June 2012.

here. The state has given up trying to ensure that all its citizens are adequately remunerated, feel socially safe and secure, can obtain full employment and participate equally in public life. The state, having abandoned its ambition to influence the socio-economic environment for the common good, has shifted its efforts to public safety. This shift, i.e. from caring for social safety to caring for public safety, has given activities in aid of 'fighting crime', 'ensuring public safety' and 'putting the criminal code in order' greater significance in public discourse and election campaigns (Żuk 2010, pp. 123–7).

Piotr Żuk's (2010, p. 128) analysis shows that the predominance of liberal, free market economics has given voice to populist political groupings – of the 'law and order persuasion' – as well as their supporters in Poland since its political and economic transformation. Social exclusion has become a personal matter and those excluded have tended to support those politicians that promise a return to a safe and secure life. 'The more drastic the social consequences of liberalisation, privatisation and deregulation in the economic domain, the more readily those who promise "safety" will be allowed to speak.' This political science analysis would explain why Polish politicians have so willingly deployed the rhetoric of harsh criminal laws and severe criminal sanctions over the last decade. Their use of such rhetoric in election campaigns is proof of their conviction that it will win votes.

Chapter 10
Criminality and the Media

Dagmara Woźniakowska-Fajst

Criminality has always been of interest to the mass media. The media, in turn, are the primary source of information on criminality (70 per cent of the population get their information from television, 15 per cent from the press and over 7 per cent from the radio) (Błachut et al. 1999, p. 420) and the justice system in Poland (Daniel 2005, p. 95). The mass media is only too willing to report on criminality. This is mostly because it is a topic that appeals to people. Criminality is exciting and often sensational, and bringing it up is an easy way to grab the attention of viewers, readers or listeners. Researchers claim that people react favourably to news about prohibited acts, as it allows them to reinforce the positive view they have of themselves by holding themselves up against someone who has violated the principles of social coexistence. The media also try to make news about crime easily digestible, e.g. through simplification and by not including deeper analyses of the causes of deviant behaviour. Moreover, all sorts of political aims can be achieved with this (see Klaus et al. 2006).

The media are definitely selective in how they present issues related to criminality, primarily focusing on brutal, sensational incidents and glaring examples of gross negligence on the part of the justice system. A more detailed discussion on this follows later in the chapter. The positive and beneficial aspects of talking about criminality, such as the aetiology of deviant behaviour, the role of the victim in causing crime, and prevention issues such as the adequate safeguarding of property, safe behaviour in everyday life and opportunities to work together with justice agencies, are rarely mentioned.

The Media Before and After the Political Transformation

There is an enormous difference between the influence the media had on public opinion in Poland in the period before the political and constitutional changes of 1989 and the impact it has had over the last 20 years. During the communist period, censorship and top-down control were part of the media's job description. Firstly, there were few news sources available to journalists. They obtained most of their information from the government-controlled Polish Press Agency and Polish Interpress Agency. As with other areas of life, coverage of criminality and court proceedings 'were made to conform to the tenets proclaimed in true socialist countries' (Witkowska-Rozpara 2011, pp. 114–16). A censorship bureau – the Central Office for Control of the Press, Publications and Entertainment in Warsaw – also operated. This agency published a register known as the *Book of Notes and Instructions* and censors were required to excise certain information in line with its instructions, e.g.:

> many of the statements concerning the inadequacy of state measures in combating the worsening alcoholism epidemic are disputed, as are the numerous alarming references to industry poisoning the natural environment, the statistics on traffic and workplace accidents, criticism of the drafting of the psychiatric act, … statements regarding anti-Semitic excesses, and articles attacking government administrative bodies and the justice system. (Strzyżewski 1977, p. 11).

Many of the guidelines additionally proscribed the publication of any news on alarming or distressing events or crisis situations that had the potential to cause societal anxiety, as well as any news on crime and deviant behaviour. Reporting on abuses perpetrated by people in positions of authority and e.g. beatings and forced confessions on the part of the 'citizen's militia' (i.e. the police force) was studiously avoided (Waltoś 1997, p. 25).

The Central Office for Control of the Press, Publications and Entertainment was abolished in April 1990 and the media was freed from being politically controlled through preventive censorship.[1] Marian Filar points out that the media was then divided into the categories of tabloid and serious. Tabloid publications are geared towards the law of supply and demand, i.e. they convey news in a way that will maximise sales (or, in the case of TV stations, appeal to the widest viewing audience). The 'serious media', on the other hand, frequently bow before the interests of particular political groupings and act as conduits for their ideological lines (Filar 2007–2008, p. 490).

The liberation of the press and the inexpressible joy of that freedom of speech unleashed journalists for an all-out war for readers, viewers and listeners that made it necessary to report on any earth shattering events. The media thus focuses exclusively on crimes that will captivate the public, i.e. on crimes that are exceptionally dramatic, cruel and tragic. This gives a misleading impression about the nature and extent of criminality. This affects all post-communist countries, not just Poland. Just as Poland now has dailies like *Fakt* and *Super Express*, Slovenia has *Slovenske Novice* and Serbia has *Novosti*. The format, layout and content of all these newspapers are modelled on *The Sun* (UK) and *Bild* (Germany). These publications are all characterised by generous helpings of violence whose only justification is their own bottom lines (Buczkowski et al. 2012, p. 40).

Apart from the daily press, there are now periodicals that write about nothing but criminality. Moreover several television channels present programmes largely or even wholly devoted to the problem of criminality.

The Media Image of Criminality

The image of criminality portrayed by the mass media is distorted and completely removed from reality. The media report on certain events in a selective manner and blow them up out of all proportion. They are happy to trumpet the fact that a crime has been committed but they follow the court proceedings and report the final judgement far less frequently, except in the case of major crimes. Even when the accused is acquitted, this information is all too often not deemed 'newsworthy' and the verdict is not publicised. The public often hears about controversial verdicts in courts of first instance but far less often about the sentences being varied or the verdicts quashed by appellate courts many months later. Journalists use techniques that enable them to present information in ways that will attract the attention of listeners, viewers and readers. Writers who research the problematic aspects of how criminality is portrayed in the media list quite a few features that media news needs if it is going to sell (Chibnall quoted by Jones 2006, pp. 80–83; Chibnall 2010, pp. 205–12).

1. *Instantaneity*. The story must relate to the present. Short press articles have no room for presenting complicated histories or referring to things that happened in the remote past. Economic crimes do not therefore enjoy a great deal of success as their complexity soon starts to bore the average reader. White collar crime and major corporate crime are virtually absent in the media for the same reason. In Poland, where economic scandals frequently hit the headlines, we are usually told more about the alleged perpetrators (who are often public figures) than the details of the acts themselves.
2. *Dramatisation*. News must be dramatic and attract attention. Catchy headlines are one way to ensure this. They also need to be more sensational and hold out a promise of something better than the mundane contents of the article beneath them. The Polish press makes use of such headlines as 'She killed out of lovesickness', 'Two-year-old locks mother out on balcony' and 'A monster was growing inside her'.[2]
3. *Personalisation*. Articles that talk about people garner more interest among readers than do articles about events. And nothing beats an innocent victim in a crime report. Stories about victimless crimes

1 Act to Repeal the Act on Control of the Press, Publications and Entertainment and to Amend the Press Act (Journal of Laws 1990 No. 29, Pos. 173).

2 J. Danilewicz, 'Zabiła z chorej miłości', *Super Express*, 16 February 2002; A. Ratajczak, 'Dwulatek więził mamę. Na balkonie', *Fakt* [online] 13 June 2011, http://www.fakt.pl/Dwulatek-wiezil-mame-Na-balkonie-artykuly,74367,1.html; K. Bonda and J. Danilewicz, 'Dojrzewał w niej potwór', *Super Express*, 19 January 2001.

do not attract the same audience. Journalists therefore try to give out personal details of the victim and his/her family so that readers can build up a rapport with them. At the very least, they try to give a cursory description of the victim and/or perpetrator, e.g. 'D's neighbours remember Magda well. She was a quiet, peaceful and secretive little girl'[3] and 'Fr. Mieczysław Kwiecień, 71, was a well-loved parish priest and a paragon of every virtue. He was modest and big-hearted' (Kowalska 2001). Journalists become indignant when the families of victims or perpetrators decline to talk to them and refuse to give out any details. Moreover, they convey this information to their readers, e.g. 'Beata's family refuse to speak with us' (*Super Express*),[4] almost making it out to be an additional aggravating circumstance.

4. *Simplification*. The media greatly simplify events, often presenting everything as black and white, and usually ignoring the complex nature of interpersonal relations. Seldom do they try to explain the causes of criminality. Journalists will even bluntly state that a certain incident is beyond comprehension, resorting to such catchphrases as 'it is truly difficult to understand what could have motivated this crime', 'we will never know what drove whoever did this' and 'it is impossible to explain this tragedy' (Klarman 2006, p. 351). If they do make an effort in this direction, however, it will be most often to focus on certain improprieties or disorders, e.g. the influence of drugs or alcohol on the perpetrator. As a rule, any questions about the functioning of society are omitted and any clarifications or qualifications are doled out 'in tablet form' in an extremely formulaic and often counterfactual manner. Agnieszka Klarman (2006, p. 351) writes about acts 'made to order', e.g. infanticide is explained by poverty, robbery by unemployment, and corruption by social acceptance. Bożena Gulla and Zdzisław Majchrzak (2007, p. 163) claim that the simplifications journalists use to get the message across are also related to the phenomenon of attributive comments, i.e. drawing general conclusions from the available data. Journalists at some newspapers (*Gazeta Wyborcza* and *Dziennik Polski* were examined) eschew simple explanations and make some attempt to understand the complex motivations that drive the perpetrators of the crimes they are describing. Tabloid (*Fakt* was examined) readers, on the other hand, can expect to find a simplified explanation that is truculent in tone and accusatory in tenor.
5. *Authenticated by authorities*. Stories relayed by journalists are often authenticated with the assistance of experts, e.g. politicians, criminal law specialists and criminologists. Expert opinions are usually short and not supported by any evidence (Jones 2006, pp. 80–83). Criminologists, psychiatrists, social psychologists, 'a reputable criminal law specialist',[5] sociologists and human rights experts have all expressed their views on criminality in the Polish media. In principle, making use of expert knowledge is obviously a positive thing. Not so easy to condone, however, is the fact that journalists often have no interest in discovering objective truth but merely want to utilise arguments that they have a priori taken to be correct. They do not, therefore, seek out experts to clarify what is happening or present an objective commentary on it but to have their words confirm a previously established proposition, e.g. that the accused must be guilty, because his/her personality traits all point in that direction. Unfortunately, academics and practitioners inadvertently lend their names to these media scripts all too often.
6. *Sex*. Sexually motivated crimes have a lot of media appeal, especially when the victim is killed or subjected to violent treatment. Sexual crime stories are exaggerated to such an extent that women live in terror of being sexually assaulted, especially by strange men in secluded places. Most rapes, however, occur in private homes and the perpetrators are usually known to the victims (Salter 2005, p. 105). Murders of a sexual nature are given inordinate attention, while sexual acts between people known to each other, but which do not end in homicide, are ignored, despite being significantly more common. These types of events are of no interest to the media. The mass media are also more willing

3 P. Gluma, 'Powiesiła się, a matka i siostra piły za ścianą' (Girl hangs herself while mother and sister drink behind wall), *Super Express*, 14 May 2007.

4 'Zadźgała nożem byłego narzeczonego. 17-letnia morderczyni' (17-year-old murderess), *Super Express*, 18 January 2007.

5 *Super Express*, 18 October 2006.

to report on an incident where the victim is an 'ordinary girl' than when she is a prostitute. A woman who provides sexual services does not quite fit the picture of an innocent victim.

7. *Violence*. This is an exceptionally lurid way of violating the rights of an individual, and at the same time, it indicates a breakdown in public order. On the one hand, the media is replete with stories about crimes involving violence (Yvonne Jewkes [2010a, p. 54], citing Paul Williams and Julie Dickinson, claims that the British press devotes 65 per cent of its crime reporting to stories connected with interpersonal violence, whereas in reality, this type of event barely accounts for 6 per cent of all crime). On the other hand, however, news about acts of this type is so common that unless an incident is linked to some other act that appeals to the media (e.g. a child victim), it will be reported in a mundane, routine manner and relegated to the middle pages of the paper.
8. *Proximity*. Jewkes relates this term to both spatial propinquity and cultural affinity. While the local media will report on a minor crime or accident, this type of 'news' is of no interest to the national media unless it results in a lot of victims or a great loss. Cultural affinity, on the other hand, denotes the appeal that an event will have to an audience from a similar cultural circle. The Polish media often reports on crude freedom of speech violations in Belarus, a neighbouring country with a sizeable Polish minority, while devoting considerably less space to the Syrian civil war than such a major event, which has been ongoing since early 2011 and which has so far claimed tens of thousands of victims and forced over a million people to flee the country, would warrant (Cumming-Bruce 2013).
9. *Exceptional or famous protagonists*. The public is not interested in run-of-the-mill heroes or villains so much as ones that are exceptional or have something that makes them stand out. They can be, e.g. reputable figures or people of high social standing. If the perpetrator is a well-known media personality then his/her 'participation' will even 'sell' a boring economic crime or something as mundane as shoplifting. The public likes stories like these, where businesspeople, politicians, celebrities or clergymen appear as either perpetrators or victims. Situations in which the perpetrator is a great deal stronger than the victim (e.g. a strong, young perpetrator and an old, infirm victim) are appealing. One tabloid reported: '14-year-old Ewelina J drank herself stupid and then abused her grandmother. The helpless old woman couldn't stand it any longer and called the police to come and take her granddaughter away'[6]; and 'For me, the most horrible thing was that these young people killed a clergyman. Some of them were still babies' (Kowalska 2001).

Overinformation and underinformation

The phenomena of overinformation and underinformation are apparent in crime reporting. Overinformation occurs when a single shocking event triggers an avalanche of news on a similar story. For example, news that a mother had killed her child while under the influence of alcohol will signal that the public is about to be inundated with stories about other mothers who have neglected their children for the next few weeks. A tragic coach accident with a lot of fatalities will prompt reports about other bus accidents (some of which were not all that serious), unroadworthy vehicles on Polish roads and/or coaches being driven by fatigued drivers. Overinformation can also create 'waves of criminality'. A certain topic might become fashionable and make a permanent comeback. The increase in reporting on, for example, crimes involving women and children may well lead to a growing conviction that there is a wave of this type of criminality, which may not necessarily be true.[7]

Underinformation is about preventing the media from publishing or broadcasting information on certain kinds of criminality or about criminality in general. This may be the result of a deliberate policy decision (as was the case during the communist period), or it may be that some more inviting topic has been given precedence, or it may even be that certain types of criminality simply do not fire the public imagination (e.g. petty theft or intricate economic crimes whose essence is incomprehensible to someone used to and biased towards a dumbed down media).

6 'Pijana nastolatka naubliżała swojej babci', *Super Express*, 14 November 2006.
7 Ibid.

Little wonder then that the mass media picture of criminality bears little resemblance to the statistical one. This also affects public awareness as to the actual nature and scale of criminality in Poland. Michał Zawadzki found that every fourth respondent he examined said that crimes against life and limb were predominant in Poland (in reality they account for approximately 3.5 per cent of the total), while almost one in three said that economic crimes were (Zawadzki 2002, p. 32) (the actual figure is approximately 15 per cent).[8] Respondents generally harboured convictions regarding homicides committed by minors that similarly failed to correspond with reality. More than 83 per cent claimed that the number of such homicides had 'frightfully' or 'significantly' increased over the previous two years (i.e. prior to 2002) whereas in fact the number had fallen (from 28 in 1999 to 16 in 2000 and 20 in 2001 (Zawadzki 2002, p. 35); minors were suspected of committing just four homicides in 2013).[9]

The sex of the perpetrator is the one factor where the media reports match the statistics: criminality is the domain of men, both in the media and the statistics (Maguire et al. 2002, p. 385). Criminal acts committed by women, though, are of more interest to the public. Researchers on this topic also note that the media portrays crimes committed by women differently from those committed by men. In the case of acts committed by women, the protagonist is frequently depicted as having emotional problems or suffering from mental illness. Female violence is also more often portrayed as irrational and emotionally driven than is male violence.

Journalists additionally omit fairly relevant facts, e.g. that most crimes involving violence occur between people who know each other. This aspect, however, is often left out of media accounts and the case is presented as having taken place between total strangers. Rape, for example, is most often described in the press as a drastic attack in a public place by an assailant completely unknown to the victim. The reality, however, is that women are most often raped in private places by men with whom they are acquainted (Williams 2004, p. 45).

The following story, which appeared in the Polish media at the beginning of 2011, is a case that illustrates the foregoing reflexions. 'Who Killed the Priest?' queried the newspaper *Fakt*.[10] 'Teenager Murders Priest', said the *naszemiasto* portal.[11] The recurring theme running through all the media was that a well loved priest had been brutally murdered and that his killer must have been a prize thug. Only after a few days, by which time the initial furore had died down, did it become apparent that the matter was not so clear cut. The teenager knew the middle-aged man from an internet chat room and the two had arranged to meet in person. The boy arrived by train and his new friend picked him up from the station and took him to a flat in an apartment building. Once there, a heated argument ensued and ended with the teenager actually killing the man. That the victim was a priest only became known afterwards (Nicpoń and Sapkowska 2011). While the facts of the case are unclear, the victim does not appear to be as squeaky clean as he did in the initial reports and the perpetrator not necessarily a degenerate.

Influence of the Media (and Politicians) on Criminal Policy

In observing the links between the media and politics, but without putting the debate into a broader context or giving any consideration to the actual interests of particular occupational or social groups, Piotr Żuk (2010, p. 128) writes, 'politics is starting to resemble a media show where the public are relegated to the role of spectators who can do no more than cheer for particular characters in political dramas'. This can also be applied to media reports on criminality. Sensational stories, short reports on lots of miscellaneous news items – what counts most in television news is the number of news items presented, not the depth of the analyses to which they are subjected – and talk show and serial conventions do not leave much room to delve into complicated relationships and dependencies or to examine social context.

8 Police Headquarters Website: http://www.statystyka.policja.pl/portal/st/842/47682/Postepowania_wszczete_przestepstwa_stwierdzone_i_wykrywalnosc_w_latach_19992010.html (accessed May 2011).

9 Police Headquarters Website: http://statystyka.policja.pl/portal.php?serwis=st&dzial=942&id=50256&sid=c5eac4ddeca7918dab4e2ab8e0b2805b (accessed March 2013).

10 *Fakt* webpage: http://www.fakt.pl/Kto-zamordowal-ksiedza-,artykuly,99590,1.html (accessed 27 March 2011).

11 *naszemiasto* portal: http://gdansk.naszemiasto.pl/tag/zamordowal-ksiedza.html (accessed March 2013).

Research shows that what the media publish or broadcast helps shape public attitudes. It has been observed, for example, that the worldview of people who often watch television is considerably more consistent with the picture presented by that medium than is the worldview of those who rarely watch television. Pretty much the same goes for attitudes towards criminality. Because television paints the world as a dangerous place and exaggerates the seriousness and frequency of crimes as well as the risk of victimisation, television viewers frequently suffer from higher levels of anxiety about crime. This higher overall level of anxiety, however, is connected with greater punitiveness and an acceptance of authoritarian methods of control (Greer 2010, p. 504). Moreover, stereotypes of criminality and the justice system (one of the sources for which are exaggerated media reports) help convince the public that not only should the law be more stringent and sentences more severe but that there should be more police and an increase in the police operational budget (Schneider 1981, p. 51).

Despite a growing sense of safety, anxiety about criminality remains at the top of the list of Polish people's concerns. This makes it a popular topic for both the mass media (as people enjoy reading and hearing about things that frighten them) and politicians, who are only too happy to make political capital out of the fears and punitiveness of their constituents without expending too much effort. Many politicians additionally believe that not responding to the emotional demands of public opinion (often made in the wake of shocking but nevertheless isolated incidents) will see them consigned to political oblivion. As a result, the criminal provisions are often not so much the expression of a rational, well thought out criminal policy for the country as knee jerk reactions to specific shocking events (see Filar 2011, pp. 327–32; Ostrowski 2014, pp. 127–8).

Making the law more stringent, however, has nothing to do with any increase in criminality (because it is not increasing) or in our sense of being under threat (because this feeling is decreasing). Nor is it a realisation of societal expectations. It is nothing more than a political game. The media, wittingly or not, repeatedly comes to the aid of politicians pursuing political interests by emphasising and exaggerating threats and demanding harsher penalties. Manipulating social perceptions is quite simple, as evidenced by the number of crimes that already provoke an exceptionally strong social reaction in many countries. In Poland, these include crimes challenging morality, e.g. incest, paedophilia and pornography, especially child pornography. Such crimes are largely criminalised for emotional reasons (Gardocki 1990, pp. 76–85).

Public opinion and the attitude of the media to a given crime, and thereby social expectations as to the severity of the punishment, sometimes differ, depending on how the character and background of the perpetrator are presented in the media. An illustrative example of this sort of double standard arose in Poland in 2009. As mentioned above, different kinds of crime temporarily become fashionable (Błachut et al. 1999, p. 415). These 'trends' sometimes begin with a single case, albeit one that outrages public opinion. This will suddenly appear in the media and spark a debate on a given topic. The problem will start to be discussed on daily news, current affairs and intervention programmes. In 2008, for example, Europe was rocked by the Josef Fritzl case.[12] Most likely as a result of the exposure this case was given in Poland, a young woman came forward with her mother and notified the police that her father had kept her at home for six years and raped her. During this time she gave birth to two children, who were given up for adoption. The discovery of a 'Polish Fritzl' (as the media frequently dubbed him) provoked an extraordinarily emotional reaction. The media frequently used epithets such as 'father/monster'[13] and 'the monster from Podlachia'.[14] This shocking story, along with an emotional statement made by the Prime Minister ('I don't think the term "human being" applies to individuals – for creatures – like this and, as a result, I don't think that human rights should apply in these sorts of cases'),[15] sparked a debate on paedophilia and effective means to combat it.

---

12 Josef Fritzl imprisoned his daughter in the basement of his home for 24 years and had seven children by her. He raised three of them with his wife, three were raised in the basement and one died immediately after birth. Fritzl was sentenced to life imprisonment.

13 'Oto polski Fritzl!', *Super Express*, 9 September 2008. Article available online: http://www.se.pl/wydarzenia/kraj/oto-polski-fritzl_71122.html (accessed October 2011).

14 Wirtualna Polska, 'Bliski koniec procesu "potwora z Podlasia"', available online: http://wiadomosci.wp.pl/kat,1342,title,Bliski-koniec-procesu-potwora-z-Podlasia,wid,11850164,wiadomosc.html?ticaid=1d312 (accessed October 2011).

15 Statement made by Prime Minister Donald Tusk at a press conference, 9 September 2008. See http://wiadomosci.gazeta.pl/wiadomosci/1,114873,5676698,Tusk__bedzie_farmakologiczna_kastracja_dla_pedofilow.html (accessed 31 October 2014).

Admittedly, the media response was not uniform. While the tabloids aggressively called for harsher punishment (Sulikowski 2009), the Prime Minister's statement was criticised (Bodnar and Graff 2008), deliberations were undertaken on the practicalities of enforcing the provisions, and there was even sympathy with the appeal of NGO campaigners who wrote an open letter to the Prime Minister in which they accused him of boosting his own image at the expense of the victim and called on him to speed up work on the *ustawa o przeciwdziałaniu przemocy w rodzinie* (Act to Counter Domestic Violence).[16] Nevertheless, over 75 per cent of the Polish population at the time supported the idea of sentencing people convicted of paedophilia to chemical castration and 94 per cent of respondents were in favour of making the penalties for these types of offences considerably more severe.[17] It should be added that the penalties for rape and for inducing a cohabitant under the age of 15 to submit to 'alternative sexual activity' or to demonstrate the performance of a sexual act for the purpose of sexual gratification (these provisions were made more stringent in 2005)[18] were all 2–12 years' imprisonment at the time. A year after the eruption of the 'Polish Fritzl' case, politicians of all stripes closed ranks and voted to amend the Criminal Code to provide for the chemical castration of convicted paedophiles and to make the penalty for this type of crime more severe. Hardly a single member of parliament voted against these amendments. Rape of a person under the age of 15 and incestuous rape now both carry a mandatory sentence of being placed in a secure institution and/or being sent for chemical castration (CC Art. 95a § 1a).

Ironically, just one day after the parliament had increased the criminal liability for paedophile acts, Roman Polański was detained at Zurich Airport pursuant to an arrest warrant from the United States on charges of raping a 13-year-old girl in 1978. Polański fled to France prior to sentencing and has not returned to the United States since. His arrest was immediately greeted with indignation in Polish and international artistic circles and hysteria in the Polish media. Director Krzysztof Zanussi, that great moral authority of Polish cinema, even went so far as to describe the girl who had been wronged by Polański in vulgar terms. Even though many objective and balanced assessments of the situation appeared in the Polish media afterwards, it is that initial hysterical reaction, full of outrage, on the part of artists and many politicians, that has stuck in our collective memory – a reaction that could not be more different from the one expressed just a year earlier, when paedophiles were labelled 'perverts'. When Polański was released on bail and placed under house arrest at his home in Switzerland, as many as 45 per cent of Poles thought the decision of the court was just.[19]

Media Broadcasting and Society's View of the Agencies of the Justice System[20]

Media broadcasting plays an important role in shaping society's view of the agencies of the justice system (Daniel 2005, pp. 89–99). The specialist literature occasionally calls on the mass media to show police officers, public prosecutors, judges and prison service personnel at work so as to instil respect for these professional groups and foster a desire to support them in their work, instead of simply chasing easy scoops (see Bronowska and Sławik 2003, p. 268). The way the media influences what Polish people know about the justice system and the people who work in it is likewise interesting. The judicial system is most often brought to public notice when it functions defectively. We often hear about judges, prosecutors and police officers in the context of dishonourable conduct and corruption. Objectively speaking, however, these instances are rare.

There is no denying that the average Pole is given a fairly negative picture of how the justice system and its agencies operate. This deluge of critical news is no doubt one of the reasons for the precipitous decline in public confidence in the judiciary. In surveys conducted in Warsaw in 1993, only 54.7 per cent of respondents

16 'Kastracja pedofilów to PR premiera kosztem ofiar', Polish Press Agency, 15 September 2008.

17 Survey conducted by Millward Brown SMG/KRC, September 2008, available online: http://wiadomosci.gazeta.pl/Wiadomosci/1,80708,5689251,Prawie_80_proc__Polakow_za_farmakologiczna_kastracja.html (accessed December 2009).

18 Act to Change the Act on the Criminal Procedure Code and the Act on the Criminal Code 27 July 2005 (Journal of Laws No. 163, Pos. 1363).

19 Survey conducted by Gemius, December 2009, from the *Newsweek Polska* website: http://www.newsweek.pl/artykuly/sekcje/polska/sondaz-newsweek-pl--w-sprawie-zwolnienia-polanskiego-polacy-podzieleni,49844,1 (accessed December 2009).

20 This section co-authored with Witold Klaus.

had any confidence in the judiciary (Bieńkowska and Wojciechowska 1993, pp. 35–7). In nationwide surveys conducted in 2002, however, as many as 29 per cent declared that the sentences handed down by the criminal courts were unjust (compared with 17 per cent of civil judgements) and every third respondent declared that the courts were functioning worse than they had been five years earlier. According to those surveyed, the cause of all this injustice was mostly the result of judges being corrupt, evidentiary hurdles that made it nigh on impossible for the parties to prove their cases, bad and unjust laws, and a lack of access to lawyers. As many as 78 per cent of respondents rated judges as not independent and as being subjected to pressure when making their judgements (of these, 12 per cent were of the view that this happens often) (Czapska 2003, pp. 38–43). Only 40 per cent of Poles expressed any confidence in the judiciary in 2010.[21]

Nevertheless, the justice system and its agencies are increasingly coming to understand the necessity of managing their own media image. Police officers know only too well that journalists are under tremendous pressure to obtain information and do not often go to the trouble of clarifying the news they have acquired or giving a police spokesperson an opportunity to issue an appropriate response (Murak 2011, p. 103, citing Wachowski 1995). The police are sufficiently cognisant of this situation to work on fully professionalising their media liaison, e.g. a Police Headquarters directive on methods and forms of media and public relations activity lays down what kinds of information can be released to journalists and under what conditions.[22] The police also place a lot of weight on having press spokespeople at other major police stations (Skibińska 2007, p. 167). These measures may well be responsible for the fairly high level of confidence that Poles have in the police: the figure has hovered around 70 per cent for several years now.[23] Łukasz Ostrowski (2014, pp. 140–41), who made a study of crime reporting in the newspaper *Fakt*, made an interesting observation. He noticed that *Fakt* journalists were as respectful and understanding towards members of the uniformed services (this included prison services staff as well as police and military personal) as they were critical of the state and its institutions and parliamentarians and bureaucrats. The reasons for their high regard of the uniformed services would obviously require a thorough analysis. It may be that journalists refrain from attacking groups whose members are valuable sources of information. Whatever the reasons for this sympathetic treatment, it is definitely one of the factors influencing the confidence that Polish people have in the uniformed services, especially the police force.

The judiciary's communication with the media is not so effective, efficient or advanced. Moreover, research shows that members of the judiciary dread communicating with society, especially when it comes to caring for the image of the courts in the media. A willingness to be 'media-friendly' might lead to populist judgements. There is a danger that judges might be more swayed by the societal predilection towards severe punishment than by the evidence adduced in court and the applicable law when sentencing, and that they would then hand down judgements that would keep the public 'satisfied' that the judiciary were doing their job (Markov 2009, pp. 18–19). The danger is such that they prefer to keep their relationship with the media at arm's length.

Figure 10.1 shows how differently society has assessed the work of the Polish police and judiciary over the last few years. While the public perception of the police has improved, confidence in the courts is significantly lower and is subject to wide fluctuations. This may be a result of the difference, described above, in the way these institutions work on their media images.

It should further be borne in mind that public confidence in the justice system cannot be separated from the questions of whether people believe in democracy and are happy to leave public decisions to politicians. If society does not trust politicians and has no faith in the quality of statutory law, it will not have any confidence in the judiciary and will also have a low opinion of how it functions (Markov 2009, p. 16). The Polish public is very critical of the parliament with some 60 per cent of the population having a low opinion of it (Kowalczuk 2010a). Similarly, 63 per cent of those sampled have a negative view of the operation of law. Three out of

21 Online reports: http://www.sprawozdanie.pl/zaufanie-polakow-do-zawodow-na-przestrzeni-ostatnich-5-lat/statystyka (accessed May 2011).

22 Police Headquarters Directive No. 13/2000 on Methods and Forms of Media and Public Relations Activity, 25 September 2000.

23 Survey conducted by OBOP, available on the Police website: http://www.statystyka.policja.pl/portal/st/905/65888/69_procent_Polakow_dobrze_ocenia_prace_Policji.htm (accessed May 2011).

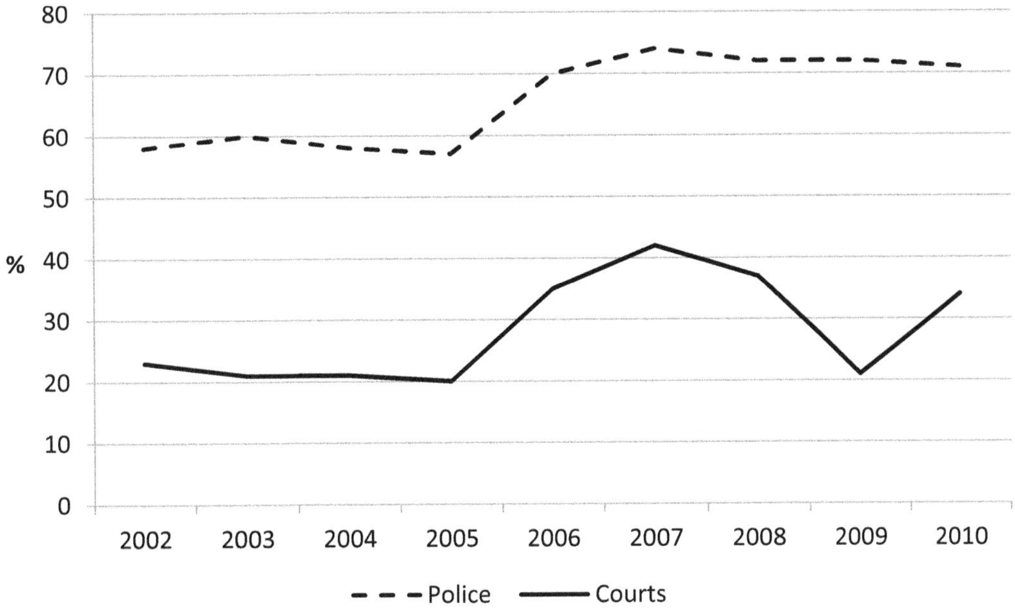

Figure 10.1 Positive assessments of the work of the police and the courts in Poland in 2002–2010

Source: Figures plotted using data from Polish Police Headquarters as per the article '69 procent Polaków dobrze ocenia pracę Policji', available online at: http://www.statystyka.policja.pl/portal/st/905/65888/69_procent_Polakow_dobrze_ocenia_prace_Policji.html (accessed March 2013).

every four respondents consider that the law is not applied equally to everybody, and that when drafting laws, parliament puts the interests of politicians and power elites first with scant regard for those of 'ordinary people' or the 'Polish state' (Cywiński 2010, pp. 170–73).

The Media and Social Life

The role of journalists in detecting and pursuing criminality, another essential function of the media, cannot be overlooked. The active part played by investigative journalists, vis-à-vis the frequently passive attitude of the investigative authorities, means that numerous crimes, many of which are economic and financial or committed by public figures, are often exposed by the media (Bronowska and Sławik 2003, p. 268). In some cases, the police only intervene after the screening of dramatic television footage showing wronged or harmed people plainly stating that they were ignored when they informed the authorities of criminal activity.

The media also raise important law-related topics that have enormous educational value. People learn about their rights, legal procedures and the options available to resolve problems legally. Even short reports on breakfast television, where lawyers are invited to provide information on some of these topics, play a large role. Popular television series are another source of legal knowledge. Idea placement contributes to this. Idea placement is analogous to product placement: just as leading actors in a film use brand name products, they also transfer knowledge about specific topics through their dialogue and behaviour. This may be knowledge about important social issues or an argument in favour of some important activity or lifestyle change (e.g. preventing cancer or sending six-year-olds to school).[24] People trust the stars of television series

24 'Ludzie ufają serialom bardziej niż ministrowi', *Rzeczpospolita* [online], 16 February 2010, available at: http://www.rp.pl/artykul/434522.html (accessed October 2010).

more than advertisements and are usually not even aware that the script is contrived. Some Polish series, for example, have subplots in which the protagonists fall victim to a crime and struggle to cope with it. Thus legal knowledge can be conveyed by this means.

Mock trials are another example whereby legal education is passed on via the media. One commercial channel used to broadcast a programme titled *Sędzia Anna Maria Wesołowska* (Judge Anna Maria Wesołowska), which examined criminal cases. This programme may have simplified issues, which is justifiable cause for complaint, but it certainly familiarised viewers with the nature, appearance and functioning of the criminal courts. Then again, Michał Zawadzki states that barely 20 per cent of the respondents he surveyed were able to obtain basic knowledge about the rules and procedures of criminal proceedings from television programmes (Zawadzki 2002, p. 29). As mentioned initially, Polish people take the media as their basic source of knowledge about the functioning of the justice system. This even applies to people personally involved in court hearings. When respondents are asked to recall court cases, they more often name high-profile trials reported in the media than cases in which they or people close to them have been involved (Daniel 2005, p. 95).

Many of the series on Polish television are licensed Polish versions of Western programmes. The police documentary series *W11 – Wydział Śledczy* (W11- Investigation Department) is a popular programme that follows the day-to-day work of a suburban police station. Each episode has a viewing audience of approximately 2 million.[25] Knowledge about criminality and police practices acquired in this manner, however, is more likely than not to be misleading. First, serious crimes are grossly over represented, and second, the conditions under which police work are presented in a completely unrealistic way. Policewomen from the Warsaw suburban station depicted in the programme say:

> '*W11*, for example, does the police a great disservice. People think it only takes a couple of days to crack a homicide case on the strength of what they see in this series. We're accused of doing nothing because a phone call can be traced in a couple of hours on *W11*. Goodness only knows who writes this stuff.' … 'More than a dozen people work on a case in *W11*. Meanwhile, I have a team of five.' (Olszewska 2011)

The media often present an exaggerated, simplified and distorted picture of how the justice system and its institutions function.

The involvement of the mass media in various kinds of campaigns aimed at raising legal awareness or increasing social sensitivity to certain issues is another virtue arising from media publications and broadcasts being ever present in society. Here it is worth mentioning the 2005 campaign against domestic violence, 'Przełam Przemoc' (Break Violence), organised by the Government Attorney for the Equal Status of Men and Women and informing the public that every act of violence, whether physical or psychological, is a crime, and the 2001 'Childhood Without Abuse' campaign organised by the Coalition of Governmental and Non-Governmental Organisations. Among the more recent initiatives we might include the 'Kocham. Nie biję' (I love them, I don't beat them) campaign supported by the National Competence Centre Foundation (Krajowe Cenrum Kompetencji), several ministers and the Children's Ombudsman. This kind of activity can produce measurable results, e.g. it can lead to a given type of crime being reported more often.

Legal Journalism: Threats and Opportunities

Finally, it is worth mentioning the people who compile the news in the media and who have come in for so much criticism in this chapter. Most journalists will state straight out that their sensational reports make the media, for which they work, more appealing (Łojko 2005, p. 113). The objection frequently raised by the legal profession, viz. that journalists who write about crime and report court cases are unprofessional and merely looking for scoops, is therefore not unwarranted. Moreover, they present a one-sided, simplified and prejudiced picture of the functioning of the court system (Daniel 2005, pp. 89–99; Łojko 2005, pp. 101–15).

25 See http://www.wirtualnemedia.pl/artykul/koniec-w11-wydzial-sledczy-serial-zniknie-z-tvn-po-10-latach-emisji (accessed 31 October 2014).

Another serious accusation levelled at journalists by lawyers is their lack of legal expertise and the many glaring errors they make when reporting criminal cases and court hearings (Daniel 2005, p. 97). This charge is not without foundation. Barely 20 per cent of Polish print journalists who write about the law have completed any formal legal studies. As if that were not bad enough, there is a general belief among the journalistic profession that innate talent, self-education and practical experience are more important than exhaustive career preparation in the practice of journalism (Łojko 2005, pp. 104–95). But a lack of professionalism on the part of journalists is sometimes not so much due to a lack of accurate knowledge about law and criminality as the enormous pressure they are under to meet print and broadcast deadlines. Their sole focus is on transmuting information into news for public consumption before a rival publisher or broadcaster beats them to the punch. This constant haste means that media reports on crime are generally superficial, devoid of any in-depth analysis and often come from unreliable sources.

Monika Gmurek (2011, pp. 98–9) highlights the fact that journalists often trust leaked information implicitly. This sort of information is often sketchy, piecemeal and taken out of context. The main concern for the media, however, is that the news they give out will remain classified or confidential for a while, as this raises it standing. They do not consider the fact that information is sometimes deliberately leaked to the media to achieve specific ends, even if only to divert journalists from lines of investigation intended to remain classified or confidential.

The demand that the level of professionalism of legal journalists be raised may well be justified, but there can nevertheless be no denying their importance in social life. Journalists not only spread knowledge about the law and the functioning of its agencies, but they frequently play a major role in uncovering criminal activity and in fighting improprieties in the justice system. Their presence in the courtroom is conducive to self-control and discipline on the part of the judges, and is a form of social control as well (Gmurek 2011, p. 111). Hans J. Schneider (1992, p. 242) encapsulates the argument for improving the quality of media news on criminality:

> Mass media news on criminality should convey a picture of crimes, criminals and victims that is more complete and closer to reality. News on criminal occurrences should be supplemented with information explaining the background of the events described. Documentary films on criminality should be broadcast at a suitable hour when there is a large viewing audience and the results of criminological research should additionally be made available to a mass audience and their practical significance explained in an accessible manner.

The fact remains, however, that criminality as media fodder has pretty much been milked for all it is worth. The press, radio and television have therefore recently gone looking for other ways to induce fear. Swine flu and even the end of the world may be prime examples.

References

Acheson, D. (ed.) (1998) *Independent Inquiry into Inequalities in Health*, London, available at: http://www.archive.official-documents.co.uk/document/doh/ih/part2c.htm, accessed 13 October 2012.

Aebi, F., Marguet, Y. and Delgrande N. (2010) *Council of Europe: Annual Penal Statistics Space II. Persons Serving Non-Custodial Sanctions and Measures in 2010*, Lausanne.

Alert, R.M., Aronson, E. and Wilson, T.D. (1997) *Psychologia społeczna. Serce i umysł*, Poznań.

Ambrozik, W. (2010) 'Współczesne koncepcje resocjalizacji a system kształcenia kadr na potrzeby praktyki', in Urban, B. (ed.) *Aktualne osiągnięcia w naukach społecznych a teoria i praktyka resocjalizacji*, Mysłowice.

Ambrozik, W., Hołyst, B. and Stępniak, P. (eds) (2001) *Więziennictwo. Nowe wyzwania*, Warszawa–Poznań–Kalisz.

Andrejew, I. (1988) *Podstawowe pojęcia nauki o przestępstwie*, Warszawa.

Andrejew, I., Lernell, L. and Sawicki, J. (1954) *Prawo karne Polski Ludowej*, Warszawa.

Andrews, D.A., Bonta, J. and Hoge, R. (1990) 'Classification for Effective Rehabilitation: Rediscovering Psychology', *Criminal Justice and Behaviour*, vol. 17, no. 1.

Andrews, D.A., Bonta, J. and Wormith, J.S. (2006) 'The Recent, Past and Near Future of Risk and/or Need Assessment', *Crime and Delinquency*, vol. 52, no. 1.

——— (2011) 'The Risk-Need-Responsivity (RNR) Model: Does Adding the Good Lives Model Contribute to Effective Crime Prevention?', *Criminal Justice and Behavior*, vol. 38, no. 7.

Anossi-Sołtysiak, M. (2007) 'Praca z indywidualnym przypadkiem jako model pracy kuratora sądowego', in Pospiszyl, K. and Konopczyński, M. (eds) *Resocjalizacja w stronę środowiska otwartego*, Warszawa.

Arystoteles (2011) *Etyka Nikomachejska*, Warszawa.

Babińska-Górecka, R. (2009) 'Problem wykluczenia społecznego a system świadczeń z pomocy społecznej', in Blicharz, J. and Boć, J. (eds) *Prawna działalność instytucji społeczeństwa obywatelskiego*, Wrocław.

Bachmat, P. (2010) 'Podstawowe zadania kuratorów sądowych w ustawodawstwie polskim', in Wójcik, D. (ed.) *Kuratela sądowa. Sukcesy i porażki*, Warszawa.

Bałandynowicz, A. (2000) 'Podstawy aksjologiczne systemu sprawiedliwego karania', *Prokuratura i Prawo*, no. 10.

———(2010) 'Kliniczny model kurateli sądowej w systemie środków probacyjnych', in *Dziewięćdziesięciolecie kurateli sądowej w Polsce. Historia – Teraźniejszość – Przyszłość. Materiały z I Kongresu Kuratorskiego, Ustka 15–17 czerwca 2009 r.*, Kraków.

Bańkowska, M. (1999) 'XX-lecie sądownictwa rodzinnego', *Przegląd Sądowy*, no. 4.

Batawia, S. (1958) *Proces społecznego wykolejania się nieletnich przestępców*, Warszawa.

Bauman, Z. (1998) 'Zbędni, niechciani, odtrąceni – czyli o biednych w zamożnym świecie', *Kultura i Społeczeństwo*, vol. 42, no. 2.

——— (2000) *Ponowoczesność jako źródło cierpień*, Warszawa.

——— (2007a) *Płynne czasy. Życie w epoce niepewności*, Warszawa.

——— (2007b) *Szanse etyki w zglobalizowanym świecie*, Kraków.

Beck, U. (2002) *Społeczeństwo ryzyka. W drodze do innej nowoczesności*, Warszawa.

——— (2005) *Risk Society: Towards a New Modernity*, London.

Bednarski, M., Kryńska, E., Pater, K. and Walewski, M. (eds) (2008) *Przyczyny pracy nierejestrowanej w Polsce*, Warszawa.

Bianchi, H. (1994) *Justice as Sanctuary: Toward a New System of Crime Control*, Bloomington, IN.

Bielecka, E. (2010) '"Galerianki" – badania i refleksje', *Pedagogika Społeczna*, no. 2.

Bielska, I. (2010) 'Przestępstwa komputerowe i internetowe. Aspekty kryminologiczne i prawne', in Kędzierska, G. and Pływaczewski, W. (eds) *Kryminologia wobec współczesnych wyzwań cywilizacyjnych*, Olsztyn.

Bieńkowska, A. (2006) 'Czego boją się Polacy', *Policja 997*, no. 17.

Bieńkowska, E. and Mazowiecka, L. (2009) *Prawa ofiar przestępstw*, Warszawa.

Bieńkowska, E. and Wojciechowska, J. (1993) 'Przestępczość i inne problemy społeczne w świetle własnych doświadczeń i poglądów mieszkańców Warszawy', *Studia Prawnicze*, no. 4.

Bieńkuńska, A. (ed.) (2012) *Ubóstwo w Polsce w 2011 r. (na podstawie badań budżetów gospodarstw domowych)*, Warszawa, available at: http://stat.gov.pl/cps/rde/xbcr/gus/WZ_ubostwo_w_polsce_2011.pdf, accessed 20 October 2014.

Bircan, T., Hooghe, M., Vanhoutte, B. and Hardyns, W. (2011) 'Unemployment, Inequality, Poverty and Crime: Spatial Distribution Patterns of Criminal Acts in Belgium, 2001–2006', *British Journal of Criminology*, vol. 51, no. 1.

Bird, O. (1967) *The Idea of Justice*, New York.

Błachut, J. (2007) *Problemy związane z pomiarem przestępczości*, Warszawa–Kraków.

Błachut, J., Gaberle, A. and Krajewski, K. (1999) *Kryminologia*, Gdańsk.

Bodnar, A. and Graff, A. (2008) 'Tusk w butach Ziobry', *Gazeta Wyborcza*, 19 September 2008.

Bojarski, M. and Radecki, W. (2006) *Kodeks wykroczeń. Komentarz*, Warszawa.

Bojarski, T. (2009) *Polskie prawo wykroczeń. Zarys wykładu*, Warszawa.

Bojarski, T., Michalska-Warias, A., Nowikowski, I., Nazar-Gutowska, K., Piórkowska-Flieger, J. and Firkowski, D. (2011) *Teoretyczne i praktyczne problemy współczesnego prawa karnego, materiały z konferencji naukowej, Lublin, 26–27.09.2011 r.*, Lublin.

Bonta J. (2002) 'Offender Risk Assessment: Guidelines for Selection and Use', *Criminal Justice and Behavior*, vol. 29, no. 4.

Bonta, J. and Andrews, D.A. (2007) *Risk-Need-Responsivity Model for Offender Assessment and Rehabilitation*, Ottawa.

Borucka-Arctowa, M. (1988) 'Zaufanie do prawa jako wartość społeczna i rola sprawiedliwości proceduralnej', in *Teoria prawa, filozofia prawa, współczesne prawa i prawodawstwa*, Toruń.

Box, S. (1987) *Recession, Crime and Punishment*, Basingstoke.

Bradley, T. (2005) 'Social Exclusion', in McLaughlin, E. and Muncie, J. (eds) *The Sage Dictionary of Criminology*, London.

Braithwaite, J. (1989) *Crime, Shame and Reintegration*, Cambridge.

——— (2003) 'Does Restorative Justice Work?', in Johnstone, G. (ed.) *A Restorative Justice Reader: Texts, Sources, Context*, Cullompton.

Brody S. (1976) *The Effectiveness of Sentencing*. Home Office Research Study 35, London.

Bronowska, K. and Sławik, K. (2003) 'Przestępczość a środki masowego przekazu', *Problemy współczesnej kryminalistyki*, vol. 6.

Browne, J. (1996) 'The Labor of Doing Time', in Rosenblatt, E. (ed.) *Criminal Injustice: Confronting the Prison Crisis*, Cambridge, MA.

Buchała, K. et al. (1995) *Komentarz do ustawy o ochronie obrotu gospodarczego*, Warszawa.

Buczkowski, K. (2007) 'Przepadek korzyści majątkowej po nowelizacji kodeksu karnego z 13 czerwca 2003 r. Wyniki badań aktowych', *Biuletyn Polskiego Towarzystwa Kryminologicznego im. profesora Stanisława Batawii*, no. 17.

——— (2010) 'Skuteczność odzyskiwania korzyści majątkowych uzyskanych przez sprawców przestępstwa – analiza przepadków orzeczonych na podstawie art. 45 k.k.', *Prawo w działaniu*, no. 8.

Buczkowski, K., Klaus, W., Kossowska, A., Rzeplińska, I. and Woźniakowska-Fajst, D. (2012) 'Politicians, Media, and Society's Perception of Crime', in Šelih, A. and Završnik, A. (eds) *Crime and Transition in Central and Eastern Europe*, New York–Heidelberg–Dordrecht–London.

Buczkowski, K., Kulma, R. and Wójcik, D. (2010) 'Badania ankietowe kuratorów zawodowych i społecznych pionu karnego i rodzinnego', in Wójcik, D. (ed.) *Kuratela sądowa. Sukcesy i porażki*, Warszawa.

Buczkowski, K. and Wojtaszek, M. (1998) *Przestępstwa gospodarcze w praktyce sądowej i prokuratorskiej*, Warszawa.

Budyn-Kulik, M., Kozłowska-Kalisz, P., Kulik, M. and Mozgawa, M. (2009) *Prawo karne materialne. Część ogólna*, Kraków.
Bulenda, T. (2005) 'Polityczno-kryminalne implikacje dotyczące bezpieczeństwa publicznego w programach partii politycznych w wyborach parlamentarnych w 2005 r.', *Przegląd Więziennictwa Polskiego*, no. 49.
——— (2010) 'Polityka karna w programach wyborczych w 2007 r.', *Przegląd Więziennictwa Polskiego*, no. 66.
Bunio-Mroczek, P. (2010) 'Nastoletnie macierzyństwo, transmisja biedy, wykluczenie społeczne', *Praca Socjalna*, special issue.
Burnett, R., Baker, K. and Roberts, C. (2007) 'Assessment, Supervision and Intervention: Fundamental Practice in Probation', in Gelsthorpe, L. and Morgan, R. (eds) *Handbook of Probation*, Cullompton.
Burnett, R. and McNeil, F. (2005) 'The Place of the Officer-Offender Relationship in Assisting Offenders to Desist from Crime', *Probation Journal*, vol. 52, no. 3.
Buszko, S. (2010) 'Zobowiązanie do naprawienia szkody, do wykonania określonych prac na rzecz pokrzywdzonego lub społeczności lokalnej', paper presented at the conference: 'Mediacja w praktyce wymiaru sprawiedliwości', 2010, Ustka.
Cartledge, C.G., Tak, P.J.P. and Tomić-Malić, M. (eds) (1981), *Probation in/en Europe: European Assembly for Probation and After-Care*, London.
Casas, R.P. (2013) *Minimum Income Standards in Enlarged EU: Guaranteed Minimum Income Schemes*, available at: http://www.eapn.i.e./pdfs/155_paper%20II%20-%20Minimum%20income%20standards%20 in%20enlarged%20EU.pdf, accessed 22 March 2013.
Case, S. and Haines, K. (2009) *Understanding Youth Offending: Risk Factor Research, Policy and Practice*, Cullompton.
Chibnall, S. (2010) 'Press Ideology: The Politics of Professionalism', in Greer, C. (ed.) *Crime and Media: A Reader*, London.
Christie, N. (1986) 'Suitable Enemy', in Bianchi, H. and van Swaaningen R. (eds) *Abolitionism: Toward a Non-Repressive Approach to Crime*, Amsterdam.
——— (2004a) 'Conflict as Property', in Fajst, M. and Płatek, M. (eds) *W kręgu kryminologii romantycznej*, Warszawa.
——— (2004b) *A Suitable Amount of Crime*, London.
Cieślak, M. (1994) *Polskie prawo karne*, Warszawa.
Ciosek, M. (2001) *Psychologia sądowa i penitencjarna*, Warszawa.
Cohen, L.E. and Felson, M. (1979) 'Social Change and Crime Rate Trends: A Routine Activity Approach', *American Sociological Review*, vol. 44, no. 4.
Coleman, R. (2009) 'Policing the Working Class in the City of Renewal: The State and Social Surveillance', in Coleman, R., Sim, J., Tombs, S. and White, D. (eds) *State, Power, Crime*, London–Thousand Oaks, CA–New Delhi–Singapore.
Consedine, J. (2004) *Sprawiedliwość naprawcza. Przywrócenie ładu społecznego*, Warszawa.
Cooley, C.H. (1964) *Human Nature and the Social Order*, New York.
Cullen, F.T. and Gendreau, P. (2001) 'From Nothing Works to What Works: Changing Professional Ideology in the 21st Century', *The Prison Journal*, vol. 15, no. 3.
Cumming-Bruce, N. (2013) 'More Than 60,000 Have Died in Syrian Conflict, U.N. Says', *New York Times*, 2 January 2013.
Currie, E. (2002) 'Crime and Market Society: Lessons from the United States', in Walton, P. and Young, J. (eds) *The New Criminology Revisited*, Houndmills.
Cywiński, Z. (2010) 'Nieegalitarne prawo w nieegalitarnym społeczeństwie', in Turska, A. (ed.) *Prawo i wykluczenie społeczne. Studium empiryczne*, Warszawa.
Czapiński, J. (2009) 'Diagnoza Szkolna 2009. Przemoc i inne problemy w polskiej szkole', in *Raport roczny programu społecznego 'Szkoła bez przemocy'*, Warszawa.
Czapiński, J. and Panek, T. (eds) (2006) *Diagnoza Społeczna 2005*, Warszawa.
Czapska, J. (2003) 'Wizerunek sądu w opinii społecznej', in Borucka-Arctowa, M. and Pałecki, K. (eds) *Sądy w opinii społeczeństwa polskiego*, Kraków.

——— (2008) 'Poczucie bezpieczeństwa mieszkańców Krakowa', in Krajewski, K. (ed.) *Poczucie bezpieczeństwa mieszkańców wielkich miast. Kraków na tle innych miast europejskich*, Kraków.
Czapska, J. and Kury, H. (eds) (2002) *Mit represyjności albo o znaczeniu prewencji kryminalnej*, Kraków.
Czapska, J. and Waltoś, S. (2007) 'O polskim populizmie penalnym, w związku z książką J. Pratta "Penal Populism" uwag kilka', in Krajewski, K. (ed.) *Nauki penalne wobec problemów współczesnej przestępczości*, Kraków.
Czarnecka-Dzialuk, B. (2010) 'Perspektywy i ograniczenia mediacji z nieletnimi' [Prospects and limitations on mediation with juveniles], in *Mediacja w praktyce wymiaru sprawiedliwości* [Mediation in judicial practice]. Słupsk Regional Court, Ustka, 4–5 October 2010, Conference materials, pp. 116–27, available at: http://www.slupsk.so.gov.pl/index.php?idg=mg,72&p=m&kword=mediacja, accessed 22 October 2014.
——— (2013) 'Perspektywy i bariery mediacji w opinii prokuratorów i sędziów', in Mazowiecka, L. (ed.) *Mediacja karne jako instytucja ważna dla pokrzywdzonego*, Warszawa.
Czarnecka-Dzialuk, B. and Walczak-Żochowska, A. (1995) 'Możliwość mediacji w sprawach o czyny karalne popełniane przez nieletnich', in Bieńkowska, E. (ed.) *Teoria i praktyka pojednania ofiary ze sprawcą*, Warszawa.
Czarnecka-Dzialuk, B. and Wójcik, D. (2001) *Mediacja w sprawach nieletnich w świetle teorii i badań*, Warszawa.
——— (2011) 'Reagowanie na czyny karalne i demoralizcję nieletnich – koncepcje teoretyczne, statystyki i opinie sędziów rodzinnych', in Siemaszko, A. (ed.) *Stosowanie prawa. Księga jubileuszowa z okazji XX-lecia Instytutu Wymiaru Sprawiedliwości*, Warszawa.
——— (2012) 'Stosowanie sądowych środkow oddziaływania wobec nieletnich w świetle koncepcji teoretycznych, statystyki oraz opinii sędziów i kuratorów rodzinnych', unpublished report of the Institute of Justice, Warszawa.
Czernicki, K. (1939) 'Przestępczość w Polsce w latach 1935–1937 według policyjnej statystyki kryminalnej', *Archiwum Kryminologiczne*, vol. 3, nos. 1–2.
Daigle, L.E. (2012) *Victimology: A Text/Reader*, Los Angeles, CA–London–New Dehli–Singapore–Washington DC.
Daly, K. (2000) 'Revisiting the Relationship between Retributive and Restorative Justice', in Strang, H. and Braithwaite, J., *Restorative Justice: From Philosophy to Practice*, Aldershot.
Danecka, M. (2007) 'O biedzie i bezrobociu', in Jarosz, M. (ed.) *Transformacja. Elity. Społeczeństwo*, Warszawa.
——— (2008) 'Ubodzy i bezrobotni', in Jarosz, M. (ed.) *Wykluczeni. Wymiar społeczny, materialny i etniczny*, Warszawa.
Daniel, K. (2005) 'Rola mediów w kształtowaniu społecznych opinii o sądach', in Magoska, M. (ed.) *Media. Władza. Prawo*, Kraków.
Deutsch, M., Coleman, P.T. and Marcus, E.C. (2006) *The Handbook of Conflict Resolution: Theory and Practice*, San Francisco, CA.
Diakowska, B. (2009) 'Przestępstwa popełniane przez "ludzi luźnych" w Warszawie u schyłku XVIII wieku na podstawie ogłoszeń w prasie warszawskiej', in *Społeczeństwo staropolskie*, vol. 2, *Społeczeństwo a przestępczość*, Warszawa.
Dolata, R. (2008) *Szkoła – segregacje – nierówności*, Warszawa.
Dölling, D., Gössel, K.-H. and Waltoś, S. (eds) (1997) *Relacje o przestępstwach i procesach karnych w prasie codziennej w Niemczech i w Polsce*, Kraków.
Domachowski, W. (2005) 'Czy istnieje przestępczość nieletnich?', in Stanik, J.M. and Woszczek, L. (eds) *Przestępczość nieletnich. Aspekty psychospołeczne i prawne*, Katowice.
Domański, H. (2004) 'Główne kierunki zmian w strukturze społecznej', in Marody, M. (ed.) *Wymiary życia społecznego. Polska na przełomie XX i XXI wieku*, Warszawa.
Doroszewski, W. (ed.) (1996–1997) *Słownik języka polskiego*, Warszawa.
Drapała, K. (2012) *Programy oddziaływania resocjalizacyjnego w zakładach poprawczych*, Warszawa (unpublished).
Dubiel, K. (2009) 'Krótka historia resocjalizacji penitencjarnej', in Marczak, M. (ed.) *Resocjalizacyjne programy penitencjarne realizowane przez służbę więzienną w Polsce*, Kraków.

Dudka, K. (2006) *Skuteczność instrumentów ochrony praw pokrzywdzonego w postępowaniu przygotowawczym w świetle badań empirycznych*, Lublin.
Dukiet-Nagórska, T. (ed.) (2006) *Zagadnienia współczesnej polityki kryminalnej*, Bielsko-Biała.
Dukiet-Nagórska, T. and Lubelski, M.J. (1982) 'Uwagi na temat kształtowania sądowego wymiaru kary w wytycznych wymiaru sprawiedliwości i praktyki sądowej', *Palestra*, nos. 1–3.
Duszczyk, M. (2010) 'Working poor – "pracujący biedni" na świecie i w Polsce', in Szarfenberg, R., Żołędowski, C. and Theiss, M. (eds) *Ubóstwo i wykluczenie społeczne – perspektywa poznawcza*, Warszawa.
Dziurnikowska-Stefańska, M. (2011) 'Stosunek studentów do naruszania przez prawników norm etyki i prawa', in Łojko, E. (ed.) *Studenci prawa o studiach i perspektywach zawodowych*, Warszawa.
Eisner, M. (1995) 'The Effects of Economic Structures and Phases of Development on Crime', in *Crime and Economy: Reports Presented to the 11th Criminological Colloquium (1994)*, Strasbourg.
Elias, N. (1976) *Uber den Prozess der Zivilisation*, Frankfurt am Main.
Esterle-Hedibel, M. (2005) 'Leaving School: A New Form of Juvenile Deviance?', *Penal Issues*, no. 16.
Eurostat (2012) *Crime and Criminal Justice: Statistics in Focus*, no. 6.
Fajst, M. and Płatek, M. (eds) *Sprawiedliwość naprawcza. Idea. Teoria. Praktyka*, Warszawa.
Falandysz, L. (1986) *W kręgu kryminologii radykalnej*, Warszawa.
Falck, S. (1992) 'The Norvegian Community Mediation Centers at a Crossroads', in Messmer, H. and Otto, H.U. (eds) *Restorative Justice on Trial: Pitfalls and Potentials of Victim-Offender Mediation: International Research Perspectives*, Dordrecht.
Falkowska, M. (2000) *Zasięg biedy i postrzeganie ludzi biednych w Polsce*, Centrum Badania Opinii Społecznej, Warszawa, available at: http://www.cbos.pl/SPISKOM.POL/2000/K_136_00.pdf, accessed 4 February 2013.
Fandrejewska, A. (2013) 'Wieś dogania już miasto', *Rzeczpospolita*, 29 March 2013.
Farrington, D.P. and Welsh, B.C. (2007) *Saving Children from a Life of Crime: Early Risk Factors and Effective Interventions*, Oxford.
Fattah, E. (1999) 'From a Handful of Dollars to Tea and Sympathy: The Sad History of Victim Assistance', in van Dijk, J., van Kaam, R.G.H. and Wemmers J. (eds) *Caring for Crime Victims: Selected Proceedings of the Ninth International Symposium on Victimology*, Monsey, NY.
——— (2002) 'From Philosophical Abstraction to Restorative Action, from Senseless Retribution to Meaningful Restitution: Just Deserts and Restorative Justice Revisited', in Weitekamp, E. and Kerner, H.J. (eds) *Restorative Justice: Theoretical Foundations*, Cullomptom.
——— (2011) 'Is Restorative Justice a Viable Option in Crimes of Violence', *Journal of Law, Politics and Sociology*, vol. 84, no. 9, available at: http://koara.lib.keio.ac.jp/xoonips/modules/xoonips/download.php?file_id=63581, accessed 10 June 2013.
——— (2012) 'The Dawning of New Era in Social Reaction to Crime: Promise, Potential and Limitations of Restorative Justice', *Archiwum Kryminologii*, vol. 34.
Feliksiak, M. (2011) *Pogorszenie nastrojów społecznych*, Warszawa, Report no. BS/25/2011, available at: http://www.cbos.pl/SPISKOM.POL/2011/K_025_11.PDF, accessed 20 October 2014.
Filar, M. (2007–2008) 'Rola mediów w kreowaniu zagrożeń i sprzyjaniu populizmowi', *Archiwum Kryminologii*, vols 29–30.
——— (2011) 'Ustawy adrenaliną pisane?', in Utrat-Milecki, J. (ed.) *Prawo i ład społeczny. Integralnokulturowa analiza zagadnienia racjonalności. Artykuły i szkice*, Warszawa.
Folkard, S., Smith, D.E., Smith, D.D. and Walmsley G. (1976) *Intensive Matched Probation and After-Care Treatment*, Home Office Research Study 36, London.
Foucault, M. (1978) *Discipline and Punish: The Birth of the Prison*, New York.
Frančić, M. (1967) *Ludzie luźni w osiemnastowiecznym Krakowie*, Wrocław–Warszawa–Kraków.
Franko Aas, K. (2007) *Globalization and Crime*, London.
Frieske, K.W. (2004a) 'Migotanie rzeczywistości: wieloznaczność "sukcesu" programów społecznej inkluzji', in Frieske, K.W. (ed.) *Utopie inkluzji. Sukcesy i porażki programów reintegracji społecznej*, Warszawa.
——— (2004b) 'Wprowadzenie: pesymistyczne wnioski teoretycznych komplikacji', in Frieske, K.W. (ed.) *Utopie inkluzji. Sukcesy i porażki programów reintegracji społecznej*, Warszawa.

——— (2008) 'Społeczna marginalność jako koszt systemowy', in Jarosz, M. (ed.) *Wykluczeni. Wymiar społeczny, materialny i etniczny*, Warszawa.

Frysztacki, K. (2009) *Socjologia problemów społecznych*, Warszawa.

Frysztacki, K., Nóżka, M. and Smagacz-Poziemska, M. (2011) *Dzieci ulicy. Studium szczególnego problemu miejskiego*, Kraków.

Fulcher, J. and Scott, J. (2005) *Sociology*, Oxford.

Gaberle, A. (2006) 'Odpowiedzialność karna nieletnich (uwagi na tle art. 10 § 2 k.k.)', in Giezek, J. (ed.) *Przestępstwo-kara-polityka kryminalna. Problemy tworzenia i funkcjonowania prawa. Księga jubileuszowa z okazji 70. rocznicy urodzin Profesora Tomasza Kaczmarka*, Kraków.

Gaetz, S. (2004) 'Safe Streets for Whom? Homeless Youth, Social Exclusion, and Criminal Victimization', *Canadian Journal of Criminology and Criminal Justice*, vol. 46, no. 4.

Gans, H.J. (1976) 'The Uses of Poverty: The Poor Pay All', in Ogletree, E.J. (ed.) *Issues in Urban Education*, vol. 1, New York.

——— (1994) 'Positive Functions of the Underserving Poor: Uses of the Underclass in America', *Politics & Society*, vol. 22, no. 3.

Gardocki, L. (1990) *Zagadnienia teorii kryminalizacji*, Warszawa.

——— (2008) *Prawo karne*, Warszawa.

Garland, D. (1990) *Punishment and Modern Society: A Study in Social Theory* (Studies in Crime and Justice), Oxford.

——— (2009) *The Culture of Control: Crime and Social Order in Contemporary Society*, Oxford.

Garland, D. and Sparks, R. (2000) 'Criminology, Social Theory and the Challenge of Our Times', *British Journal of Criminology*, vol. 40, no. 2.

Gawlicz, K. and Starnawski, M. (2011) 'Oblicza pracy – oblicza biedy', in Szarfenberg, R. (ed.) *Ubóstwo i wykluczenie społeczne w Polsce. Raport krajowy Polskiej Koalicji Social Watch i Polskiego Komitetu European Anti-Poverty Network*, Warszawa.

Gelsthorpe, L. and Morgan, R. (eds) (2007) 'Introduction', in Gelsthorpe, L. and Morgan, R. (eds) *Handbook of Probation*, Cullompton.

Geremek, B. (2006) *The Margins of Society in Late Mediaeval Paris*, Cambridge.

Giddens, A. (1994) *Poza lewicą i prawicą*, Poznań.

——— (2009) *Sociology*, Cambridge.

Glover, C. (2008) *Crime and Inequality*, London.

Główny Urząd Statystyczny (2010) *Rocznik Demograficzny 2010*, Warszawa.

Główny Urząd Statystyczny Rzeczypospolitej Polskiej (1936) *Mały Rocznik Statystyczny*, Warszawa.

Gmurek, M. (2011) *Oskarżenie na zamówienie. Medialno-polityczny układ w przedstawianiu problematyki przestępczości zorganizowanej*, Toruń.

Gmurzyńska, E. (2011) 'Sprawiedliwość a mediacja. Wybrane zagadnienia związane z realizowaniem koncepcji sprawiedliwości w mediacji', in Gudowski, J. and Weitz, K. (eds) *Aurea praxis aurea theoria. Księga pamiątkowa ku czci Profesora Tadeusza Erecińskiego*, vol. 2, Warszawa.

Goffman, E. (2006) 'Charakterystyka instytucji totalnych', in Jasińska-Kania, A., Nijakowski, L.M., Szacki, J. and Ziółkowski, M. (eds) *Współczesne teorie socjologiczne*, Warszawa.

——— (2011) *Instytucje totalne*, Warszawa.

Golczyńska-Grondas, A. (1999) 'Specyfika pracy przedstawicieli służb społecznych w obszarach zagrożenia', in Warzywoda-Kruszyńska, W. (ed.) *(Żyć) Na marginesie wielkiego miasta*, Łódź.

——— (2002) 'Postawy przedstawicieli służb społecznych. Szanse i ograniczenia w działaniach przeciw biedzie', in Tarkowska, E. (ed.) *Przeciw biedzie. Programy, pomysły, inicjatywy*, Warszawa.

Goldschneider, M. (2009) 'Lęk przed przestępczością w Warszawie w świadomości ludzi starszych i studentów', *Biuletyn Polskiego Towarzystwa Kryminologicznego*, no. 17.

——— (2010) 'Przestępczość w wielkim mieści. Empiryczna weryfikacja teorii ekologicznych w kryminologii', dissertation, Instytut Nauk Prawnych PAN.

Golinowska, S. (2010) 'Podatność młodzieży na ubóstwo i wykluczenie społeczne', *Kultura i Społeczeństwo*, vol. 54, no. 3.

Gottfredson, M. and Hirschi, T. (1990) *A General Theory of Crime*, Stanford, CA.

Gozdór, G., Kuć, M. and Świtka, J. (eds) (2007) *Społeczno-moralna potrzeba bezpieczeństwa i porządku publicznego*, Lublin.

Górniak, K. and Kalbarczyk, A. (2007) 'System edukacji wobec ubóstwa i wykluczenia społecznego', in Tarkowska, E. (ed.) *Ubóstwo i wykluczenie społeczne młodzieży*, Warszawa.

Górniok, O. (1995) *Ustawa o ochronie obrotu gospodarczego z komentarzem*, Warszawa.

Grabek, A. (2007) 'Trzcinka i pas wrócą do szkół', *Dziennik*, 7 May 2007, available at: http://www.dziennik.pl/Default.aspx?TabId=14&ShowArticleId=43271, accessed 11 May 2009.

Granosik, M. (2012) '"Mówię, jak jest, robię, co mi każą" – o interpretacyjnym rozdarciu współczesnego pracownika socjalnego', in Rymsza, M. (ed.) *Pracownicy socjalni i praca socjalna w Polsce. Między służbą społeczną a urzędem*, Warszawa.

Greer, C. (2010) 'News Media Criminology', in McLaughlin, E. and Newburn, T. (eds) *The SAGE Handbook of Criminological Theory*, Los Angeles, CA–London–New Delhi–Singapore–Washington DC.

Gromek, K. (2001) 'Probacja czy kuratela albo środki alternatywne – próba optymalizacji systemu w ujęciu ewolucyjnym', in *Materiały z konferencji z 20–21 października 2000 r. 'Probacyjne środki polityki karnej – stan i perspektywy'*, Warszawa.

——— (2002) *Kuratorzy sądowi. Komentarz do ustawy z 27 lipca 2001*, Warszawa.

Grotowska-Leder, J. (1998) 'Zachowania aspołeczne w enklawach biedy', in Warzywoda-Kruszyńska, W. (ed.) *Żyć i pracować w enklawach biedy (Klimaty łódzkie)*, Łódź.

——— (1999) 'Dynamika biedy (Jak długo jest się klientem pomocy społecznej?)', in Warzywoda-Kruszyńska, W. (ed.) *(Żyć) Na marginesie wielkiego miasta*, Łódź.

——— (2006) 'Gettyzacja wielkomiejskiej przestrzeni jako współczesne zagrożenie społeczne', in Królikowska, J. (ed.) *Problemy społeczne w grze politycznej. Współczesne zagrożenia społeczne – diagnoza i przeciwdziałanie*, Warszawa.

Grove, L., Tilley, N. and Tseloni, A. (2012) 'Crime, Inequality, and Change in England and Wales', in van Dijk, J., Farrell, G. and Tseloni, A. (eds) *The International Crime Drop: New Directions in Research*, Basingstoke–New York.

Grover, C. (2008) *Crime and Inequality*, Cullompton–Portland, OR.

Gruszczyńska, B. (2004) 'Crime in Central and Eastern European Countries in the Enlarged Europe', *European Journal on Criminal Policy and Research*, vol. 10, nos. 2–3.

——— (2005) 'Trendy przestępczości w krajach Unii Europejskiej', *Przegląd Więziennictwa Polskiego*, no. 49.

——— (2007) *Przemoc wobec kobiet w Polsce. Aspekty prawnokryminologiczne*, Warszawa.

——— (2010) 'Statystyczny obraz kurateli w Polsce', in Wójcik, D. (ed.) *Kuratela sądowa. Sukcesy i porażki*, Warszawa.

Gruszczyńska, B. and Gruszczyński, M. (2005) 'Crime in Enlarged Europe: Comparison of Crime Rates and Victimization Risks', *Transition Studies Review*, vol. 12, no. 2.

Gruszczyńska, B. and Heiskanen, M. (2012) 'Trends in Police-recorded Offences', *European Journal of Criminal Policy and Research*, vol. 18, no. 2.

Gruszczyńska, B. and Marczewski, M. (1997–1998) 'Efektywność warunkowego, przedterminowego zwolnienia', *Archiwum Kryminologii*, vols 23–4.

Gruszczyńska, B., Marczewski, M., Ostaszewski, P., Siemaszko, A. and Woźniakowska-Fajst, D. (2010) 'Stalking w Polsce. Rozmiary – Formy – Skutki. Raport z badania nt. uporczywego nękania', *Archiwum Kryminologii*, vol. 32.

Gulla, B. and Majchrzyk, Z. (2007) 'Atrybucje przyczynowe zachowań dewiacyjnych kobiet w środkach masowego przekazu', in Pospiszyl, I. and Szczepanik, R. (eds) *Zachowania dewiacyjne dziewcząt i kobiet*, Łódź.

Hałas, R.G. (2006) *Odpowiedzialność karna nieletniego na tle kodeksu karnego z 1997 r.*, Lublin.

Hancock, L. (2009) 'Crime Prevention, Community Safety and the Local State', in Coleman, R., Sim, J., Tombs, S. and White, D. (eds) *State, Power, Crime*, London–Thousand Oaks, CA–New Delhi–Singapore.

Hedderman, C. (2007) 'Past, Present and Future Sentences: What Do We Know About Their Effectiveness', in Gelsthorpe, L. and Morgan, R. (eds) *Handbook of Probation*, Cullompton.

Henry, S. (2006) 'Crime', in E. McLaughlin and J. Mucie (eds) *The SAGE Dictionary of Criminology*, London.

Hirschfield, P.J. (2008) 'Preparing for Prison? The Criminalization of School Discipline in the USA', *Theoretical Criminology*, vol. 12, no. 1.
Hołyst, B. (ed.) (1981) *Opinia publiczna i środki masowego przekazu a ujemne zjawiska społeczne*, Warszawa.
Hopkins, B. (2006) *Just Schools: A Whole School Approach to Restorative Justice*, London–Philadelphia, PA.
Izdebski, Z. (2008) 'Czego doświadczają polscy nastolatkowie', in Izdebski, Z. (ed.) *Zagrożenia okresu dorastania*, Zielona Góra.
Jakubowska-Hara, J. (2009a) 'Kara grzywny jako alternatywa pozbawienia wolności', in Jakubowska-Hara, J. and Skupiński, J. (eds) *Alternatywy pozbawienia wolności w polskiej polityce karnej*, Warszawa.
——— (2009b) 'Wstęp', in Jakubowska-Hara, J. and Skupiński, J. (eds) *Alternatywy pozbawienia wolności w polskiej polityce karnej*, Warszawa.
Jankowski, B. (2010) 'Łódzkie enklawy biedy – 10 lat później', *Praca Socjalna*, special issue.
Jankowski, Z., Kalinowski, P. and Kubiak, R. (1982) *Postępowania szczególne w sprawach o przestępstwa i wykroczenia w czasie obowiązywania stanu wojennego (Komentarz do dekretu z dnia 12 grudnia 1981 r.)*, Warszawa.
Jaroszewska, E. (2010) 'Bezdomni jako zbiorowość wykluczona społecznie', in Szarfenberg, R., Theiss, M. and Żołędowski, C. (eds) *Ubóstwo i wykluczenie społeczne – perspektywa poznawcza*, Warszawa.
Jasiński, J. (1982) 'Przemiany polityki karnej sądów powszechnych rozwijanej na tle przepisów nowej kodyfikacji karnej (1970–1980)', *Archiwum Kryminologii*, vols 8–9.
——— (1993) 'Obraz polityki karnej lat osiemdziesiątych i początku lat dziewięćdziesiątych (1980–1991)', *Archiwum Kryminologii*, vol. 19.
Jedynak, T. (2008) 'Efektywność Kuratorskiej Służby Sądowej w Polsce a standardy dotyczące sankcji i środków alternatywnych. Materiały z konferencji "Polski system probacji – Stan i perspektywy rozwoju". Popowo 27–28 października 2008', *Biuletyn Kuratorski. Pismo kuratorów sądowych*, no. 2.
——— (2010) 'Aktualny stan kurateli w Polsce. O potrzebie unormowania zadań kuratorów rodzinnych', in *Dziewięćdziesięciolecie kurateli sądowej w Polsce. Historia – Teraźniejszość – Przyszłość. Materiały z I Kongresu Kuratorskiego, Ustka 15–17 czerwca 2009 r.*, Kraków.
Jedynak, T. and Martuszewicz, A. (2007) 'Od rozporządzenia do ustawy o kuratorach sądowych', in Jedynak, T. and Stasiak, K. (eds) *Zarys metodyki pracy kuratora sądowego*, Warszawa.
Jehle, J.M. (1996) 'Dieselben Probleme, VerschiedeneLosungen? Der Justitielle Sozialdienst im Europaischen Vergleich. Bewahrungs Hilfe Fachzeitschrift fur Bewagrungsgerichts und Straffaligenhilfe', *Jahrgang*, no. 4.
Jescheck, H. (1979) 'Die Krise der Kriminalpolitik', *Zeitschrift für die gesamte Strafrechtswissenschaft*, vol. 91.
Jewkes, Y. (2010a) *Media and Crime*, London.
——— (2010b) 'The Construction of Crime News', in Greer, C. (ed.) *Crime and Media: A Reader*, London.
Jones, C. and Novak, T. (2009) 'Power, Politics and the Welfare State', in Coleman, R., Sim, J., Tombs, S. and White, D. (eds) *State, Power, Crime*, London–Thousand Oaks, CA–New Delhi–Singapore.
Jones, S. (2006) *Criminology*, Oxford.
Kaczmarek, T. (2009) 'Racjonalny ustawodawca wobec opinii społecznej a populizm penalny', in Sienkiewicz, Z. and Kokot, R. (eds) *Populizm penalny i jego przejawy w Polsce*, Wrocław.
Kaczyńska, E. (1994) *Człowiek przed sądem. Społeczne aspekty przestępczości w Królestwie Polskim (1815–1914)*, Warszawa.
Kalinowski, M. and Pełka, J. (1996) *Zarys dziejów resocjalizacji nieletnich*, Warszawa.
Kalka, J. (2011) 'Młodzież a szkoła', in *Młodzież 2010*, Warszawa.
Kamiński, J. (1997) 'Kuratorzy społeczni w systemie resocjalizacji skazanych w warunkach wolności dozorowanej', *Nowe Prawo*, nos. 7–8.
Kamler, M. (2010) *Złoczyńcy. Przestępczość w Koronie w drugiej połowie XVI i pierwszej połowie XVII wieku (w świetle ksiąg sądowych i miejskich)*, Warszawa.
Kant, I. (1785) *Groundwork for the Metaphysic of Morals*, available at: http://www.earlymoderntexts.com/pdfs/kant1785chapter2.pdf, accessed 15 May 2014.
Kaźmierczak, T. (2006) 'Praca socjalna a kapitał społeczny', in Królikowska, J. (ed.) *Problemy społeczne w grze politycznej. Współczesne zagrożenia społeczne – diagnoza i przeciwdziałanie*, Warszawa.

——— (2011) 'Praktyka aktywizacji w ośrodkach pomocy społecznej', in Rymsza, M. (ed.) *Czy podejście aktywizujące ma szansę? Pracownicy socjalni i praca socjalna w Polsce 20 lat po reformie systemu pomocy społecznej*, Warszawa.

——— (2012) 'Pracownicy socjalni, kapitał ludzki, profesjonalna praktyka', in Rymsza, M. (ed.) *Pracownicy socjalni i praca socjalna w Polsce. Między służbą społeczną a urzędem*, Warszawa.

Kelling, G.L. and Coles, C.M. (1996) *Fixing Broken Windows: Restoring Order and Reducing Crime in Our Communities*, New York.

Kemshall, H. and Wood, J. (2007) 'High-risk Offenders and Public Protection', in Gelsthorpe, L. and Morgan, R. (eds) *Handbook of Probation*, Cullompton.

Kępka, S. (2006) 'Kuratela sądowa: wychowująca czy kontrolno-represyjna. Ujęcie formalnoprawne', in Bielecka, E. (ed.) *Profilaktyka i readaptacja społeczna. Od teorii do doświadczeń praktyków*, Białystok.

Kiersztyn, A. (2008) *Czy bieda czyni złodzieja? Związki między bezrobociem, ubóstwem a przestępczością*, Warszawa.

King, Nancy J. (2007) 'Introduction', in Gelsthorpe, L. and Morgan, R. (eds), *Handbook of Probation*, Cullompton.

Klarman, A. (2006) 'Wątki kryminologiczne w medialnej argumentacji perswazyjnej w aspekcie kształtowania świadomości społecznej', in *Nowa kodyfikacja prawa karnego*, vol. 19, Wrocław.

Klaus, W. (2009a) *Dziecko przed sądem. Wymiar sprawiedliwości wobec przestępczości młodszych nieletnich*, Warszawa.

——— (2009b) 'Wykorzystanie sprawiedliwości naprawczej w zapobieganiu przemocy rówieśniczej w szkole', in Mazowiecka, L. (ed.) *Mediacja*, Warszawa.

——— (2010) 'Integracja – marginalizacja – kryminalizacja, czyli o przestępczości cudzoziemców w Polsce', *Archiwum Kryminologii*, vol. 32.

Klaus, W., Kossowska, A., Rzeplińska, I. and Woźniakowska, D. (2008) 'Criminal Policy Based on Fear of Crime: Case of Poland', in Kury, H. (ed.) *Fear of Crime: Punitivity New Developments in Theory and Research*, Bochum.

Klaus, W., Kossowska, A., Rzeplińska, I., Woźniakowska, D. and Wójcik, D. (2006) 'Zagrożenie przestępczością – mity, rzeczywistość, reakcja społeczna', in Czapliński, W. (ed.) *Prawo w XXI wieku. Księga pamiątkowa 50-lecia Instytutu Nauk Prawnych PAN*, Warszawa.

Klaus, W., Rzeplińska, I. and Woźniakowska-Fajst, D. (2011) 'Punitivity in Polish Law, Public Opinion, and Penal Policy', in Kury, H. and Shea, E. (eds) *Punitivity: International Developments*, Bochum.

Klaus, W. and Woźniakowska-Fajst, D. (2012) 'Związki pomiędzy wiktymizacją oraz ubóstwem i wykluczeniem społecznym', *Archiwum Kryminologii*, vol. 34.

Kłos, B. (2003) 'Minimalny dochód gwarantowany w państwach członkowskich Unii Europejskiej', *Informacja Biura Studiów i Ekspertyz Kancelarii Sejmu*, no. 1022, available at: http://biurose.sejm.gov.pl/teksty_pdf_03/i-1022.pdf, accessed 22 March 2013.

Kojder, A. (1995) *Godność i siła prawa*, Warszawa.

Kołaczek, B. (2004) *Dostęp młodzieży do edukacji. Zróżnicowania, uwarunkowania, równanie szans*, Warszawa.

Kołakowska-Przełomiec, H. (1984) *Zapobieganie przestępczości: studium kryminologiczne*, Wrocław–Warszawa–Kraków–Gdańsk–Łódź.

Kołakowska-Przełomiec, H. and Wójcik, D. (1990) *Selekcja nieletnich przestępców w sądach rodzinnych*, Warszawa.

Kołakowski, L. (2003) *Mini wykłady o maxi sprawach*, Kraków.

Komendant-Brodowska, A., Giza-Poleszczuk, A. and Baczko-Dombi, A. (2011) *Przemoc w szkole. Raport z badań*, Warszawa, available at: http://www.szkolabezprzemocy.pl/pliki/333-sbp2-szkoly-ost-wersjadoc.pdf, accessed 29 April 2013.

Konopczyński, M. (1996) *Twórcza resocjalizacja*, Warszawa.

——— (2012) 'Twórcza resocjalizacja – Zarys koncepcji metodycznej', *Probacja*, no. 2.

Kossowska, A. (1978) 'Przestępczość na terenie wielkiego miasta', in Jasiński, J. (ed.) *Zagadnienia nieprzystosowania społecznego i przestępczości w Polsce*, Wrocław–Warszawa–Kraków–Gdańsk.

——— (1982) 'Rodziny wieloproblemowe – charakterystyka 222 rodzin z dzielnicy Praga-Północ', *Archiwum Kryminologii*, vols 8–9.
——— (1992) *Funkcjonowanie kontroli społecznej. Analiza kryminologiczna*, Warszawa.
——— (1996) 'Crime in Poland in the Period of Rapid Social Change', in Szamota-Saeki, B. and Wójcik, D. (eds) *Impact of Political, Economic and Social Change and Its Image in Society, 51th International Course of Criminology, 12–16 September 1995 Warsaw*, Warszawa.
——— (2006) 'Uwarunkowania i konsekwencje lęku przed przestępczością', in Królikowska, J. (ed.) *Problemy społeczne w grze politycznej*, Warszawa.
——— (2013) 'Wykluczenie społeczne a przestępczość – wybrane aspekty', in Rzeplińska, I. and Rzepliński, A. (eds) *Pozbawienie wolności – funkcje i koszty. Księga pamiątkowa dedykowana prof. dr hab. Teodorowi Szymanowskiemu*, Warszawa.
Kotarbiński, T. (1987) 'Drogowskazy etyki niezależnej', in Kotarbiński, T. (ed.) *Pisma etyczne*, Wrocław–Warszawa–Kraków–Gdańsk–Łódź.
Kotlarska-Michalska, A. (2004) 'Nowe role pracownika socjalnego w nowych obszarach pracy socjalnej', in Brągiel, J. and Sikora, P. (eds) *Praca socjalna – Wielość perspektyw: Rodzina-Multikulturowość-Edukacja*, Opole.
Kowalczuk, K. (2010a) *Oceny instytucji publicznych*, Warszawa, Report no. BS/125/2010, available at: http://www.cbos.pl/SPISKOM.POL/2010/K_125_10.PDF, accessed 20 October 2014.
——— (2010b) *Opinie o poczuciu bezpieczeństwa i zagrożeniu przestępczością*, Warszawa, Report no. BS/80/2010, available at: http://www.cbos.pl/SPISKOM.POL/2010/K_080_10.PDF, accessed 21 October 2014.
——— (2012a) *Polacy o skali ubóstwa w kraju*, Warszawa, available at: http://www.cbos.pl/SPISKOM.POL/2012/K_051_12.PDF, accessed 14 March 2013.
——— (2012b) *Polacy o sprawiedliwości społecznej*, Warszawa, available at: http://www.cbos.pl/SPISKOM.POL/2012/K_031_12.PDF, accessed 2 May 2013.
Kowalska, D. (2001) 'Nie było dla nich świętości', *Super Express*, 24 July 2001.
Kozarzewski, P. (2008) 'Wykluczenie edukacyjne', in Jarosz, M. (ed.) *Wykluczeni. Wymiar społeczny, materialny i etniczny*, Warszawa.
Krajewski, K. (1992) 'Kara i współczesne społeczeństwo (wokół książki D. Garlanda)', *Państwo i Prawo*, no. 7.
——— (1994) *Teorie kryminologiczne a prawo karne*, Warszawa.
——— (2001) 'Przemoc w doświadczeniach życiowych młodzieży', in Gaberle, A. (ed.) *Przestępczość i zachowania dewiacyjne dzieci i młodzieży w Krakowie*, Kraków.
——— (2002) 'Punitywność społeczeństwa polskiego', in Czapska, J. and Kury, H. (eds) *Mit represyjności albo o znaczeniu prewencji kryminalnej*, Zakamycze.
——— (2007–2008) 'Przestępczość przeciwko mieniu Polsce w latach 1924–2005 w świetle danych statystyki policyjnej', *Archiwum Kryminologii*, vols 29–30.
——— (2007a) 'Czy więzienie jest skuteczne? Uwagi na marginesie amerykańskiej dyskusji na temat wpływu kary pozbawienia wolności na rozmiary przestępczości', in Krajewski, K. (ed.) *Nauki penalne wobec problemów współczesnej przestępczości*, Kraków.
——— (2007b) 'Spór o politykę karną w Polsce, problem kary pozbawienia wolności z warunkowym zawieszeniem jej wykonania i alternatyw kary pozbawienia wolności', *Przegląd Więziennictwa Polskiego*, no. 54.
——— (2008a) 'Niepokoje, lęki, strach przed przestępczością i rozmiary wiktymizacji w pięciu badanych miastach', in Krajewski, K. (ed.) *Poczucie bezpieczeństwa mieszkańców wielkich miast. Kraków na tle innych miast europejskich*, Kraków.
——— (ed.) (2008b) *Poczucie bezpieczeństwa mieszkańców wielkich miast. Kraków na tle innych miast europejskich*, Kraków.
Kromolicka, B. (2003) 'Wybrane bariery działania społecznego pracowników socjalnych', in Kantowicz, E. and Olubński, A. (eds) *Działanie społeczne w pracy socjalnej na progu XXI wieku*, Toruń.
Królikowski, M. (2005) *Sprawiedliwość karania w społeczeństwach liberalnych. Zasada proporcjonalności*, Warszawa.
——— (2006) 'Sprawiedliwość retrybutywna wobec sprawiedliwości naprawczej', *Ius et Lex*, no. 4.

Kryńska, K. (ed.) (2009) *Flexicurity w Polsce. Diagnoza i rekomendacje. Raport końcowy z badań*, Warszawa.

Krzyszkowski, J. (1998) 'Środowiskowa pomoc społeczna w Łodzi. Determinanty funkcjonowania, koncepcje zmian', in Warzywoda-Kruszyńska, W. (ed.) *Żyć i pracować w enklawach biedy (Klimaty łódzkie)*, Łódź.

Kubiak, J.R. and Kasprzycki, W. (1977) 'Sądy rodzinne – Idea i regulacja prawna', *Nowe Prawo*, no. 7–8.

Kuć, M. (2007) 'Poczucie bezpieczeństwa jak problem kryminologiczny i wiktymologiczny', in Gozdór, G., Kuć, M. and Świtka, J. (eds) *Społeczno-moralna potrzeba bezpieczeństwa i porządku publicznego*, Lublin.

Kulesza, J.A. (2010) 'Pozbawienie praw publicznych', in Melezini, M. (ed.) *System Prawa Karnego*, vol. 6, *Kary i środki karne. Poddanie sprawcy próbie*, Warszawa.

Kulesza, M. (2008) 'Wpływ klimatu szkoły na przejawianie przez uczniów agresji i przemocy w szkole', in Libiszowska-Żółtkowska, M. and Ostrowska, K. (eds) *Agresja w szkole. Diagnoza i profilaktyka*, Warszawa.

Kunicka-Michalska, B. (2009) 'Kara ograniczenia wolności jako alternatywa pozbawienia wolności', in Jakubowska-Hara, J. and Skupiński, J. (eds) *Alternatywy pozbawienia wolności w polskiej polityce karnej*, Warszawa.

Kurdybacha, Ł. (1951) *Dzieje kodeksu Andrzeja Zamoyskiego*, Warszawa.

Kurowska, A. (2008) 'Skąd się bierze bieda?', *Zeszyty Forum Obywatelskiego Rozwoju*, no. 5.

Kurowski, P. (2013) *Poziom i struktura zmodyfikowanego minimum egzystencji w 2012 roku (na podstawie danych średniorocznych)*, Warszawa, available at: https://www.ipiss.com.pl/wp-content/plugins/download-monitor/download.php?id=1691, accessed 27 March 2013.

Kury, H. (2002) 'Postawy punitywne i ich znaczenie', in Czapska, J. and Kury, H. (eds) *Mit represyjności albo o znaczeniu prewencji kryminalnej*, Zakamycze.

——— (ed.) (2008) *Fear of Crime: Punitivity New Developments in Theory and Research*, Bochum.

Kurzępa, J. (2010) *Młodzież pogranicza – 'świnki', czyli o prostytucji nieletnich*, Kraków.

Kuźmicz, E. and Stasiowski, J. (2008) *Pracujący biedni. Komunikat z badań*, Warszawa, available at: http://www.cbos.pl/SPISKOM.POL/2008/K_182_08.PDF, accessed 4 February 2013.

Kwaśniewski, J. (2010) 'Wpływ norm prawnych na procesy wykluczenia społecznego', in Turska, A. (ed.) *Prawo i wykluczenie społeczne. Studium empiryczne*, Warszawa.

Lacey, M. (2002) 'Reflections on Work in Progress', in Ward, D., Scott, J. and Lacey, M. (eds) *Probation: Working for Justice*, Oxford.

Lelental, S. (2009) 'Faktyczne i potencjalne rozmiary przeludnienia jednostek penitencjarnych', in Pohl, Ł. (ed.) *Aktualne problemy prawa karnego. Księga pamiątkowa z okazji Jubileuszu 70 Urodzin Profesora Andrzeja J. Szwarca*, Poznań.

——— (2010) 'Kurator sądowy jako organ postępowania wykonawczego. Rola i zadania kuratora według autorów kodeksu karnego wykonawczego', in *Dziewięćdziesięciolecie kurateli sądowej w Polsce. Historia – Teraźniejszość – Przyszłość. Materiały z I Kongresu Kuratorskiego, Ustka 15–17 czerwca 2009 r.*, Kraków.

Lem, S. (2006) *Rasa drapieżców. Teksty ostatnie*, Kraków.

Lepianka, D. (2002a) 'Funkcje gminnego ośrodka pomocy społecznej w Kościelcu w opinii pracowników i mieszkańców gminy', in Korzeniewska, K. and Tarkowska, E. (eds) *Lata tłuste, lata chude ... Spojrzenia na biedę w społecznościach lokalnych*, Warszawa.

——— (2002b) 'Polacy a biedacy – społeczny obraz ubóstwa i stosunek społeczeństwa polskiego do osób ubogich', in Tarkowska, E. (ed.) *Przeciw biedzie. Programy, pomysły, inicjatywy*, Warszawa.

Lernell, L. (1978) *Współczesne zagadnienia polityki kryminalnej. Problemy kryminologiczne i penologiczne*, Warszawa.

Lin, M.-J. (2008) 'Does Unemployment Increase Crime? Evidence from U.S. Data 1974–2000', *The Journal of Human Resources*, vol. 43, no. 2.

Lind, E.A. and Tyler, T.R. (1988) *The Social Psychology of Procedural Justice*, New York.

Lipton, D., Martinson, R. and Wilks, J. (1975) *The Effectiveness of Correctional Treatment: A Survey of Treatment Evaluation Studies*, New York.

Lisowska, A. (2011) 'Dolnoślązacy wobec problemów społecznych regionu', in Popow, M., Kowzan, P., Zielińska, M., Prusinowska, M. and Chruściel, M. (eds) *Oblicza biedy we współczesnej Polsce*, Gdańsk.

Lister, R. (2004) *Poverty*, Cambridge.

Lizak, Z. (2001) 'Medialny wizerunek więziennictwa', in Ambrozik, W., Hołyst, B. and Stępniak, P. (eds) *Więziennictwo. Nowe wyzwania*, Warszawa–Poznań–Kalisz.

Lösel, F. (2012) 'The Offender Treatment and Rehabilitations: What Works?', in Maguire, M., Morgan, R. and Reiner, R. (eds) *The Oxford Handbook of Criminology*, Oxford.

Łabieniec, P. (2008) 'O statusie etyki zawodowej I kodeksow etyki zawodowej', in Izdebski, H. (ed) *Etyka prawnika. Stanowiska i perspektywy*, Warszawa.

Łojko, E. (2005) 'Dziennikarze i prawnicy', in Magoska, M. (ed.) *Media. Władza. Prawo*, Kraków.

Łukaszewicz, A. (2012) 'Koniec z politycznym marketingiem w kodeksach', *Rzeczpospolita*, 21 February 2012.

Machel, H. (2009) 'Aktualne tendencje resocjalizacji penitencjarnej w polskich zakładach karnych', in Lelental, S. and Szczygieł, G.B. (eds) *X lat obowiązywania kodeksu karnego wykonawczego*, Białystok.

Madey, M. (1936) 'Opieka nad więźniami', *Głos Sądownictwa*, no. 3.

Maguire, M. (2007) 'The Resettlement of Ex-Prisoners', in Gelsthorpe, L. and Morgan, R. (eds) *Handbook of Probation*, Cullompton.

Maguire, M., Morgan, R. and Reiner R. (2002) *The Oxford Handbook of Criminology*, Oxford.

Majcherczyk, A. (2008) 'Organizacja i wyniki wdrożenia Treningu Zastępowania Agresji ART. do praktyki penitencjarnej polskiego więziennictwa', *Przegląd Więziennictwa Polskiego*, no. 60.

Makarewicz, J. (1922) *Zbrodnia i kara*, Lwów.

——— (2009) *Wstęp do filozofii prawa karnego w oparciu o podstawy historyczno-rozwojowe*, Lublin.

Mańka, B. (2010) 'Zobowiązanie do naprawienia szkody, do wykonania określonych prac na rzecz pokrzywdzonego lub spoleczności lokalnej', paper presented at the conference 'Mediacja w praktyce wymiaru sprawiedliwości', 2010, Ustka.

Marczak, M. (ed.) (2009) *Resocjalizacyjne programy penitencjarne realizowane przez służbę więzienną w Polsce*, Kraków.

Marczewski, M. (2010) 'Opinie zawodowych kuratorów o problemach swej pracy', in Wójcik, D. (ed.) *Kuratela sądowa. Sukcesy i porażki*, Warszawa.

Marek, A. (1975) *Prawo wykroczeń w zarysie*, Warszawa.

——— (1978) 'Rola amerykańskiej probacji i jej efektywność', *AUNC Prawo*, vol. 16, no. 89.

——— (1980) '"Nowy realizm" w polityce kryminalnej Stanów Zjednoczonych – założenia i efekty', *Państwo i Prawo*, no. 4.

——— (1986) *Prawo karne*, Warszawa.

——— (1994) 'Problemy reformy polskiego prawa wykroczeń. Refleksje na tle historycznym i prawnoporównawczym', in Ćwiąkalski, Z., Waltoś, S. and Zoll, A. (eds) *Problemy odpowiedzialności karnej. Księga pamiątkowa ku czci Profesora Kazimierza Buchały*, Kraków.

——— (1996) *Prawo wykroczeń*, Warszawa.

——— (1999) 'Podstawy prawa karnego krajów anglosaskich', in Górniok, O. (ed.) *U progu nowych kodyfikacji karnych, Księga pamiątkowa ofiarowana Profesorowi Leonowi Tyszkiewiczowi*, Katowice.

——— (2007) *Prawo karne*, Warszawa.

——— (2008) *Kodeks karny*, Warszawa.

——— (2009a) 'Funkcje kary pozbawienia wolności na tle zmian polityki karnej', in Lelental, S. and Szczygieł, G. (eds) *X Lat obowiązywania Kodeksu karnego wykonawczego*, Białystok.

——— (2009b) 'Niepowodzenie prób kompleksowej nowelizacji kodeksu karnego jako efekt sporu między populizmem a racjonalizmem', in Sienkiewicz, Z. and Kokot, R. (eds) *Populizm penalny i jego przejawy w Polsce*, Wrocław.

——— (2010a) 'Pojęcie i formy probacji. Zagadnienia ogólne', in Melezini, M. (ed.) *System Prawa Karnego*, vol. 6, Warszawa.

——— (2010b) 'Pojęcie prawa karnego, jego funkcje i podział', in Marek, A. (ed.) *System Prawa karnego, Zagadnienia ogólne*, vol. 1, Warszawa.

Markov, D. (2009) 'Review of the Importance of Public Confidence as a Tool for Policy Assessment', in Jokinen, A. (ed.) *Review of Need: Indicators of Public Confidence in Criminal Justice for Policy Assessment*, Helsinki.

Markwart, A. (2010) *Kara – sprawiedliwa i ... ? Instytut Filozofii, Wydział Filozoficzny, Uniwersytet Jagielloński*, V Konferencja Młodych Uczonych, Kraków, available at: http://www.profuturo.agh.edu.pl/pliki/Referaty_V_KKMU/NSiH/r699–706_Markwart.pdf, accessed 10 June 2013.

Marody, M. (2011) 'Kilka uwag o problemach wyznaczających rozwój, ustalenie sytuacji społeczno-politycznej', in Krzemiński, I. (ed.) *Wielka transformacja. Zmiany ustroju w Polsce po 1989 r.*, Warszawa.

Marszałek, M. (2011) 'Krytyka polityki mieszkaniowej w Wałbrzychu z perspektywy jego mieszkanek', in Szarfenberg, R. (ed.) *Ubóstwo i wykluczenie społeczne w Polsce. Raport krajowy Polskiej Koalicji Social Watch i Polskiego Komitetu European Anti-Powerty Network*, Warszawa.

Martinson, R. (1974) 'What Works: Questions and Answers, about Prison Reform', *Public Interest*, vol. 35.

Martuszewicz, A. and Rzepniewski, A. (2003) 'Ustawa o kuratorach sądowych. Fakty i komentarz do wybranych zasad ustrojowych kurateli sądowe', in *Kurator w społeczeństwie obywatelskim – Biuletyn Biura Studiów i Ekspertyz Kancelarii Sejmu*, no. 7 (51).

Mary, P. and Nagels, J. (2012) 'Penalization and Social Policies', in Snacken, S. and Dumortier, E. (eds) *Resisting Punitiveness in Europe? Welfare, Human Rights and Democracy*, London–New York.

Matthews, R. (2005) 'The Myth of Punitiveness', *Theoretical Criminology*, vol. 9, no. 2.

Matyjas, B. (2004) 'Diagnoza społeczna jako podstawa pracy socjalnej w środowisku', in Brągiel, J. and Sikora, P. (eds) *Praca socjalna – Wielość perspektyw: Rodzina-Multikulturowość-Edukacja*, Opole.

——— (2008) 'Polityka społeczna i praca socjalna wobec rodziców i ich dzieci zagrożonych wykluczeniem społecznym (na przykładzie środowiska wiejskiego)', in K. Marzec-Holka, K., Rutkowska, A. and Jachimowska, M. (eds) *Praca socjalna i polityka społeczna – obszary współdziałania wobec wykluczenia społecznego*, Bydgoszcz.

Mazowiecka, L. (2012) *Państwowa kompensata dla ofiar przestępstw*, Warszawa.

Mazur, M. (2008) 'Realizacja orzeczeń o warunkowym zawieszeniu wykonania kary pozbawienia wolności bez oddania skazanego pod dozór', in Zagórski, J. (ed.) *Wykonywanie środków probacji i readaptacji skazanych w Polsce*, Warszawa.

McLaughlin, E. and Muncie, J. (eds) (2006) *The SAGE Dictionary of Criminology*, London.

McLaughlin, E. and Newburn, T. (eds) (2010) *The SAGE Handbook of Criminological Theory*, Los Angeles, CA–London–New Dehli–Singapore–Washington DC.

McNeill, F., Raynor, P. and Trotter, C. (2010) 'Conclusion: Where Are We Now?', in McNeill, F., Raynor, P. and Trotter, C. (eds) *Offender Supervisior: New Direction in Theory, Research and Practice*, New York.

Meier, R. (ed.) (1977) *Theory in Criminology: Contemporary Views*, London.

Melezini, M. (2003) *Punitywność wymiaru sprawiedliwości karnej w Polsce w XX wieku*, Białystok.

——— (2005) 'O punitywności wymiaru sprawiedliwości karnej w okresie II Rzeczypospolitej Polskiej', in Pływaczewski, E.W. (ed.) *Aktualne problemy prawa karnego i kryminologii*, Białystok.

——— (2007) 'Represyjność polityki karnej w okresie obowiązywania nowej kodyfikacji karnej', in Krajewski, K. (ed.) *Nauki penalne wobec problemów współczesnej przestępczości. Księga Jubileuszowa z okazji rocznicy urodzin profesora Andrzeja Gaberle*, Warszawa.

——— (2010a) 'Systematyka kar i środków karnych. Zagadnienia ogólne', in Melezini, M. (ed.) *System Prawa Karnego*, vol. 6, *Kary i środki karne. Poddanie sprawcy próbie*, Warszawa.

——— (2010b) 'Środki karne', in Melezini, M. (ed.) *System Prawa Karnego*, vol. 6, *Kary i środki karne. Poddanie sprawcy próbie*, Warszawa.

Melossi, D. and Selmini, R. (2009) '"Modernisation" of Institutions of Social and Penal Control in Italy/Europe: The "New" Crime Prevention', in Crawford, A. (ed.) *Crime Prevention Policies in Comparative Perspective*, Cullompton–Portland, OR.

Merrington, S. and Stanley, S. (2007) 'Effectiveness: Who Count What?', in Gelsthorpe, L. and Morgan, R. (eds) *Handbook of Probation*, Cullompton.

Michałowska, E. (1999) 'Przemoc w rodzinie w warunkach zmiany społecznej wyzwaniem dla pomocy społecznej', in Warzywoda-Kruszyńska, W. (ed.) *(Żyć) Na marginesie wielkiego miasta*, Łódź.

Michałowski, R. (1977) 'Perspective and Paradigm', in Meier, R. (ed.) *Theory in Criminology: Contemporary Views*, London.

Mieszkowski, J.T. (1936) 'Społeczne skutki bezrobocia', *Tygodnik Ilustrowany*, no. 5.

Mik, B. (2003) *Nowela antykorupcyjna z dnia 13 czerwca 2003 r. Rys historyczny i podstawowe problemy interpretacyjne*, Kraków.

Mika, S. (1969) *Skuteczność kar w wychowaniu*, Warszawa.

Ministerstwo Edukacji Narodowej (2007) *Rządowy program poprawy stanu bezpieczeństwa w szkołach i placówkach 'Zero tolerancji dla przemocy w szkole'*, Warszawa, available at: http://bip.men.gov.pl/men_bip/akty_prawne/uchwala_20070306_zalacznik.pdf, accessed 26 April 2013.

——— (2008) *Rządowy program na lata 2008–2013 'Przyjazna i bezpieczna szkoła'*, Warszawa, available at: http://bip.men.gov.pl/men_bip/akty_prawne/ uchwala_20080819_zalacznik.pdf, accessed 26 April 2013.

Moczydłowski, P. (2006) 'Przestępca na uwięzi. Elektroniczny monitoring sprawców przestępstw', *Zeszyty Naukowe Ius et Lex*, no. 2.

Mooney, J. (2002) 'Moral Panics and the New Rights: Single Mothers and Feckless Fathers – Is This Really the Key to the Crime Problem', in Walton, P. and Young, J. (eds) *The New Criminology Revisited*, Houndmills.

Morrison, B. (2007) *Restoring Safe School Communities: A Whole School Response to Bullying, Violence and Alienation*, Sidney.

Mościskier, A. (1978a) 'Przestępczość w procesie szybkich zmian społecznych, na przykładzie rejonów intensywnie uprzemysławianych', in Jasiński, J. (ed.) *Zagadnienia nieprzystosowania społecznego i przestępczości w Polsce*, Wrocław–Warszawa–Kraków–Gdańsk.

——— (1978b) 'Rozwój ekonomiczny, uprzemysłowienie i urbanizacja a przestępczość', in Jasiński, J. (ed.) *Zagadnienia nieprzystosowania społecznego i przestępczości w Polsce*, Wrocław–Warszawa–Kraków–Gdańsk.

Mudrecka, I. (2004) 'Wspólne obszary pracy socjalnej i profilaktyczno-resocjalizacyjnej', in Brągiel, J. and Sikora, P. (eds) *Praca socjalna – Wielość perspektyw: Rodzina-Multikulturowość-Edukacja*, Opole.

Mycka, K. (2008) 'Podstawowe problemy w systemie polskiej probacji', paper presented at the conference 'Probacyjne środki polityki karnej – stan i kierunki rozwoju w kontekście standardów europejskich', 27–28 October 2008, Popowo.

Namiotkiewicz, W. (1960) 'Uwagi w sprawie polityki represyjnej', *Prawo i Życie*, vol. 22.

Nelken, D. (ed.) (1994) *The Futures of Criminology*, London.

Newburn, T. (2007) *Criminology*, Cullompton–Portland, OR.

Nicpoń, M. and Sapkowska, M. (2011) 'Dlaczego Eryk B. zabił księdza z Gdańska?', *Dziennik Bałtycki*, 1 April 2011.

Niełaczna, M. (2011) *Zmiany za murami? Stosowanie standardów postępowania z więźniami w Polsce*, Warszawa.

Nowakowska, A.K. (2004) 'Zachowania nauczycieli wobec agresji w szkole i ich przyczyny', in Rejzner, A. (ed.) *Agresja w szkole – spojrzenie wieloaspektowe*, Warszawa.

Olech, A. (1998) 'Przygotowanie zawodowe pracowników socjalnych i kierowników ośrodków pomocy społecznej', in Porowski, M. (ed.) *IPSiR Dzisiaj, Księga jubileuszowa*, Warszawa.

Olszewska, K. (2011) 'Recydywiści się kłaniają', *Wysokie Obcasy*, 6 September 2011, available at: http://wyborcza.pl/1,75248,10214533,Recydywisci_sie_klaniaja.html, accessed 31 October 2014.

Orwell, G. (1933) *Down and Out in Paris and London*, available at: http://www.planetebook.com/ebooks/Down-and-Out-in-Paris-and-London.pdf, accessed 21 October 2014.

Ostrihanska, Z. (1980) 'Norma poszanowania cudzej własności w zachowaniu uczniów szkół państwowych', *Państwo i Prawo*, vol. 7.

——— (1986) 'Problemy współczesnej kurateli sądowej', *Biuletyn Polskiego Towarzystwa Kryminologicznego im. Profesora Stanisława Batawii*, no. 5.

——— (2006) 'Treść dozoru kuratora sądowego. (Refleksja na podstawie zmian w kurateli angielskiej)', in Czapliński, W. (ed.) *Prawo XXI wieku. Księga pamiątkowa 50-lecia Instytutu Nauk Prawnych Polskiej Akademii Nauk*, Warszawa.

——— (2008) 'Diagnoza w pracy kuratora sądowego', in Jedynak, T. and Stasiak, K. (eds) *Zarys metodyki pracy kuratora sądowego*, Warszawa.

Ostrihanska, Z. and Greczuszkin, A. (1999) *Praca z indywidualnym przypadkiem w nadzorze rodzinnego kuratora sądowego*, Lublin.

Ostrihanska, Z. and Rzeplińska, I. (1988) *Pasożytnictwo społeczne – stereotypy i fakty*, Warszawa.

Ostrihanska, Z. and Wójcik, D. (1984) 'Karalność uczniów nieprzystosowanych społecznie', *Archiwum Kryminologii*, vol. 11.

——— (1993) 'Włamania do mieszkań w opinii osób poszkodowanych', in Bieńkowska, E. (ed.) *Wiktymologia w Europie. Materiały pierwszej międzynarodowej konferencji na temat wiktymologii w Europie Wschodniej i Zachodniej, Konstancin k/Warszawy, 17–23 marzec 1991*, Warszawa.

Ostrowska, K. and Surzykiewicz, J. (2005) *Zachowania agresywne w szkole. Badania porównawcze 1997 i 2003*, Warszawa.

Ostrowski, Ł. (2014) 'Tak kończą bandyci: obraz kary kryminalnej w publikacjach dziennika "Fakt"', in Filar, M. and Utrat-Milecki, J. (eds) *Kulturowe uwarunkowania polityki kryminalnej*, Warszawa.

Owen, T. (2007) 'Culture of Crime Control: Through a Post-Foucauldian Lens', *Internet Journal of Criminology*, available at: http://www.internetjournalofcriminology.com/owen%20-%20culture%20of%20crime%20control.pdf, accessed 21 October 2014.

Palmer, T. and Levis, R.V. (1980) *An Evaluation of Juvenile Diversion*, Cambridge.

Paszkiewicz, A. (1990) 'Efektywność i uwarunkowania wykonywanego nadzoru kuratora', in Górnikiewicz, J. et al. (eds) *Działalność profilaktyczna i resocjalizacyjna sądów rodzinnych*, Białystok.

Pawełczyńska, A. (1964) *Przestępczość grup nieletnich*, Warszawa.

Peno, M. (2009) 'Wybrane problemy reakcji karnej w społeczeństwie postindustrialnym. Prawo karania – sprawiedliwość – zasada ultima ratio', *Studia Prawnoustrojowe*, no. 10.

Pieniążek, M. (2008) 'Fenomenologiczne podstawy etyki zawodowej prawnika', in Izdebski, H. (ed.) *Etyka prawnika. Stanowiska i perspektywy*, Warszawa.

Pilch, T. (2009) 'Kara w wychowaniu', in Utrat-Milecki, J. (ed.) *Kara w nauce i kulturze*, Warszawa.

Plato. *The Republic*, translated by Benjamin Jowett, availabale at: http://ebooks.adelaide.edu.au/p/plato/p71r/complete.html, accessed 15 May 2014.

Płatek, M. (2005) 'Teoria sprawiedliwości naprawczej', in Fajst, M. and Płatek, M. (eds) *Sprawiedliwość naprawcza. Idea. Teoria. Praktyka*, Warszawa.

——— (2009) 'Dlaczego w Kazachstanie nie rosną banany – czyli o mediacji w Polsce', in Mazowiecka, L. (ed.) *Mediacja*, Warszawa.

Pomiankiewicz, J. (2011) 'Stres i wypalenie zawodowe funkcjonariuszy Służby Więziennej', *Forum Penitencjarne*, no. 152.

Post, B. (2007) 'Zawiedzione nadzieje: reforma edukacji', in Jarosz, M. (ed.) *Transformacja. Elity. Społeczeństwo*, Warszawa.

Pring, R. (2009) 'Sprawiedliwość naprawcza w szkołach', in Utrat-Milecki, J. (ed.) *Kara w nauce i kulturze*, Warszawa.

Probant, S.C. (2008) 'European Prison Populations Table', *Newsletter of the European Society of Criminology*, vol. 7, no. 1.

Program społeczny 'Szkoła bez przemocy' (2009) *Raport roczny programu społecznego 'Szkoła bez przemocy'*, Warszawa.

Przyłęcki, P. (2012) *Populizm w polskiej polityce. Analiza dyskursu polityki*, Warszawa.

Ptak, K. (2010) 'Propozycje zmian systemowych w zakładach poprawczych a treści programowe na specjalności pedagogika resocjalizacyjna', in Urban, B. (ed.) *Aktualne osiągnięcia w naukach społecznych a teoria i praktyka resocjalizacyjna*, Mysłowice.

Pytka, L. (1998) *Raport o stanie wdrożenia reformy resocjalizacyjnej w zakładach poprawczych*, Warszawa.

——— (2001) 'Resocjalizacja – anachronizm, utopia czy nowe wyzwanie socjopedagogiczne', in Urban, B. (ed.) *Dewiacje wśród młodzieży. Uwarunkowania i profilaktyka*, Kraków.

Pyżalski, J. (2007) *Nauczyciele – uczniowie: dwa spojrzenia na dyscyplinę w klasie*, Kraków.

Racław, M. (2011) 'Ludzie instytucji i ludzie w instytucji. Pracownicy socjalni o swojej pracy', in Dudkiewicz, M. (ed.) *Pracownicy socjalni: pomiędzy instytucją pomocy społecznej a środowiskiem lokalnym*, Warszawa.

——— (2012) 'Zmiany w pracy socjalnej z rodziną – w stronę kontroli stylu życia i zarządzania marginalizacją', in Rymsza, M. (ed.) *Pracownicy socjalni i praca socjalna w Polsce. Między służbą społeczną a urzędem*, Warszawa.

Radosz, S. (2007) *Internet – broń w rękach terrorystów*, available at: http://www.wiadomosci24.pl/artykul/internet_bron_w_rekach_terrorystow_20523.html, accessed 1 October 2011.

Radzinowicz, L. (1935–1937a) 'Przestępczość w Polsce w latach 1924–1933 na podstawie policyjnej statystyki kryminalnej', *Archiwum Kryminologiczne*, vol. 2, nos. 1–2.

——— (1935–1937b) 'Struktura przestępczości w Polsce według statystyki sądowej', *Archiwum Kryminologiczne*, vol. 2, nos. 3–4.

——— (1937) 'Kryzys polskiej polityki kryminalnej', *Głos Sądownictwa*, no. 2.

——— (1966) *Ideology and Crime*, New York.

——— (1969) 'Wpływ warunków ekonomicznych na przestępczość w Polsce w latach 1928–1934', *Czasopismo Prawno-Historyczne*, vol. 21, no. 2.

Ram, C.D. (2012) *Meeting the Challenge of Crime in the Global Village*, Helsinki.

Raś, D. (2011) *Rodziny ubogie i przestępczość od XVI do XX wieku. Warunki życia, badania psychologiczno-społeczne, dobroczynność i wychowanie młodzieży*, Kraków.

Rawls J. (1971, 1999), *A Theory of Justice*, revised edition, Cambridge, MA.

Raynor, P. (2002) 'Community Penalties: Probation, Punishment and What Works?', in Maguire, M., Morgan, R. and Reiner, R. (eds) *The Oxford Handbook of Criminology*, Oxford.

——— (2006) 'The Background to NOMS Effective Practice, Evaluation and the Politics on Penal Reform', paper presented at a conference in Greifswald, 19 October 2006.

——— (2012a) 'Community Penalties and Offender Management', in Maguire, M., Morgan, R. and Reiner, R. (eds) *The Oxford Handbook of Criminology*, Oxford.

——— (2012b) 'Is Probation Still Possible?', *The Howard Journal of Criminal Justice*, vol. 51, no. 2.

Raźniewski, P. (2009) 'Instytucja pomocy społecznej jako narzędzie kontroli społecznej', *Prace IPSiR UW*, vol. 14.

Rodak, M. (2009) 'Międzywojenna polska debata kryminologiczna – poszukiwanie społecznych przyczyn przestępczości i sposobów jej zwalczania', *Archiwum Kryminologii*, vol. 31.

Roxin, C. (1990) 'Nowe kierunki polityki karnej', *Przegląd Prawa Karnego*, no. 4.

Rubington, E., Martin, S. and Weinberg, M.S. (eds) (2003) *The Study of Social Problems*, Oxford.

Rymsza, M. (2012) 'Praca socjalna, służby społeczne, pomoc społeczna w Polsce. Stan obecny i perspektywy rozwoju', in Rymsza, M. (ed.) *Pracownicy socjalni i praca socjalna w Polsce. Między służbą społeczną a urzędem*, Warszawa.

Rzeplińska, I. (1985) *Recydywiści w okresie nadzoru ochronnego*, Warszawa.

——— (1997) *Konfiskata mienia. Studium z historii polityki kryminalnej*, Warszawa.

——— (2007) 'Nieletni skazani w warunkach art. 10 § 2 k.k.', in Krajewski K. (ed.) *Nauki penalne wobec problemów współczesnej przestępczości. Księga Jubileuszowa z okazji 70. rocznicy urodzin Profesora Andrzeja Gaberle*, Warszawa.

——— (2007–2008) 'Sylwetki społeczne nieletnich – późniejszych dorosłych sprawców przestępstw', *Archiwum Kryminologii*, vols 29–30.

——— (2010) 'Przestępczość i jej kontrola – co wynika z dwudziestolecia RP', in Domański, H. and Kozłowski, P. (eds) *Po 20 latach. Polska transformacja z perspektywy ekonomicznej, socjologicznej i prawniczej*, Warszawa.

Rzepliński, A. (1989) *Sądownictwo w Polsce Ludowej, między dyspozycyjnością a niezawisłością*, Warszawa.

——— (1990) *Sądownictwo w PRL*, London.

Rzepniewski, A. (2008) 'Praca socjalna kuratora dla dorosłych przy realizowaniu pomocy postpenitencjarnej', in Jedynak, T. and Stasiak, K. (eds) *Zarys metodyki pracy kuratora sądowego*, vol. 3, *Kurator dla dorosłych jako instytucja systemu karnego*, Warszawa.

Sakowicz, A. (2010) 'Zakaz wstępu na imprezę masową', in Melezini, M. (ed.) *System Prawa Karnego*, vol. 6, *Kary i środki karne. Poddanie sprawcy próbie*, Warszawa.

Salmi, V. and Kivivuori, J. (2006) 'The Association between Social Capital and Juvenile Crime: The Role of Individual and Structural Factors', *European Journal of Criminology*, vol. 3, no. 2.

Salmonowicz, S. (2011) *W cieniu Klio i Temidy. Studia z historii prawa*, Toruń.

Salter, A.C. (2005) *Drapieżcy. Pedofile, gwałciciele i inni przestępcy seksualni*, Poznań.

Sampson, R.J. and Groves, W.B. (1989) 'Community Structure and Crime: Testing Social-Disorganization Theory', *The American Journal of Sociology*, vol. 94, no. 4.

Savolainen, J. (2000) 'Inequality, Welfare State, and Homicide: Further Support for the Institutional Anomie Theory', *Criminology*, vol. 38, no. 4.

Sawicka, K. (2010) 'Model kurateli sądowej. Podstawowe założenia i źródła inspiracji', in *Dziewięćdziesięciolecie kurateli sądowej w Polsce. Historia – Teraźniejszość – Przyszłość. Materiały z I Kongresu Kuratorskiego, Ustka 15–17 czerwca 2009 r.*, Kraków.

Schneider, H.J. (1981) 'Wpływ środków masowego przekazu na opinię publiczną o przestępczości i wymiarze sprawiedliwości w sprawach karnych', in Hołyst, B. (ed.) *Opinia publiczna i środki masowego przekazu a ujemne zjawiska społeczne*, Warszawa.

——— (1992) *Zysk z przestępstwa. Środki masowego przekazu a ujemne zjawiska społeczne*, Warszawa.

——— (1997–1998) 'Przyczyny przestępczości. Nowe aspekty międzynarodowej dyskusji o teoriach kryminologicznych', *Archiwum Kryminologii*, vols 23–4.

Šelih, A. (2012) 'Crime and Crime Control in Transition Countries', in Šelih, A. and Završnik, A. (eds) *Crime and Transition in Central and Eastern Countries*, New York.

Sherman, W. and Strang, H. (2007) *Restorative Justice: The Evidence*, London, available at: http://www.smith-institute.org.uk/file/RestorativeJusticeTheEvidenceFullreport.pdf, accessed 10 June 2013.

Siedlecka, E. (2008) 'Kastracja leczy czy kaleczy?', *Gazeta Wyborcza*, 12 September 2008.

Siellawa-Kolbowska, K.E. (2007) *Ocena projektu rządowego programu 'Zero tolerancji dla przemocy w szkole'*, Warszawa, available at: http://www.isp.org.pl/files/18365688600523030011703 3 1644.pdf, accessed 26 April 2013.

Siemaszko, A. (1993) *Granice tolerancji. O teoriach zachowań dewiacyjnych*, Warszawa.

——— (2001) *Kogo biją, komu kradną. Przestępczość nie rejestrowana w Polsce i na świecie*, Warszawa.

——— (2004) 'Polska polityka kryminalna – konieczność rewolucyjnych zmian', in *Materiały z konferencji 1–2 grudnia 2003 r. 'Zapobieganie i zwalczanie przestępczości w Polsce przy zastosowaniu probacyjnych środków karania' Senat Rzeczypospolitej Polskiej*, Warszawa.

——— (2007–2008) 'International Crime Victim Survey '04/05. Polska na tle wybranych krajów Unii Europejskiej', *Archiwum Kryminologii*, vols 29–30.

——— (ed.) (2008) *Geografia występku i strachu. Polskie Badanie Przestępczości '07*, Warszawa.

——— (ed.) (2010) 'Stalking w Polsce. Rozmiary – formy – skutki. Raport z badania nt. uporczywego nękania', *Archiwum Kryminologii*, vol. 32.

Siemaszko, A., Gruszczyńska, B. and Marczewski, M. (1999) *Atlas przestępczości w Polsce 2*, Warszawa.

——— (2009) *Atlas przestępczości w Polsce 4*, Warszawa.

Sienkiewicz, Z. (2010a) 'Z problematyki środków karnych', in Konarska-Wrzosek, V., Lachowski, J. and Wójcikiewicz, J. (eds) *Węzłowe problemy prawa karnego, kryminologii i polityki kryminalnej. Księga pamiątkowa ofiarowana Profesorowi Andrzejowi Markowi*, Warszawa.

——— (2010b) 'Zakaz prowadzenia pojazdów', in Melezini, M. (ed.) *System Prawa Karnego*, vol. 6, *Kary i środki karne. Poddanie sprawcy próbie*, Warszawa.

Sierocka, B. and Drewniak, M. (2006) *Dzieci ulicy. Raport z socjologicznych badań terenowych*, Kraków, available at: http://www.archiwum.mlodziez.info/images/mpppm.pl/DZIECI_ULICY_30 .11.pdf, accessed 15 April 2013.

Siewierski, M. (1947) *Mały kodeks karny i postępowanie doraźne wraz z przepisami o Komisji Specjalnej do walki z nadużyciami i innymi dodatkowymi. Komentarz*, Łódź.

Sitarz, O., Jaworska-Wieloch, A., Lorek, D., Sołtysiak-Blachnik, A. and Zawiejski, P. (2012) 'Mediacje karne w opiniach stron postępowania oraz sędziów i prokuratorów – wyniki badań ankietowych. Część I.', *e-Czasopismo Prawa Karnego i Nauk Penalnych*, no. 3.

Skiba, R. et al. (2006) *Are Zero Tolerance Policies Effective in the Schools? An Evidentiary Review and Recommendations*, an official report of the American Psychological Association.

Skibińska, A. (2007) 'Wizerunek Policji w środkach masowego przekazu jako element budowy zaufania publicznego i poczucia bezpieczeństwa. Przykład Wielkiej Brytanii i Polski', in Szymaniak, A. and Ciepiela, W. (eds) *Policja w Polsce. Stan obecny i perspektywy*, vol. 1, Poznań.

Skorupka, J. (2013) *O sprawiedliwości procesu karnego*, Warszawa.

Skupiński, J. (1967) 'Przekazanie niektórych przestępstw do orzecznictwa karno-administracyjnego', *Państwo i Prawo*, no. 1.

——— (1992) *Warunkowe skazanie w prawie polskim na tle porównawczym*, Warszawa.

——— (2009a) 'Kara bezwzględnego pozbawienia wolności i populacja więzienna w Polsce. Współczynniki prizonizacji w Polsce i w Europie', in Jakubowska-Hara, J. and Skupiński, J. (eds) *Alternatywy pozbawienia wolności w polskiej polityce karnej*, Warszawa.

——— (2009b) 'Problem alternatyw pozbawienia wolności w obecnej i przyszłej polskiej polityce kryminalnej (uwagi końcowe)', in Jakubowska-Hara, J. and Skupiński, J. (eds) *Alternatywy pozbawienia wolności w polskiej polityce karnej*, Warszawa.

——— (2009c) 'Warunkowe zawieszenie wykonania kary pozbawienia wolności', in Jakubowska-Hara, J. and Skupiński, J. (eds) *Alternatywy pozbawienia wolności w polskiej polityce karnej*, Warszawa.

Smagacz, M. (2007) *Młodzież w centrum handlowo – rozrywkowym. Raport z badań socjologicznych*, Kraków, available at: http://www.archiwum.mlodziez.info/images/mpppm.pl/GALERIA_RAPORT _08.01.pdf, accessed 15 April 2013.

Sochacka, J. (2010) 'Chuligaństwo stadionowe jako samodzielne zjawisko społeczne i przedmiot regulacji prawnych. Zarys problematyki', *Archiwum Kryminologii*, vol. 32.

Sójka-Zielińska, K. (2009) *Historia prawa*, Warszawa.

Stang, H. and Sherman, L.W. (2007) 'Restorative Justice to Reduce Victimisation', in Welsh, B.C. and Farrington, D.P. (eds) *Preventing Crime: What Works for Children, Offenders, Victims and Places*, New York.

Stanik, J.M. and Woszczek, L. (eds) (2005) *Przestępczość nieletnich. Aspekty psychospołeczne i prawne*, Katowice.

Stankiewicz, A. (2006) 'Polaków strachy własne', *Rzeczpospolita*, 25 July 2006.

Stańdo-Kawecka, B. (2007) *Prawo karne nieletnich. Od opieki do odpowiedzialności*, Kraków.

——— (2010a) 'O koncepcji resocjalizacji w polskiej literaturze polemicznie', *Probacja*, no. 1.

——— (2010b) 'Ruch "What Works" i "nowa resocjalizacja" – nowa perspektywa w polityce karnej?', in Konarska-Wrzosek, V., Lachowski, J. and Wójcikiewicz, J. (eds) *Węzłowe problemy prawa karnego, kryminologii i polityki kryminalnej. Księga pamiątkowa ofiarowana Profesorowi Andrzejowi Markowi*, Warszawa.

Staręga-Piasek, J. (2005) 'Pomoc społeczna. Próba oceny funkcjonowania pomocy społecznej w zwalczaniu ubóstwa i wykluczenia społecznego', in Golinowska, S., Tarkowska, E. and Topińska, I. (eds) *Ubóstwo i wykluczenie społeczne. Badania. Metody. Wyniki*, Warszawa.

Staręga-Piasek, J. and Wóycicka, I. (2011) 'Niektóre problemy związane z systemem minimalnych dochodów w Polsce', in Szarfenberg, R. (ed.) *Ubóstwo i wykluczenie społeczne w Polsce. Raport krajowy Polskiej Koalicji Social Watch i Polskiego Komitetu European Anti-Poverty Network*, Warszawa.

Stasiak, K. (2008) 'Wprowadzenie. 1. Ewolucja kurateli sądowej od początków do wejścia w życie rozporządzenia z 1986 r.', in Jedynak, T. and Stasiak, K. (eds) *Zarys metodyki pracy kuratora sądowego*, Warszawa.

——— (2010) 'Ewolucja systemu kurateli sądowej w Polsce w latach 1919–2009 – kamienie milowe', in *Dziewięćdziesięciolecie kurateli sądowej w Polsce. Historia – Teraźniejszość – Przyszłość. Materiały z I Kongresu Kuratorskiego, Ustka 15–17 czerwca 2009 r.*, Kraków.

Staśkiewicz, W. (2010) 'Wykluczenie prawne w procesie tworzenia prawa', in Turska, A. (ed.) *Prawo i wykluczenie społeczne. Studium empiryczne*, Warszawa.

Stępniak, P. (1992) *Funkcjonowanie kurateli sądowej. Teoria a rzeczywistość*, Poznań.

——— (1998) *Wymiar sprawiedliwości i praca socjalna w krajach Europy Zachodniej*, Poznań.

——— (2001) 'Pomiędzy resocjalizacją a pracą socjalną. Dylematy współczesnej penitencjarystyki', in Hołyst, B., Ambrozik, W. and Stepniak, P. (eds) *Więziennictwo nowe wyzwania*, Warszawa–Poznań–Kalisz.

——— (2005–2006) 'Probacja – pomiędzy modelem idealnym a realiami społecznymi', *Pampaedia. Leszczyńskie Studia Humanistyczne*, nos. 2–3.

——— (2007) 'Misja Służby Więziennej a jej zadania wobec aktualnej polityki kryminalnej i oczekiwań społecznych. (IV Polski Kongres Penitencjarny, Kalisz 22–24 listopada 2006 r.)', *Przegląd Więziennictwa Polskiego*, no. 54.

——— (2008) 'Praca socjalna czy socjalna resocjalizacja. W poszukiwaniu nowego modelu', in Szecówka, A., Koukola, B. and Kwiatkowski, P. (eds) *Teoria i praktyka resocjalizacyjna wobec współczesnych zachowań dewiacyjnych w Polsce i Republice Czeskiej*, Wrocław.

——— (2009a) 'Nowelizacja ustawy o kuratorach sądowych a Europejskie Reguły dotyczące Sankcji i Środków Alternatywnych', *Probacja*, no. 2.

——— (2009b) 'Wokół kontrowersji w definiowaniu probacji', *Państwo i Prawo*, no. 12.

——— (2012) 'Systemowa pozorność resocjalizacji penitencjarnej w świetle badań empirycznych. Propozycja zmian', *Archiwum Kryminologii*, vol. 34.

Stojanowska, W. and Strzembosz, A. (1978) 'O nowe zasady organizacji i postępowania przed sądem rodzinnym', *Zeszyty Naukowe IBPS*, no. 10.

Strzembosz, A. (1984) 'Polskie sądy rodzinne w świetle badań empirycznych', *Archiwum Kryminologii*, vol. 11.

Strzyżewski, T. (1977) 'Czarna księga cenzury PRL (Black Book of Polish Censorship)', *ANEKS Political Quarterly*, London.

Sulikowski, J. (2009) 'Kastracja! Bez litości dla pedofilów', *Fakt*, 26 September 2009.

Surzykiewicz, J. (2000) *Agresja i przemoc w szkole. Uwarunkowania socjoekologiczne*, Warszawa.

Szacki, J. (1983) *Historia myśli socjologicznej*, Warszawa.

——— (2002) *Historia myśli socjologicznej*, Warszawa.

Szamota-Saeki, B. (2007–2008) 'Wpływ prawa karnego na przekonania moralne społeczeństwa w świetle wybranych badań empirycznych', *Archiwum Kryminologii*, vols 29–30.

Szarfenberg, R. (2010) 'Marginalizacja i wykluczenie społeczne – panorama językowo-teoretyczna', in Szarfenberg, R., Theiss, M. and Żołędowski, C. (eds) *Ubóstwo i wykluczenie społeczne – perspektywa poznawcza*, Warszawa.

Szarfenberg, R. and Kurowska, A. (2010) 'Ubóstwo a wielowymiarowa deprywacja, nierówność i wykluczenie społeczne', in Szarfenberg, R., Theiss, M. and Żołędowski, C. (eds) *Ubóstwo i wykluczenie społeczne – perspektywa poznawcza*, Warszawa.

Szecówka, A. (2007) 'Treść i forma przekazu medialnego a przestępczość i zachowania dewiacyjne', *Przegląd Więziennictwa Polskiego*, no. 56/57.

Szelhaus, S. (1969) *Młodociani recydywiści. Społeczne czynniki procesu wykolejania*, Warszawa.

Szewczyk, M. (2007) 'Jaka alternatywa dla krótkoterminowej kary pozbawienia wolności', in Krajewski, K. (ed.) *Nauki penalne wobec współczesnej przestępczości, Księga jubileuszowa z okazji 70 rocznicy urodzin Profesora Andrzeja Gaberle*, Warszawa.

——— (2010) 'Kara ograniczenia wolności', in Melezini, M. (ed.) *System Prawa Karnego*, vol. 6, *Kary i środki karne. Poddanie sprawcy próbie*, Warszawa.

Sztompka, P. (2002) *Socjologia. Analiza społeczeństwa*, Kraków.

——— (2005) *Socjologia zmian społecznych*, Kraków.

Sztuka, M. (2007) 'Efektywność oddziaływań w zorientowanym korekcyjnie modelu instytucji penitencjarnej. Doświadczenia amerykańskie', *Czasopismo Prawa Karnego i Nauk Penalnych*, no. 1.

——— (2010) 'Prace nad adaptacją instrumentarium risk assessment do warunków polskich', in *Dziewięćdziesięciolecie kurateli sądowej w Polsce. Historia – Teraźniejszość – Przyszłość. Materiały z I Kongresu Kuratorskiego, Ustka 15–17 czerwca 2009 r.*, Kraków.

Sztumpf, J. (1933) 'Cele i znaczenie środków zabezpieczających w polskim Kodeksie Karnym', *Przegląd Więziennictwa Polskiego*, no. 1.

Szumski, J. (1980) 'Przekwalifikowywanie przestępstw w wykroczenia. Konsekwencja w sferze polityki karnej', *Państwo i Prawo*, no. 5.

Szwarc, A.J. (ed.) (2008) *Represyjność polskiego prawa karnego. Materiały Zjazdu Katedr Prawa karnego (Gniezno 26–29 września 2006 r.)*, Poznań.

Szymanowska, A. (2003) *Więzienie i co dalej*, Warszawa.

——— (2008) *Polacy wobec przestępstw i karania*, Warszawa.

Szymanowska, A. and Szymanowski, T. (1996) *Opinia społeczna w Polsce o niektórych kontrowersyjnych zachowaniach patologicznych, przestępstwach i środkach kontroli prawno-karnej*, Warszawa.

Szymanowski, T. (2001) 'Podstawy prawne i problemy funkcjonowania kurateli w Polsce', in *Materiały z Konferencji 'Probacyjne środki polityki karnej – stan i perspektywy' (20–21 października 2000 r.)*, Warszawa.

——— (2002) 'Ustawa o kuratorach sądowych na tle pozostałych przepisów normujących ich zadania i obowiązki', *Przegląd Więziennictwa Polskiego*, nos. 34–5.
——— (2005a) 'Kuratorzy sądowi i zadania przez nich wykonywane po dokonanej reformie', *Archiwum Kryminologii*, vol. 27.
——— (2005b) *Polityka karna i penitencjarna w Polsce w okresie przemian prawa karnego*, Warszawa.
——— (2007) 'Opinia społeczna w Polsce o zmianach prawa karnego', *Państwo i Prawo*, no. 5.
——— (2010a) 'Polityka karna w Polsce współczesnej w świetle przepisów prawa i danych empirycznych', in Marek, A. (ed.) *System Prawa Karnego*, vol. 1, *Zagadnienia ogólne*, Warszawa.
——— (2010b) *Recydywa w Polsce. Zagadnienia prawa karnego, kryminologii i polityki karnej*, Warszawa.
——— (2010c) 'Znaczenie kuratorskiej służby sądowej w realizacji zadań polityki karnej i penitencjarnej', in *Dziewięćdziesięciolecie kurateli sądowej w Polsce. Historia – Teraźniejszość – Przyszłość. Materiały z I Kongresu Kuratorskiego, Ustka 15–17 czerwca 2009 r.*, Kraków.
——— (2012) *Przestępczość i polityka karna w Polsce w świetle faktów i opinii społeczeństwa w okresie transformacji*, Warszawa.
Śliwowski, J. (1936) 'Przestępczość w Polsce i jej zwalczanie', *Głos Sądownictwa*, no. 1.
——— (1958) *Kodeks karzący Królestwa Polskiego (1818 r.). Historia jego powstania i próba krytycznej analizy*, Warszawa.
Świda, W. (1960) *Wpływ zmiany ustroju na przestępczość (w świetle przestępczości w Kaliszu i powiecie kaliskim)*, Wrocław.
——— (1989) *Prawo karne*, Warszawa.
Tarkowska, E. (2002) 'Czy dziedziczenie biedy? Bariery i szanse edukacyjne młodzieży z wiejskiej gminy Kościelec', in Korzeniewska, K. and Tarkowska, E. (eds) *Lata tłuste, lata chude ... Spojrzenia na biedę w społecznościach lokalnych*, Warszawa.
Taylor, I. (2002) 'Free Market and the Costs of Crime: An Audit of England and Wales', in Walton, P. and Young, J. (eds) *The New Criminology Revisited*, Houndmills.
Tilley, N., Tseloni, A. and Farrell, G. (2011) 'Income Disparities of Burglary Risk: Security Availability during the Crime Drop', *British Journal of Criminology*, vol. 51, no. 2.
TNS OBOP (2007) *Polacy wobec zjawiska przemocy w rodzinie oraz opinie ofiar, sprawców i świadków o występowaniu i okolicznościach występowania przemocy w rodzinie. Wyniki badań TNS OBOP dla Ministerstwa Pracy i Polityki Społecznej*, Warszawa, available at: http://www.bezuprzedzen.org/doc/polacy_wobec_zjawiska_przemocy_w_rodzinie.pdf, accessed 17 October 2012.
Tonry, M. (2007) 'Polityka karna, kultura polityczna a zasady konstytucyjne', *Archiwum Kryminologii*, vol. 28.
——— (2011) *Retributivism Has a Past: Has It a Future?*, Oxford.
Tuziak, B. (1996) 'Przestępczość w Rzeszowie w latach 1990–1995', *Archiwum Kryminologii*, vol. 22.
Tyszkiewicz, L. (2003) 'Ewolucja kurateli sądowej w Polsce', in Zgryzek, K. and Hofmański, P. (eds) *Współczesne problemy procesu karnego i wymiaru sprawiedliwości. Księga ku czci Profesora Kazimierza Marszała*, Katowice.
——— (2004) 'Spór wokół resocjalizacji i pracy socjalnej w polskiej polityce kryminalnej', in Ambrozik, W. and Stępniak, P. (eds) *Służba więzienna wobec problemów resocjalizacji penitencjarnej, III Krajowe Sympozjum Penitencjarne*, Poznań–Warszawa–Kalisz.
Ulman, Z. (1960) 'Głos w dyskusji nad polityką represyjną', *Prawo i Życie*, vol. 23.
Utrat-Milecki, J. (2007) 'Penologiczne podstawy probacji', *Przegląd Więziennictwa Polskiego*, nos. 56–7.
van Dijk, J., Farrell, G. and Tseloni, A. (2012a) 'Conclusions – Understanding International Crime Trends: A Summing Up', in van Dijk, J., Farrell, G. and Tseloni, A. (eds) *The International Crime Drop: New Directions in Research*, London.
——— (eds) (2012b) *The International Crime Drop: New Directions in Research*, London.
van Dijk, J., van Kersten, J. and Smit, P. (2007) *Criminal Victimisation in International Perspective: Key Findings from the 2004–2005 ICVS and EU ICS*, WODC, available at: http://unicri.it/services/library_documentation/publications/icvs/publications/ICVS2004_05report.pdf, accessed 21 October 2014.
van Dijk, J. and Vollaard, B. (2012) 'Self Limiting Crime Waves', in van Dijk, J., Farrell, G. and Tseloni, A. (eds) *The International Crime Drop: New Directions in Research*, London.
Veillard-Cybulsky, H. and M. (1968) *Nieletni przestępcy w świecie*, Warszawa.

Ville, R., Zwekic, H. and Klaus, J.F. (1997) *Promoting Probation Internationally*, Rome–London.

Wachowski, I. (1995) 'Policja a środki masowego przekazu', *Biuletyn Policji*, no. 3 (39).

Wacquant, L. (2009) *Prisons of Poverty*, Minneapolis, MN.

——— (2010) 'Crafting the Neoliberal State: Workfare, Prisonfare, and Social Insecurity', *Sociological Forum*, vol. 25, no. 2.

——— (2011) 'The Wedding of Workfare and Prisonfare Revisited', *Social Justice*, vol. 38, nos. 1–2.

Waltoś, S. (1997) 'Karnoprocesowa problematyka sprawozdawczości prasowej w Polsce', in Dölling, D., Gössel, K.-H. and Waltoś, S. (eds) *Relacje o przestępstwach i procesach karnych w prasie codziennej w Niemczech i w Polsce*, Kraków.

Warylewski, J. (2010) 'Kierunki i szkoły w nauce prawa karnego', in Marek, A. (ed.) *System Prawa Karnego*, vol. 1, *Zagadnienia Ogólne*, Warszawa.

Warzywoda-Kruszyńska, W. (1999) 'Dorastać w biedzie – obrazy z życia różnych pokoleń łodzian', in Warzywoda-Kruszyńska, W. (ed.) *(Żyć) Na marginesie wielkiego miasta*, Łódź.

——— (2010) 'Enklawy biedy – mechanizm powstawania i trwania', *Praca Socjalna*, special issue.

Warzywoda-Kruszyńska, W. and Kruszyński, K. (2011) 'Dziedziczenie biedy i wykluczenia społecznego – w perspektywie lokalnej polityki społecznej', in Szarfenberg, R. (ed.) *Ubóstwo i wykluczenie społeczne w Polsce. Raport krajowy Polskiej Koalicji Social Watch i Polskiego Komitetu European Anti-Poverty Network*, Warszawa.

Waszkiewicz, P. (2006) 'Jak bezpiecznie żyje się za ogrodzeniem? Poczucie bezpieczeństwa mieszkańców warszawskich osiedli zamkniętych', *Biuletyn Polskiego Towarzystwa Kryminologicznego*, no. 15.

Wągiel-Linder, G. (2011) 'Europejskie absolutorium', *Forum Penitencjarne*, no. 9.

Widacki, J. (2002) 'Polscy politycy o bezpieczeństwie (między demokracją a demagogią)', in Czapska, J. and Kury, H. (eds) *Mit represyjności albo o znaczeniu prewencji kryminalnej*, Kraków.

Wiktorska, P. (2010) *Czekając na wokandę. Warunkowe przedterminowe zwolnienie młodocianych*, Warszawa.

Williams, K.S. (2004) *Criminology*, Oxford.

Wirth, L. (1929) *The Ghetto*, Chicago, IL.

Witkowska, K. (2007) 'Informacja o przestępczości w środkach masowego przekazu', in Chudziński, B. and Marszałek-Kawa, J. (eds) *Znaczenie informacji w społeczeństwie obywatelskim. Wybrane aspekty prawne*, Toruń.

Witkowska-Rozpara, K. (2011) *Przestępczość, środki masowego przekazu a polityka karna*, Warszawa.

Wnuk-Lipiński, E. (2005) *Socjologia życia publicznego*, Warszawa.

Wojciechowski, J. (1995) *Ustawa o ochronie obrotu gospodarczego z komentarzem*, Warszawa.

Wojtasik, Ł. (2009) 'Przemoc rówieśnicza z użyciem mediów elektronicznych – wprowadzenie do problematyki', *Dziecko krzywdzone*, no. 1 (26).

Woźniak, W. (2012) *Nierówności społeczne w polskim dyskursie politycznym*, Warszawa.

Woźniakowska-Fajst, D. (2010) *Nieletnie. Niebezpieczne, niegrzeczne, niegroźne?*, Warszawa.

——— (2011) 'Nieletnie dziewczęta 10 lat później – badania katamnestyczne', *Archiwum Kryminologii*, vol. 33.

Wójcik, D. (2008) 'Problematyka wczesnego zapobiegania przestępczości nieletnich', in Andrzejewski, M., Kociucki, L., Łączkowska, M. and Schulz, A. (eds) *Księga Jubileuszowa Profesora Tadeusza Smyczyńskiego*, Toruń.

——— (2009) 'Poglądy sędziów na temat mediacji w sprawach karnych', in Mazowiecka, L. (ed.) *Mediacja*, Warszawa.

——— (2010) *Kuratela sądowa. Sukcesy i porażki*, Warszawa.

——— (2014) 'Stosowanie w postępowaniu karnym narzędzi diagnostyczno-prognostycznych służących oszacowaniu ryzyka powrotności do przestępstwa', *Prawo w działaniu*, vol. 16.

Wright, M. (2005) *Przywracając szacunek sprawiedliwości*, Warszawa.

——— (2010) *Towards Restorative Society: Problem-solving Response to Harm*, available at: www.makejusticework.org.uk/wp-content/uploads/Martin-Wright-Towards-a-Restorative-Society.pdf, accessed 10 June 2013.

Wróbel, W. (2006) 'Wina i zawinienie, a strona podmiotowa czynu zabronionego, czyli o potrzebie posługiwania się w prawie karnym pojęciem winy umyślnej i winy nieumyślnej', in Giezek, J. (ed.) *Przestępstwo-*

kara-polityka kryminalna. Problemy tworzenia i funkcjonowania prawa. Księga jubileuszowa z okazji 70. rocznicy urodzin Profesora Tomasz Kaczmarka, Kraków.
——— (2009) 'Czy powrót do racjonalizmu? Projekty nowelizacji kodeksu karnego w perspektywie zmian dokonanych w prawie karnym w latach 2005–2007', in Sienkiewicz, Z. and Kokot, R. (eds) *Populizm penalny i jego przejawy w Polsce*, Wrocław.
Wróbel, W. and Zoll, A. (2010) *Polskie prawo karne. Część ogólna*, Kraków.
Wróblewski, B. (1922) *Wstęp do polityki kryminalnej*, Wilno.
Young, J. (1999) *The Exclusive Society*, London.
——— (2002) 'Crime and Social Exclusion', in Maguire, M., Morgan, R. and Reiner, R. (eds) *The Oxford Handbook of Criminology*, Oxford.
Zagórski, J. (2008) 'Dozór kuratora sądowego przy warunkowym zawieszeniu kary pozbawienia wolności', in Zagórski, J. (ed.) *Wykonywanie środków probacji i readaptacji skazanych w Polsce*, Warszawa.
——— (2010) 'Stan kurateli sądowej dla dorosłych w świetle badań Rzecznika Praw Obywatelskich', in *Dziewięćdziesięciolecie kurateli sądowej w Polsce. Historia – Teraźniejszość – Przyszłość. Materiały z I Kongresu Kuratorskiego, Ustka 15–17 czerwca 2009 r.*, Kraków.
Zahorska, M. (2009) 'Równi, równiejsi i … najmniej równi, czyli o społecznych barierach w dostępie do edukacji', *Polityka Społeczna*, vol. 36.
Zalewski, D. (2002) 'Życie z preambułą: o tępieniu fikcji', in Tarkowska, E. (ed.) *Przeciw biedzie. Programy, pomysły, inicjatywy*, Warszawa.
Zalewski, W. (2006) *Sprawiedliwość naprawcza. Początek ewolucji polskiego prawa karnego?*, Gdańsk.
——— (2008) 'Recenzja pracy John Pratt "Penal Populism", London 2007', *Państwo i Prawo*, no. 3.
——— (2009) 'Populizm penalny – próba zdefiniowania zjawiska', in Sienkiewicz, Z. and Kokot, R. (eds) *Populizm penalny i jego przejawy w Polsce. Materiały Ogólnopolskiego Zjazdu Katedr Prawa Karnego. Szklarska Poręba 24–27 września 2008*, Wrocław.
Zalikowska, I. (2009) '"Atlantis" – Program edukacyjno-terapeutyczny', in Marczak, M. (ed.) *Resocjalizacyjne programy penitencjarne realizowane przez służbę więzienną w Polsce*, Kraków.
Załuski, W. (2009) *Ewolucyjna filozofia prawa*, Warszawa.
Zawadka, G. and Blikowska, J. (2013) 'Przestępcy wolą prać, niż kraść', *Rzeczpospolita*, 11 January 2013.
Zawadzki, M. (2002) 'Rzeczywistość kryminalna prezentowana w telewizji a opinia publiczna (analiza kryminologiczna z uwzględnieniem wyników badania ankietowego mieszkańców Gdańska)', *Biuletyn Polskiego Towarzystwa Kryminologicznego*, no. 11.
Zehr, H. and Gohar, A. (2002) *The Little Book of Restorative Justice*, Intercourse, PA, available at: http://www.unicef.org/tdad/littlebookrjpakaf.pdf, accessed 10 June 2013.
Ziembiński, Z. (1996) *Sprawiedliwość społeczna jako pojęcie prawne*, Warszawa.
Zienkiewicz, A. (2007) *Studium mediacji. Od teorii ku praktyce*, Warszawa.
Zimring, F. (2007) *The Great American Crime Decline*, Oxford.
Zoll, A. (1998) 'Założenia polityczno-kryminalne w świetle wyzwań współczesności', *Państwo i Prawa*, no. 9.
——— (2011) 'Potrzeba racjonalności w reformowaniu prawa karnego', in *Teoretyczne i praktyczne problemy współczesnego prawa karnego, materiały z konferencji naukowej, Lublin, 26–27.09.2011 r.*, Lublin.
Zub, M. (ed.) (2011) *Badanie ścieżek migracyjnych klientów pomocy społecznej i powiatowych urzędów pracy oraz możliwości wprowadzenia zintegrowanych usług aktywizacji zawodowej. Raport z badań*, Warszawa.
Żakowski, J. (2007) 'Rzecz o szczuciu. Raport', *Polityka*, 10 March 2007.
Żemojtel-Piotrowska, M. and Piotrowski, J. (2011) 'Biedny, więc roszczeniowy czy roszczeniowy, więc biedny? O możliwych związkach postaw roszczeniowych ze statusem socjo-ekonomicznym i wykluczeniem społecznym', in Popow, M., Kowzan, P., Zielińska, M., Prusinowska, M. and Chruściel, M. (eds) *Oblicza biedy we współczesnej Polsce*, Gdańsk.
Żuk, P. (2010) 'Czy każda krytyka neoliberalizmu jest populizmem. O pułapkach demokracji w Polsce', in De Waele, J.M. and Pacześniak, A. (eds) *Populizm w Europie. Defekt i przejaw demokracji?*, Warszawa.

Index

For Product Safety Concerns and Information please contact our EU
representative GPSR@taylorandfrancis.com
Taylor & Francis Verlag GmbH, Kaufingerstraße 24, 80331 München, Germany

www.ingramcontent.com/pod-product-compliance
Ingram Content Group UK Ltd.
Pitfield, Milton Keynes, MK11 3LW, UK
UKHW050050200926
475702UK00019B/2764
* 9 7 8 1 0 3 2 0 9 8 7 5 3 *